JUDGING JEHOVAH'S WITNESSES

Judging Jehovah's Witnesses

Religious Persecution and
the Dawn of the Rights Revolution

Shawn Francis Peters

 UNIVERSITY PRESS OF KANSAS

Published by the University Press of Kansas (Lawrence, Kansas 66049),
which was organized by the Kansas Board of Regents and is operated and
funded by Emporia State University, Fort Hays State University, Kansas
State University, Pittsburg State University, the University of Kansas, and
Wichita State University

Library of Congress Cataloging-in-Publication Data

Peters, Shawn Francis, 1966–

    Judging Jehovah's Witnesses : religious persecution and the dawn of the
rights revolution / Shawn Francis Peters.

      p. cm.

    Includes bibliographical references (p.) and index.

    ISBN 0-7006-1008-1 (cloth : alk. paper)

      1. Jehovah's Witnesses—United States—History—20th century.
2. Persecution—United States—History—20th century. 3. Freedom
of religion—United States—History—20th century. I. Title.

BX8525.7 .P48 2000

289.9′2′0973—dc21

99-048616

Printed in the United States of America

10 9 8 7 6 5 4 3 2 1

The paper used in this publication meets the minimum requirements of the
American National Standard for Permanence of Paper for Printed Library
Materials Z39.48-1984.

I think the Jehovah's Witnesses ought to have an endowment in view of the aid which they give in solving the legal problems of civil liberties.—*Harlan Fiske Stone, Associate Justice, U.S. Supreme Court*

Contents

Acknowledgments

I am indebted to a number of generous people who aided in the researching, writing, and editing of this book. I hope that I can properly acknowledge their help.

As always, Susan Crawford, my partner and best friend, was extraordinarily supportive. Without her patience, emotional support, legal expertise, and keen copy-editing skills, I doubt that this book ever would have seen the light of day. More times than I care to remember, she saved me from making glaring mistakes of both style and substance.

I have been lucky enough to spend much of the last decade at three wonderful schools—the University of New Hampshire, the University of Iowa, and the University of Wisconsin—and several colleagues at those institutions supported my work. Among them were Helene Collins, Mike DePorte, Sue Hertz, and Andy Merton at UNH; Sara Cody, Jason Duncan, Ellis Hawley, Dan Lewis, and John Raeburn at Iowa; and James Baughman, Deborah Blum, Donald Downs, Robert Drechsel, Sharon Dunwoody, Lance Holbert, and Ronald Numbers at Wisconsin. I'm also indebted to the office staffs of the English Department at UNH, the American Studies Program at Iowa, and the School of Journalism and Mass Communication at Wisconsin. Their hard (and sometimes unappreciated) work made my life a lot easier.

My friends outside the academy were perhaps even more unselfish than my colleagues within it, and I am happy to recognize their assistance. Jen Lyon, Jacqueline Waraksy, Kristin Oberg, and Ted and Melissa Maillett never failed to provide encouragement. Ted and Melissa also were gracious enough to allow me to stay at their home when I conducted research in Washington, D.C. Marjorie Alexander twice helped me to find work in Des Moines. Along with Marjorie, Laura Castro de Cortés, Kathleen Duffy, and Amy Myers made my tenure at the Des Moines Art Center an enjoyable one.

In piecing together this story, I came to rely on the wisdom and expertise of a number of librarians and archivists. The library staffs at the University of New Hampshire, the University of Iowa, and the University of Iowa College of Law bore the brunt of my innumerable questions and interlibrary loan requests. At various times, I also imposed on librarians at Amherst College, the Des Moines Public Library, Drake University, the University of Massachusetts at Amherst, the University of Pennsylvania, Rutgers University, Smith College, and the University of Wisconsin. The staff of the Manuscript Division of the Library of Congress facilitated my research on Felix Frankfurter, Robert Jackson, and Harlan Fiske Stone. The staff of the Seeley G. Mudd Library at Princeton University greatly expedited my research on the American Civil Liberties Union, and I am grateful for that library's permission to quote from the ACLU Papers.

The photographs in this book were supplied by the Watchtower Bible and Tract Society, and I am appreciative for its permission to reproduce them. Katrina Bartley of the society's public affairs office has my gratitude for hunting down the images and arranging for their reproduction. Benjamin Sasso, the image services director, did an excellent job of helping me on short notice.

Two Jehovah's Witnesses were particularly generous with their time. Lillian Gobitas Klose not only shared her memories with me but also supplied photographs and photocopies of several important documents. Walter Chaplinsky was similarly helpful.

Lisa Gillard Hanson of Rutgers University Press helped me to navigate safely through the shoals of academic publishing. Michael Briggs, editor-in-chief of the University Press of Kansas, did everything to make my first experience as an author a smooth one. I won't soon be able to repay him for his faith in this book.

Finally, the members of my family deserve a note of special thanks for their support and forbearance over the past several years.

Introduction:
A Turning Point for
Religious Liberty

Halfway through summer 1942, thirteen men huddled together in a building located at 510 South Main Street in Pittsburgh's West End. Devout Christians, they thumbed through well-worn Bibles and discussed the Scriptures for the better part of an hour, all the while murmuring earnest questions and suggestions to one another like schoolboys cramming for an exam. The solemn men who assembled on that Saturday night were Jehovah's Witnesses, and they were extraordinarily devoted to their faith, a controversial and widely misunderstood brand of millennialism practiced by roughly 40,000 people in the United States in the early 1940s. Throughout the World War II era, the Witnesses were frequent targets of verbal and physical abuse because they believed that saluting the "graven image" of the American flag amounted to idolatry.[1] The harassment did little, however, to temper their boundless enthusiasm for reading and interpreting the touchstone of their hardscrabble lives, the Bible. On many Saturday nights, while their neighbors were relaxing in the Iron City's many taverns and movie theaters, the Witnesses eagerly filed into their "Kingdom Hall," as it was called, and pored over the Scriptures.[2]

When the Bible study broke up that night in Pittsburgh, the Jehovah's Witnesses piled into three cars and headed for nearby Imperial, where they planned to distribute pieces of religious literature produced at their faith's headquarters in Brooklyn, New York. They brought with them bundles of periodicals, including the latest issues of *The Watchtower* and *Consolation* magazines, as well as tracts entitled "Hope," "Judge Rutherford Uncovers Fifth Column," "End of Axis Powers," and "Comfort All That Mourn." Distributing such materials in exchange for nominal cash donations—or simply giving them away to people who couldn't afford to pay—was the most meaningful work imaginable for the Witnesses because it gave them the opportunity to fulfill the obligation placed upon the disciples by Christ in Matthew 24:14: "And this gospel of the kingdom will be preached throughout the whole world, as testament to all nations; and then the end will come." Proselytizing was a labor of love for the Witnesses, but it often could be a risky endeavor, particularly when they were accosted by skeptics and forced to explain their apparent lack of reverence for the American flag. Two local Witnesses, John Golinie and Frank Kikosicsky Jr., had been accosted a few days earlier while proselytizing in Imperial, and stories of similar confrontations in other communities were legion among members of their faith. The Witnesses, however, were nothing if not stubborn, and the abuse seemed only to strengthen their resolve. That they were persecuted, as the earliest Christians had been, appeared to confirm that theirs was the most righteous of causes.[3]

The Witnesses' trip from the West End was brief, and by 7:30 P.M. all of them—including Golinie and Kikosicsky, who were happy to resume their preaching with the help of reinforcements—had taken up positions in downtown Imperial. For the first half hour or so, the Witnesses were able to work peacefully, "presenting the literature without any interference whatever," according to Witness G. C. Flick. Victor Lendin preached in front of a hardware store; Barton Ensley distributed tracts across the street, near a drugstore; and Steve Chornenky roamed outside a small shop and hawked printed material. Meanwhile, Golinie and Kikosicsky propagandized at their usual spot, near the Imperial State Bank on Main Street, pressing literature into the hands of passersby and boldly denouncing other religions as shams or degenerate "rackets." This kind of proselytizing was a cornerstone of the Witnesses' faith, and they took to the streets as often as possible. Wherever they went, the evangelists delivered the same startling message: Armageddon was fast approaching, and man's only hope of attaining salvation before that cataclysmic day of reckoning lay in fully embracing the teachings of the Bible.[4]

The Jehovah's Witnesses first sensed trouble in Imperial when Golinie and Kikosicsky were angrily challenged by a teller who lived in an apartment above the local bank. The Witnesses' return to Imperial infuriated the teller, and he screamed at them, "Get the hell out of here! I don't want you here; this is bank property." The Witnesses stood their ground and explained that their distribution of literature on the sidewalk in front of the bank was perfectly legal. They reminded the irate teller that the U.S. Supreme Court recently had handed down opinions in several cases involving the civil liberties of Witness proselytizers, and those decisions—citing the protections of press, speech, and religion furnished by the First and Fourteenth Amendments—generally supported their right to propagandize freely in public places, including sidewalks. Eventually, though, the two Witnesses moved on, hoping to defuse the increasingly tense situation by taking up another post on the street, this one away from the bank and near a telegraph pole. An Imperial constable arrived at the scene within ten minutes. He questioned the Witnesses and suggested that they had violated local law by distributing literature without having first obtained a valid municipal permit. They stood firm and protested again, Golinie saying that they "had a perfect right to do this work and stand here," but the constable arrested the Witnesses anyway and took them into custody.[5]

As the evening wore on, men and boys began trickling into downtown Imperial to hector the remaining Jehovah's Witnesses. Some passersby insulted the evangelists by suggesting that they were subversives or spies; others simply denigrated or mocked the Witnesses' uncommon beliefs. For a time, several carloads of boisterous adolescents cruised up and down Main Street, the youths craning their necks and shouting epithets and threats as they sped past. The Witnesses' discomfort mounted with each passing car, but, resolute in their faith, they continued to offer the latest issues of *Consolation* and *The Watchtower*. The Witnesses tried to respond to insulting questions about their alleged lack of patriotism with thoughtful answers based on their understanding of the Scriptures, and they exchanged copies of tracts for small donations. But with the crowd in downtown Imperial swelling and growing more hostile by the minute, most of the literature went unread. One livid man shredded a copy of *Consolation* and hurled it at Witness Barton Ensley. While a crowd of rowdy onlookers hooted and cheered, another magazine was set aflame in the middle of the street.[6]

The town's fire siren pealed at approximately 8:15 P.M. and stopped the evangelists in their tracks. As G. C. Flick remembered, "cars came from every direction" after the siren went off. Within moments, groups of abusive men converged upon and then pummeled the Witnesses. Dispersed throughout the downtown area, they made easy targets when throngs of assailants set upon them. In their subsequent accounts of the mobbing, none of the Witnesses ventured to guess how many vigilantes had attacked them in Imperial, but from their testimony it seems clear that at least fifty men—and perhaps as many as one hundred or more—swarmed over and brutalized the proselytizers, punching and kicking them, sometimes even dragging them helplessly through the streets.[7]

Among the besieged Witnesses, G. C. Flick had perhaps the greatest reason for concern. "I did not know exactly what to do," he explained, "as I have a crippled arm and could not even properly defend myself, much less assist anyone else." With the situation spiraling out of control, Witness William Torso urged Flick to leave the scene of the riot and telephone the nearby state police barracks for help. After slipping through the crowd, both men sped away in Torso's car, but not without a pang of remorse; Flick felt that, despite his handicap, he should have stayed behind and helped the Witnesses who were under attack. As they drove off in search of help, Torso and Flick picked up several Jehovah's Witnesses who had already been trounced by the mob. Squeezing into the car, all of them told similarly dismal stories of their encounters with vigilantes. When the attack had begun, William Comodor and Walter Moss rushed to help another Witness, Victor Lendin, fend off an assailant. Comodor was overmatched and soon found himself getting the worst of a painfully lopsided brawl. "The man started to beat me up," he said, "and some of his companions started to beat me also. One of the men had a sharp knife or rock and hit me in the nose, cutting the side of it. They knocked me to the ground and started to kick me about the body. . . . I was bleeding very badly, and my shirt was badly stained [with my own blood]." Dazed from his wounds, he scrambled into the car carrying Torso, Flick, and the other Witnesses to apparent safety. Though relieved by their own good fortune, the men in the car worried about those who had been left behind, fearing that they would be seriously injured by the mob, perhaps even killed.[8]

The Jehovah's Witnesses absorbed blows from all sides when the vigilantes surged toward them that night in Imperial. A band of men accosted Frank Kikosicsky and accused him of distributing Nazi propaganda. He was then ordered to leave town immediately. Before long, members of the crowd "began shoving me along," Kikosicsky recounted, "and someone struck me from behind several times in the back of the head." The beating resumed after he was given a moment to take off his glasses. "I protected myself as much as I could," he said, "but every time I got any kind of advantage, someone else would interfere. They finally knocked me down several times. Every time I got up, blows were rained on my face, eyes, head, etc., until I was finally knocked completely out." He was "pushed and dragged and kicked" all the way to the local police station, where he was joined by several other punch-drunk Witnesses who had staggered in for a reprieve from the mobbing. Although they had done nothing illegal, the men were held in custody for several hours, grilled about their activities and the content of their literature, and asked to produce valid draft registration cards. Some of these victims had been seriously wounded in the attack, but they were not released from police custody and allowed to seek medical treatment at a nearby hospital until early the following morning.[9]

G. C. Flick and William Comodor were concerned about the safety of the Witnesses who had not escaped in their car, and they drove back into downtown Imperial after they had telephoned the state police for help. They saw a horrific scene on the outskirts of town: a group of men were chasing and stoning several defenseless Jehovah's Witnesses as they fled on foot. Flick and Comodor pulled over, and their grateful friends clambered in as a shower of rocks and other debris bounced off the car's hood and windshield. With eight men packed inside, the car was dangerously overloaded and difficult to drive, so the Witnesses pulled into a parking lot after they had safely outdistanced the crowd. According to Comodor, some of the Witnesses were disoriented and "stained with blood," and they washed up in the men's room of a nearby nightclub. Meanwhile, Flick dashed across the road, telephoned his wife, and asked her to drive over and pick up some of the victims. As the Witnesses regrouped, William Torso and Walter Vrusk—both still worried about the victims who might have remained in harm's way—drove back into downtown Imperial, but a second prolonged blast from the town's fire siren interrupted their rescue effort. Vrusk and Torso feared another violent outburst and retreated, turning around to pick up the Witnesses they had just deposited in the parking lot.

Checking their rearview mirror as they sped away, they found themselves being chased by several carloads of men—as well as, incredibly, Imperial's fire truck. The vehicle was packed with vigilantes who hoped to assault the Witnesses yet again.[10]

The mob caught up with Vrusk and Torso just as the Witnesses' car careened into the parking lot. Trapped inside their vehicle, Vrusk and Torso rolled up the windows and attempted to drive away, but the fire truck blocked their path. Vigilantes quickly encircled them and set upon the car with a variety of improvised weapons, including axes from the fire truck. As Vrusk described it, "One of the mob leaders punched his fist right through the window and said, 'Come on out. We're taking you guys for a ride.' Two other fellows broke the other windows of the car. . . . Then they . . . grabbed Bill Torso. Two men grabbed his arms, while one held an axe, ready to thrust it into his skull." Vrusk could hear men yelling, "Get the ropes! Bring the flags!"[11]

G. C. Flick, burdened by his crippled arm, was particularly vulnerable when the vigilantes renewed their assault on the Jehovah's Witnesses and brutalized them with "fists, knives, axes, and crowbars." He later described what happened to him and his fellow Witnesses during the second wave of the vigilantes' attack:

> I was lined up against a building along with four or five others . . .
> and there was a big fellow on each side of me and one in front of
> me. I was commanded to salute the flag. I started to explain why
> I could not, and was immediately hit on the left side of the face.
> Before I could right myself, I received another blow directly in the
> face. Another man then took a swing at me, but he missed and I
> fell to the ground. I was then stood on my feet and put in a line
> with the others who had been similarly treated in the meantime
> by three or four kidnappers. My nose and forehead were badly
> bruised, nose and mouth bleeding. One of the kidnappers told me
> that he would take me to the doctor at once if I would salute the
> flag. I told him that this would be the easy way out, so he threw
> me back against the house.

William Comodor saw assailants meting out the same kind of punishment to other Witnesses. "They got hold of Walter Hess and stood him up against a pole and started to beat his face, and then they tried to make him salute the flag," Comodor said. "Then they started on the others and gave them the same treatment, beating them and trying to make them salute the flag." Comodor himself also suffered again at the hands of vigilantes: "They kept dragging me, trying to make me salute the flag. They only stopped beating me because I was pretty badly battered up."[12]

A few of the Jehovah's Witnesses fled yet again during the chaos of the assault, some of them running from the melee and curling up in hiding places for several hours. Still unwilling to compromise their beliefs by saluting the American flag, the remaining Witnesses were loaded into the fire truck and told by vigilantes that "they were going to hang us," as William Comodor remembered. The Witnesses held firm even after this apparent death sentence. They continued to refuse to salute, at least in part because they feared God's wrath more than the mob's fury; being lynched, they felt, was preferable to incurring punishment from the Almighty for idolizing the flag. Fortunately for the victims, several state police patrol cars intercepted the fire truck as it headed toward a secluded area outside Imperial, and the Witnesses were grudgingly freed by their captors before they could be further harmed. Reeling from the assault, they were taken into custody and driven to the nearby state police barracks for questioning. Comodor was appalled by the condition of the men he saw there: Victor Lendin was "badly bruised and hardly able to walk"; Frank Kikosicsky "looked terrible—his face was swollen and his eyes were barely open"; both of Steve Chornenky's eyes had been blackened, and his face and back were "all swollen." State police officers interrogated the Witnesses until approximately 3:00 A.M. on Sunday. Afterward, they groggily headed to Allegheny General Hospital for treatment. Nursing a variety of injuries, most of the Witnesses were reunited with their worried families just before dawn, but John Golinie and Frank Kikosicsky were so afraid of returning to Imperial that they spent the rest of the night sleeping on the floor of the West End Kingdom Hall.[13]

At least one Jehovah's Witness who stayed in Imperial that night later regretted his decision not to flee. John Kikosicsky Jr. had avoided the brunt of the mobbing by remaining at home for most of the evening, although he too had been forced to fend off sporadic attacks by vigilantes. Near midnight, a group of rowdy men—many of them drunk, Kikosicsky observed—pulled up in front of the house in a pair of fire trucks. Foiled earlier in the evening by the state police's rescue of the other Witnesses, the rioters now focused their rage on Kikosicsky's house. After dousing the structure with water from a fire hose, the attackers unleashed a fusillade of rocks, shattering most of the windows and terrifying Kikosicsky's sleeping children. Kikosicsky rushed his family to the basement for safety as vigilantes burst in upstairs and rampaged, destroying whatever they could find. While Kikosicsky and his family slipped out a basement window and summoned police, men upended furniture and broke windows and crockery; someone even demolished a banjo by smashing it into a mirror. The house was a disaster when the family returned at 2:30 A.M. "The doors were shattered, curtains torn, windows and frames broken, quilts were all over the floor, glass was scattered everywhere, and on the beds were buckets of glass," Kikosicsky said. "A shelf was broken on the stove. The mattresses and bed clothing were all wet from the hoses. The wallpaper was also damaged by the water." As dawn approached, weary family members picked through the debris and tried to salvage what they could.[14]

The kind of mistreatment endured by Jehovah's Witnesses in Imperial, Pennsylvania, was shocking but not unusual. For several grim years in the early and mid-1940s, vigilantes in nearly every state of the Union brutalized hundreds of members of their faith in similarly fierce attacks. Targeted largely because they refused to salute the American flag, Witnesses throughout the United States were pummeled in situations ranging from riots involving hundreds of people to scuffles among a handful of men. Amazed at both the scope and the savageness of the persecution of Witnesses during the World War II era, the faith's most prominent attorney remarked in dismay that hundreds of his coreligionists were "beaten, kidnapped, tarred and feathered, throttled in castor oil, tied together and chased through the streets, castrated, maimed, hanged, shot, and otherwise consigned to mayhem."[15] Witnesses were so widely and viciously abused during the war years that some observers outside the faith— most of whom were careful to distance themselves from the victims' controversial beliefs—compared their plight to the persecution of religious minorities in Nazi Germany. "Nothing parallel to this extensive mob violence has taken place in the United States since the days of the Ku Klux Klan in the 1920s," the American Civil Liberties Union (ACLU) reported in 1941. "No religious organization has suffered such persecution since the days of the Mormons."[16]

The U.S. Supreme Court's notorious ruling in the *Gobitis* flag-salute case, handed down in June 1940, helped to ignite some of the worst anti-Witness violence of the period. *Gobitis* arose from the expulsion of Witness schoolchildren from a public school in Minersville, Pennsylvania, after they refused to participate in compulsory flag-salute exercises. In an opinion written by Justice Felix Frankfurter, the Supreme Court dismissed the Witnesses' claim that the Minersville School District's compulsory flag-salute regulation violated their right to free exercise of religion, which was protected by the First Amendment. Frankfurter's majority opinion in *Gobitis* dealt the Witnesses a heavy blow, in part because its timing was so unfortunate. In spring 1940, a number of European countries, including France, were in the process of being overrun by Germany, and many Americans believed that a secret network of Nazi spies and saboteurs—a Fifth Column, it was called—was at work in the United States. In many small communities, the Witnesses, who not only spurned the flag salute but also denigrated "patriotic" groups like the American Legion, were accused of distributing un-American propaganda and thus attempting to lay the groundwork for a German invasion. Frankfurter's opinion in the *Gobitis* case did not directly impugn the Witnesses' loyalty, but in many small towns it was misinterpreted as official confirmation of their disloyalty.[17]

Thanks to the incendiary combination of the Fifth Column scare and the *Gobitis* opinion, spring and summer 1940 proved to be especially grueling for the Jehovah's Witnesses. Civil liberties groups in all but four states reported anti-Witness rioting in that period. "What stands out as indisputable fact," the *Christian Century* asserted, "is that in many widely separated parts of the country, mob action has been stirred up against these people and scenes of disgraceful violence have occurred."[18] In June 1940, the Justice Department's Civil Rights Section was swamped with reports of hundreds of anti-Witness disturbances, many of them led or encouraged by police officers. Just days after the release of the Supreme Court's opinion in *Gobitis*, vigilantes ransacked and then burned a Witness Kingdom Hall in Kennebunk, Maine, sparking several days of rioting in the area. In subsequent weeks, large and violent anti-Witness demonstrations also erupted in Litchfield, Illinois; Rockville, Maryland; Jackson, Mississippi; and Richwood, West Virginia. With accounts of mobbings of Witnesses crossing his desk almost daily, a bewildered Solicitor General Francis Biddle reported that "self-constituted bands of mob patrioteers are roaming about the country, setting upon these people, beating them, driving them out of their homes."[19]

By September 1940, according to the American Civil Liberties Union's estimates, more than 1,000 Witnesses had been attacked in 236 separate incidents across the country. Although Witnesses in Illinois, Indiana, Ohio, and Oklahoma fared poorly, their coreligionists in Texas encountered the worst vigilantism, reporting a total of 41 assaults involving 304 victims between May and September 1940. This kind of "mayhem," as Witness attorney Hayden Covington called it, continued through fall and winter of that year, and by the end of 1940 a total of more than 1,500 Witnesses in the United States had been victimized in 335 separate attacks.[20] Mobbings and other forms of vigilantism became less frequent as World War II progressed (in part because fears of the Nazi Fifth Column ebbed), but the ACLU and the Justice Department continued to field reports of anti-Witness incidents long after V-J Day. The best estimates suggest that a total of between 800 and 2,000 attacks on Jehovah's Witnesses were reported in the United States during the early and mid-1940s. As the ACLU pointed out on numerous occasions, no religious minority in the United States had suffered so intensely from raw bigotry since the Mormons had been driven out to Utah a century earlier.[21]

The ACLU was so troubled by this outburst of religious persecution that it vigorously defended the Witnesses throughout the early and mid-1940s. Its leaders consistently spoke out against the widespread oppression of Witnesses, and on numerous occasions they implored local, state, and federal authorities to rein in and punish vigilantes who had participated in anti-Witness disturbances. Although many civil libertarians rallied to their defense, the Witnesses usually had far less luck when they asked state and local authorities to provide them with protection. In case after case, officials ranging from policemen and sheriffs to attorneys general and governors either ignored the Witnesses' requests for assistance or actively participated in the suppression of their civil liberties. Witnesses swamped the federal government with hundreds of complaints of abuse, but it too failed to do much on their behalf. On at least three separate occasions, Solicitor General Biddle publicly denounced violence against Witnesses and equated it with the worst excesses of Nazism, yet the Justice Department's fledgling Civil Rights Section (CRS) proved to be extraordinarily reluctant to prosecute anti-Witness vigilantes under federal civil rights laws. Justifying their hesitancy, CRS attorneys explained that the victims' pervasive unpopularity made it virtually pointless to bring such cases before juries.[22]

To make matters even worse for Jehovah's Witnesses, their persecution in the early and mid-1940s was not limited to physical punishment meted out in vigilante attacks. Religious discrimination permeated the lives of Witnesses of all ages, including schoolchildren and the elderly. Authorities in dozens of states and communities, for instance, enacted new laws or applied existing ones to suppress their First Amendment freedoms of religion, speech, and assembly. As one member of the U.S. Supreme Court noted in an opinion handed down in 1944, the Witnesses were "harassed at every turn by the resurrection and enforcement of little used ordinances and statutes," including long-dormant antisedition laws.[23] Furthermore, employers and coworkers often discriminated against Witnesses in their workplaces. Throughout the war years, the American Civil Liberties Union and the Justice Department received hundreds of complaints from highly qualified women and men who had been fired from or forced to quit their longtime jobs because they would not salute the American flag. Expulsions of Witness pupils from public schools—which were sometimes accompanied by assaults from livid teachers and school administrators—became so widespread in the late 1930s and early 1940s that Witnesses in dozens of communities were forced to operate their own makeshift educational institutions, called Kingdom Schools. Witness parents in several states were charged with neglect or disorderly conduct following the flag-salute expulsions of their children, and a few faced the prospect of sizable prison terms for their alleged crimes. Young Witnesses who registered for the military draft faced rampant discrimination as well. Even when Witnesses were able to present abundant evidence that they, like other recognized clergy, deserved minister's exemptions from military service, local draft boards and the federal Selective Service bureaucracy tended to dismiss their claims. As a result, thousands of Witnesses were parceled off to prison for violating the federal draft law enacted by Congress in 1940.[24]

Buffeted by a gale of intolerance in the United States in the early and mid-1940s, the Jehovah's Witnesses proved to be amazingly resilient. They were so unyielding and so deeply committed to their faith that widespread persecution did not squelch their passion for evangelizing. And, to their credit, when the Witnesses responded to religious persecution, they did not resort to vigilantism and coercion, as their critics so often did. Instead of meeting violence and bigotry with lawlessness of their own, the Witnesses pursued judicial recognition of their rights with the same righteous determination that marked their efforts to disseminate the teachings of the Bible. Realizing that, as Nebraska's governor once told the beleaguered Witnesses in his state, their "only recourse [was] the courts," they sought redress by mounting an intense legal counterattack against all forms of religious discrimination.[25] When they were arrested under bogus charges, Witnesses asserted stout defenses in court and repeatedly appealed their convictions. They also sought injunctions that would bar the enforcement of laws that were being used for no other purpose but to suppress their freedoms of religion, speech, assembly, and press. In the process, the Witnesses compelled courts at all levels, including the U.S. Supreme Court, to reinforce judicial protections for civil liberties—no small accomplishment for a group of largely unlettered and politically powerless zealots who were widely believed to be in league with Hitler.

The Witnesses' legal efforts resulted in hundreds of favorable rulings in municipal, state, and lower federal courts. Led by the resourceful Hayden Covington, a band of Witness attorneys worked tirelessly in courtrooms throughout the country to combat the manifestations of religious bigotry that were devastating so many members of their faith. Their brave efforts in cities like Connersville, Indiana, and Harlan, Kentucky, helped to safeguard the Witnesses' civil liberties from a flood tide of persecution. Although their many lower-court victories were significant both practically and symbolically, the Witnesses' most noteworthy legal accomplishments came before the final arbiter of American constitutional

rights, the U.S. Supreme Court. From 1938 to 1946, when the persecution of Jehovah's Witnesses was reaching almost epidemic pro-
portions in some parts of the United States, the Court handed down
twenty-three opinions covering a total of thirty-nine Witness-
related cases. It was a testament to the Witnesses' far-reaching unpopularity in this era (and perhaps their own contentiousness) that
they became embroiled in a wide range of disputes—flag salute
cases, free speech cases, leafleting ordinance cases, sedition cases,
draft law cases, tax cases, and even child labor-law cases. The
women, men, and children whose rights lay at the heart of these
cases did not always prevail when they appeared before the Supreme
Court; sometimes they lost, and with devastating consequences. But
as one scholar has noted, the Witness cases as a group nonetheless
had a "profound impact on the evolution of constitutional law" by
helping to bring minority and individual rights—areas long overlooked by the Supreme Court—out of the shadows and into the forefront of constitutional jurisprudence.[26]

In spring 1940, the Supreme Court handed down watershed rulings in two Witness cases. At the time, the Court's misguided opinion in the *Gobitis* flag-salute case stirred the greatest controversy:
anguished civil libertarians contended that the ruling was the result
of mounting hysteria over the war in Europe, but jingoists welcomed
it as a fitting tribute to the sacredness of the flag (as well as an indictment of those who failed to respect such a revered emblem). The
tempest over *Gobitis*, which climaxed in a wave of anti-Witness violence in spring and summer 1940, in some ways overshadowed the
Court's notable ruling in another Witness case, *Cantwell v. Connecticut*. In that opinion, the Supreme Court completed the important task of incorporating the First Amendment's protections of
speech, press, and religion into the due process clause of the Fourteenth Amendment, thus shielding those rights from infringement
by the states.[27]

The Witnesses' oppression continued throughout the war era, and
a torrent of their appeals reached the Supreme Court over the next
six years. By no means were all of these cases landmarks, but many
had a lasting impact on constitutional jurisprudence. In *Chaplinsky
v. New Hampshire*, for example, the Court first articulated the
"fighting words" exception to the First Amendment's protections of
speech.[28] That same year, in a dissent in the Court's first *Jones v.*

Opelika ruling, Chief Justice Harlan Fiske Stone advanced the idea
that the freedoms guaranteed by the First Amendment were so important to the functioning of democracy that they deserved to be
accorded a "preferred position" in the constitutional hierarchy.[29]
Thanks in part to several subsequent cases involving the First
Amendment freedoms of Witness proselytizers, Stone's arguments
for strengthening constitutional protections for individual and minority rights eventually were endorsed by a majority of his fellow
justices; and in 1943 they voted to reverse their rulings in both *Jones*
and *Gobitis*.[30] With those dramatic reversals, the Court took what
one account has called "some significant steps . . . in expanding the
liberties of Americans."[31]

It would be naive to suggest that the Witnesses were motivated
by anything other than self-interest when they defended their rights
in courtrooms across the United States in the early and mid-1940s.
As they pressed courts to enhance judicial protections for civil liberties, Witness litigants were primarily attempting to mitigate their
own suffering and ensure that they could propagate their beliefs—
and thus ready the world for Armageddon—without interference.
(Although their appeals did a great deal to bolster the First Amendment's protections of religious liberty, the Witnesses clearly did not
intend to facilitate the work of other religious organizations, which
they frequently disparaged as satanic "rackets.") Moreover, the Witnesses almost surely viewed their campaign in the courts as a
means to shake off some of the unfortunate stereotypes that dogged
them during the war era. Becoming intrepid champions of the First
Amendment allowed the Witnesses to refute rumors that they harbored anti-American sympathies and participated in Fifth Column
activities. It also provided them with a new forum for proselytizing—the courtroom. When they were called upon to testify in legal
proceedings, many Witnesses felt that they had been given a mar-
velous opportunity to praise the power of the Scriptures.

Whatever their intentions, the Witnesses served more than the
interests of their own peculiar faith when they turned to the courts
in the early and mid-1940s and sought legal protection for their civil
liberties. In an article published in the *Virginia Law Review* in 1943,
Francis H. Heller argued that the Witness cases could mark a "turning point for religious liberty" in the United States. Assessing their
potential impact, he suggested that they might play a crucial role in

Vigilantes attack a Jehovah's Witness meeting in Illinois in the early 1940s.

prompting the Supreme Court to "introduce a new set of constitutional values that will inevitably and probably permanently affect the American way of life."[32] Witness cases like *Cantwell v. Connecticut*, *West Virginia v. Barnette*, and *Jones v. Opelika* fulfilled Heller's expectations by helping to set the stage for a revolution in constitutional jurisprudence. "Harbingers of change, the [Witness] cases were part of a larger trend to expand individual civil liberties, a movement that grew under the pressures of World War II and eventually crested in the Warren Court era of the 1950s and 1960s," historian Merlin Owen Newton has written in a revealing study of two Witness cases, *Jones v. Opelika* and *Marsh v. Alabama*. "The decisions represented not only victories for the Jehovah's Witnesses," Newton concluded, "but also turning points in the nation's constitutional commitment to individual rights and indexes of the increasingly activist role of the Court as the guardian of personal liberty."[33] Coming at a critical juncture in constitutional history—it has been aptly described as the "seedtime of a modern constitution"—the

Witness cases helped to usher in an era in which the Supreme Court took unprecedented strides to protect civil and minority rights.[34] Without the guidance provided by these early "turning points," the high Court might have followed a far different path in the second half of the twentieth century.

Several ironies emerge from a close study of the persecution of Jehovah's Witnesses and the indelible mark it left upon American law. Because they refused to salute the American flag or serve in this country's armed forces, Witnesses routinely faced a host of shocking accusations, including charges that they were not a religious group but a subversive Fifth Column laying the groundwork for a Nazi invasion of North America. More the result of wartime jitters than hard evidence, the spurious indictments of the Witnesses' patriotism resulted in a wide and often brutal range of abuses, including physical violence, jailings, expulsions, and workplace discrimination. Ironically (and tragically), when they encroached upon the Witnesses' civil rights, those who accused the evangelists of lacking loyalty ran roughshod over some of their nation's most treasured liberties. Conversely, by repeatedly challenging discrimination in the courts, the Witnesses prompted a series of state and federal court rulings that bolstered the basic democratic freedoms articulated in the Bill of Rights. Thus, while the purported defenders of "Americanism" subverted both the letter and spirit of the Constitution, a group roundly condemned as spies and traitors remained true to that same charter and ultimately strengthened it.

That this took place in the United States during World War II, the country's all-consuming struggle against fascist Japan and Germany, is paradoxical as well. The gruesome persecution of religious minorities in Germany (including Bible Students, as Witnesses were known there) horrified many Americans and prompted them to tout the religious liberties enjoyed by members of all faiths in this country. Although such claims served a valuable rhetorical purpose as the nation rallied for war, they glossed over the fact that the worst outbreak of religious persecution seen in the United States in this century—the widespread abuse of Jehovah's Witnesses—was taking place as the nation prepared for and then entered the conflict with the Axis powers. The internment of thousands of Japanese Americans in relocation camps and the racial segregation of the armed forces exposed similarly disturbing contradictions between Americans' critique of fascism abroad and the appalling violations of civil liberties occurring in their own country.

The Jehovah's Witnesses themselves, of course, provide some of the greatest and perhaps most disturbing ironies. By and large, freedom of expression and freedom of conscience were not hallmarks of the Witnesses' own faith, which could be painfully repressive. Although they championed religious liberty and free expression when they campaigned in the courts in the early and mid-1940s, the Witnesses practiced a rigid faith that left virtually no room for ideological flexibility or dissent. In fact, those Witnesses who openly questioned the tenets or practices of their faith often found themselves "disfellowshipped," that is, excommunicated, and spurned. A number of disgruntled former members of the faith, most notably Barbara Grizutti Harrison, have written perceptive books and articles describing their agonizing struggles to cope with the brutal contradiction between the Witnesses' public advocacy of civil liberties and their private suppression of those very same freedoms. Whipsawed by that paradox, some Witnesses found themselves living what Harrison has called "a life in which one is not free to move around, explore, argue, flirt with ideas and dismiss them, [and] form passionate alliances and friendships according to no imperative but one's own nature and volition." In Harrison's experience—and in that of many others who became so disenchanted with the faith that they ultimately repudiated it—genuine freedom was a rare commodity in the Witnesses' world.[35] One memoirist bitterly equated his three decades as a Witness to slavery.[36]

As Harrison and others have argued, both adults and children were often expected to suppress their natural inquisitiveness and demonstrate an unswerving commitment to all facets of the Witnesses' labyrinthine faith—no small burden, given that their leaders instituted countless changes in doctrine and prophecy over the years. In retrospect, it seems clear that many Witness youngsters, including some whose stories are told in this volume, made enormous sacrifices, both in the long and short terms, to practice a faith they could not completely fathom. For instance, while some Witness children apparently reveled in defying school authorities and refusing to salute the American flag, others were enormously reluctant to abandon patriotic rituals at their schools and thus "stand out as being so completely different from my classmates," as one later described it. "I dreaded the start of each school day when everyone in the class would stand and pledge allegiance to the flag," this former Witness recalled. "Everyone except me. . . . The pressure to conform was enormous."[37] Harrison has written that for her, "the simple act of going to a theater or to a ball game was filled with dreaded expectation, because the national anthem might be played, the flag saluted." In time, she came to a painful realization—that because of her faith, she "could never expect not to be different from other people." Witnesses who grew up in such a burdensome environment often felt the disastrous effects for years afterward. Harrison, the most eloquent of the former Witness memoirists, has written that her childhood provided "about as good a preparation for real life as spending a commensurate amount of time in a Skinner Box on the North Pole."[38]

Although I examine such ironies in this book, I make no attempt to provide a comprehensive account of the Witnesses' history or their sometimes puzzling doctrines. (That has been done capably by several other authors, including M. James Penton in his indispensable *Apocalypse Delayed: The Story of the Jehovah's Witnesses*.) Instead, I focus on a narrow and troubling chapter of the Witnesses' history—their persecution throughout the United States in the early and mid-1940s—and gauge its formidable impact on American law. As legal histories go, this narrative is unconventional in that it relies most heavily upon the Witnesses' own accounts of their struggles in communities like Minersville, Pennsylvania, Connersville, Indiana, and Rochester, New Hampshire, to overcome religious discrimination and forge meaningful lives for themselves and their families. Largely forgotten for the past fifty years, their simple but eloquent voices tell a remarkable story, one that lays bare the extremes of cowardice and courage so often found in nations engrossed by war.

1. Jehovah Is My God and the Bible Is My Creed

Long after he had packed up and moved to Arizona with his wife, Walter Gobitas was fondly remembered by residents of Minersville, Pennsylvania, his hometown. In the early 1970s, a local man, Warren Schollenberger, recalled that Gobitas's friends and neighbors in the aptly named mining borough had always appreciated his cheerful demeanor. Ravaged by the hard-coal industry, Minersville was a grim and often desolate place, particularly during the Great Depression, but the area's pervasive gloom had rarely seemed to bother the good-natured Gobitas. "You could be down in a rut," Schollenberger explained, "but if Wally came along, he would cheer you up." He remembered Gobitas (whose surname would be misspelled "Gobitis" throughout his family's battles in the courts) as a great talker who had often employed a shopkeeper's version of the Socratic method when customers entered his store, the Economy Grocery, located at 15 Sunbury Street. "Wally loved discussion," Schollenberger said. "He was well-read, and he was good at drawing things out of people. Sometimes he would take the opposite side of an issue to make you think harder about your side. He did it just to draw information out of you, not to be difficult."[1] It had been generally understood in Minersville that the friendliness wasn't merely a sales ploy; Gobitas, townspeople knew, was inquisitive, and he genuinely enjoyed bantering with his customers.[2]

As much as he loved to converse with patrons and indulge in his other passion, reading, Walter Gobitas never shirked his responsibilities at the Economy Grocery, and it flourished. The son of hardworking Lithuanian immigrants, he spent almost every waking moment at the store. Lillian Gobitas Klose, his daughter, remarked that "his life was centered on the store." Her father was a "workaholic," she said, laboring long hours so that his independent business could

weather the formidable challenge posed by chains like A & P, a be-
hemoth that frequently swallowed smaller competitors. "You had to
be that way," Lillian said of her father's diligence, "to survive." The
children—Lillian, the eldest, was followed by five siblings—helped
out at the store every day and did their best to lighten their father's
load. Walter Gobitas sometimes received discarded hogs' heads from
a local slaughterhouse and cooked them in an enormous kettle that
the children referred to as "the witch's pot." At the time, Lillian
detested this chore, but she and her siblings dutifully removed
the eyes and jowls so that each head could be transformed into some
of the store's cold cuts, which drew shoppers from throughout
Schuylkill County. To make the meat products, Gobitas and his wife
toiled "all kinds of late hours," as Lillian remembered, working well
into the night to grind sausage, for instance, and stuff it into casings.
In retrospect, Lillian didn't mind the herculean efforts that everyone
in the family had to put into the store. She later wrote that despite
the long hours it required, "having a grocery store was much nicer"
than having to send their father off to work each morning in one of
the local hard-coal mines.[3]

Lillian had few complaints about her childhood in Minersville.
Aside from the horrors of "the witch's pot," she enjoyed working in
the Economy Grocery, and she got along well with her parents and
siblings. "We survived, and we had a good life," she said. "It was a
pleasant time." Thanks to the modest success of the store, which
expanded several times in order to meet the increasing demands of
customers, Walter Gobitas was able to provide for his family, and he
somehow found the time to teach his children how to maintain their
balance on ice skates and bicycles. (Not that the family could afford to invest much in sporting goods during the Great Depression:
"Each one of us didn't get a bicycle. We had a *family* bicycle," Lillian
said with a laugh.) He also supervised a variety of home-improve-
ment projects, providing lumber or wallpaper when one of the children wanted to fix up a room. For her part, Ruth Gobitas taught her
daughters homemaking skills, and they spent hours tackling chores
around the house. It was hard and sometimes tedious work, but the
girls made the best of it. "My sister Jeanne and I, we would do moun-
tains of ironing to help mother," Lillian said. "While we were working at night, we would put on one of the radio shows, like Red Skel-
ton, and really just have a good time."[4]

The Gobitas family quietly aided many distressed families in Minersville when the Great Depression crippled the linchpin of the region's economy, the already enfeebled anthracite coal industry. As hard-coal production plunged to its lowest levels since the 1890s, the mines laid off tens of thousands of unskilled workers in the 1930s, and they were hard pressed to find work and support their families. (The anthracite region's woes were hardly unique, of course; unemployment skyrocketed throughout Pennsylvania, idling close to a quarter of the state's workforce in 1935 and leaving 1.7 million people on the state's welfare rolls.)[5] Walter Gobitas, dismayed by the grinding poverty he saw every day on the streets of Minersville, used his modest resources to help unemployed men and their families pull through the storm. Customers who were strapped for cash often bought their goods "on the book" at the Economy Grocery, swallowing their pride and promising to pay Gobitas if and when they could scrape together enough money. Such arrangements were so routine that narrow rows of debtors' accounts gradually filled a small yellow ledger maintained by Lillian. Walter Gobitas was notoriously lenient, and impoverished families were rarely cut off from credit, even if they had failed to pay their bills for several months. "Some people never paid," Lillian later wrote, "but he never went after them." Although he had his own brood of children to clothe and feed, her father rarely grumbled about having to extend credit or forgive debts at the Economy Grocery; the times were brutal, and he and his family had been far more fortunate than many of their luckless neighbors. Gobitas knew only too well that some impoverished people in Minersville had been reduced to begging for food or "bootlegging" coal from abandoned mine shafts.[6]

Gobitas's compassion extended well beyond his charitable treatment of straitened customers at the Economy Grocery. Friends and extended family members were frequent guests at his dinner table, and he often persuaded them to settle in and stay for longer periods. Temporarily homeless because their new house was under construction, Lillian Gobitas's maternal grandparents paid a lengthy visit to her family in 1931, when she was seven years old. Grammy and Grampop, as they were called, brought with them a set of quirky religious beliefs and stacks of accompanying literature; Lillian's mother was a Methodist, but her grandparents had been ardent Bible Students for almost thirty years. (Members of the faith did not adopt the name "Jehovah's Witnesses" until a short time later.) Walter Gobitas was so intrigued by his in-laws' unusual faith that he furtively entered their room and scrutinized their belongings when they left the house to proselytize. The literature that he read during those forays into Grammy and Grampop's room outlined a faith unlike any he had encountered before, and he was transfixed. Writing later about her father's conversion from Catholicism, Lillian recalled that he had not only read the literature but "devoured" it, burying himself in passages from Isaiah and happily envisioning the grandeur of the earthly paradise that would bloom after the subjugation of "the beast" and his charges at Armageddon. "The truth," Lillian recalled, "was a pure delight to him." Gobitas was soon exclaiming to his startled children, "Look at what the Bible says!" and reading verses aloud, his voice rising in excitement when he came upon a particularly revealing or inspirational passage. It didn't take long for his fervor to spread to the rest of the family. Swept away by their father's enthusiasm, the children abandoned Methodist services, as did their mother. Soon the entire family was studying the Bible together at home, usually complementing their reading of the Scriptures with a careful review of Watch Tower tracts and periodicals. As she later put it, Lillian was "overjoyed" to discover her grandparents' faith, for it seemed to open up a whole new world—one in which spiritual rather than temporal wealth was treasured most highly.[7]

To grasp the intricacies of their complex faith, each member of the Gobitas family became a devoted student of the Bible. Several nights each week, they pored over it among themselves and with some of the eighty or so other Witnesses who lived in the area and gathered at the Kingdom Hall in Pottsville, Pennsylvania. During these sessions, the Witnesses read the Bible exhaustively—and literally. For proof that Satan would reign as invisible ruler of the temporal world until he was vanquished by God at Armageddon, they consulted 2 Corinthians (4:4), John (12:31), and 1 John (5:19). Evidence that the wicked would be eternally destroyed during this clash was provided by Matthew (25:41–46) and 2 Thessalonians (1:6–9). As Witnesses, the Gobitas family believed that after the sinful and their champion were eradicated at Armageddon, only a "little flock" of 144,000 people would ascend to heaven and rule with Christ, and this too was apparent from the Scriptures—Luke (12:32), Revelation

(5:9, 10 and 14:1, 3), and 1 Corinthians (15:40–53). Other tenets of their faith—that, for instance, total immersion at baptism signifies complete dedication to God or that Christians should obey all man-made laws that are in harmony with God's laws—were similarly proven simply by consulting the Scriptures. Even the name of the faith, they learned, could be traced to a particular passage—Isaiah 43: 10–11, in which God refers to himself as "Jehovah" and declares, "Ye are my witnesses."[8]

Having read in Luke that Jesus and his disciples had devoted themselves to "preaching and declaring the good news of the kingdom of God" by journeying among the people, Walter Gobitas understood that he too must become an unrelenting evangelist. Fired by a convert's zeal, he applied his considerable skills as a salesman to a new calling: like all Witnesses (who did not recognize a formal distinction between clergy and laymen), he was now a "minister of the Gospel" working to spread the message of the Bible. At her mother's urging, eight-year-old Lillian followed his lead and began proselytizing in neighboring boroughs in 1932. Young but intrepid, she earnestly approached homeowners with "testimony cards" bearing a brief message extolling the wisdom of the Bible as well as touting the usefulness of Watch Tower tracts, which she carried along in a satchel. "I have an important message," Lillian would say. "Would you please read this?" It required grit and persistence, but Lillian enjoyed "witnessing" and came to view it as the sincerest form of worshiping her Creator. Walking from door to door with armloads of literature, she felt as though she was upholding the laudable tradition established by Jeremiah, Samuel, and Timothy, brave youngsters whose preaching had been noted in the Scriptures. It was risky work; even young Witnesses were targets for abuse. At least initially, most people in Minersville, knowing the Gobitas family and appreciating their generosity, tolerated their eccentric new faith, but beyond the borough lay far more hostile territory. On a Sunday morning in 1935, Lillian and more than forty other Jehovah's Witnesses evangelized in New Philadelphia, Pennsylvania. Decades later, she could recount the scene vividly, recalling that the Witnesses

were mobbed in the town of New Philadelphia and put into cells in the fire house. There were about forty of us that went into New Philadelphia to do witnessing from house to house. I remember being at a door, all alone, when this police car came up and the householder was kind of aghast at this little girl being taken away. I was eleven at the time. The police called me into the car and took me past the mob into the fire house. I remember one girl punched me and the mob was trying to break down the door of the fire house. There must have been close to a thousand people. . . . Finally, at the end of the day the mob dispersed. The police kept the men, and the women and children could go home.

If there was a silver lining to her harrowing experience in New Philadelphia, it was that Lillian met and befriended another young Jehovah's Witness, Eleanor Walaitis, when the evangelists were holed up in the fire house. The two became lifelong friends.[9]

Ruth and Wally Gobitas were loving parents, and they did their best to make witnessing enjoyable for their children. "They always mixed fun with it," Lillian said, recalling how family members frequently stowed bathing suits and picnic baskets in the family car when they went witnessing on Sundays. After a long, tiring morning of preaching the Gospel from door to door, the family often stopped at a lake or swimming hole to relax. At one secluded spot near Pottsville, the family spread out its meal on picnic tables near a country schoolhouse and enjoyed the cool waters of a brook. Lillian appreciated such idyllic moments, particularly on days when the family proselytized among her friends and classmates in Minersville itself. In general, Lillian loved going from house to house and sharing her faith, but in Minersville she often found herself worrying what her non-Witness peers thought of her beliefs and her proselytizing. During one particularly discouraging encounter in the borough, Lillian rang the doorbell of a house and overheard a clearly annoyed young woman inside mutter, "Oh, it's that Lillian Gobitas." The woman came to the door and they had a pleasant conversation, but Lillian, knowing that she was viewed as a pest, came away feeling somewhat embarrassed, a feeling she never quite overcame in Minersville. "So when it was the turn for us to witness in Minersville," she said years later, "oh, I dreaded it."[10]

A speech delivered in summer 1935 by their leader Joseph Rutherford had an enormous long-term impact on Jehovah's Witnesses throughout the country, including Lillian Gobitas and her family. Addressing a convention in Washington, D.C., Rutherford praised the bravery of German Witnesses (still known as Bible Students), thousands of whom were enduring persecution for failing to offer sufficient tribute to the Third Reich. Banned as "troublemakers" and "quacks" by Hitler in 1935, Bible Students steadfastly refused to engage in idolatry by offering the "German greeting," or "Hitler salute." They paid dearly for their stubbornness. "Foremost amongst the opponents of Nazism were the Jehovah's Witnesses, of whom a higher proportion (97 percent) suffered some form of persecution than any of the other church [in Germany]," J. S. Conway has noted in a volume examining the fate of religion under the Third Reich. "No less than a third of the whole following were to lose their lives as a result of their refusal to conform or compromise."[11] Most Bible Students remained intractable even after they had been dispatched to concentration camps. Remarkably uncompromising, they received smuggled literature and bore witness within the death camps, further risking their already endangered lives to ensure that other inmates were exposed to the grandeur of the Scriptures. The Bible Students' valor throughout the Nazi era left a lasting impression on Rutherford, and he urged American Witnesses to draw an important lesson from their courage. Responding to a question at the Witnesses' 1935 convention, Rutherford stressed the relevance of the Bible Students' example by drawing a parallel between the "Hitler salute" and an analogous ceremony practiced throughout the United States—the flag salute. At that time, schoolchildren did not clasp their hands over their hearts while reciting the Pledge of Allegiance but offered a military-style salute and then slowly extended their arms forward at eye level. As Rutherford (and a number of other observers, including the American Civil Liberties Union) noted, the salute bore a disturbing similarity to the one rejected by the German Bible Students, and in his estimation it also deserved to be spurned as a form of idolatry. "He claimed that it was unfaithfulness to God to ascribe salvation by saluting an earthly emblem," Lillian recalled of Rutherford's speech. "He said he wouldn't do it."[12]

Ironically, although Walter Gobitas and his family traveled to Washington and attended most of the 1935 convention, they missed Rutherford's comments on the flag salute. (Always sensitive to his children's interests, Gobitas had arranged for a trip to the zoo that day.) After learning of Rutherford's criticism, Lillian and her brother Billy worried that their participation in patriotic rituals at school amounted to sacrilege. Deeply troubled, they discussed flag-saluting with their parents and read relevant passages from the Bible, including Exodus 20:4–6, Matthew 22:21, and John 5:21. For them, the passage from Exodus seemed to provide their answer:

> Thou shalt not make unto thee any graven image, or any likeness of any thing that is in heaven above, or that is in the earth beneath, or that is in the water under the earth. Thou shalt not bow down thyself to them, nor serve them: for I the Lord thy God am a jealous God, visiting the iniquity of the fathers upon the children unto the third and fourth generation of them that hate me.

According to Lillian, Walter and Ruth Gobitas counseled their inquisitive children, pointing out passages from the Bible and interpreting them when Lillian and Billy were puzzled, but they did not pressure the youngsters into openly opposing the flag salute. "This wasn't something my parents forced on us," Lillian wrote. "They were very firm about that, that what you do is your decision, and you should understand what you're doing. I did a lot of reading and checking in the Bible and I really took my own stand." By September 1935, both Lillian and Billy had resolved to heed Rutherford's admonition; they would not salute the American flag or recite the Pledge of Allegiance at their school. But Lillian hesitated, fearing that she might jeopardize her status there. "I was very chicken," she later confessed. A successful and popular student (she had been elected president of her seventh grade class, and her report card sported a column of A and A+ grades), she worried "that my worldly friends would drop me if I took my stand." One thought dominated Lillian's mind as she weighed the enormous costs of refusing to salute: "Oh, if I stop saluting the flag, I will blow all this!" In part because they were reluctant to become pariahs, Lillian and her brother "sheepishly" participated in flag-salute ceremonies for several weeks, raising their arms and mouthing the words of the Pledge of Allegiance if a teacher glanced in their direction. The compromise left Lillian feeling incredibly guilty, and she eventually confessed her cowardice to a fellow Witness. "Lillian," she was told, "Jehovah hates a hypocrite."[13]

A short time later, in early October, Rutherford reiterated his opposition to flag-saluting. He revisited the topic after Witness

Carleton Nicholls, a third-grader in Lynn, Massachusetts, was expelled from the Breed School for refusing to participate in pledge exercises. (The youngster had asserted that man-made symbols such as the American flag were unworthy of reverence because they represented nothing less than "the work of the devil.") With his characteristic fondness for overstatement, Rutherford laid out an emphatic case against the flag salute, suggesting that it was a profanation foisted on Americans by "a sect of so-called patriots," none of them genuine Christians. "The distinctive doctrine of the flag-saluting cult is the deification of the flag," Rutherford said. "It not only advocates the offering of respect, service, honor, reverence and devotion to the flag, but attempts to coerce worship to its god." Rutherford's conclusion was plain: "Jehovah's Witnesses conscientiously object and refuse to salute the flag and pledge allegiance to it." He said that the Massachusetts schoolboy had made a "wise choice" in deciding to abandon the flag salute and suggested that other Witnesses "who act wisely will do the same thing."[14] Rutherford's talk hit home with Lillian Gobitas as she agonized over her decision. "He explained that we respect the flag but that going through rituals before an image or emblem was actually idolatry," she later wrote. "Our relationship with Jehovah would strictly forbid this."[15]

On 22 October 1935, a beaming Billy Gobitas returned home from school and announced that he had finally mustered the courage to follow in the footsteps of the German Bible Students and Carleton Nicholls. "I stopped saluting the flag!" he breathlessly told his family. "The teacher tried to put up my arm, but I held on to my pocket." Billy's mettle inspired Lillian. "I really felt that it was the right thing to do—I just didn't have the courage to go ahead. So that spurred me," she said of her brother's decision. The next morning, with a nervous lump in her throat, she spoke with her teacher, Anna Shofstal, and divulged that she too would henceforth refuse to salute the flag because it seemed so clearly at odds with her religious beliefs. "Miss Shofstal, I can't salute the flag anymore," Lillian said. "The Bible says at Exodus chapter 20 that we can't have any other gods before Jehovah God." To Lillian's immense relief, Shofstal hugged her and praised her valor, but her young classmates simply "were awful," as she later explained. Many were appalled when, without explanation, she took her seat and remained silent during pledge exercises later that morning. "Soon everyone was staring at me," Lillian remembered. "But I felt elated." A few curious students later approached Lillian, and she eagerly told them how her deep commitment to her religious beliefs had led her to take such an un-usual—and decidedly unpopular—step. Impressed by the strength of her faith, these classmates proved to be understanding and support-ive, but others shunned Lillian and Billy. As she had feared, they became outcasts among a few of her peers. Some youngsters show-ered the Gobitas children with pebbles as they walked to and from school, while others derisively shouted, "Here comes Jehovah!" whenever they passed. Sixth-grader Edmund Wasliewski, another Minersville Witness who refused to salute at school, endured simi-lar abuse.[16]

Like all Jehovah's Witnesses, Lillian Gobitas and her family traced their faith's roots to the earliest Christian evangelists, the apos-tles. In America, their more recent forebears could be found among millennialists like the Puritans and the Millerites.[17] Charles Taze Russell, the founder of the Jehovah's Witnesses, followed the path that had been blazed by prophets William Miller and Ellen Harmon White in the mid-nineteenth century, a time when "the idea of the millennium remained a part of the ideological reservoir that shaped American public consciousness," according to one account.[18] In 1870, after dabbling with the Presbyterians and Congregationalists, Russell drifted away from mainstream religion and scrutinized the teachings of one of the Millerites' many progeny, the Seventh-day Adventists. Not yet twenty years old, the clothing merchant's son soon initiated Bible-study meetings of his own, bringing together a half-dozen Pittsburgh-area men who were interested in reading the Bible and discerning its prophecies regarding the Advent. While he remained firmly convinced that Christ's return was imminent, Russell's interpretation of the Scriptures differed in significant ways from that of the Seventh-day Adventists. For instance, he and the other members of the Pittsburgh Bible Class, as it was called, antici-pated that the Savior would be as invisible as "a thief in the night," not present in the flesh, when he returned at the Second Coming.[19]

Russell eventually charted his own theological course, and in 1873, in the first of his many publishing efforts, he offered an outline of his beliefs in the booklet "The Object and Manner of the Lord's Return." After tinkering with and refining his prophecy, Russell eventually settled on an elaborate chronology that is perhaps best summarized by one of its most careful students, former Witness Barbara Grizutti Harrison:

> Russell preached that 6,000 years of man's existence on earth had ended in 1872 . . . and that the seventh millennium had begun in 1873. The glorified Christ became invisibly present in 1874. . . . For forty years, the "saints," God's consecrated ones, would be "harvested," until, on October 1, 1914, the evil worldly system would collapse, God would have His everlasting day, and there would be a general "Restitution" for all mankind—but not before the "living saints" (Russell and his followers) would be suddenly and miraculously caught away bodily to be with their Lord, in 1878.[20]

On Good Friday 1878, Russell and the other "living saints" reportedly prepared for their ascension into heaven by donning white robes and standing on the Sixth Street Bridge in Pittsburgh, where they waited for several embarrassing hours. Russell later denied having been present, but the incident was reported in local newspapers and fed the perception that he was little more than a charlatan.[21]

In *The American Religion*, Harold Bloom has lambasted Russell as a "fairly brazen imposter" whose nearly incoherent writings grossly "offend anyone's sense of human dignity."[22] Russell's faults as a writer were perhaps the least of his shortcomings. Accusations of sexual and financial improprieties, for example, dogged him throughout his adult life. Russell's notorious difficulties with his long-suffering wife Maria, aired during a series of sensational libel, separation, and alimony suits near the turn of the century, became a particular source of embarrassment for both the pastor and his flock. (Russell's stature couldn't have been enhanced when a Pennsylvania judge concluded that his "continual arrogant domination" of his wife was enough to "render the life of any sensitive Christian woman a burden and make her life intolerable.")[23] Despite his frequent missteps, he gradually built the Watch Tower Bible and Tract Society into a small but vigorous religious empire by catering to— and in some ways reinvigorating—the country's longstanding appe-

tite for millennial prophecy. Under his sometimes erratic stewardship, what began as a modest Bible-study group developed into a vibrant religious movement with thousands of zealous followers.
By 1940 it boasted approximately 40,000 adherents in the United
States.[24]

As a prophet of the millennium, Russell proved to be a far luckier
man than most of his predecessors. Although Armageddon did not
arrive in 1914, in that year Europe was engulfed by a war that lasted
for four years, claimed hundreds of thousands of lives, and laid waste
to much of the Continent. The timely outbreak of that conflict
helped stave off the kind of "great disappointment" among believers
that had fractured the Millerites in the 1840s, and it gave Russell a
chance to tweak his prophecy of the world's end. Like many prophets
before him, Russell responded to the glitch in his forecast by reex-
amining the Scriptures and issuing a new, and presumably more reliable, prediction for Armageddon. "Because 1914 did not bring the
end of the world as Russell had expected but did see the outbreak of
the First World War," M. James Penton has written in his history of
the Witnesses, "he revised his expectations and suggested that the
war would lead to Armageddon." Russell now prophesied that with
the European war having acted as a prelude, the destruction of Baby-
lon would begin in earnest in 1918. At Armageddon, the "little
flock"—the group of 144,000 anointed ones referred to in Revelation—would ascend to heavenly glory.[25]

Russell, however, died two years before the rapture was to take
place, succumbing to a prolonged illness in fall 1916; and Joseph
Rutherford succeeded him as Watch Tower leader.[26] Rutherford,
often called "Judge" in deference to a brief stint he had spent on the
bench in Missouri, picked up on a number of Russell's most cherished themes and "stayed the course," according to Merlin Owen
Newton. "Imposing an iron discipline, he soon gained almost total
control over the goals, literature, method of organizing, and finances
of the Watch Tower establishment. Then, having vanquished his opponents within the faith, he unified his followers by [initiating] a
hard-hitting attack on the enemies beyond it." Lashing out at a diz-
zying variety of targets, Rutherford excoriated mainstream religions
as "rackets" and, true to Russell's example, took the widely unpopular position of opposing America's entry into World War I. (For Witnesses, the only war worth fighting was the sacred one waged by God

against "the beast" at Armageddon.) Because of their sharp attacks on the war effort, Rutherford and seven other Watch Tower directors wound up in federal prison as violators of the Espionage Act of 1917. After receiving a twenty-year sentence in 1918, Rutherford declared, "This is the happiest day of my life," and perhaps it was, for persecution at the hands of a degenerate government allowed him to step out of the shadow of his predecessor and assume the mantle of a heroic Christian martyr. Rutherford remained in control of the organization throughout his prison term, which turned out to be brief; an appeals court overturned the convictions in May 1919, and the federal government eventually dropped all its charges.[27]

Emerging from prison weakened by pneumonia but in firm command of the faith, Rutherford undertook a number of important doctrinal and practical initiatives, none of them more significant than his recognition of millions of people as "Jonadabs." Charles Russell had focused his energies on preparing the "elect" for their eventual ascent into heaven with Christ after Armageddon. According to historian David Manwaring, Rutherford developed the idea that beyond these "saints from birth . . . there is a much larger group of people who have sinned much, not through evil intent but through ignorance and wrong training." Saving Jonadabs from dissolution would not give them a place with the elect in heaven, but it would prepare them for the next best thing: eternal lives in an earthly paradise ruled by the Savior as his "kingdom of heaven on earth." As Manwaring has written, the distinction drawn by Rutherford between the elect and the "Great Multitude" of Jonadabs "revolutionized Witness values and practices." In this new scheme, millions of people who were not predestined for heavenly splendor could at least enjoy earthly bliss—provided they were rescued from the clutches of corrupt churches, exposed to the teachings of the Bible, and given an opportunity to save others themselves.[28]

Rutherford maintained that the rescue of millions of Jonadabs could be accomplished only through incessant proselytizing. Speaking to a convention in 1922, he urged Witnesses to "herald the message far and wide. The world must know that Jehovah is God and that Jesus Christ is King of kings and Lord of lords. . . . Behold, the King reigns! You are his publicity agents. Therefore advertise, advertise, advertise the King and his kingdom." Elaborating on the significance of Rutherford's speech, a subsequent issue of *The Watch*

Tower concluded that "the obligation is laid upon every one of the consecrated from this time forward to act as a publicity agent for the King and the Kingdom." By the mid-1930s, Witness propagandists were stocked with plenty of rhetorical ammunition—tracts, magazines, booklets, Bibles, records and record players, bookmarks, "sound cars" capable of blaring prerecorded messages—as they went about the task of saving Jonadabs and mitigating Satan's baleful influence. Witness "publicity agents" initially confined themselves to door-to-door proselytizing, but early in 1940 they began witnessing on street corners and public squares, a shift in strategy that left them far more vulnerable to vigilante attacks.[29]

Witnesses came to regard proselytizing, not participation in traditional Sunday-morning church services, as the highest form of worship of their Creator. "I consider it my Christian duty to preach the Gospel, not by standing up in church and preaching," one Iowa Witness explained in 1940, "but by going from house to house with literature and asking people if they will read it."[30] That the world was hurtling toward Armageddon made them even more eager to spread what they called "the most urgent message of all time": the teaching of the Scriptures. Statistics kept by the faith's headquarters revealed the strength of the Witnesses' commitment to proselytizing. In 1939, Witnesses who had organized themselves into 2,425 "companies" (or individual congregations) traveled more than 2 million miles while distributing literature. That year, they made no fewer than 1,285,327 "back calls" (return visits to people who had previously expressed an interest in their materials); sold roughly 150,000 recordings of Rutherford's lectures on various topics; and distributed 27 million publications throughout the United States. The widespread dissemination of printed materials proved to be the backbone of the Witnesses' preaching campaign. Between 1931 and 1939, they distributed almost 216 million pieces of literature, many of them books and booklets ostensibly authored by Rutherford. "With an organization that any publisher would envy, Judge Rutherford has built himself up into the best-seller of best-sellers," one observer remarked in 1940. "Some of his books have passed the 2,500,000 mark [in sales], and most booklets, according to the title pages, have a first printing of 10,000,000 copies."[31]

The Witnesses' fervor as propagandists was remarkable—and quite often disturbing. Witnesses did not canvass small towns so much as they simply overwhelmed them, sometimes descending with as many as 1,000 zealous proselytizers at a time. In describing the impact of these small armies of evangelists, a recent Witness history has proudly noted that the "effect was like that of the symbolic swarm of locusts referred to in the Scriptures."[32] In his book *Religion,* Rutherford went to considerable lengths to explain why the comparison between Witness proselytizers and locusts was an appropriate one:

> [Witnesses] do not loot or break into houses, but they set up their phonographs before the doors and windows and send the message of the kingdom right into the houses into the ears of those who might wish to hear. Locusts invade the homes of the people and even eat the varnish off the wood and eat the wood to some extent. Likewise God's faithful witnesses, likened unto the locusts, get the kingdom message right into the house and they take the veneer off the religious things that are in that house . . . and show them that the doctrines that have been taught to them are wood, hay and stubble, destructible by fire, and they cannot withstand the heat.[33]

That the Witnesses aggressively sought out Jonadabs on Sunday mornings, when more traditional forms of worship were in full swing, made them still more exasperating. Even their staunchest defenders conceded that the Witnesses could be extraordinarily bothersome as they preached the Gospel in public. The Reverend John Haynes Holmes, a vocal champion of the Witnesses' civil liberties, admitted that their persistent evangelizing sometimes "came close to disturbing the public peace." He maintained that "they are a peculiarly aggressive, even obnoxious set of people, at least as judged by ordinary standards of polite, conventional life," and that the general public often found their tactics "disquieting, upsetting, alarming."[34] Although the ACLU lamented the abuse of Witnesses and pleaded for the protection of their civil liberties, the organization conceded that they proselytized "by annoying methods."[35]

Listeners who were not unsettled by the Witnesses' predictions about the conflagration at Armageddon often were stunned by their vituperative attacks on the "hypocrisy of Christendom's clergy." The "most reprehensible men on earth," the clergy had foisted

"Satanic doctrine" on mankind for thousands of years and fomented war after war by wickedly "encouraging the rulers to believe that the king reigns by divine right" and is thus infallible. Foremost among the many religious figures pilloried by Rutherford were the debauched leaders of the "harlot" Roman Catholic Church. In one typical screed he assailed the church's leadership as "the wickedest organization of liars, murderers and gangsters that has ever cursed the planet," a heinous gang "attempting to grab control of the nations of earth" through a variety of underhanded methods, including the encouragement of global war. Many of Rutherford's writings equated the church with a degenerate "whore" whose licentiousness had wreaked havoc on mankind, corrupting millions who lacked the wisdom and fortitude to live according to the teachings of the Bible. "Since the World War the old harlot has daily increased her boastful, scornful attitude and arrogance in parading herself before the people of the earth," Rutherford wrote in *Enemies*. "The harlot, that is, the Roman Catholic organization, goes up and down the earth with her instruments of sound under the leadership of the Devil and in opposition to the faithful followers of Christ Jesus. . . . The harlot puts forth her best endeavors to crush everything that makes known the truth as god has put it in his Word."[36]

Rutherford claimed that the depraved "Roman Catholic Hierarchy" and its deluded subordinates were laying siege to both Christianity and the First Amendment by "taking the lead in compulsory flag-saluting, and building images or monuments." Here, as he saw it, was yet another example of the great "racket" of religion working "clearly in opposition to the commandments of Almighty God." In *Enemies*, published in 1937, two years after his watershed speech praising the steadfastness of the German Bible Students, Rutherford again made his case against flag-saluting, this time hinting at the Almighty's possible reaction to such blasphemy:

> The making of images . . . and using them in what is supposed to be worship of God is a direct violation of God's law and shows that those who thus practice are unwittingly falling to the Devil. The saluting of flags or men or other like objects, or bowing down to them, is attributing protection and salvation to creatures or things, and that is a religious formalism and in open violation of God's law. No creature can divide his affections or devotion be-

tween God and anything. Jehovah God is his only protector and is the Life-giver, and he is therefore a "jealous god," or zealous for righteousness, and will not permit his name or his Word to be sullied by any part of the Devil's operations or schemes.

But while they would not want to incur the wrath of a "jealous god" by participating in one of Satan's most unholy "operations or schemes," the Witnesses were sensitive to charges that their abhorrence of the flag salute betrayed a lack of loyalty to the United States. Consequently, the same materials that excoriated members of the "Catholic Hierarchy" as incorrigible hoodlums were full of reminders that Witnesses were upstanding citizens who loved their country and happily honored its laws, provided, of course, that such laws conformed with the word of God. If not, then Witnesses were obliged as devout Christians to break them, regardless of the earthly consequences. It was far better to be arrested or expelled from school or pummeled by vigilantes, they reasoned, than to forfeit life's ultimate reward, a place in Christ's kingdom, by compromising their beliefs.[37]

As they attempted to reconcile their deep religious convictions with the patriotic expectations of their communities, the Witnesses made a rare attempt to meet their critics halfway. They formulated an alternative to the Pledge of Allegiance that was meant to help defuse misunderstandings about their fidelity to the United States. During pledge exercises, Witnesses were to stand at attention, doff their hats, and recite a brief statement affirming their loyalty to both God and country:

> I have pledged my unqualified allegiance and devotion to Jehovah the Almighty God and to his Kingdom for which Jesus commands all Christians to pray. I respect the flag of the United States and acknowledge it as a symbol of freedom and justice for all. I pledge allegiance and obedience to all the laws of the United States that are consistent with God's law as set forth in the Bible.[38]

Despite its reasonableness, the Witnesses' alternative pledge failed to mollify many self-appointed arbiters of patriotism, especially war veterans belonging to groups like the American Legion and the

Veterans of Foreign Wars. As the Witness schoolchildren who abandoned flag-saluting at their public school in Minersville, Pennsylvania, quickly discovered, jingoists viewed their equivocations as signals of outright disloyalty.

According to Lillian Gobitas, authorities at their school "watched for two weeks" in fall 1935 without subjecting the young Witnesses to formal disciplinary action. But the superintendent of schools, Charles E. Roudabush, was incensed by their behavior, and he resolved to punish them for it.[39] Employed by the local school system since 1914, Roudabush had long been known in Minersville as a relentless disciplinarian, and he did little to sully that reputation for toughness as he dealt with the Witnesses. In October 1935, Roudabush asked the state's Department of Public Instruction to determine if he possessed the legal authority to penalize the Witnesses if they balked at saluting the American flag. An official in that agency consulted with Pennsylvania's attorney general, Charles J. Margiotti, and quickly issued an order that apparently gave Roudabush the authority to punish the recalcitrant Witnesses if they had broken a formal school regulation—at that point, something Minersville's public schools lacked. "Refusal of any pupil who owes allegiances to our national government to participate in the exercise [of flag-saluting]," Margiotti explained, "should be considered an act of insubordination and treated as any other refusal to obey the lawful regulations of our schools." In short, if Minersville's school board formalized local tradition by adopting a flag-salute regulation, the superintendent could censure Edmund Wasliewski and the Gobitas children as he would any other disobedient pupils.[40]

Armed with Margiotti's opinion, Roudabush summoned the Jehovah's Witnesses to a school board meeting on 6 November 1935. In anticipation of that showdown, Walter Gobitas met privately with two school board members, Thomas McGurl and his brother John, and asked that his children be spared punishment. Lillian and Billy, he explained, were simply devout Christians doing their best to honor the sacred lessons they had learned from the Scriptures. Gobitas later said that the two men had not been very receptive to his call for religious tolerance, pleading with him, "Come on, Wally, can't you get off this thing? We're under a lot of pressure. If you could just forget this flag thing, it would save us all a lot of trouble."[41] Gobitas scoffed at the notion of abandoning his beliefs and decided to make the case for his family before the full school board.

Nervous but resolute, he argued that even though they were loyal Americans who greatly respected the flag and the freedoms it represented, the Witnesses' allegiance to their faith left them no choice but to refrain from saluting a man-made object. "We are not desecrating the flag," he said. "We show no disrespect for the flag, but cannot salute it. The Bible tells us this, and we must obey." Lillian and Billy seconded their father's arguments with brief letters that cut to the core of the flag-salute dispute. Lillian wrote:

1. The Lord clearly says in Exodus 20: 3, 5, that you should have no gods besides Him and that we should serve Him.

2. The constitution of the United States is based upon religious freedom. According to the dictates of my conscience, based on the bible, I must give my full allegiance to Jehovah God.

3. Jehovah is my god and the bible is my creed. I try my best to obey the Creator.[42]

Billy wrote in a similar vein:

I do not salute the flag because I have promised to do the will of God. That means that I must not worship anything out of harmony with God's law. In the twentieth chapter of Exodus it is stated, "Thou shalt not make unto thee any graven image, nor bow down to them nor serve them for I the Lord thy God am a jealous God visiting the iniquity of the fathers upon the children unto the third and fourth generation of them that hate me." I am a true follower of Christ. I do not salute the flag not because I do not love my country but I love my country and I love God more and I must obey His commandments.[43]

The Witnesses' touching appeals were shunted aside. Lillian later wrote that in his oral report to the school board, Roudabush, as stern as ever, "insisted that our stand amounted to insubordination" and made no effort to accommodate the Witnesses' controversial religious beliefs. The school board was only too willing to follow his lead. It unanimously formalized a flag-salute measure, ruling that "all teachers and pupils of the [Minersville] schools be required to salute the flag of our country as a part of the daily exercises." In keeping with Roudabush's sentiments, the same measure held that "refusal to salute the flag shall be regarded as an act of insubordination and shall be dealt with accordingly." The superintendent wasted little time in invoking his new authority to mete out punishment against the Witnesses. Moments after the board approved the flag-salute regulation, Roudabush declared, "I hereby expel from the Minersville schools Lillian Gobitas, William Gobitas and Edmund Wasliewski for this act of insubordination, to wit, failure to salute the flag in our school exercises."[44] Roudabush and the board told the children and their families that the expulsions were effective immediately. "They said at the meeting, Don't even come to school tomorrow!" Lillian recalled.[45]

As he stormed out of the school board meeting, Walter Gobitas delivered a kind of rallying cry for Witnesses who had resolved to protect their beleaguered families from intolerance. His voice suffused with anger, he yelled, "I'm going to take you to court for this!"[46] In spring 1937, more than a year after Charles Roudabush expelled his children, Gobitas made good on his angry promise. Represented by Olin Moyle, the Jehovah's Witnesses' national legal counsel, and Philadelphia attorney Harry M. McCaughey, Gobitas submitted a bill of complaint against the school district in the U.S. District Court in Philadelphia. Acting individually and as "next friend" of Lillian and Billy, Gobitas asserted that the enforcement of a compulsory flag-salute measure violated the rights guaranteed to the youngsters under both the Eighth and Fourteenth Amendments to the Constitution by denying them freedom of speech and religion and by subjecting them to cruel and unusual punishment. Gobitas asked the court to enjoin the school district from enforcing the onerous and unconstitutional flag-salute regulation against the Witness children and thus to restore their right to "enjoy full religious freedom in the manner dictated by conscience." The courts botched the spelling of Walter Gobitas's surname, and the case was known as *Gobitis v. Minersville School District*.[47]

Skirmishing between Gobitas and the school board erupted even before the case went to trial early in 1938. Three weeks after Gobitas filed his bill of complaint, the Minersville School District filed a motion with Judge Albert Maris to dismiss it. The motion to dismiss, prepared by the Philadelphia law firm Rawle and Henderson under the supervision of attorney Joseph Henderson, attacked Gobitas's complaint on jurisdictional grounds as well as on its merits.[48] Before the case could proceed to trial, it was left to Maris, a Quaker who had served in World War I, to rule on the school district's claim that the case should be thrown out even before it reached trial. Although he reserved judgment on part of the school district's argument regarding jurisdiction, Maris left little doubt as to where he stood on the merits of the case, expressing concern in his ruling that the Minersville school board had used "our beloved flag, the emblem of religious liberty, to impose a religious test as a condition of receiving the benefits of public education. And this has been done without any compelling necessity of public safety or welfare." As he denied the motion to dismiss Gobitas's complaint, Maris gutted the school board's principal defenses of the compulsory flag-salute measure. He refused, for instance, to countenance the notion that the school board was empowered to decide whether or not the refusal to salute the American flag was an inherently "religious" choice. As Maris saw it, the protections of the First Amendment guaranteed that such a determination could be made only by the Witnesses themselves. Since "liberty of conscience means liberty for each individual to decide for himself what is to him religious," permitting "public officers to determine whether the views of individuals sincerely held and their acts sincerely undertaken on religious grounds are in fact based on convictions religious in character would be to sound the death knell of religious liberty," Maris wrote. "To such a pernicious and alien doctrine this court cannot subscribe." He determined that in "refusing for conscience sake to salute the flag, a ceremony which they deem an act of worship to be rendered to God alone," the Witness children in Minersville were

> within the rights of conscience guaranteed to them by the Pennsylvania Constitution. The conclusion is inescapable that the requirement of that ceremony as a condition of the exercising of their right or the performance of their duty to attend the public schools violated the Pennsylvania Constitution and infringed the liberty guaranteed them by the Fourteenth Amendment.

The first round of a long, exhausting fight in the courts thus went to Walter Gobitas and his children.[49]

The motion to dismiss having failed miserably, *Gobitis v. Miners-ville School District* went to trial in Maris's courtroom on 15 February 1938. Since their faith—with all its controversial and sometimes misunderstood tenets—stood at the center of the case, Walter Gobitas and his children testified at length. Despite their nervousness, they were able to outline their religious beliefs calmly and succinctly, in part because they felt so at ease before Maris, whom Lillian Gobitas later described as "a very agreeable person, not formidable at all." Following the testimony of their father, who had explained how he had devoted himself to teaching his children "to believe and study the Bible for a long time," Billy and Lillian cited a number of passages from Scripture as they justified their refusal to salute. Lillian ignited a brief furor when she referred to a particularly telling verse from the Book of John, one in which children are admonished to "keep yourselves from idols." Henderson, the school district's lead counsel, vigorously objected, claiming that the Witnesses' testimony had degenerated into a Bible-study session; but Maris, doing his best to understand the Witnesses' faith, overruled him. Also taking the stand for the plaintiffs was Frederick W. Franz, a prominent Witness who had been dispatched to Philadelphia from the faith's headquarters in Brooklyn. Despite strident objections from Henderson, who unsuccessfully maintained that his testimony was immaterial, Franz reiterated the Gobitas family's claims that flag-saluting amounted to idolatry.[50]

The lone witness for the defense was Superintendent Charles Roudabush. The passage of time since the expulsions had done nothing to cool Roudabush's fury toward Walter Gobitas and his children; decades after the trial, Lillian recalled that he had been "very feisty on the stand, very angry and hostile." In a startling exchange with the judge, the superintendent asserted that Lillian and Bill held such "perverted views" about the flag salute because they had been "misled" and "indoctrinated" by their deluded parents. Dismissing the Witnesses' claims to the contrary (as well as Judge Maris's conclusion in his ruling denying the motion to dismiss), Roudabush clung to the idea that the flag salute "is not a religious exercise in any way and has nothing to do with anybody's religion. . . . As I see it, your Honor, I feel that this is not a matter of religion at all, it has nothing to do with religion, and I think the objection by the Jehovah's Witnesses [to the compulsory ceremony] is uncalled for."[51]

Lillian later wrote that despite this display of Roudabush's manifest hostility to her family and its faith, "we never felt any animosity on our part toward him." As the trial came to a close, they simply hoped that "he would eventually see the error in his ways" and embrace Christ's teachings.[52]

Maris's final ruling in *Gobitis v. Minersville School District*, issued in June 1938, reaffirmed the forceful call for religious tolerance he had issued earlier in denying the school district's motion to dismiss. In order to clarify why "loyal American citizens" such as Gobitas and his children "sincerely and honestly believed that the act of saluting a flag contravenes the law of God," Maris outlined some of their basic religious beliefs, even quoting one of the Witnesses' favorite passages from Exodus to explain their reluctance to engage in idolatry. Having taken the time to listen to their testimony and to study the subtleties of their unusual faith, he was able to appreciate that the Witnesses' refusal to participate in flag-salute exercises "was based solely upon their sincerely held religious convictions that the act was forbidden by the express command of God as set forth in the Bible." While the Witnesses had a valid reason for refraining from saluting—they believed that doing so could result, as Maris put it, in their "eternal destruction"—the school district could offer no constitutionally viable justification for encroaching on their religious liberty by enforcing a compulsory flag-salute measure. Maris scoffed at Roudabush's argument that the rule was required to maintain a degree of discipline and safety in the schools. "I think it is . . . clear from the evidence," he wrote, "that the refusal of these two earnest Christian children to salute the flag cannot even remotely prejudice or imperil the safety, health, morals, property or personal rights of their fellows." Although he did not claim to admire or even fully to understand their beliefs, Maris was firmly convinced that the Witnesses' rights under the Fourteenth Amendment were being violated by the flag-salute measure. He granted the injunction requested by Wally Gobitas.[53]

Maris's ruling gained favorable editorial attention from Philadelphia's main newspapers, the *Inquirer* and the *Bulletin*, but it enraged Charles Roudabush. The superintendent found it incomprehensible that Maris had praised the Witnesses—they demonstrated "sincerity of conviction and devotion to principle," the judge had written, as well as "sturdy independence of thought and action"—

while pillorying the school board's position as not only unconstitutional but also inherently undemocratic. ("Our country's safety surely does not depend on the totalitarian idea of forcing all citizens into one common mold of thinking and acting or requiring them to render lip service of loyalty in a manner which conflicts with their sincere religious convictions," Maris had written. "Such a doctrine seems to me utterly alien to the genius and spirit of our nation and destructive of that personal liberty of which our flag itself is the symbol."[54]) Seething in the wake of defeat, Roudabush issued a vitriolic statement assailing both the ruling and the Witnesses whose rights had been shielded by it. As always, he did not mince words: children who failed to honor their flag were "aliens," he fumed, and they simply did not "belong in the public schools which are tax supported." Openly doubting the validity of the Witnesses' faith, he also suggested that teachers in Minersville's public schools possessed "as much right to teach and require elements of patriotism as a parent has to indoctrinate the children with false religion." Given Roudabush's displeasure with Maris's ruling, his eagerness to appeal it surprised no one. The school district, with its legal bills mounting, turned to patriotic organizations for financial assistance, and it received substantial contributions from the Patriotic Order of the Sons of America and from the Order of Independent Americans. Their underwriting, apparently offered in the interest of saving the flag from the scourge of religious zealotry, allowed the school district to file an appeal with the Third Circuit Court of Appeals late in summer 1939.[55]

With the case going to the appellate court, Maris's injunction barring enforcement of the flag-salute regulation was stayed, and the Witness children were forced to remain out of school. At first, the Gobitas children studied at home under the tutelage of Jenny Wylonis, a young, eager Witness who had often performed housekeeping duties for their mother. Though she lacked much in the way of experience or formal training, Wylonis was unruffled in her new post as teacher, and she patiently tutored Billy and Lillian as they pored over their texts at home each day. Luckily, both children had been allowed to keep their schoolbooks after their expulsions, and they clambered upstairs each day for their lessons. When Roudabush learned of this somewhat informal arrangement, he dispatched a curt letter to Walter Gobitas declaring that his children "would be

A group of Jehovah's Witness children who attended the Kingdom School near Minersville, Pennsylvania, in 1939.

sent to reform school," as Lillian later put it, if they were not taught by a qualified teacher. A crisis seemed imminent, but help came from Paul and Verna Jones, Witnesses who lived on a farm some thirty miles from Minersville. To accommodate the growing number of young Witnesses (including four of their own children) who had been banished from local public schools because of their refusal to salute, Paul Jones offered to modify his home and transform it into a Kingdom School, run in accordance with God's word by the Witnesses themselves. The institution complemented the standard subjects with intense spiritual instruction grounded in the lessons of the Bible. After Jones collected supplies from local Witnesses and leveled the wall separating his living and dining rooms, the fledgling institution could serve forty students in grades one through eight. Erma Metzger—Lillian fondly remembered her as a "young teacher from Allentown who was interested in the [biblical] truth"—taught everyone. The school often was a haphazard arrangement, but it proved to be a blessing for the Gobitas children as their case inched its way through the federal courts; there seems little doubt that

Roudabush would have eagerly seized on any pretext to dispatch them to reform school.[56]

In the middle of the Great Depression, operating the Kingdom School required enormous sacrifices of time and energy from everyone involved. Having converted their home into a bustling school, Paul and Verna Jones bore perhaps the heaviest load. Many students, including Lillian and Bill Gobitas, lived too far away from the farm to return home each evening after classes, and they boarded with the Jones family. Lillian, who was joined at the Kingdom School by Eleanor Walaitis, the friend she had made during the New Philadelphia mobbing, later wrote that her time on the farm had been filled with both hardships and happiness.

> The Joneses had four children of their own; yet they took in at least ten others. We slept three to a bed and turned over by signal and mutual agreement! Another Witness family nearby took in nearly as many, and soon school attendance grew to over 40. There was a lot of fun and giggling, but there were chores too. We were up at 6 A.M. The boys helped outside, and the girls had kitchen duty. Our parents came Friday after school to take us home for the weekend.

Other students stayed at the nearby farm of Witness Charles Steigerwalt. Decades later, Steigerwalt's son Earlin marveled at his mother's resourcefulness, which was instrumental to the Kingdom School's success. With more than a dozen children in her care, she was a whirlwind of activity around the house, cooking, cleaning, and laundering from dawn to dusk—and frequently into the night. Her son was left to wonder how she mustered the energy to rise from bed each morning.[57]

The Kingdom School's future appeared to be in jeopardy when Paul Jones died unexpectedly, but Walter Gobitas stepped into the breach. Lillian recalled that when her father learned of his fellow Witness's death, he telephoned Jones's widow and discussed how they might keep the school afloat. Gobitas suggested that Verna Jones would be able to free herself from the burden of single-handedly caring for so many boarders if students at the school could live at home and ride a bus each day. Always a resourceful handyman, Gobitas converted an Economy Grocery delivery truck into a makeshift bus by installing planks in its bed, and soon Witness children were crowding onto them as he drove the route to and from the school each day. Because it required numerous detours down country lanes, the thirty-mile trip from Minersville to the Jones farm took the better part of an hour, but the young riders didn't seem to mind; they enjoyed jostling one another and gossiping. "We had a blast on the school bus," Lillian said. "We had a lot of fun."[58]

2. Felix's Fall-of-France Opinion

As the Witnesses scrambled to educate their children, their case against the Minersville School District ground on in federal court. Like Superintendent Charles E. Roudabush, they enlisted outside help as the appeal progressed, chiefly from the American Civil Liberties Union. Its amicus curiae brief, written by ACLU general counsel Arthur Garfield Hays, Jerome M. Britchey, and William G. Fennell, offered a short but compelling argument for upholding Judge Albert Maris's injunction. As the ACLU saw it, forcing the young Witnesses to choose between adhering to the central tenets of their faith or attending public school was symptomatic of the "rising tide of political dictatorship and religious intolerance" that was threatening to swamp civil liberties both abroad and in the United States. And the school district's protestations to the contrary notwithstanding, the constitutionally protected right to free exercise of religion clearly lay at the heart of the Walter Gobitas family's claim. "If there could be any clearer case of a deprivation of civil rights because of religious principles, it is difficult to imagine what it might be," the brief maintained. "Why were the children expelled? Because they did not salute the flag; and they did not salute because their religious beliefs, in their own sincere and deep-seated conviction and faith, forbade it. The conclusion is inescapable that the principle of religious liberty and toleration is violated by this regulation, as applied." To bolster their argument, the brief's authors struck the kind of emotional chord so favored by Witness leader Joseph Rutherford, comparing the compulsory flag salute with the "outstretched arm of fascism and nazism where one stands in fear of his life or the concentration camp if he does not comply with the dictator's wish and whim."[1]

In November 1939, the Third Circuit Court of Appeals unanimously affirmed Maris's ruling. Written by Judge William Clark, the appeals court's opinion was a wide-ranging affair that drew upon

sources from Cicero to the work of modern legal scholars like Paul
Freund to eviscerate the school board's rationale for mandating the
flag salute, a ceremony the court explicitly compared to "the salute
... of the Hitler regime." Perhaps the most powerful section of
Clark's argument was its all-out assault on the "at least doubtful
efficacy" of compulsory flag-saluting as a means of instilling genuine national loyalty in schoolchildren. Directly rejecting one of the
central contentions offered by the Minersville School District, Clark
claimed that mandated "patriotic" exercises were "neither logically
consistent with, nor pedagogically indispensable to, the dissemination of courage or loyalty." To Clark, it seemed apparent that those
admirable qualities could not be inculcated with a brief ceremony.
If anything, he wrote, forcing reluctant pupils such as the Gobitas
children to participate in flag-salute exercises against their will was
actually counterproductive in terms of fostering loyalty because the
victims of coercion, having seen their civil liberties compromised,
might develop "an antagonistic attitude" toward their oppressors.
And, like Maris, Clark was reluctant to privilege the "material" interests of the state over the "spiritual" needs of the Witness children. Quoting George Washington, he concluded that the school
board had "failed to 'treat the conscientious scruples' of all children with ... 'great delicacy and tenderness,'" violating their civil
liberties in the process. Issued to shield those basic democratic
rights, which were explicitly safeguarded by the First and Fourteenth
Amendments, Maris's injunction barring enforcement of the compulsory flag-salute measure was valid.[2]

Clark's ruling stung Roudabush, who dismissed it as "a hodge-
podge of perverted quotations," and the school board considered its
final option, an appeal to the U.S. Supreme Court. Early in 1940, as
the board weighed the costs of taking the flag-salute case to Washington, pledges of financial support came from two local patriotic
groups, and the appellants decided to forge ahead. Although it had
already ruled in several prior flag-salute cases, the Court granted
certiorari, and both sides of the dispute mustered their arguments
for a final hearing of the case now known as *Minersville School District v. Gobitis*. In his brief, Joseph Henderson, the school board's
attorney, urged the Court to adhere to precedent and dispose of the
case as it had *Gobitis*'s predecessors—by upholding the constitutionality of compulsory flag-salute regulations. He also trotted out sev-

eral of the arguments that had failed so miserably in the lower federal courts, including the notion that compulsory "patriotic exercises" were a reasonable and effective means to "inculcate . . . a love
of country" in all students, regardless of their religious beliefs. For
its part, the Gobitas family, now represented by Witness leader
Joseph Rutherford and Hayden Covington, Olin Moyle's successor as
the faith's national legal counsel, reiterated its religious objections
to flag-saluting and noted the ceremony's similarity to the salute offered in Nazi Germany. "The vital question in the . . . case," the
brief argued, "is this: Shall the creature man be free to exercise his
conscientious belief in god and his obedience to the law of Almighty
God, the creator, or shall the creature man be compelled to obey the
law or rule of the state, which law of the state, as the creature believes, is in direct conflict with the law of Almighty God?" The answer, clearly, was the former.[3]

In his thoughtful study of the *Gobitis* case, David Manwaring has
termed the Witnesses' effort "a discouragingly bad brief. It ignored
all the most crucial constitutional issues, and seemed calculated to
produce a negative emotional effect with its repeated recourse to argument ad hominem." Indeed, the brief was a prototypical Witness
text in terms of intemperance and hyperbole, casting the advocates
of compulsory flag-saluting as champions of oppressive and "arbitrary totalitarian rule of the state."[4] Filling in many of the gaping
holes left by the Witnesses' slipshod document were amicus curiae
briefs filed by the American Civil Liberties Union and the American Bar Association's (ABA's) Committee on the Bill of Rights. As
it urged the high Court to deny the school district's final appeal, the
ACLU's brief stressed that the "right to entertain the belief, to adhere to the principle, and to teach the doctrine, that the act of saluting a flag contravenes the law of Almighty God, is a part of the
liberty referred to in the Fourteenth Amendment to the Constitution of the United States." Echoing the lower-court opinions, the
ACLU's brief questioned the efficacy of mandating the flag salute
as a means of fostering genuine patriotism, and it wondered if expelling the Witness youngsters would "instruct the youth of Pennsylvania in loyalty to the flag and Constitution of the United
States."[5] In its brief, the ABA maintained that "there is no such public need for the compulsory flag salute as to justify the overriding
of the religious scruples of the children. . . . We believe that the letter

and spirit of our Constitution demand vindication of the individual liberties which are abridged by the challenged regulation."[6]

Joseph Rutherford spoke for the Gobitas family during oral arguments. Shortly after Rutherford launched into his argument before the Supreme Court, Justice James McReynolds interrupted him. McReynolds growled that he was "hearing with difficulty," and Rutherford was forced to repeat a few of his introductory remarks to the Court, most of them meant to clarify possible misapprehensions about the Witnesses' background and beliefs. "In fairness to this Court I should say Jehovah's Witnesses are not a sect or a cult," Rutherford said, his voice rising for the cranky McReynolds's benefit. "Jehovah's Witnesses are those who bear testimony to the name of Almighty God, whose name alone is 'Jehovah.' They have been in existence for at least five thousand years." From the outset, it was apparent that Rutherford was eager to cede responsibility for a full discussion of the substantive legal issues at stake in the case to the ACLU's George Gardner, who had been granted time for oral argument as a friend of the court. Liberated from the burden of addressing matters of law, the Witness leader was content to sermonize, rattle off quotations from Scripture, and address the duty of devout Christians to abide by God's will, regardless of the potentially grievous temporal consequences. As was typical for Rutherford, there were a number of bewildering digressions (he felt compelled, for instance, to relate in some detail the story of Daniel's deliverance from the lions' den), but his basic argument in support of Walter Gobitas and his children was relatively straightforward: "The law of God is supreme. And if a man believes that God's law is supreme and conscientiously deports himself accordingly, no human authority can control or interfere with his conscience." If it stumbled and permitted the Minersville School District to meddle with such sacred—and constitutionally protected—rights, Rutherford intoned, the Court would commit "an error that will lead this people of the United States into a totalitarian class and destroy all the liberties guaranteed by the Constitution." To Rutherford's credit, it was a painfully accurate prediction of the public's explosive reaction to the Court's decision in the flag-salute case and its calamitous impact on the Witnesses' civil liberties.[7]

The Gobitas children had traveled from Pennsylvania to Washington to hear the oral arguments, and they were dazzled by Ruther-

William, *left*, and Lillian Gobitas stand with their father, Walter, after they were expelled from school for failing to salute the American flag.

ford's oratory. "I'll never forget," Lillian later wrote, "how he compared us Witness children with the faithful prophet Daniel, Daniel's three Hebrew companions, and other Bible characters." Lillian considered Rutherford's effort "electrifying," and decades later she marveled at how the justices had "listened so attentively. They gave him complete attention."[8] But members of the Supreme Court apparently found Rutherford and Gardner to be somewhat less than persuasive. Justice Felix Frankfurter's misgivings about the Witnesses' position were clear almost from the moment the Court granted certiorari in *Gobitis*. Although both lower courts had eloquently refuted Charles Roudabush's specious claim that the case had "nothing to do with religion," Frankfurter apparently agreed with the superintendent's assessment. "Is it at all probable," Frankfurter wrote to one of the Brethren during oral argument in the case, "that the framers of the Bill of Rights would have thought that a requirement to salute the flag violates the protection of the 'free exercise of religion'?"[9] Though he apparently did not challenge Rutherford's meandering oration, Frankfurter unloaded a fusillade of pointed questions at Gardner, whose amicus curiae brief had stressed that the Minersville regulation had violated the protections of religious liberty conferred on the Witnesses by the First and Fourteenth Amendments. The details of their exchange apparently were not recorded, but a dejected Gardner, having seen his argument dissected by Frankfurter, later called it an "uninspired and unsatisfactory discussion."[10]

As he initiated discussion of *Gobitis* at the Court's weekly conference, Chief Justice Charles Evans Hughes confessed that he "came up to this case like a skittish horse to a brass band," if only because the Court had already decided three roughly similar compulsory flag-salute cases within the preceding five years and had upheld their constitutionality in each instance. After acknowledging his initial hesitancy, the chief justice spoke with his usual forcefulness and clarity; and he offered a persuasive argument that sought to legitimize Charles Roudabush's much-reiterated claim that the case had "nothing to do with religion." Hughes set the tone for the Court's approach to *Gobitis* by telling the conference that "there is no legitimate impingement on religious belief here. What is required of those who salute the flag is a legitimate object"—namely, participation in a ceremony designed to promote national unity. To the chief justice, the case ultimately boiled down to "the question of state power" and how it could be legitimately wielded; it "had nothing to do with religion." (Here, of course, Hughes echoed verbatim Charles Roudabush's central contention throughout the flag-salute controversy.) Never wavering in his argument, he told the conference that in this instance, with the school district simply enforcing a regulation that was designed to contribute to the public good, the Court lacked the constitutional mandate to strike down the measure as a violation of the First or Fourteenth Amendments. "We have no jurisdiction as to the wisdom of [the flag salute regulation]," Hughes said. "I don't want to be dogmatic about this but I simply cannot believe that the state has not the power to inculcate this social objective." Believing that the Minersville rule was "inappropriate for judicial meddling," Hughes informed the conference that he favored a reversal of the appeals court ruling and thus would vote to strike down the injunction issued by Maris.[11]

After Hughes spoke, justices James McReynolds, Harlan Fiske Stone, Owen Roberts, Stanley Reed, and Hugo Black were given the opportunity to share their own views on *Gobitis*. The five men passed, suggesting that they accepted the chief justice's reasoning and would cast their votes with him to rule in favor of the school district. When it was his turn to speak, Justice Frankfurter seconded Hughes's arguments and, in what the chief justice later termed a "moving statement," advocated a reversal of the appeals court ruling. Frankfurter noted that the flag salute was far from an empty or a pointless ceremony, as had been suggested by the Witnesses and the ACLU. By achieving "inculcation of loyalty in the young citizen of the country," he told the conference, it served a unique and invaluable purpose in terms of what Hughes later described as "instilling love of country in our pluralistic society." Frankfurter also underscored the chief justice's warning that the Court should not engage in "judicial meddling" and usurp the authority of legislators and local lawmakers, whose links to the will of the people were far stronger than those forged by judges. The Court's two most junior members, justices William Douglas and Frank Murphy, were given the chance to speak their minds after Frankfurter, but they said nothing, and Hughes was left with the impression that he commanded a unanimous majority. Although his own feelings about *Minersville School District v. Gobitis* were strong, Hughes was so impressed by Frankfurter's persuasive and "moving" address to the conference that he gave the former Harvard Law School professor the task of writing the Court's opinion.[12]

It seems clear that Frankfurter's approach to the *Gobitis* case was shaped as much by his fervent patriotism as it was by his understanding of the Constitution. As a boy, Frankfurter had emigrated to the United States from Vienna, and he was never shy about expressing his profound affection for his adopted homeland. Passersby were often startled to hear him happily whistling "Stars and Stripes Forever" as he walked the corridors of the Supreme Court's building, and on his deathbed he urged a biographer, "Let people see . . . how much I loved my country."[13] Frankfurter was particularly enamored of the American flag, the emblem that lay at the heart of the *Gobitis* case; in his opinion for the Court, he called it "the symbol of our national unity, transcending all internal differences, however large, within the framework of the Constitution."[14] Frankfurter's heartfelt devotion to Old Glory as a symbol of all that was noble and good about America was perhaps best expressed in a maudlin speech he delivered in 1944 as part of the District of Columbia's "I Am an American Day" celebration. In his address, Frankfurter divulged that his prose simply was insufficient for the task at hand. "Love of country, like romantic love," he confessed, "is too intimate an emotion to be expressed publicly except in poetry." Not surprisingly, Frankfurter had a particular poem in mind, an overwrought work by Franklin K. Lane that "put into words the meaning of America, making the flag our spokesman." Quoting Lane, Frankfurter said to the crowd, "I am not the flag, not at all. I am but its shadow."[15]

Without question, the kind of passionate "love of country" that Frankfurter shared while quoting Lane's poem was in full bloom late in spring 1940, when the Supreme Court considered *Minersville School District v. Gobitis*. A European by birth and a Jew, Frankfurter was preoccupied by the expanding war in Europe and its potentially devastating impact on American security. Having overrun the Low Countries and Norway with almost breathtaking ease, Nazi forces were poised to vanquish France, Germany's last significant foe on the Continent; such a conquest, many feared, would allow Hitler to launch a cross-Channel invasion of England and perhaps establish sovereignty over all of Europe. Despite the spread of isolationist sentiment in the United States following the cataclysm of World War I, most policymakers in Washington were coming to understand that their nation's fate, for better or for worse, was inextricably linked to that of Europe's besieged democracies. No one recognized this more than Frankfurter, who was so troubled by the war that he balanced his Supreme Court responsibilities with a spirited effort to shore up his adopted country's defenses. Frankfurter was nothing if not well connected in Washington—his protégés could be found in influential positions throughout the three branches of the federal government—and in spring 1940 he exploited his many links to the levers of power in the capital to help ready the country for a war that seemed, in his eyes, inevitable.

As Richard Danzig has noted in his excellent studies of the relationship between the war in Europe and the genesis of the *Gobitis* opinion, nothing better typified Frankfurter's backstage maneuvering in this period than his efforts to have the venerable Henry Stimson named secretary of war.[16] On 3 May 1940, Frankfurter brought Stimson, once his boss and mentor, to lunch with President Franklin D. Roosevelt at the White House, where the three men "talked quite openly . . . about a number of confidential foreign policy developments," as Stimson put it in his diary.[17] No stranger to flattery, Frankfurter later expressed his appreciation by thanking Roosevelt for "taking me out of my marble prison," the Supreme Court, where one of his main chores lay in drafting and circulating the majority opinion in the *Gobitis* case. Three weeks later, on 26 May, Frankfurter wrote to Roosevelt and suggested that the president underscore the urgency of the country's nascent war effort by overhauling his entire cabinet, starting with his isolationist secretary of war, Harry Woodring. Frankfurter settled on Stimson as the most logical replacement for Woodring and visited the White House to tout his candidacy on 1 June, two days before the Court handed down its opinion in the *Gobitis* case. It was a measure of Frankfurter's influence (as well as Stimson's stature) that Roosevelt announced the Stimson-for-Woodring switch in mid-June, around the time that France finally succumbed to the Germans.[18]

Frankfurter's preoccupation with the conflict in Europe was obvious to many of those who observed him that spring. In his published diary, Secretary of the Interior Harold Ickes provided a brief but telling account of Frankfurter's absorption with the war. In late May, Ickes hosted a lunch attended by Frankfurter, the poet Archibald MacLeish, and their wives. As Ickes later put it, the group "talked almost exclusively about the war situation because we feel keenly that here is a crisis that is bound to affect America," and Frankfurter was one of the more animated participants in the discussion. On 2 June, the day before the Court handed down its opinion in *Gobitis*, Frankfurter dominated a late-night skull session at MacLeish's home in which the war was again the central topic. Although Ickes was not in attendance, he soon learned that Frankfurter and Robert Jackson, who was then serving as Roosevelt's attorney general, had participated in a tense exchange over the war. "Apparently there was a good deal of feeling between Bob Jackson and Felix," Ickes wrote. "The latter is not really rational these days on the European situation."[19]

Perhaps because he was so engrossed by the war in Europe, Frankfurter privately touted the notion that the Supreme Court had an obligation to consider the critical importance of national security when it weighed the constitutional issues at stake in *Gobitis*. Frankfurter's feelings on this score were most thoroughly expressed in a letter he sent to fellow justice Harlan Fiske Stone on 27 May 1940 (the day after he wrote to President Roosevelt and noted that "hardly anything else has been on my mind" except the war).[20] Having discovered that Stone intended to author a lone dissent in *Gobitis* and assert that the Witnesses' right to free exercise of religion had in fact been violated by the school district, Frankfurter claimed to have undertaken "an anxious re-examination of my own views." Frankfurter had reconsidered "the whole matter," he wrote, "because I am not happy that you should entertain doubts that I cannot share or meet in a domain where constitutional power is on one side and my private notions of liberty and toleration and good sense are on the other." He told Stone that while "the vulgar intrusion of law in the domain of conscience is for me a very sensitive area," he was more convinced than ever that the kind of civil liberties normally given free reign by the Constitution in peacetime might be reasonably constrained by the state as it grappled with the exigencies of war. Frankfurter asserted that "time and circumstances are surely not irrelevant considerations in resolving the conflicts that we do have to resolve in this particular case." Viewed within the strictures presented by these current (and increasingly dire) wartime "circumstances," the Minersville case was, as Frankfurter saw it, essentially a matter of making the delicate "adjustment between legislatively allowable pursuit of national security and the right to stand on individual idiosyncracies [*sic*]." Frankfurter pointed to one of his heroes, Justice Oliver Wendell Holmes Jr., who had struggled with this same issue while drafting several World War I–era opinions before coming to understand "that he had a right to take into account the things that he did take into account"—presumably the state's prerogative to sustain itself by taking extraordinary measures to safeguard national security in wartime. Given "the framework of present circumstances and those that are clearly ahead of us," Frankfurter wrote to Stone, members of the present Supreme Court would do well to emulate Holmes when they determined if the Constitution protected the Gobitas family's "idiosyncracies."[21]

In his attempt to sway the reluctant Stone, Frankfurter paired his concerns about national security with a spirited call for judicial restraint. It was clear from both his letter to Stone and the final version of the *Gobitis* opinion that Frankfurter's desire to protect civil liberties from the "vulgar intrusion of law" had been subsumed by his reluctance to circumscribe the broad powers normally exercised by popularly elected legislative bodies. "What weighs with me strongly in this case," he explained to Stone, "is my anxiety that, while we lean in the direction of the libertarian aspect, we do not exercise our judicial power unduly, and as though we ourselves were legislators by holding with too tight a rein the organs of popular government." Both Frankfurter and Stone understood that this was a sensitive issue for the Supreme Court, which had come under intense fire during the formative years of the New Deal for repeatedly frustrating efforts made by President Roosevelt and Congress to regulate commerce and thus stimulate the economy out of its doldrums. A confidant of Roosevelt who had himself played a major role in drafting several New Deal measures, Frankfurter had lamented the Supreme Court's meddling as disastrously intrusive, and he plainly had no intention of engaging in similar obstruction after his own ascension to the nation's highest bench. Accordingly, Frankfurter informed Stone that the principal "responsibility for [establishing] a combination of firmness and toleration" had to be placed "directly home where it belongs—to the people and their representatives themselves," not the judiciary. In the end, he simply could not "resist the conviction that we ought to let the legislative judgment stand and put the responsibility for its exercise where it belongs."[22]

During his career at Harvard, Frankfurter had been known as one of the country's preeminent civil libertarians, and he invoked that reputation to assure Stone that he too had felt more than a little sympathy for the arguments advanced by the Gobitas family. "For various reasons . . . a good part of my mature life has thrown whatever weight it had against foolish and harsh manifestations of coercion and for the amplest expression of dissident views, however absurd or offensive those may have been to my own notions of rationality and decency," he wrote. "I say this merely to indicate that all my bias and predisposition are in favor of giving the fullest elbow room to every variety of religious, political, and economic view." But despite his liberal inclinations, Frankfurter could not conclude that the Witnesses' civil liberties had been seriously violated by a requirement that they simply offer "a gesture of respect for the symbol of our national being," the American flag, especially since "all channels of affirmative free expression [were] open to both children and parents."

Frankfurter had not reached this conclusion off-handedly; the issues at the core of *Gobitis* were difficult for him to resolve, and he confessed to Stone that "nothing has weighed as much on my conscience, since I have come to this Court, as has this case." Having set aside all "bias and predisposition" and having grappled long and hard with his conscience, he was ready to stand behind an opinion that would serve as "a vehicle for preaching the true democratic faith of not relying on the Court for the impossible task of assuring vigorous, mature, self-protecting and tolerant democracy"—an opinion that would, in short, recognize the limits of judicial power and highlight the authority of the people themselves, speaking through their elected representatives, to shape public policy.[23]

Frankfurter's willingness to cede the judiciary's power to check unconstitutional abuses of legislative authority permeated the Court's majority opinion in *Gobitis*. Approaching the case far differently than the Gobitas family and the American Civil Liberties Union, which had framed *Gobitis* in terms of the Supreme Court's obligation to recognize the protections afforded to the Witnesses' civil liberties by the First and Fourteenth Amendments, Frankfurter maintained that the Minersville dispute was largely a matter of determining when and how the courts could legitimately infringe on the "legislative judgment" normally exercised by lawmakers. Like Roudabush and Hughes, Frankfurter was able to dismiss the notion that the "vital question" of the case concerned the Gobitas children's right to freely exercise a "conscientious belief in God" without unreasonable interference by the state. Rather, he wrote for the Court, "The precise issue . . . for us to decide is whether the legislatures of the various states and the authorities in a thousand counties and school districts of this country are barred from determining the appropriateness of various means to evoke that unifying sentiment without which there ultimately can be no liberties, civil or religious." A firm advocate of judicial restraint, Frankfurter was reluctant to employ the power of the judiciary, as he put it, to "exercise censorship" over those kinds of basic legislative functions, particularly when they were being used to promote such a worthwhile goal: "promotion of national cohesion" in support of the lofty democratic principles embodied by the American flag. Since, after all, "the courtroom is not the arena for debating issues of educational policy," he was not about to attempt to establish the Supreme Court as "the school board for the country." Chosen by their communities and more closely attuned to the needs of students and their families, elected school boards and legislatures, not appointed judges, were in the best—and most constitutionally valid—position to pass judgment on the soundness of public policy. "The wisdom of training children in patriotic impulses by those compulsions which necessarily provide so much of the educational process," Frankfurter wrote, "is not for our independent judgment."[24]

Keenly aware of those limitations on the power of the judiciary, Frankfurter acknowledged in his *Gobitis* opinion that the Supreme Court had been forced to "reconcile two rights"—the right of citizens such as the Gobitas children to freely exercise their religious beliefs and the right of legislative bodies to make laws without excessive meddling by the courts—"in order to prevent either from destroying the other." Though the protections of religious liberties conferred by the First and Fourteenth Amendments were indeed "precious," Frankfurter wrote, they were hardly unlimited, as the Court had recognized many times before. Thus, in a case such as the one at hand, "when the conscience of the individual collides with the felt necessity of society," the Court's "judicial conscience is put to its severest test" by the necessity to strike an adequate balance between individual rights and the state's "authority to safeguard the nation's fellowship." In exercising this authority, legislative bodies often enacted measures "deemed . . . essential to secure and maintain that orderly, tranquil, and free society without which religious toleration itself is unattainable." Frankfurter was vehement in his assertion that the Constitution protected these prerogatives as much as it shielded civil liberties. "We are dealing with an interest," he argued, "inferior to none in the hierarchy of legal values."

Frankfurter conceded that in "safeguarding conscience we are dealing with interests so subtle and so dear [that] every possible leeway should be given to the claims of religious faith." At the same time, however, the Court had a duty to recognize that even such a treasured freedom had its limits, especially when it came into conflict with the legitimate interests of the state. "Conscientious scruples have not, in the long struggle for religious toleration, relieved the individual from obedience to a general law not aimed at the promotion or restriction of religious beliefs," he wrote. "The mere possession of religious convictions which contradict the relevant concerns of a political society does not relieve the citizen from the discharge of political responsibilities." By enforcing the flag-salute measure, the Minersville School Board was not demanding that the Witnesses abandon their faith but was merely requiring them to participate in "an exercise appropriate in time and place and setting, and one designed to evoke in them appreciation of the nation's hopes and dreams, its sufferings and sacrifices"—a ceremony, in short, that was meant "to evoke that unifying sentiment without which there can ultimately be no liberties, civil or religious." In so doing, it was in no way violating the Witnesses' First or Fourteenth Amendment freedoms, for the state could "in self-protection utilize the educational process for inculcating those almost unconscious feelings which bind men together in a comprehending loyalty, whatever may be their lesser differences and difficulties." Reversing the lower court rulings, the Supreme Court allowed the expulsions of the Witness children in Minersville to stand.[25]

Even before it was formally released to the public, Frankfurter's opinion in the Pennsylvania flag-salute case anguished two young men who revered him and shared many of his political inclinations. Frankfurter's clerk, Edward Prichard Jr., was a "young man with exuberant libertarian loyalties," according to one account. Prichard was so disturbed by Frankfurter's approach to *Gobitis* that he furtively removed a draft of the opinion from the justice's chambers and spirited it to the Washington apartment of Joseph Rauh Jr., his predecessor as Frankfurter's clerk. His breath short and his body drenched in sweat, Prichard handed Rauh the opinion and said, "Felix has made a terrible mistake. You have to speak to him." After reading the pilfered opinion, Rauh agreed to speak to Frankfurter about it; he too was troubled by Frankfurter's reasoning and its implications for civil liberties. But Rauh explained that he also would be obliged to tell Frankfurter that Prichard had brought him the draft of the *Gobitis* opinion. Fearing that Frankfurter would be enraged by the news that his clerk had so grossly compromised the Supreme Court's secrecy, Prichard made an agonizing decision; he and Rauh would keep their qualms to themselves. Over the coming weeks and months, they took cold comfort in knowing that numerous other civil libertarians shared their misgivings.[26]

In 1953, Frankfurter ruefully suggested to an interviewer that Stone had been persuaded to dissent in *Gobitis* by Allison Dunham, his able law clerk. According to Frankfurter, "Dunham had fierce feelings on the subject," and he eventually persuaded Stone to break with the majority. Dunham himself scoffed at the idea that Stone—who had served as dean of Columbia University's law school and as attorney general before joining the Supreme Court in 1925— would have deferred to his clerk in a case involving such weighty constitutional issues. It was Dunham's impression that Stone, vexed by what he saw as a clear infringement of the Witness children's civil liberties, "had made up his mind to vote as he did" even before the Court discussed *Gobitis* at its conference. Dunham did acknowledge, however, that he had not wanted Stone to suffer the majority opinion in silence. Profoundly troubled by Frankfurter's arguments and their potential impact on civil liberties, the clerk prevailed upon Stone "to write a dissent as distinguished from noting his dissent." Having been prodded by his clerk, Stone drafted perhaps the most noteworthy opinion of his long career as a member of the Supreme Court, an eloquent defense of civil liberties and minority rights that still ranks as one of the Court's finest dissents.[27]

Although he rebuffed Frankfurter ("The case is peculiarly one of the relative weight of imponderables," he wrote in response to the 27 May letter, "and I cannot overcome the feeling that the Constitution tips the scales in favor of religion"), Stone was by no means a critic of judicial restraint.[28] During what historian William Leuchtenburg has described as an "unwontedly destructive sixteen-month period" in the mid-1930s, Stone had repeatedly dissented as the Supreme Court laid waste to numerous New Deal initiatives, including the Railroad Retirement Act, the Guffey Coal Act, and the Municipal Bankruptcy Act. "The Supreme Court during these months frequently went out of its way to frustrate the Roosevelt administration," according to Leuchtenburg. "It revived doctrines that had languished for decades or employed rubrics that had never before been used to invalidate an act of Congress."[29] Stone's dismay with the Court's persistent obstructionism climaxed in a dissenting opinion in *United States v. Butler* (1936), in which he provided what one observer called "a classic justification of judicial restraint every bit as eloquent as any ever uttered by Holmes or Brandeis."[30] The majority opinion in *Butler*, written by Justice Owen Roberts, had struck down a key section of the Agricultural Adjustment Act by a narrow (and absurd, many thought) reading of both the Tenth Amendment and Article 1 of the Constitution. Stone, joined in dissent by justices Louis Brandeis and Benjamin Cardozo, blasted Roberts's reasoning as a "tortured construction of the Constitution" and declared that "courts are not the only agency of government that must be assumed to have capacity to govern." As it had so many times during the 1930s, the Court had in *Butler* resorted to "judicial fiat" to frustrate a New Deal legislative initiative that had broad popular support. This was anathema to Stone, and in his dissent he felt compelled to remind the majority that the Court would do well to recognize the boundaries of its authority. He noted in one memorable passage:

> The power of the courts to declare a statute unconstitutional is subject to two guiding principles of decision which ought never to be absent from judicial consciousness. One is that courts are concerned only with the power to enact statutes, not with their wisdom. The other is that while unconstitutional exercise of power by the executive and legislative branches of the government is subject to judicial restraint, the only check upon our own exercise of power is our own sense of self-restraint. For the removal of unwise laws from the statute books appeal lies, not to the courts, but to the ballot and to the processes of democratic government.[31]

Much to Stone's dismay, Frankfurter, though dealing with minority rights and not with economic regulation, seized upon this line of argument when crafting his opinion in *Gobitis*. He acknowledged as much in his 27 May letter, telling Stone, "I have tried in this opinion to really act on what will, as a matter of history, be a lode-star for due regard between legislative and judicial powers, to wit, your dissent in the *Butler* case."[32]

Yet the touchstone for Stone's approach to *Gobitis* was not his dissent in *Butler* but a well-known footnote he had added to the Supreme Court's opinion in *United States v. Carolene Products.* Decided in 1938, *Carolene Products* was an unspectacular case involving the right of the federal government to prohibit the interstate shipment of a product known as "filled milk" (a mixture of animal fats and skimmed milk). In the fourth footnote of the Court's opinion, Stone momentarily veered away from the basic issues in the case to suggest that the Court might exercise "more exacting judicial scrutiny" when determining the constitutionality of statutes directed at various "discrete and insular" minority groups. He further indicated that a "correspondingly more searching judicial inquiry" might be in order when prejudice directed toward such groups tended to inhibit "the operation of those political processes ordinarily to be relied upon to protect minorities."[33] Buried in an otherwise obscure opinion, Stone's caveat, hinting at the need for greater scrutiny of measures aimed at restricting civil and minority rights, was a watershed in constitutional jurisprudence. With it, the Court recognized what Frankfurter acknowledged in his letter to Stone as an "important distinction,"[34] signaling that the sometimes lax standards of constitutional review it had employed while judging economic regulation might not be applicable in cases involving individual rights. And to Stone, the circumstances of the *Gobitis* case merited precisely the kind of strict scrutiny he had advocated in his *Carolene Products* footnote. He noted in his dissent:

> We have previously pointed to the importance of a searching judicial inquiry into the legislative judgment in situations where prejudice against discrete and insular minorities may tend to curtail the operation of those political processes ordinarily to be relied on to protect minorities. . . . Here we have such a small minority entertaining in good faith a religious belief, which is such a departure from the usual course of human conduct, that most persons are disposed to regard it with little toleration or concern. In such circumstances careful scrutiny of legislative effort to secure conformity of belief and opinion by a compulsory affirma-

tion of the desired belief, is especially needful if civil rights are to receive any protection.

In other words, the standard he had articulated in "footnote four" guided his interpretation of *Gobitis*.[35]

Picking up on a theme developed by Frankfurter in both his 27 May letter and in the majority opinion, Stone conceded that the "constitutional guaranties of personal liberty are not always absolutes"—in wartime, for instance, the federal government could compel men to serve in the military, and in order to ensure public safety it could "suppress religious practices dangerous to morals." (In making this same point in his letter, Frankfurter had used almost identical language, claiming that the Court was not considering "the domain of absolutes."[36]) When imposed prudently, strictures of this nature were crucial to the smooth and equitable functioning of an orderly society. But as the Supreme Court had noted on several previous occasions, "where there are competing demands of the interests of government and of liberty under the Constitution, and where the performance of governmental functions is brought into conflict with specific constitutional restrictions, there must, when that is possible, be reasonable accommodation between them so as to preserve the essentials of both." Moreover, given their central role in preserving constitutional rights from abuse, "it is the function of the courts to determine whether such accommodation is reasonably possible." Ideally, the legislatures themselves, being chosen by the people and thus responsive to their liberties, would willingly provide such balance, but the courts had an obligation to intercede when the state's overzealous pursuit of its perceived interests threatened to swamp individual rights. Such was the role of the judiciary in a system kept in equilibrium by a network of checks and balances.[37]

Firm in his belief that the judiciary had a duty to check the authority of legislatures before their power unreasonably infringed on the rights of individuals, Stone had little doubt that the lower federal courts had acted properly in enjoining enforcement of Minersville's compulsory flag-salute measure. Though the state had a legitimate interest in promoting patriotism and maintaining discipline in the schools, the federal judiciary would abdicate its constitutional function by allowing that interest to subordinate "the right of this small and helpless minority, including children having a strong religious conviction, whether they understand its nature or not, to refrain from an expression obnoxious to their religion." It was not a matter, as Frankfurter had argued, of the Court usurping the authority of elected officials and somehow establishing itself as "the school board for the country," a role for which it was ill-equipped. Instead, Stone merely hoped that the Court would fulfill one of its most fundamental and important responsibilities by invalidating legislation that plainly and unnecessarily violated the protections codified in the Bill of Rights and the Fourteenth Amendment.[38]

Two paragraphs at the heart of Stone's dissent best summarized his dismay over Frankfurter's reluctance to shield civil liberties by limiting the power of legislative bodies. In them he skillfully wove together his application of the principles of footnote four, a ringing defense of civil liberties, and an implicit indictment of Frankfurter's myopic concern with maintaining judicial restraint.

> The guaranties of civil liberty are but guaranties of freedom of the human mind and spirit and of reasonable freedom and opportunity to express them. They presuppose the right of the individual to hold such opinions as he will and to give them reasonably free expression, and his freedom, and that of the state as well, to teach and persuade others by the communication of ideas. The very essence of the liberty which they guaranty is the freedom of the individual from compulsion as to what he shall think and what he shall say, at least where the compulsion is to bear false witness to his religion. If these guaranties are to have any meaning they must, I think, be deemed to withhold from the state any authority to compel belief or the expression of it where that expression violates religious convictions, whatever may be the legislative desirability of such compulsion.
>
> History teaches us that there have been but few infringements of personal liberty by the state which have not been justified, as they are here, in the name of righteousness and the public good, and few which have not been directed, as they are now, at politically helpless minorities. The framers were not unaware that under the system which they created most governmental curtailments of personal liberty would have the support of a legislative judgment that the public interest would be better served by its curtailment than by its constitutional protection. I cannot

conceive that in prescribing, as limitations upon the powers of government, the freedom of the mind and spirit secured by the explicit guaranties of freedom and speech and religion, they intended or rightly could have left any latitude for a legislative judgment that the compulsory expression of belief which violates religious convictions would better serve the public interest than their protection.

His patriotism heightened by the outbreak of war, Frankfurter was willing to give the Minersville School District wide latitude because its ostensible purpose in requiring the flag salute was, as he saw it, fundamental to the preservation of the American system of governance. For Stone, that noble end could not justify the means—the coercion of a largely powerless minority and a forced compromise of its most cherished religious beliefs. With such a basic civil liberty in peril, it was imperative for the Supreme Court to adhere to the principles set forth in the *Carolene Products* footnote.[39]

Stone was not the only member of the Supreme Court to harbor serious misgivings about what some of the Court's clerks were derisively calling "Felix's Fall-of-France Opinion."[40] Although he too had said nothing during the Court's discussion of the Minersville case at conference, Justice Frank Murphy, elevated to the Court only a few months earlier from his post as attorney general, drafted a dissent of his own and highlighted many of the same arguments advanced by Stone. Even in an open and democratic society, Murphy acknowledged, a person's actions often "are subject to the will of the group," but "in the realm of attitude and opinion . . . the individual is allowed wide freedom" because beliefs were shielded by the protections of the Bill of Rights. Turning one of Frankfurter's central assumptions on its head, Murphy asserted that the ominous specter of the European war made it even more important for the Court to shield civil liberties from encroachment by the state, particularly when such an intrusion had little if any substantive impact in terms of maintaining national security:

Especially at this time when the freedom of individual conscience is being placed in jeopordy [*sic*] by world shaking events, it is of vital importance that freedom of conscience and opinion be protected against all considered regulations that have no practical

efficacy and bear no necessary or substantial relation to the maintenance of order and safety of our institutions.

Murphy's dissent might have provided a powerful complement to
Stone's, but, new to the Supreme Court and perhaps cowed by the
venerable combination of Hughes and Frankfurter, he never circulated it among the other justices. In the end, Murphy joined the majority. (One of his biographers has suggested that a private admon-
ishment from Hughes might have led the Court's newest member
to shelve the dissent.) Wracked by doubt, Murphy compared his
somewhat reluctant change of heart to the experience of Christ at
Gethsemane—an incident sometimes called "the agony in the gar-
den."[41]

Alone in dissent once Murphy surrendered to the majority, Stone
was informed on the day that the *Gobitis* opinions were to be
handed down that Frankfurter intended to read his opinion from the
bench. As he had once explained in a letter to Frankfurter, Stone
believed that "the elaborate oral delivery of opinions was a great
waste of time," and he thus favored a far simpler approach—"merely
announcing the name of the case, the way in which it came to us
(certiorari, appeal, certificate, etc.), the precise question presented,
and the decision. This takes about two minutes." Yet Frankfurter's
egregious misreading of the fundamental constitutional issues at
stake in *Gobitis* stirred something deep within Stone, and he gradually became convinced that his dissent merited more than a short
mention, particularly if Frankfurter chose to read the majority opinion. "He began to think of reading his opinion also," Dunham, his
clerk, said of Stone. "During the course of the morning it became
clear that he was getting more and more worked up." Surprisingly,
Frankfurter ultimately chose not to read the majority opinion from
the bench, but Stone had become so agitated that he could not follow
suit. The tenor of his voice revealing his intense feelings about the
case, Stone read his dissent in full to a hushed courtroom and expressed his unwillingness to "surrender . . . the constitutional protection of the liberty of small minorities to the popular will," as the
Court's majority had.[42] Describing Stone's impassioned delivery, his
biographer, Alpheus Mason, has written that his "emotions rose to
heights he seldom exhibited."[43]

Incensed by Frankfurter's apparent betrayal, civil libertarians were quick to praise Stone's effort as a landmark dissent, and congratulatory mail flooded his chambers. John Haynes Holmes, chairman of the American Civil Liberties Union, lauded the "dignity, power and truth" of Stone's opinion and claimed that it was "destined to rank as one of the great dissenting opinions in American history."[44] Thurman Arnold, then an assistant attorney general (and later a founder of one of Washington's most powerful law firms), was similarly moved. "I think that your dissenting opinion in the salute-to-the-flag case is not only sensible but courageous. I congratulate you," Arnold wrote in a brief letter. "It shows a sense of proportion which people are too apt to lose in these days. Ten years from now everyone who knows you will be proud that you dissented."[45] A Congregational minister, Charles Hager, struck a similar chord, telling Stone, "I dare believe that the time will come when your children, if you have them, will be as proud of your dissent in this case as on any other act of your progressive career." (Hager, like Stone, was a graduate of Amherst College, and he confessed that he was so proud of the stand taken by his fellow alumnus that he had nearly belted out the college cheer.) As was typical for most people who commented on the *Gobitis* opinions, Hager paired his praise for Stone with an expression of disbelief over Frankfurter's bewildering breach of faith. "Especially am I surprised and disappointed with Frankfurter," he wrote.[46]

There was a smattering of applause for the majority opinion in the press. *The Washington Post*, for instance, agreed with Frankfurter, editorializing that the Bill of Rights did not license "any group to interfere with legitimate functions of the state under the guise of practicing their religion."[47] Most newspapers, however, condemned the *Gobitis* opinion in unequivocal terms. According to a survey noted in Mason's splendid biography of Stone, over 170 papers endorsed Stone's dissent and rebuked the Court's majority.[48] The *St. Louis Post-Dispatch* announced,

We think this decision of the United States Supreme Court is dead wrong. We think its decision is a violation of American principle. We think it is a surrender to popular hysteria. If patriotism depends upon such things as this—upon violation of a fundamental right of religious freedom—then it becomes not a noble emotion of love for country, but something to be rammed down our throats by the law.[49]

Although wondering if it might be "heresy" to offer such an apparently impertinent suggestion about members of the Supreme Court, who purportedly suppressed the "ordinary human frailties and emotions" when weighing matters of law, the *Des Moines Register* intimated that the majority opinion in *Gobitis* was "a by-product of the new circumstances that have developed in the world in the last month or two"—namely, the spread of war in Europe.[50]

The editors of the *Christian Century* were so distressed by Frankfurter's opinion that they condemned it in two separate editorials in summer 1940. One critique, "The Court Abdicates," acknowledged Frankfurter's undeniable talents as a jurist but doubted the soundness of his approach to the Minersville flag-salute case. Despite its author's skills, the *Gobitis* opinion had potentially disastrous implications for unpopular minority groups, particularly in wartime. "Courts that will not protect even Jehovah's Witnesses," the magazine warned, "will not long protect anybody."[51] In another editorial, the *Christian Century* downplayed the connection between the Fifth Column scare and the *Gobitis* ruling, and it also noted that "it is impossible not to view with respect an opinion written by the conspicuously liberal Justice Frankfurter and concurred in by so large a majority of the Court." But after bowing to Frankfurter and the other members of the *Gobitis* majority, the editorial reproved both their efforts and the gruesome activities of the vigilantes who were so incensed by the Witnesses' refusal to salute the American flag. Their intransigence, the journal cautioned, "is not half as dangerous to this country as the equally conscientious and equally misguided zeal of the patriots who, mistaking one formula of loyalty for the thing itself, are more anxious to have a symbol of liberty saluted than to have liberty maintained."[52]

Perhaps the fiercest criticism of the majority opinion was leveled at Frankfurter by civil libertarians and New Dealers who had rarely questioned his bona fides as a liberal. Narrow-mindedness and insensitivity to minority rights were to be expected from an archconservative such as Justice McReynolds; from Frankfurter, who had defended the likes of Tom Mooney and Sacco and Vanzetti, it amounted to sacrilege. The British socialist Harold Laski, a longtime friend and admirer of Frankfurter, wrote to Stone, "First and foremost, I want to tell you how right I think you are in that educational case from Pennsylvania and, to my deep regret, how wrong I think Felix is."[53] Shortly after the *Gobitis* opinions were handed down, an obviously perplexed Roger Baldwin, director of the American Civil Liberties Union (which Frankfurter had helped found), released to the press a letter he had written to Joseph Rutherford. In it, Baldwin publicly disclosed his "shock" in discovering that the Supreme Court had "brush[ed] aside the traditional right of religious conscience in favor of a compulsory conformity to a patriotic ritual. The language of the prevailing opinion unhappily reflects something of the intolerant temper of the moment." Claiming that Frankfurter had articulated a constitutional doctrine that "seems fraught with great danger for civil liberties," the ACLU resolved to lend its support to efforts aimed at modifying or repealing local flag-salute measures such as the one enacted in Minersville.[54]

The *New Republic*, another of Frankfurter's progeny, also weighed in with a series of editorials excoriating the majority opinion in *Gobitis*. The fact that Frankfurter had been one of the magazine's founders seemed only to heighten its sense of outrage at his apparent abandonment of liberalism. A scathing editorial noted that the "country is now in the grip of war hysteria," with many Americans "in great danger of adopting Hitler's philosophy in the effort to oppose Hitler's legions." The magazine cited the *Gobitis* opinion as evidence that the nation's highest Court had drifted "dangerously close to being a victim of that hysteria" by sacrificing religious liberty in the name of national security. Another *New Republic* article mocked Frankfurter for "heroically saving America from a couple of schoolchildren whose devotion to Jehovah would have been compromised by a salute to the flag." And in what must have been an especially painful jab at Frankfurter, the magazine also compared the Supreme Court to a German tribunal that had punished Witnesses for refusing to perform the Nazi salute. The editors were "sure that the majority members of our Court who concurred in the Frankfurter decision would be embarrassed to know that their attitude was in substance the same as that of the German tribunal."[55]

It did not take long for Frankfurter to learn how passionately many people disagreed with his opinion in *Gobitis*. On 5 June 1940, just two days after the Court had handed down its opinion, he traveled to Mt. Kisko, New York, to attend the wedding of Phil and Katharine Graham. At a lunch just before the ceremony, Frankfurter became embroiled in a heated argument over the *Gobitis* decision with several members of the wedding party, including the bride and groom. "Felix loved and encouraged loud and violent arguments, which everyone usually enjoyed," Katharine Graham recalled in a memoir, "but this time the argument went over the edge into bitter passion." According to her recollection, several members of the wedding party were "deeply disturbed—even shocked—by Felix's position," and they angrily rebuked him for authoring the opinion in *Gobitis.* Frankfurter, sensitive to charges that he had forsaken civil libertarianism, defended himself at one point by sputtering, "Everyone always talks about me as a liberal, but I never was one." The debate over the case was so intense that one of Phil Graham's friends wept while trying to convince the obdurate Frankfurter that he had erred in upholding the constitutionality of the Minersville flag-salute measure. When the wedding party learned that their argument was delaying the ceremony, Frankfurter brought matters to a close by clutching the bride and saying, "Come along, Kay. We will go for a walk in the woods and calm down." When they returned, the couple exchanged vows.[56]

News of the Supreme Court's decision staggered Lillian Gobitas and her family. "It never really occurred to us that the Court's decision would be anything but favorable," she remembered. "After all, we had won the previous two cases [in the lower courts]." At work in the kitchen with her mother, Lillian heard a radio broadcast announcing the decision. They "just stood there, frozen in disbelief" by the news. "We couldn't speak for a few minutes, and then we ran downstairs and told dad and Bill." As word of the decision spread, the family faced renewed dangers. Early one morning, Walter Gobitas received a warning from a friend: vigilantes would descend upon the Economy Grocery and wreck it if he and his children didn't proclaim their willingness to salute the American flag. Gobitas refused to yield. As sure as ever of his faith, he summoned help from local authorities and dispatched his younger children to safety. With a state police cruiser outside, the store was unharmed, but the family soon faced another threat—a boycott of the store. Lillian later said that "business fell off drastically," and her brother remembered that "the boycott . . . took its toll financially." To pay his mortgage, Walter Gobitas had to borrow money from his sister, a Roman Catholic who was somewhat bewildered by the Witnesses' beliefs. "Eventually, things came back," Lillian said, and customers returned to the Economy Grocery.[57]

Lillian later noted that though her family suffered in the wake of the Supreme Court's decision, other Witnesses fared far worse. "We were not prepared for the wave of persecution that followed the decision," she said. "That was unreal. I always say that it became 'open season' on Jehovah's Witnesses."[58] War hysteria, the *Gobitis* opinion, and the Witnesses' sometimes perplexing beliefs and practices proved to be a volatile mix in communities like Kennebunk, Maine. After the flag-salute opinion was handed down, Witnesses there and in dozens of other communities across the United States fell victim to brutal vigilante assaults. As Peter Irons has noted in his study of the Minersville flag-salute case, "Supreme Court decisions are often criticized, and some are disobeyed, but few have ever provoked as violent a public reaction as the *Gobitis* opinion."[59]

3. They're Traitors—
the Supreme Court Says So

As the war in Europe intensified in spring and summer 1940, "a widespread Fifth Column phobia" spread throughout the United States, according to historian Francis Michael MacDonnell. Based in part on the assumption that the Germans had skillfully used espionage and sabotage to undermine the defenses of their European victims, "stories of the Axis Fifth Column inundated America," MacDonnell has written, and precipitated alarm about the possibilities of subversion on American soil. "Fears about a hidden enemy boring from within and preparing the way for a hostile invasion extended from the White House to the public at large."[1] A public opinion poll published in *Fortune* in July 1940 indicated the scope of the public's fears: nearly three quarters of the survey's respondents believed that Germany had "already started to organize a 'Fifth Column' in this country" as part of a plan to mount a full-scale invasion.[2] President Roosevelt's public warnings about the threat of German subversion only served to make matters worse. "One word: Of course we have this Fifth Column thing," he asserted in a May 1940 press conference, "[and it] is altogether too widespread through the country."[3] In a fireside chat broadcast that same month, Roosevelt issued another dire admonition about the danger posed by Fifth Column activities, claiming that a nation's "strength can be destroyed" if such treachery is left unchecked.[4]

"Following the collapse of one European democracy after another," the American Civil Liberties Union reported, "fear of elements hostile to democracy aroused attacks in this country on alleged Fifth Columnists and Trojan Horses—phrases instantly popular which were recklessly misused to attack all sorts of unpopular groups." During this "time of intense feeling," as the ACLU called it, few groups triggered more intense suspicion than the Jehovah's Witnesses.[5] In the minds of many people who encountered them on front porches and street corners, the Witnesses' unusual beliefs and practices, particularly their refusal to salute the American flag or serve under it as members of the armed forces, appeared to be signs of disloyalty. That the Witnesses repeatedly denigrated ostensibly patriotic groups like the American Legion—it was commonly referred to in their splenetic tracts and periodicals as the "un-American Legion"—seemed only to confirm that their true allegiance lay with some foreign power.

In Texas, Witnesses were generally considered to be Fifth Columnists, and vigilantes in dozens of small communities brutalized them. On 22 May 1940, an irate crowd of 400 people forced three proselytizers out of Del Rio after they attempted to distribute Witness tracts and play recordings of Joseph Rutherford's speeches on their portable phonographs. A wildly inaccurate wire service account of the incident called the Witnesses "professed Nazi agents," claimed that they had compelled "housewives to listen to pro-Nazi phonograph recordings," and reported that one of the Witnesses had mocked the American flag as "a dirty rag."[6] When word of the confrontation reached the ACLU, director Roger Baldwin telegraphed Del Rio's mayor, J. S. Bradford, in hopes of quelling speculation about the Witnesses' alleged ties to Germany. "The facts clearly indicate," Baldwin wrote, "that these persons were not Nazi agents but representatives of Jehovah's Witnesses, a religious sect engaged in the lawful pursuit of distributing their literature."[7] The ACLU's efforts had little effect in Del Rio, where sentiment against the "three radical transients," as they were described in a letter to a local newspaper, continued to run strong. Incensed by the "Trojan Horse tactics" employed by these "sinister agents," Del Rio resident John Dobkins argued that his "community does not need that class of cattle, and the sooner the entire population of good red-blooded American citizens make up their minds that we don't need them, the better off the entire nation will be."[8]

In May and June 1940, with the Fifth Column scare reaching its peak, vigilantes in Texas waylaid Jehovah's Witnesses in numerous mob actions similar to the incident in Del Rio.[9] In almost every instance, law enforcement officials either actively participated in the harassment or failed to intervene and protect the victims.[10] Police nonfeasance was so widespread in Texas that the American Civil

Liberties Union asked Gov. W. Lee O'Daniel to deploy the vaunted Texas Rangers to ensure the Witnesses' safety.[11] Elliott Roosevelt, the president's son, also spoke out to urge fair treatment of the Witnesses in Texas. In a radio address, Roosevelt "greatly deplored" the recent outbreak of anti-Witness disturbances in the state and cautioned that "it is pitifully easy to crush out freedom in an overzealous attempt to preserve it."[12]

Perhaps the worst anti-Witness incident in Texas occurred in Odessa. On 1 June 1940, a large group of Witnesses converged on that city to attend a "zone assembly"—a kind of local convention— at a park and an auditorium. By nightfall, approximately sixty Witnesses had been herded by sheriff's deputies to the local jail, where they were lectured about Americanism and held overnight. More Witnesses, including Virgil Walker and H. C. Beattie, arrived in Odessa early on 2 June, and they were taken into custody as well by a group of deputies and Sheriff Reeder Webb. Walker later said that when he had tried to explain that the Witnesses were "just Christians," not subversives, Webb had struck him and angrily shouted that members of his faith were nothing more than "[expletive] Nazi spies."[13] Other Witnesses suffered through similarly rough treatment. Beattie reported that one older Witness, drawn to the zone assembly because he had hoped to be baptized, had been "ordered to 'shut up' " by a deputy when he attempted to explain the Witnesses' reasons for coming to Odessa, "and then one of these patriotic lawmen displayed a sample of his great courage and bravery by slapping this sixty-one-year-old man, and leaving marks on his face which were plainly noticeable the remainder of the day." By midmorning, a group of as many as seventy-five Witnesses were assembled at the county jail. At that point they were loaded onto a large flat-bed truck and slowly driven toward the county line. Hundreds of cars, most of them overflowing with jeering townspeople, followed. When the caravan reached Ector County's border, the Witnesses were unloaded and "told to start walking," as Beattie put it. The sheriff's parting words were customarily blunt: "When the sun quits shining on your navel and shines on your hind part, keep going! And if I ever see a one of you in Odessa again, it will not be good for you."[14]

Despite the rising heat, which became sweltering as the day wore on, the Witnesses set out on a brutal march along a railroad bed. Beattie later described the scene:

We were . . . forced to walk along the railroad [for] four or five miles in extreme heat in which some of the weak and afflicted ones became unable to stand and had to be carried by others. The mob followed along the highway, prevented our stopping for rest, and the only refreshment enjoyed was hot, muddy water from shallow pools along the railroad.[15]

Virgil Walker was among the Witnesses who succumbed to the heat. "I gave out walking," he recalled, "and some brothers carried me along until I was picked up by some friends." Drenched with perspiration, the marchers enjoyed a bit of a respite when they reached the outskirts of Midland and took shelter on the farm of a fellow Witness.[16] Witness J. O. Spaulding said, "We all ate and drank and then left for home by 4 P.M. The mob threw rocks at our cars as we came out of the gate, going home."[17] Writing in the *Christian Century* about the Odessa disturbance, Rev. John Haynes Holmes of the ACLU was astonished. "This sounds like the Jews in Germany," he proclaimed, "but it happens to be Jehovah's Witnesses here in America!"[18]

The Witnesses targeted by vigilantes in Texas were not the only members of their faith to suffer when wartime apprehensions of a Nazi Fifth Column swept across the United States in spring 1940. As the fighting in Europe intensified and spurred widespread fears of subversion, residents of Kennebunk, Maine, began to exchange fantastic rumors about Gertrude and Edwin Bobb and the other Witnesses who had established a new Kingdom Hall in the village. Wary villagers whispered that the strange newcomers—whose Kingdom Hall in Saco, Maine, had been ransacked the previous year—were not religious fanatics at all but Fifth Columnists, cunning agents of the Nazis or Soviets who had plastered the walls of their headquarters with lurid pictures of Hitler and Stalin. Such images reportedly were meant to inspire the Witnesses as they plotted a campaign of sabotage. "It was charged that the Witnesses had in their possession maps of Kennebunk and vicinity on which had been carefully marked the locations of bridges, public buildings and other works of strategical importance," an incredulous John Haynes Holmes wrote. "This evidently with the idea of starting the nazi revolution for the overthrow of the Washington government in a New England village ninety miles north of Boston!" (As Holmes acknowledged, the

Witnesses did in fact own maps, but the only sites marked on them were "homes of citizens to be visited for interviews and tract distribution."] Doubts about the Witnesses' loyalty were also fueled by their dissemination of the 29 May 1940 issue of *Consolation*, which discussed *Minersville School District v. Gobitis* in some detail and trumpeted the Witnesses' opposition to flag-saluting. For many of those who mistrusted the Witnesses, the provocative journal seemed to offer convincing evidence that they were indeed Nazi propagandists.[19]

As the rumors spread, the Witnesses began to receive unmistakable hints that villagers "were going to drive us out [of Kennebunk] as they had done in Saco," according to Gertrude Bobb. On 20 May, Bobb and her husband were followed and taunted as they proselytized, and on the following evening she discovered that her car had been vandalized. Through friends and acquaintances, the Bobbs received word that local members of the American Legion were planning to attack the Kingdom Hall. "This is serious. You can expect anything," one worried friend told Gertrude Bobb. Tensions worsened on Memorial Day. Automobiles "circled the building the whole day," Gertrude Bobb recalled. "There were carloads of Boy Scouts yelling 'Jehovah!'" Determined to protect themselves, the Witnesses had equipped the Kingdom Hall with spotlights; these were used to discourage villagers from vandalizing the building after nightfall. Although Memorial Day passed without a major disturbance, a group of men set upon the Kingdom Hall late the following evening, "crashing in the front, breaking the windows and even the walls," Bobb said. She scrambled over broken glass and debris to flick on the spotlights, and the assailants fled—only to return a short time later with a cache of empty beer bottles. "As they stepped into the yard to throw them, a shot was fired from the building," Bobb recalled. "The . . . men dropped the bottles and fled and we never found out who they were."[20]

The Witnesses discussed their increasingly desperate situation with village and state police officers and virtually begged them for protection. "If I were you, bud, and wanted to live a little longer, I'd lay off the shooting," a state policeman told Edwin Bobb. "These New Englanders all have rifles, and they'll come down and shoot the [Kingdom Hall] full of holes." Having warned the Witnesses to hold their fire, the officer conceded that they could not rely on the state police for protection. "He went on to say that our lives were in danger," Gertrude Bobb remembered. "He said he was telling this to us because he was afraid the whole thing was getting beyond the point where the state police could control it." The officer's words of caution prompted the Witnesses to appeal to the county attorney, Joseph Harvey.[21] Harvey told the Witnesses that "they had the right to assemble and to conduct their affairs without unwanted interruption," as he later explained, yet he took no substantive action to safeguard those basic civil liberties. Harvey even scolded the Witnesses, pointing out "that there had been complaints that they were going from door to door in certain parts of the county branding other religions as a racket and making seemingly unnecessary reference to the fact that they paid no attention to man-made laws, which included saluting the American flag or pledging one's allegiance to it."[22] As a last resort, the Witnesses brought their concerns to the attention of Maine's governor, Lewis O. Barrows, and the state's attorney general, but neither man intervened. Barrows, for instance, merely referred the troubled Witnesses back to the state police, who had already ignored their request for help. Writing to his ACLU colleague Roger Baldwin, John Haynes Holmes expressed his frustration with the indifference of state and local officials. "The authorities were grossly negligent," Holmes noted. "The Witnesses, [harassed] and beset through a period of two weeks, sought in vain for protection. They petitioned the local police, the state police, and the Government, and got nothing but a run-around."[23]

Meanwhile, vigilantes began to harry Witnesses in neighboring villages. After two National Guard officers reported that they had uncovered subversive activities in nearby Sanford, a huge crowd mobbed two Witnesses, sacked their office, and burned hundreds of Witness tracts and pamphlets in a large public bonfire.[24] According to an ACLU report, a police officer told one of the victims of the Sanford disturbance that it was "the worst thing that ever happened in Sanford, that even the Ku Klux Klan had never created such a commotion."[25]

Tensions in Kennebunk, after simmering for several weeks, finally boiled over early on 9 June, just hours after the anti-Witness incident in Sanford and less than a week after the Supreme Court handed down its opinion in *Minersville School District v. Gobitis*. Throughout the evening of 8 June, several carloads of "hoodlums," as Gertrude Bobb referred to them, circled the Kingdom Hall and feigned attacks. "These cars would come up almost to the front porch," she said, "but they stayed there a moment and then swerved out into the road again. This sort of thing kept up until 2:30 in the morning, when a car pulled up in front of the Kingdom Hall, and three men got out and started for the hall." The automobile "was loaded to the gunwales with rocks and stones," according to John Haynes Holmes, and when its occupants—Everett Nadeau Jr., Frederick MacDonald, and Dwight Robinson—disembarked, they launched a barrage of the small projectiles at the building.[26] Weary and unnerved after a long night of harassment, Witnesses ignored the state policeman's warning to "lay off the shooting" and opened fire on the men with at least three guns. Angrily justifying their use of force, the Witnesses later claimed that they had acted purely in self-defense, firing only when "the rocks started to fly," as Gertrude Bobb recalled.[27] Edwin Bobb contended that in firing at the trespassers, he was simply protecting his family and property; Joseph Leathers, another Witness who had holed up inside the Kingdom Hall, maintained that the gunfire had been provoked by the lawlessness of "a gang of religious fools" who loathed the Witnesses' fierce commitment to disseminating Christian teachings. Whatever their justifications, the Witnesses' gunfire struck Robinson and MacDonald, both of whom were wounded in the legs and hips. Nadeau managed to flee to a nearby house without being injured, a remarkable escape, given the intensity of the Witnesses' shooting. The police officers who inspected the shooting victims' car later reported that it had been struck by nearly thirty shots from the Kingdom Hall.[28]

State police officers arrived at the Kingdom Hall soon after Robinson and MacDonald sought treatment for their gunshot wounds at a hospital in nearby Biddeford. "They took our names and addresses and the guns and left. About 4:30 A.M., we went to bed, but we decided that the mob would be after us, so we started to get our car, which was about a mile away," Gertrude Bobb said. "The state police picked us up, telling us we were under arrest." A half-dozen Witnesses were arrested and charged with assault with the intent to kill. Their bail was "heavy," according to Holmes: $5,000 each, an astronomical sum for people of such modest means.[29] Three of the accused men's wives, including Gertrude Bobb, were forced to join them in Kennebunk's tiny jail because police feared that the women would be mobbed if they appeared in public. When Gertrude Bobb asked to leave the jail briefly—she wanted to use a nearby drugstore's pay phone—police wisely told her to stay put. "They said that we didn't realize the seriousness of the situation," she recalled, "and that our lives were in danger and not worth a nickel out in the streets."[30] Eventually, police ushered the women onto a bus bound for Portland, Maine, and shifted the men to the more secure county jail in Alfred.[31]

The police officers' belated cautiousness might have saved Gertrude Bobb and some of the other Witnesses from serious harm. As word of the shootings spread throughout Kennebunk in the early morning hours, hundreds of incensed villagers—"led by American Legion boys, most of them drunk," Holmes told Baldwin—began converging on the jail.[32] The crowd staged a brief demonstration there, then headed toward the Kingdom Hall once it was learned that the alleged shooters had been transferred to the county jail. In a front-page story published the following day, the *Boston Globe* described how the vigilantes ravaged the hall and abused two bystanders:

> The mob made two visits and set two fires. The first burned out part of the building's interior but was extinguished quickly. The second . . . completed the destruction. Before each of the fires the mob ransacked the building . . . and removed tracts, furnishings and members' personal belongings. These were burned in piles in a street of this ordinarily placid town. A man and woman were "roughed up" in the second sacking of the headquarters. Identified only as Biddeford members of the Witnesses, they were taken to the town line and released. . . . Neither was hurt, police said, but the man's shirt was "torn from his back." Hours after firemen doused the last ember, club-carrying townspeople milled around the building, and someone affixed a small American flag to the charred front of the hall.

Although its exterior walls remained standing, the fires essentially gutted and destroyed the Kingdom Hall. Nearly all of the Witnesses' propaganda materials and the Bobbs' personal belongings were either consumed in the two main blazes or destroyed in smaller fires set in the streets.[33]

Then the rioting spread. After the Kennebunk disturbance died down, a large contingent of vigilantes drove to Biddeford and hounded more Jehovah's Witnesses. Amid cries of "salute the flag," the mob stoned the apartment building occupied by Witness John Anthony and his two daughters. After verbally abusing him, rioters dragged Anthony from his bed and prepared to tar and feather him, but police intervened, sending the vigilantes off in search of new prey. "Let's go over to Elm Street," one rioter suggested. "There's another one [of the Witnesses] over there." Witness Benjamin Jariz became the next object of the mob's fury: rioters first stoned his bungalow, then dragged him outside and trounced him. Jariz's wife was not directly harmed in the assault, but she reportedly suffered a heart attack after finding shelter at a neighbor's home.[34]

Anti-Witness rioting continued in the area on Monday 10 June. "By the second night," *Time* reported, "mobs were hunting victims" in southern Maine.[35] Their rage at the Witnesses still not exhausted, vigilantes drove from Kennebunk to Wells in an effort to "get all these Fifth Columnists," as one participant put it. They assembled at the home of Clarence Grant, an employee of the Kittery Navy Yard who was mistakenly believed to be a Witness. When rioters confronted Grant outside his home with shouts of "you are a Jehovah's Witness!" and demanded that he prove his loyalty by saluting the American flag, Grant responded, "Of course. I have no objection." Grant's offer mollified no one. "The crowd then retreated from my door," he later told police, "and started throwing stones." Grant hoped to scare off the "hysterical hoodlums" in the crowd by brandishing an unloaded rifle, but the ploy backfired miserably. "With this they started to surge toward the house. I hastily loaded the rifle and fired as I thought into the ground." Grant's warning shot was errant, however, and it wounded two teenagers who were participating in the riot. As they were rushed to a local hospital for treatment, Grant delivered himself to the nearest state police barracks, where he was questioned and eventually released.[36] Unlike the Witnesses who fired at and wounded MacDonald and Robinson in Kennebunk, Grant faced no charges for shooting the two young rioters in Wells. Defending Grant's use of force, a sympathetic state police captain deplored the reckless "hoodlumism" of local men and complained that the crowd in Wells had simply "gone too far."[37]

The disturbances in Sanford, Kennebunk, Biddeford, and Wells made headlines across the United States. *Time*'s account, "Witnesses in Trouble," asserted that after several days of rioting, "little Witness literature [had been] left unburned in Maine."[38] An astounded New York newspaper editorialized that vigilantes were operating in Maine

> in the best Ku Klux Klan tradition. They have broken into the bedrooms of members of the Jehovah sect, forcing the members to salute the flag, and often flogging them for refusing. . . . Six members of the Jehovah's Witnesses have been arrested for assault with the intent to kill—all because they chose to defend their homes and their ideals from an illegal invasion at night.[39]

Governor Barrows was so embarrassed by such terrible publicity that he finally lurched into action. Although he had dismissed the Witnesses' pleas for relief in the days leading up to the Kennebunk tempest, Barrows ordered extra state policemen into the area and readied the National Guard. In an announcement that must have made local Witnesses groan in disbelief, he said from Augusta, "We cannot permit a breakdown of order, and our citizens must be protected."[40]

The governor's tardy intervention, motivated at least in part by a realization that Maine's critical summer tourist season might be jeopardized by widespread rioting, helped to quell the disturbances in the southern part of the state. It did little, however, to placate the American Civil Liberties Union, which issued a stinging rebuke of the "lawlessness displayed against Jehovah's Witnesses not only in Maine but all over the country." Roger Baldwin stated that if "some members of the sect fired on a crowd in Kennebunk, they should be punished by legal means"—and not further vigilantism—"after [being given] full opportunity to prove that they acted in self-defense. Legal processes must be preserved." To Baldwin, the persecution of Witnesses in Maine and Texas as Fifth Columnists was a tragic manifestation of war hysteria, and it needed to be controlled by aggressive measures before the victims' civil liberties were completely squelched.

> It is a symptom of the hysteria of the moment that Jehovah's Witnesses, of all minorities, should be so savagely and widely attacked on wholly false grounds. The sect is bitterly anti-Nazi. Its members in Germany have been executed and imprisoned, yet they are attacked here as Nazi agents. It arouses religious opposition by its pamphleteering against other creeds, but it is de-

voutly Christian. It refuses to salute the flag as a man-made symbol, yet its members are patriotic and law-abiding citizens. Its rights of propaganda have been sustained by the Supreme Court . . . but its members are arrested for doing only what the Supreme Court protects.

Baldwin ended his statement with a challenge: "The civil rights of Jehovah's Witnesses are a first charge on all those zealous for the defense of democracy in this crisis."[41]

Under the headline "Religious Riots in Maine," the *New York Herald Tribune* published one of the more perceptive analyses of the anti-Witness disturbances in southern Maine. As was true with almost every account of the disorders, the *Herald Tribune* readily acknowledged that the victims were not entirely blameless. Its editorial noted that by so eagerly assailing other faiths and flaunting their opposition to the flag salute, the Witnesses "have often gone out of their way to look for trouble." But though Witnesses could be provocative and cantankerous, "they have the constitutional right to worship as they choose," and state and local officials, particularly the state police, had a sworn duty to protect them. Their negligence and the public's outright hostility, the paper argued, could be traced to a pair of sources—the "national 'fifth column' hysteria" and Felix Frankfurter's opinion in *Minersville School District v. Gobitis*, handed down just as anti-Witness sentiments in the Kennebunk area were reaching their apogee. According to the *Herald Tribune*, the *Gobitis* opinion had been read in Maine as a call to arms against Witnesses.

> We have the "liberal" members of the Supreme Court to thank— at least in part—for the religious riots which have been breaking out in Maine. This conservative old New England state has seen little lynching or other lawlessness; but the Supreme Court's recent decision that the Jehovah's Witnesses must salute the flag seems to have convinced several hundred Maine rustics that it is their personal responsibility to see this decree carried out.[42]

John Haynes Holmes also pointed his finger at the Supreme Court. "It is no accident," he claimed, "that this long and violent succession of outrages against the Witnesses in recent weeks was coincident with the unfortunate decision of the Supreme Court refusing

Jehovah's Witnesses survey the wreckage of a Kingdom Hall in Saco, Maine, after a mob attack.

to interfere with the action of school authorities in demanding the salute."[43]

Halfway through 1940, Beulah Amidon reported in *Survey Graphic* on the precarious state of civil liberties in the United States. As a worried nation prepared for war, Amidon wrote, members of political, religious, and ethnic minority groups, including Jehovah's Witnesses, were in danger of becoming "scapegoats for the intolerance that is a common human reaction in times of tension and anxiety." Granted, any number of well-established legal safeguards remained to protect their civil liberties, but "an intimidated sheriff, a graft hungry police chief, and prejudiced judge or jury can defeat the letter and the spirit of the constitutional guarantees of the rights of minorities," leaving them nearly defenseless.[44]

This discouraging point was brought home forcefully when Amidon traveled to an unnamed hamlet in the Deep South and observed vigilantes physically and verbally abusing "a sorry little procession" of seven Witnesses. It was a gruesome but increasingly common sight in mid-1940: eager to eliminate potential Fifth Columnists from their community, vigilantes assaulted Witness proselytizers after they refused to salute the American flag or to disavow the allegedly subversive themes developed in their tracts and periodicals. As the victims limped their way out of town, the crowd following them "jeered and shouted and occasionally threw pieces of wood or rubble from the roadside." To Amidon's dismay, no one intervened on the Witnesses' behalf.

> A shirt-sleeved sheriff, a gun on his hip, leaned against a telephone pole, watching the scene. He made no move to join the crowd, or to check it. A half brick hit one of the women between her shoulders. She gasped and staggered. Two of the men caught her and dragged her along. The crowd jeered, and then the jumbled voices blended in the deep, rhythmic bay of the mob. The victims began to shuffle more quickly, to glance right and left in quick terror.

Appalled by this "ugly scene," Amidon asked the sheriff what had caused the disturbance. "Jehovah's Witnesses. They're running them out of here," he said. "They're traitors—the Supreme Court says so. Ain't you heard?" Although Amidon was amazed that the sheriff had so grossly misinterpreted the Supreme Court's *Gobitis* opinion, she recognized that his mistake—and its horrific consequences—were not at all unusual. "North and South, East and West," she wrote, "the Court decision has served to kindle mob violence against Jehovah's Witnesses."[45]

As Amidon reported, the anti-Witness disturbances that rocked southern Maine were duplicated in dozens of other communities across the United States in the months following the release of the *Gobitis* opinion. Writing in the *Christian Century*, John Haynes Holmes noted that the "lawless attacks" on Witnesses in Kennebunk and its neighboring villages were repeated "with less provocation, fiercer violence and more disastrous results in many other places in the country."[46] With the Fifth Column scare reaching its zenith, the weeks immediately preceding and following the *Gobitis* decision proved to be the most calamitous for Witnesses during the war years. On 11 June 1940, two days after the disturbance in Kennebunk, the ACLU formally requested that "the Civil Liberties Unit of the Department of Justice investigate the background of the 42 reported cases of violence against Jehovah's Witnesses in 21 states in the last month." Unfortunately, anti-Witness vigilantism became even more prevalent after the ACLU made its call for federal intervention. Between 12 June and 20 June, two Justice Department attorneys later wrote, "hundreds of attacks upon the Witnesses" were reported. What they lamented as "an uninterrupted record of violence and persecution," aided partly by the refusal of police officers in many communities to discharge their duties and shield Witnesses from vigilantism, continued throughout summer and fall 1940.[47] In a document forwarded to the Justice Department, the ACLU noted that 1,488 Witnesses in 335 communities had been attacked by vigilantes between May and October. All but four states saw anti-Witness disorders during that period.[48]

The Witnesses' suffering was barbarous enough to attract the attention of First Lady Eleanor Roosevelt, and she wrote passionately about it in her syndicated newspaper column, "My Day." "Something curious is happening to us in this country," she observed on 22 June 1940, "and I think it is time we stopped and took stock of ourselves." What Roosevelt bemoaned as "hysteria about 'fifth columnists,'" fueled in large part by the success of the Nazi military efforts in Europe, was sweeping the country, and it posed a serious threat to civil liberties. For proof, she wrote, one need look no further than a recent news report about the abuse of Jehovah's Witnesses in Wyoming. In a typically brutal assault involving the "unconstitutional and ill considered" activities of vigilantes, a half-dozen Witnesses in that state had been "dragged from their homes and forced to pledge allegiance to the flag." The Wyoming incident left the First Lady shaking her head. "Must we drag people from their homes," she wondered, "to force them to do something which is in opposition to their religion?"[49]

As both the First Lady's column and the ACLU's statistics suggested, June 1940 was the cruelest month of the war period for Jehovah's Witnesses in Illinois, Maryland, West Virginia, and dozens of other states. Policemen and members of the American Legion expelled a small band of Witness evangelists from Litchfield, Illinois, a small town located south of Springfield, on 1 June. Early on Sunday

16 June, twenty-one carloads of defiant Witnesses returned, bringing with them recordings and literature, including copies of *The Watchtower, Consolation,* and the tracts "Government and Peace" and "Religion as a World Remedy." Packs of furious townspeople, led in some instances by members of the American Legion, besieged many of the Witnesses before they could knock on a single door, "and most of the men were beaten before the entire company was placed in the town jail," the *St. Louis Post-Dispatch* reported. Asked to explain why the Witnesses had been ambushed, one vigilante later said, "Why, they wouldn't even salute the flag! We almost beat one guy to death to make him kiss the flag."[50]

Throughout the day, rioters in Litchfield thrashed Witnesses like Will Mittendorf when they refused to salute the American flag or repudiate the content of their literature. "Two fellows approached the car and demanded that I open the door or they would break it in," said Mittendorf, a Navy veteran. "I unlocked the door, and as I did one fellow hit me in the eyes as he pulled me out of the car. Immediately about eight fellows began beating me." Witness Clara Morford watched in horror as the assailant pulled Mittendorf from his automobile.

> He dragged Will from the car and took hold of his head. Several others joined in, beating him on all sides, knock[ing] him to the ground. He was able to get up, started grunting, falling headlong into the street. Will groaned and they started kicking him and beating him again. [At] that time, the people came from their houses and came to join in the mob. This crowd of men was comprised of about thirty or thirty-five men beating on Will.[51]

Once the pounding had subsided, both Witnesses were led to the local jail, where vigilantes battered Mittendorf once more. "I was again beaten and knocked down several times," Mittendorf said, "until I finally staggered into the jail, out of the reach of the mob."[52]

Bob Fischer and several other Witnesses attempted to flee the disturbance in Litchfield, but vigilantes foiled their escape by chasing their car for several miles and blocking the road. "Then they pulled all of us, women as well as men, out of the car and beat up the men for about ten minutes and pushed the women around," Fischer said. An assailant grabbed the keys to Fischer's automobile and prepared to drive the Witnesses back to the jail in Litchfield. "Just before the car started up," Fischer recalled, "one of the mobsters threw a book case full of books through the car window, breaking the glass and hitting me on the head." As the attack continued, many of the "mobsters devoted their attention to destroying our literature and personal property," the victim said. "Fists came from every direction, and they threw us on the ground, kicking us all over."[53] At one point a rioter draped an American flag over the hood of Fischer's car. When the Witness stubbornly refused to salute, vigilantes grabbed his head and repeatedly slammed it against the flag-covered hood. Recounting the scene, another Witness said that she had seen members of the crowd "beating Robert Fischer's head against the car . . . for about thirty minutes. The chief of police sat in his car while all this was going on."[54]

George Taylor, Litchfield's chief of police, waited for the disturbance to play itself out before summoning help from a nearby town and the state police barracks in Springfield. By day's end, state police reinforcements had escorted all the Witnesses—approximately thirty-five women and twenty-five men—to Hillsboro, the county seat, where they were fingerprinted and eventually released. The beleaguered Witnesses were forced to ride buses from Hillsboro back to their homes in the St. Louis area because rioters had overturned the evangelists' vehicles and pounded them with curbstones, paving material, and baseball bats. One incensed man even drove a Witness's late-model Chrysler into a nearby reservoir. In a letter to Ira Latimer of the Chicago Civil Liberties Committee, Witness officials "conservatively" estimated that property damage from the Litchfield riot totaled $8,000.[55]

On the night of 19 June 1940, just three days after the anti-Witness fracas in Litchfield, several dozen vigilantes surged into a Kingdom Hall in suburban Washington, D.C., and broke up a Witness Bible-study session. Despite the presence of two uniformed Montgomery County police officers, whose headquarters stood directly across the street from the Rockville, Maryland, Kingdom Hall, a group of approximately fifty rioters "raided the meeting hall when members of the religious sect refused to salute the flag," according to the *Washington Post*'s front-page account of the disturbance. "Desks, chairs, typewriters, literature and records were destroyed by the crowd, said by police to include ex-service men and 'leading citizens' of Rockville."[56] No serious injuries were reported, but damage to the Witnesses' property was extensive. As Witness officials complained in a letter to Maryland's governor, "The place was wrecked."[57] The two Montgomery County police officers who were at the scene apparently made no attempt to stop or disperse the crowd until after it had trashed the Kingdom Hall. One angry victim, echoing the complaints voiced by the victims of the Litchfield disturbance, protested that the officers had watched "with arms folded" as the mob descended upon and sacked the hall. "During the whole affair," another Witness reported, "not one of the police officers as much as lifted his hand to try to stop the riot." In the headline to its report on the attack, the *Post* made much the same observation, noting, "Rockville Crowd Raids Hall of Sect as Police Look On."[58]

The Rockville disturbance astounded the editors of the *Washington Post*. In deploring the "disgraceful riot" and the obvious negligence of county police, whose headquarters stood "within a stone's throw" of the Kingdom Hall, the *Post* excoriated both the rioters and the police officers who had failed to stop the attack. "The members of the mob no doubt believed they were acting in a patriotic manner," an editorial noted. "In truth, they were insulting the American flag far more than those against whom their actions were directed." Most of the *Post*'s venom, though, was reserved for county Police Chief Charles Orne and his subordinates. Making the kind of comparison that became common as the persecution of the Witnesses worsened during the war years, the editorial claimed:

If the behavior of the Rockville rioters was shocking, even more so was the complacent attitude taken by the police of that town. . . . The similarity between the attitude of the Montgomery County police and those of Nazi Germany is all too striking. It was the custom in the Third Reich for the custodians of the law to look on half approvingly while youthful gangsters destroyed the fundamentals of liberty under the specious pretext of patriotism. That such tolerance of brutality should be permitted in the near neighborhood of Washington is something to think about.

Seconding a call made by local Witnesses, the *Post* maintained that justice might be best served if the federal government investigated the circumstances of the riot and paid particular attention to the negligence of county police.[59]

Prodded by a chorus of such complaints and the threat of an investigation by the Justice Department's Civil Rights Section, Montgomery County police arrested ten Rockville residents on 21 June and charged them with unlawful assembly and disorderly conduct. It was the police themselves, however, who soon became the primary target of an investigation launched by the Montgomery County Board of Commissioners. Their probe proved to be one of the most speedy, even-handed, and thorough of any post-*Gobitis* disturbance. Having affirmed their "determination to guarantee to the people of this county that as sworn officers of the law we shall continue to exert every effort to assure prompt and adequate law enforcement and to guarantee them the constitutional rights of a free people," the commissioners held several public hearings and then dismissed Police Chief Charles Orne for his halfhearted response to the Rockville disorder.[60] In a separate proceeding, a police trial board fined the two police officers who had failed to quell the riot.[61] Praising the "good work at Rockville," the *Washington Post* applauded Montgomery County for its equitable handling of the riot investigation. The paper commended the commissioners for taking "a firm stand for democratic rights and constitutional government" and for giving the county's police officers a "sharp warning that unless they can vigorously and impartially protect minority groups in the exercise of their rights they have no place on that county's police force."[62]

Largely because of the explosive combination of the Fifth Column scare and the release of the *Gobitis* flag-salute opinion, anti-Witness disturbances continued to erupt throughout the country as June 1940 wore on. A few of these incidents, such as the attack on Witnesses that took place late in the month in Richwood, West Virginia, were extraordinarily brutal. Witnesses Stanley Jones and C. A. Cecil visited Richwood on 28 June in order to "distribute literature . . . and carry on the usual work of pioneers of [the] Jehovah's Witnesses," Cecil recalled. Cecil and Jones rented a room in town and then took to the streets to worship, "calling separately from home to home, or from person to person, until about noon of that day," Cecil said. The Witnesses were stopped on Main Street by state trooper Bernard McLaughlin, who took them into custody at the state police barracks and questioned them about the nature of their business. A number of local men, including Lee Reese, Martin Catlette, and Louis Baber, members of Richwood's American Legion post, soon arrived at the barracks and joined in the interrogation. Reese and Catlette, a Nicholas County sheriff's deputy, proved to be particularly antagonistic, accusing the Witnesses of being Fifth Columnists and then ordering them to leave town immediately. According to Cecil, Reese mentioned a recent mobbing of Witnesses in Oklahoma and "suggested similar action" might be called for to protect Richwood from the menacing outsiders. Reese intimated that if the Witnesses did not depart from Richwood immediately, "the American Legion would handle the matter," presumably by force, and "the law wasn't going to interfere" with the veterans' vigilantism. Cecil and Jones managed to talk their way out of the barracks without being harmed, but McLaughlin, the state trooper, yelled after them, "You damned reds, get out of here!"[63]

Cecil and Jones returned to their homes in Mt. Lookout, West Virginia, that night, but they came back to Richwood the following morning with several other Witnesses, including John Leedy, Harding Legg, Robert Shawver, and four members of the Stull family, Walter, Arthur, Howard, and Carlton. Arriving in Richwood, the men were dismayed to learn that the room rented the previous day by Cecil and Jones had been broken into and ransacked by a group of men led by Lee Reese, the volatile Legionnaire. Jones, Cecil, and Carlton Stull searched for the office of Richwood's mayor, where they hoped to debunk the rumor that they were disseminating "communistic literature" and to solicit "police protection, cooperation and kindness," as Cecil later put it. Before they could track down the mayor, Catlette intercepted the Witnesses and detained them in the mayor's office. While Bert Stewart, Richwood's chief of police, guarded the door, Catlette telephoned several fellow Legionnaires and summoned them to the office. "We have three of these damned sons-of-bitches," he said. "The others are at large, and [other veterans] are out looking for them to herd them up." His voice rising in anger, the sheriff's deputy berated the Witnesses after he had hung up the telephone. "You damned birds are going to get out of town," he fumed. "You don't know what you've gotten yourselves into. You'll know you have been in Richwood."[64]

A group of veterans, led by Louis Baber, tracked down the remaining Witnesses and escorted them into the mayor's office. Nervous but still resolute, the Witnesses stubbornly maintained that they had broken no laws by proselytizing; in fact, they said, the U.S. Supreme Court had specifically upheld their right to worship by distributing literature in public. Their arguments fell flat. When Carlton Stull gamely attempted to bolster his position by quoting a verse from the Bible, Catlette slapped the Witness and ordered him to shut up. After abusing Stull, the sheriff's deputy removed his badge, placed it in his pocket and announced, "What is done from here on will not be done in the name of the law." As the room filled with his fellow members of the American Legion, Catlette forced the Witnesses to surrender their possessions, which included "our petition sheets, a map of Richwood, a key to the Kingdom Hall at Mt. Lookout, [and] our pocket knives," Cecil recalled. The Witnesses grew increasingly apprehensive when "someone brought two guns into the room and another a rope. Catlette said he had to have something to settle his nerves and took a drink of whiskey from a bottle." Fortified by the drink, the sheriff's deputy encircled the right hand of each Witness with the rope and bound the victims together at intervals of two feet. According to Cecil, Catlette snarled that he meant to "rope you people like cattle." After the vigilantes had constrained the Witnesses with the rope, they began forcing the victims to ingest large doses of castor oil. Carlton Stull tried to writhe his way free, but several captors subdued him and forced him to swallow an eight-ounce serving. Cecil fared even worse: because he was an especially defiant prisoner, questioning Catlette's right to detain them and balking at most of the deputy sheriff's orders, the vigilantes compelled him to drink two eight-ounce bottles of castor oil. He later urinated blood and sought treatment at a hospital, as did several of the other victims.[65]

The nauseous and terrified Witnesses were marched outside to Richwood's post office, where a large crowd had gathered. After bringing the procession to a halt, Catlette recited the preamble to the American Legion's constitution and led the gathering in a flag-salute ceremony. The Witnesses could not have been blind to the irony of this moment; the document read by Catlette in the middle of a grotesque vigilante incident urged members of the Legion "to make right master of might [and] to promote peace and good will on earth." The Witnesses refused to offer the salute with their free

hands, so Catlette ordered them to march to the boardinghouse
where Cecil and Jones had previously rented a room. "At least five
hundred people followed," according to Cecil. "A time or two they
stopped us to let traffic through, but [the vigilantes] held up traffic
most of the time." To keep the Witnesses in step as they marched,
Catlette barked out a military cadence: "One, two, three, four; one,
two, three, four." Although vigilantes had cleared out most of the
Witnesses' proselytizing materials during the previous day's raid, the
boardinghouse room still contained a number of items, including food, bedding, and household supplies. These the Witnesses were
forced to pick up and carry back into the middle of Richwood.[66]

The procession stopped near the town square, and Legionnaire
Lee Reese ascended a pole to address the crowd. "We're carrying
on this demonstration," he said, "to show the people of Richwood
that if anyone is in sympathy with the work [the Witnesses] are doing, there is room for them on the end of this rope, and they will
go out of town with them." At this, according to Cecil, "the crowd
cheered," but the Witnesses did notice that at least a few spectators
were uncomfortable with the vigilantes' behavior. As the Witnesses
trudged toward the outskirts of town after the conclusion of Reese's
brief speech, several men offered to carry their belongings, and a
woman protested that they deserved a "fair trial," not "heathenish"
abuse from vigilantes. (True to form, Reese responded to this outburst by threatening to bind her with the rope as well.) Although
such gestures of sympathy were welcomed by the victims, the crowd
remained largely hostile; weary and humiliated, the Witnesses enjoyed little relief. Their march ended when they reached their cars,
which had been seized by vigilantes earlier in the day and driven
to the city limits. The victims were disheartened to learn that the
vehicles had been doused with castor oil and defaced with crudely
painted swastikas and epithets—"Hitler's spies," "Fifth Column,"
"Heil Hitler," and "Beware."[67]

The widespread abuse of Jehovah's Witnesses in spring and summer 1940 worried Frederick L. Gibson, a minister from Grand
Island, Nebraska. It wasn't that Gibson, a Baptist, thought very
highly of the victims. "Among the hundreds of irrational groups that
have come to notice in these depression years, the Jehovah's Wit-

nesses are probably the most ignorant and irritating," he told his
congregation at First Baptist Church one Sunday in June 1940. "No
intelligent person will accept their ideas about the sudden coming
of the end of the world, about all organized churches being the agencies of the devil, about its being a sin to salute the emblem of free
government." To be sure, the Witnesses espoused weird doctrines,
and their behavior could be "insolent, irritating, and nasty," as Gibson later wrote to a friend. Gibson's exasperation with the Witnesses
was unmistakable, yet it disturbed him to see "a religious group . . .
denied its constitutional right of petition, of assembly, [and] of worship," as had happened recently to Witnesses in the Grand Island
area. A group of war veterans planned to intimidate local Witnesses
by violently disrupting one of their upcoming Bible-study sessions.
"In hysteria a group of ex-service men decided that either the meeting would be broken up by the police or by mob violence," Gibson
noted. "The feeling was such that the police evidently feared violent
deaths." Fortunately, police intervened at the last minute, and the
veterans were unable to inflict any damage on the Witnesses or their
property.[68]

The episode passed, and although Gibson's worst fear—"a mob
murder"—was not realized, he was bewildered by the misguided response of Grand Island authorities to the near-disaster. Police had
reacted to the aborted vigilante assault by jailing and fining several
Witnesses instead of the veterans who had threatened them. "It is a
strange commentary on the hysteria that has swept our country,"
Gibson told his congregation, "that officers of the law, according
to their own testimony, will arrest and prosecute the intended victim of reported violence rather than the intended criminals." Without going so far as to endorse their unpopular faith, the minister
deplored the mistreatment of Witnesses in Grand Island because it
seemed so clearly at odds with the country's long and commendable
history of religious tolerance. Gibson later explained that he had appealed to his congregation on behalf of the Witnesses because he
feared that "hysteria has done away temporarily with constitutional
liberties."[69]

From a far less detached perspective, Jehovah's Witness Oliver
Siebenlist seconded Gibson's worried assessment of the erosion of
civil liberties in Grand Island. Just after Gibson delivered his ser-
mon lamenting the abuse of local Witnesses, Siebenlist wrote an in-

dignant letter to Nebraska's governor, Robert LeRoy Cochran, and complained bitterly about the "unlawful and malicious" conduct of local veterans and public officials. Siebenlist reported that on 22 June 1940, twenty Jehovah's Witnesses in Grand Island had been physically assaulted and then jailed for merely collecting signatures for a petition. Witnesses who tried to provide bail for the prisoners were locked up as well, and police held the entire group incommunicado. As always, veterans were in the thick of things, threatening the Witnesses and baiting them with promises of further vigilantism, but police seemed unconcerned. "The head of the American Legion post was at the police station and made threats of mob violence, and [he] was permitted to abuse Jehovah's Witnesses," Siebenlist protested. "No effort was made to arrest him." Police later stepped up their pressure on Witnesses in the community, first barring a planned Bible study on 23 June and then prohibiting "assembly or activity [of] Jehovah's Witnesses in the entire county," as the Witnesses noted in a telegram to Solicitor General Francis Biddle. Such "malicious interference" with the Witnesses' First Amendment freedoms clearly rankled Siebenlist, and he begged the governor to step in. "Jehovah's Witnesses are Christians, not criminals," he wrote to Cochran. "Can't our state law stop arrests of people who are guilty of nothing except coming to a peaceful assembly of Christian people for Bible study?"[70] Reluctant to help a group as widely reviled as the Witnesses, Cochran sidestepped the dispute by claiming that he was powerless to intervene in a local matter. "The executive branch of the government does not have authority to impose [its] judgment or discretion upon local law enforcing agencies," the governor explained to Siebenlist. "Your only recourse is the courts."[71]

With state and local officials doing little to safeguard Witnesses' First Amendment rights, members in Nebraska suffered at the hands of vigilantes throughout summer 1940. That August, S. A. Senk informed the American Civil Liberties Union that he and Ray Pillars had been accosted while they distributed Witness tracts in Grand Island and instructed to leave town immediately. Senk was lucky enough to escape violence, but Pillars was taken out of town and thrashed by vigilantes. "His head was badly bruised and bleeding," Senk wrote after inspecting his friend's wounds. "Blood was [all] over his shirt." To Senk's disbelief, police refused to investigate the

Witnesses' complaint, and the assailants went unpunished.[72] Another Jehovah's Witness wrote to the solicitor general to report the ongoing mistreatment of Witnesses in Nebraska City, Syracuse, Auburn, and other communities. Summarizing complaints lodged by roughly two dozen members of her Witness "company," Mrs. J. C. Kantz asserted that Witnesses had at various times been harassed by a Catholic priest, war veterans, a marshal, a city councilman, and an unidentified woman who had run through the streets of Auburn and lambasted their faith. "As matters now stand," she alleged, "our people are in danger of violence when continuing their work in places where grasping individuals or misinformed officials or war-veterans have established a law of their own, contrary to established law and order."[73] The ACLU received so many complaints from Witnesses like Kantz and Siebenlist that it wired protests to authorities in at least two Nebraska counties, reminding them that "mob action in your county resulting in interference with free movement and peaceful activities of Jehovah's Witnesses constitutes [a] violation of civil rights. Trust you will take all necessary steps to punish persons guilty and to protect civil rights of all citizens."[74]

The abuse of Jehovah's Witnesses in Nebraska reached a grisly climax in late summer 1940. Two men appeared at the home of Albert Walkenhorst on 27 August, identified themselves as fellow Witnesses, and asked if he had a minute to spare; they wanted him to join them outside for a discussion of the Bible. They seemed earnest and claimed to be involved "in the same work of Witnessing the Kingdom" that so captivated Walkenhorst, but it was a trap: the assailants seized the unsuspecting Witness as he stepped out his front door and hustled him to a nearby grove of trees. According to a note later written by the victim from his bed at Lutheran Hospital in Norfolk, Nebraska, the attackers "proceeded to perform an operation of taking out one of my testicles." After castrating Walkenhorst, one of the men joked, "There, that will hold you for a while."[75]

4. A Shocking Episode of Intolerance in American Life

Solicitor General Francis Biddle in June 1940 publicly condemned the wave of anti-Witness mobbings that followed the release of the Supreme Court's opinion in the *Gobitis* flag-salute case. Having received dozens of complaints from Witnesses who had been arrested, assaulted, and harassed in places like Odessa, Texas, and Kennebunk, Maine, Biddle recognized that the country's sudden preoccupation with spying and subversion, spurred at least in part by the dire warnings issued by the president and FBI Director J. Edgar Hoover, had begun to endanger the civil liberties of members of small, powerless minority groups, the Witnesses being most prominent among them. As they braved violence and harassment in every region of the country, the solicitor general spoke out in an effort to preserve their increasingly tenuous rights to speak, assemble, and worship freely. In a speech broadcast nationally, Biddle reported that the Witnesses, though law-abiding, "have been repeatedly set upon and beaten" by vigilantes who were so caught up in war hysteria that they thought nothing of flouting the Constitution and dishing out "mob punishment." Because these "outrages," as the solicitor general termed them, were as intolerable as they were widespread, Robert Jackson, the attorney general, had "ordered an immediate investigation," one that would presumably bring many of the vigilantes to justice and help safeguard the Witnesses from further abuse. Like so many observers of the Witnesses' suffering in spring and summer 1940, Biddle warned that if "alert and watchful" Americans truly wanted to protect their most cherished freedoms from the threat of fascism, they had to remain "cool and sane" when confronted by the Witnesses and other provocative dissenters. "We shall not defeat the Nazi evil," Biddle cautioned, "by emulating its methods."[1]

A few weeks later, in a speech before the Pennsylvania Bar Association, Biddle again mentioned "the swiftly increasing cases of mob violence in connection with Jehovah's Witnesses." The solicitor general noted that the Witnesses "consider it improper to offer obeisance to anyone but their Creator, and refuse, as a consequence, to salute the flag," a gesture of defiance that could incense patriotic Americans, especially those who were troubled by the menacing prospect of Nazi aggression. "To us to whom the flag means so much that is passionate and beautiful," he acknowledged, "I can see how such an attitude might be deeply offensive." But if Biddle could understand why some of his anxious countrymen might view the Witnesses' unorthodox beliefs with disdain, or even anger, he was dumbfounded by the violent aftermath of the *Gobitis* opinion. "Self-constituted bands of mob patrioteers are roaming about the country, setting upon these people, beating them, driving them out of their homes," he said to the assembled attorneys. As troubling as the attacks themselves was the indifference or outright hostility to the victims demonstrated by many peace officers. Biddle mentioned one attack in which "a sheriff, pretending to lead [the Witness victims] out of harm from the barn where they had taken shelter, terrified and powerless, brought them straight back to where the mob was waiting." Sounding the refrain that appeared in each of his major addresses on the subject, the solicitor general stressed that in a nation still guided by the principles delineated in the Constitution, "we shall not tolerate such nazi methods" of suppressing dissent, even if war seemed imminent. Biddle said that the attorney general shared his views and had instructed the FBI to conduct an "immediate investigation" to determine if the Justice Department could prosecute any anti-Witness vigilantes for violating federal civil rights statutes.[2]

A year later, Biddle again expressed his alarm over the Witnesses' persecution and what it signified for the nation as a whole. In a speech before the National Conference on Social Work, Biddle reiterated his protest against the widespread mistreatment of a harmless religious minority, calling it a black mark on the country's reputation for religious tolerance. Speaking on 2 June 1941, he lamented the "outrages committed against the members of the sect known as Jehovah's Witnesses," exasperating but devout Christians who were guided by "the misplaced zeal of martyrs." It was clear to Biddle that as bigotry and war hysteria overwhelmed small towns, police officers and other local authorities, though sworn to enforce the law equitably, were being particularly negligent guardians of the Witnesses' civil rights. "Where state officials should have been active in preventing this cruel persecution," he groused, "they have in many instances permitted it to occur, and in some have been the leaders of the mob." Biddle discerned the brutal irony of the persecution of the Witnesses: "This betrayal of the rights of citizens is done in the name of patriotism, and failure to salute the flag is made an excuse to desecrate the principles of which the flag is a symbol." In order to endure the crisis brought on by the war, the nation would have to remain true to those principles both in word and in deed, even if it meant allowing a detested minority like the Witnesses to spread their apparently weird faith. "Hitler's methods cannot preserve our democracy," he added, "which demands justice for all alike."[3]

Unfortunately for the Jehovah's Witnesses, the Justice Department failed to fulfill the promise augured by the solicitor general's speeches. As Biddle had promised, the department's overworked and understaffed Civil Rights Section investigated several egregious anti-Witnesses incidents in the early 1940s, but it proved to be extraordinarily reluctant to mount prosecutions under federal civil rights laws. As a result, the hundreds of reports of abuse lodged by Witnesses with the federal government in the early and mid-1940s resulted in only a single modestly successful prosecution—that of the sheriff's deputy and police chief who spearheaded the shocking anti-Witness incident that had taken place in Richwood, West Virginia, just weeks after the Supreme Court handed down its opinion in the *Gobitis* flag-salute case. With the federal government largely refusing to commit significant resources to the protection of their civil liberties, the Witnesses forged an alliance with the American Civil Liberties Union, and it became their staunchest ally. The ACLU's leaders and rank-and-file members were greatly alarmed by both the breadth and the severity of the Witnesses' oppression, and they provided the victims with unflagging support throughout the war years. Liberal members of the clergy also rallied to the Witnesses' defense. The vigilance of the Witnesses' champions served as an important counterweight to the efforts of the American Legion, which all but declared open war on alleged subversives like the Witnesses once European democracies began falling to the Germans in spring 1940.

That the Legion's hostility was left unchecked by lackadaisical local, state, and federal authorities helped to convince the Witnesses that their best hope for preserving their civil liberties lay in waging a battle of their own—in state and federal courts across the country.

R arely afraid to champion the rights of unpopular and misunderstood minorities, the American Civil Liberties Union rushed to the Witnesses' defense almost from the moment their troubles began to mount in 1940.[4] David Manwaring has written that the ACLU "did its best on the Witnesses' behalf," frequently offering substantial rewards (usually $500) for information leading to the arrest and conviction of anti-Witness vigilantes and engaging in a tenacious "campaign to persuade the Justice Department's Civil Rights Section to take active steps to stem the tide of persecution." Manwaring has noted that neither of these tactics had an overwhelming practical impact: in part because of the federal government's continued unwillingness to prosecute, few participants in anti-Witness disturbances were convicted of any crimes.[5] The ACLU thus had to settle for modest victories as it battled to protect the Witnesses from discrimination and violence. It could claim, for instance, that public knowledge of its well-publicized rewards discouraged additional outbreaks of vigilantism. In one 1941 report, the ACLU maintained that "in no community where these offers of reward were made public and where Jehovah's Witnesses returned to conduct their canvassing, as they always do, were any further incidents reported." Furthermore, the ACLU's frequent protests against anti-Witness vigilantism, which were widely noted in newspapers and magazines, served to legitimize the Witnesses' grievances. If nothing else, its imprimatur aided victims by bolstering the credibility of their complaints at a time when suspicion of the Witnesses ran deep.[6]

In two pamphlets published in the early 1940s, the American Civil Liberties Union thoroughly documented the Witnesses' struggles and advocated the protection of their civil liberties. Primarily a compendium of victims' testimony, *The Persecution of Jehovah's Witnesses* (1941) included lengthy affidavits from some of the Witnesses who had been abused in Kennebunk, Litchfield, and Jackson in the weeks following the release of the Supreme Court's opinion in the *Gobitis* case. As they recounted their travails, these Witnesses told the "story of a shocking episode of intolerance in American life," the pamphlet's introduction stated, "reflecting a tendency against which both officials and citizens should constantly be on guard." Beyond simply giving Witnesses an opportunity to provide compelling firsthand accounts of their suffering, the ACLU was careful to explore the causes of the rash of violent anti-Witness incidents. *The Persecution of Jehovah's Witnesses* pointed to two overlapping causes for their widespread difficulties—their well-known aversion to flag-saluting and the fears of subversion bred by the expansion of the European war:

> The cause of this extraordinary outbreak was the "patriotic" fear aroused by the success of the Nazi armies in Europe and the panic which seized the country at the imagined invasion of the United States. From California to Maine this emotion expressed itself in searching out "Fifth Columnists"—phrases which sprang into almost immediate popularity to characterize those thought to be opposed to national defense.

Once the hunt for subversives was under way in earnest, vigilantes in dozens of small communities targeted the purportedly disloyal Witnesses in a long series of brutal assaults. *The Persecution of Jehovah's Witnesses* reported that in 1940, nearly 1,500 Witnesses endured a total of 335 separate mobbings in 44 states. "Not since the persecution of the Mormons years ago," the ACLU argued, "has any religious minority been so bitterly and generally attacked as the members of Jehovah's Witnesses—particularly in the spring and summer of 1940."[7]

The Persecution of Jehovah's Witnesses was complemented in 1942 by a second grim report, *Jehovah's Witnesses and the War.* The follow-up pamphlet represented an "extraordinary record of attacks upon the liberties of a religious organization," according to the ACLU. "The attacks constitute a challenge to democratic liberty and religious tolerance." Because they employed "annoying methods" while proselytizing and refused to salute the American flag or serve in the armed forces, the Witnesses were forced to endure "wartime attacks on their freedom of conscience" through mobbings and other forms of harassment. Acts of outright vigilantism against the Witnesses declined after the raucous spring and summer of 1940,

Jehovah's Witness J. B. Good, imprisoned in 1941, looking out from a jail cell in Marianna, Arkansas.

but they continued to suffer from violent attacks throughout 1941 and 1942, "almost always in small communities where prejudice and action are easily organized, and hard to check," the pamphlet asserted. Some of these later outbursts were especially barbarous. In Little Rock, Arkansas, for instance, men wielding "guns, sticks, black-jacks and pipe" dragged Witnesses from their automobiles, beat them, and then left some of the thrashed victims in a ditch. A remarkably comprehensive document, *Jehovah's Witnesses and the War* also cataloged more subtle manifestations of religious bigotry that were plaguing the evangelists throughout the United States. In addition to assaulting Witnesses in vigilante actions, critics of the faith were firing them from their jobs, arresting them on implausible charges such as "riotous conspiracy," and expelling them from public schools, all because they balked at saluting the American flag. Such abuses, according to the ACLU, "present in new form the ancient conflict that at times arises between men's convictions of their duty to God and the commands of the state." If democratic freedoms were to survive the war, the state would have to nurture—not suppress—the right of dissenters to harbor such convictions.[8]

Following the principled example set by the organization's national leaders, members of individual ACLU affiliates defended Witnesses in dozens of communities across the country. In June 1940, for instance, the ACLU's Southern California branch protested the disruption of a Witness Bible-study session in Elsinore. With police looking on, vigilantes had broken up the meeting and then simply driven the victims out of town. The local ACLU branch quickly came to the Witnesses' assistance, asking both Culbert Olson, California's governor, and Earl Warren, the state's attorney general, to ensure their safety. Two years later, the same branch intervened when Charles Ellis, a Redondo Beach police sergeant, "brutally assaulted August Schmidt, a Jehovah's Witness, in his home, on the way to the police station, and later inside the station itself," according to one report. Despite the unpopularity of the victim's faith, the branch helped to secure a grand jury indictment of Ellis on two charges of assault. "Tried before the Superior Court, he was found guilty of one charge and fined $100.00," the branch noted in its year-end report. "The penalty seemed to us very light, but the conviction has had a salutary effect and there have been no further cases of the sort."[9] Claiming that "there's a dangerous intolerance afloat," the

Ohio League for Constitutional Rights came to the Witnesses' defense in summer 1940, when their persecution was at its worst. In an open letter to supporters, Robert Mathews, a member of the state-wide civil liberties organization's executive committee, noted that the Witnesses' activities had been suppressed in both the Soviet Union and in Germany and that their abuse in the United States had become "distressingly like their treatment in those dictator countries." A group of Witnesses recently had been mobbed in Steubenville, Ohio, for instance, and plans for a Witness convention at the state fairgrounds in Columbus had been scrapped after the state, citing the Witnesses' purported lack of patriotism, canceled the permit. Mathews acknowledged that the Witnesses "hold certain religious convictions which most of us don't agree with, some of which we even disapprove." Yet, as he pointed out, they were a "harmless religious sect," and their beliefs were sincere, not seditious. Although they undoubtedly were annoying, their activities were "not foreign inspired, not Nazi or Communist." With that in mind, Ohioans who were troubled by the fact that the Witnesses' "rights of assembly, of free speech, and of religious worship can . . . be lightly cast aside in the face of a national hysteria" had a duty to voice their concerns to Gov. John Bricker.[10]

The pervasiveness and intensity of the Witnesses' unpopularity during the war years meant that not all such local efforts could be successful. Twenty-four-years-old and responsible for coordinating Jehovah's Witness activities in nine southwestern Iowa counties, Reginald Bourne brought his wife and infant daughter from Omaha, Nebraska, to Carson, Iowa, a small town twenty miles east of Council Bluffs, in spring 1940. On 4 June (the day after the Supreme Court handed down its opinion in the *Gobitis* flag-salute case), a group of several dozen angry men confronted and threatened Bourne and his family at their trailer. "Two sheriff's deputies were in the mob, and one member of the mob had a pint of gasoline in his pocket with the intent of burning the trailer," an executive of the Iowa Civil Liberties Union wrote to his colleagues in New York. "A Methodist minister tried to restrain the crowd, and probably did prevent their burning the trailer." After that crisis had passed, Pottawattamie County sheriff Riley Nelson, having received several dozen complaints that Bourne was "not patriotic" and had refused to salute the American flag, called on the Witnesses to determine if their proselytizing represented a serious threat to public safety. Nelson listened to Bourne's recordings and concluded that they were basically harmless, yet he counseled the Witness to "avail himself of the opportunity" to flee Carson before serious violence flared. "It looked like an ugly situation," Nelson later explained, "and might have been worse if one of the Carson pastors hadn't held the boys in check." The sheriff offered to escort Bourne back to Omaha, where a large group of Witnesses met weekly to study the Scriptures, but he declined and chose to make the trip without protection. Nelson's refusal to buck mob sentiment and protect Bourne's civil liberties provoked an impassioned response from the Iowa Civil Liberties Union (ICLU), which charged that the sheriff had permitted a gross "violation of freedom of assembly, of speech, and of conscience." Following an ICLU meeting in Des Moines on 8 June, Willard Johnson, the organization's chair, wrote to Nelson, "In these days of mounting hysteria against minority groups whose rights are protected by the Constitution of the United States, it is the duty of citizens and officials to see that those constitutional guarantees are not nullified by mob sentiment." Johnson's letter was noted in a *Des Moines Sunday Register* story about Bourne's expulsion from Carson, but it came too late to do much good for the Witness. Fearing for the safety of his wife and child, he was forced to remain in Omaha.[11]

Although their role was not always as visible as the American Civil Liberties Union's, clergy from a variety of denominations also defended the Witnesses' right to speak and worship freely. The Reverend John Haynes Holmes, who had been one of the ACLU's founders and served on its board of directors for several decades, was among the Witnesses' most eloquent advocates. In his autobiography, Holmes noted that he had long felt a profound concern for what could "best be described as 'the social question'—the high resolve to make this world a better world by abolishing its evil and fostering its good." War and other forms of violence ranked high on the list of depravities that Holmes hoped to eliminate. An avowed pacifist, he felt strongly that "force and violence are futile" and antithetical to the most basic precepts of Christianity.[12]

Whatever his misgivings about the victims' obstreperous behavior, the pacifist in Holmes was so disconcerted by the Witnesses' suffering in spring and summer 1940 that he met in Washington with Hayden Covington, the faith's leading attorney, and pored over detailed accounts of the vigilante assaults that erupted after the *Gobitis* decision. The Witnesses' stories appalled him in part because they were so similar to the chilling accounts provided by the victims of religious persecution in Nazi Germany. "Men and women of various ages and conditions have been raided in their homes and meeting places," he wrote in the *Christian Century*, "set upon by organized mobs led in some cases by officers of the law, held in prison without bail or access to legal counsel, beaten and otherwise physically injured. They have had their property seized and destroyed, their halls stoned and burned, and they themselves have more than once been driven out of town and scattered over the countryside." As he marveled at such abuses, Holmes could not help but think about "some of the persecutions which are going forward on a larger scale in Europe." It seemed apparent—and absolutely startling—to him that both the Witnesses in America and the Jews in Germany were falling victim to brutal manifestations of religious bigotry.[13]

What made Holmes's article for the *Christian Century* so remarkable was not so much his account of anti-Witness atrocities but his praise for the victims' ability to maintain an unswerving fidelity to the true spirit of Christianity. Although he was forced to concede that they were "a peculiarly aggressive, even obnoxious set of people" who often launched "bitter and unfair attacks on Catholics," Holmes argued that the Witnesses were, for all their faults, "among the few Christian groups in the world today who stand ready to die, as did the early Christians, for the faith that is within them." Yes, the Witnesses were zealots, but so too were the earliest Christians, gallant and persistent people who faced much the same kind of antagonism as they attempted to disseminate Christ's teachings. "The Witnesses preach exactly what the early Christians preached eighteen hundred years ago to a society which had no more belief in religion, least of all the Christian religion, than our society has in our time," Holmes wrote. "As these early Christians were regarded as dangerous, more particularly to the state and its government, so Jehovah's Witnesses are regarded as dangerous today in the same way." As he praised the Witnesses for their steadfastness, Holmes addressed perhaps the most controversial tenet of their faith—that they could, as he put it, "recognize as worthy of reverence nothing that is made of man's hands, since that is idolatry that is expressly denounced in the pages of Holy Writ." He found it hard to fathom that the Witnesses' reluctance to salute the American flag on such grounds could be called into question. Again, Holmes compared the Witnesses to their earliest Christian forebears: "Are not the Witnesses in the best tradition of the Christian spirit in refusing this salutation to the flag? What were the early Christians doing but this very thing when they refused to put their pinch of salt upon the altars of the Roman emperor?"[14]

Had it not been for the anti-Witness incidents that wracked southern Maine in June 1940, Holmes might have kept his unorthodox views to himself. The disturbance in Kennebunk, where Holmes had maintained a summer residence for a number of years, was particularly unsettling for him; he knew the village well, and it hardly seemed to be a hotbed of vigilantism. "Old families abound; traditions and local customs are everywhere; life is prevailingly sober, conservative, self-respecting," he wrote of Kennebunk. To Holmes, the eruption of violence in such a tranquil place indicated that the Witnesses were in desperate trouble, at least in part because state and local authorities were unwilling to protect them. The day after the Kingdom Hall in Kennebunk burned, he wrote to the ACLU's Roger Baldwin, "About this Kennebunk matter! There must have been some very lax policing. And this means, of course, that the State Police were at fault, as the local force consists of only two officers, if I remember rightly. . . . This is bad, and the Governor should be told so."[15] Ten days later, Holmes wrote to Baldwin once more about the tumult in Kennebunk and reiterated his contention that by ignoring the Witnesses' entreaties in May and June, local "authorities were grossly negligent" and thus culpable for the disturbance. As summer 1940 wore on, and Witnesses continued to suffer because of their beliefs, Holmes struggled to fathom the bigotry engulfing dozens of small communities like Kennebunk. "The regular element of Kennebunk," he told Baldwin on 20 June, "are still describing the Witnesses as Nazis; the so-called better elements are humiliated and indignant, and see the issue clearly." Holmes, shocked by the mistreatment of the Kennebunk Witnesses and the destruction of their property, counted himself among the latter group, and he resolved to aid the victims by championing their civil rights.[16]

Following the Kennebunk debacle, Holmes helped to persuade a number of prominent religious figures, including the theologian

Reinhold Niebuhr, to advocate the positions outlined in the ACLU's *Persecution of Jehovah's Witnesses* and *Jehovah's Witnesses and the War*. A coalition of twenty-two Protestant, Catholic, and Jewish leaders endorsed the second publication and sought to "commend it to the attention of all liberty-loving Americans."[17] Motivated by the same spirit of tolerance, individual members of the clergy did what they could to mitigate the Witnesses' suffering. In addition to lending his imprimatur to the ACLU's efforts, Frederick May Eliot sent a letter urging his fellow Unitarians to "speak out in vigorous protest against any assault upon the rights of these fellow-citizens of ours." Eliot readily acknowledged that the Witnesses might have provided "real provocation" for vigilantism by being "annoying and irritating on many occasions." Nevertheless, "the fact remains," he wrote, "that a comparatively small number of devout, perhaps fanatical, people have roused in this country of ours a wave of intense and bitter animosity, so that mob violence and all the familiar paraphernalia of religious persecution have once again appeared." Eliot hoped that his fellow ministers, realizing the gravity of the situation, would look beyond the victims' obstreperous behavior and work with members of their congregations to safeguard the Witnesses' civil liberties. "I hope you will do all in your power," he wrote, "to make your church and your people a strong influence for fair play to everyone—even those who may seem to be deliberately seeking to provoke attack." The *Michigan Christian Advocate* struck much the same tone in an editorial published in summer 1940, arguing that while the Witnesses may have "violated some minor laws and ordinances, they have not done so with any malicious intent and they certainly do not justify the more lawless acts of mob violence committed against them." As it bemoaned their suffering at the hands of vigilantes, the periodical praised the Witnesses for offering a "challenge to our pagan complacency" by so zealously disseminating the basic precepts of Christianity.[18]

Although they were sometimes slow to admit it, the Witnesses needed all the help they could get from allies like the American Civil Liberties Union and liberal members of the clergy. The Witnesses' beliefs and practices earned them some fervent adversaries during the war years, and these foes mounted strenuous efforts to suppress their civil liberties. None of the Witnesses' detractors were more strident than the members of the American Legion, the nation's largest organization of veterans. In small communities across the country, members of the Legion frequently challenged the patriotism of Witnesses, demanded that they repudiate their faith by saluting the American flag, and then violently abused those who refused to comply. When he delivered a radio address urging Texans to respect the Witnesses' civil liberties, U.S. Attorney Clyde Eastus singled out members of the Legion for their confrontational tactics. "You American Legion boys have been presenting the Jehovah's Witnesses with the American flag, and have asked them to salute it, and they have refused to do it," Eastus said. "This starts trouble. *You should not do that.*" Having received complaint after complaint from Witnesses who had been pummeled by Legionnaires, he felt compelled to admonish members of the veterans' organization: "You gentlemen are acting too hasty, you let your patriotism get the best of your judgment."[19]

In fact, the Legion's hostility, grounded in the gross misapprehension that anyone who refused to salute Old Glory must be in league with Hitler, represented a formidable problem for Witnesses throughout the United States. David Manwaring, in his study of 843 "incidents of alleged persecution" reported by Witnesses in the early 1940s, estimated that Legionnaires participated in 176 of the attacks, "or over a fifth of the total."[20] That estimate might have seemed overly conservative to an observer writing in the *Nation* in 1940. "In nearly every account of the prevalent violence," H. Rutledge Southworth noted, "we read . . . that American legionnaires led the attacks."[21] The Legion's national leaders never explicitly instructed veterans to mob or harass purported subversives, but their reluctance even mildly to censure the vigilantes within their ranks undoubtedly contributed to the oppression of the Witnesses. "National headquarters made no effort," historian William Pencak has written in his account of the Legion's formative years, "to discourage the widespread attacks and expulsions [of Witnesses]. . . . By ignoring Legion violence, National Headquarters undoubtedly fueled it."[22]

Homer Chaillaux, head of the Legion's National Americanism Commission, ranked among the organization's most active campaigners against the Witnesses. To the leaders of the American Civil Liberties Union, Chaillaux was perhaps most notorious for his duplicitous handling of a dispute between Legion members and a group of Witnesses in Jackson, Mississippi, in June 1940. On 25 June the ACLU's Arthur Garfield Hays telegraphed the Justice Department, Mississippi governor Paul Johnson, and Raymond Kelly, national commander of the American Legion. In the three messages, Hays stressed the unmistakable threat posed by Legion-led vigilantes to a group of Witnesses who were attempting to hold a convention in Jackson, Mississippi's capital.[23] Chaillaux, apparently fabricating a pretext for ignoring Hays's appeal for calm, erroneously claimed that the ACLU had referred to "Jacksonville," not Jackson, in its plea on behalf of the Witnesses. "I hope that all of your information is not as erroneous as your telegram in which you refer to Jacksonville, Mississippi," Chaillaux informed Hays. "We find that we do not have any post of the American Legion in Jacksonville because there is no such town in Mississippi. This being the case, it would be impossible for us to follow through as you have suggested." Hays marked the Legion's reply with a question mark, but its import was plain: the Legion would do nothing to restrain its increasingly frenzied members in Jackson.[24]

As Hays had feared, vigilantes followed through on their threats and ejected the Jehovah's Witnesses from Jackson early on 27 June. With Chaillaux's implicit approval, members of the American Legion overran the Witnesses' trailer camp at dawn. The victims were ordered to pack up their belongings and then marched out of town. Approximately two dozen Witnesses, a New Orleans newspaper reported, "were escorted from Jackson . . . by a large group of citizens and told to leave the state."[25] Forcibly removed from the camp, the victims were escorted west through several counties, across the Mississippi River and into Louisiana, where more veterans greeted the procession with further harassment. "They would not allow the women and children to go to toilets or to secure food," one victim later wrote. "Several of the Legionnaires went ahead, and at every town we were met by officers and ordered on."[26] An incredulous Hays labeled the expulsions a "clear violation of the federal kidnapping law."[27]

In that instance and numerous others, Chaillaux demonstrated little respect for the Witnesses' civil rights, perhaps because he felt that they were a "supposed" religious group propagating nothing less sinister than a "doctrine of disloyalty." Determined to suppress the Witnesses' proselytizing, he not only urged Legionnaires to lobby for anti-Witness ordinances in their communities but also made a point of distributing literature highlighting what he termed "the true facts" about the Witnesses' thoroughly un-American activities. When he learned that Legionnaires had confronted and verbally abused Witnesses, Chaillaux urged them to "keep up the good work."[28]

Lynn Stambaugh, the Legion's national commander, was only slightly more tactful than Chaillaux in expressing his distaste for Witnesses and their faith. Shortly after the Japanese attacked Pearl Harbor late in 1941, Arthur Garfield Hays contacted Stambaugh and suggested that they meet in New York to discuss the deplorable anti-Witness activities engaged in by so many Legionnaires. Hays apparently hoped that Stambaugh might exercise his authority over individual posts and reprimand Legionnaires who participated in anti-Witness vigilantism. But the national commander begged off meeting with Hays, claiming in a half-hearted letter that his busy schedule would not permit him to travel to Manhattan "for the next thirty days, thus preventing the possibility of the personal conference you suggest." He then explained that "acts of violence alleged to have been committed by local posts of the organization can be dealt with, without any hesitation whatever"—but only through proper channels. Complaints about the misconduct of Legionnaires first had to be addressed to the state (or "department") Legion commanders, Stambaugh wrote. Since his office "intervene[d] only when asked to do so by Department officials," it would be inappropriate for him to disregard the chain of command and prematurely take action against individual Legionnaires for their supposed crimes against Witnesses. Having offered that clumsy dodge, Stambaugh indicated that he was unlikely to worry much about the Legion's widespread suppression of the Witnesses' civil liberties. "Quite frankly," he wrote Hays, "I feel this is not the time for Jehovah's Witnesses or any other organization to be engaged in a nationwide program teaching disloyalty to our Flag, disloyalty to the defense of the United States when our supreme effort is needed for the unification of all elements toward our national safety."[29]

Taking their cue from Chaillaux and Stambaugh, Legionnaires throughout the country did their best to harass Witnesses and frustrate their efforts to speak, worship, and assemble.[30] In the weeks following the Supreme Court's decision in *Gobitis*, Legionnaires in

Harrisburg, Illinois, announced that they would enforce a virtual ban on the Witnesses' most basic form of worship, proselytizing. The George Hart Post of the Legion resolved "that in the future no Jehovah's Witnesses or any other sect having similar belief shall distribute any literature or play any recordings in the city of Harrisburg or surrounding territory stating that they will neither salute the flag nor take up arms in defense of this country in the event of armed invasion." The Legionnaires' decree also forbade local Witnesses from soliciting "membership to their organization, either in the city of Harrisburg or any surrounding territory."[31]

Soon after the Legion post issued the proclamation, veterans in Harrisburg began carrying out its edicts, and local Witnesses suffered immeasurably. In a lengthy complaint sent to Solicitor General Biddle in July 1940, several Witnesses presented what they called "an account of intimidation by threats of boycott, mob violence and property destruction." Members of the American Legion, including Jack Edwards, a deputy sheriff and the commander of the George Hart Post, figured prominently in most of "these unwarranted, unlawful and un-Christian attacks" on their civil liberties. Mrs. Helen Jordan lodged a typical complaint, reporting that on 23 June Edwards accosted her as she proselytized and warned that members of the Legion "were going to 'get'" Witnesses if they continued to spread their pernicious beliefs in the area. Perhaps more serious than such confrontations were the boycott threats repeatedly leveled at businesses employing, or owned by, Witnesses. Duncan Felts, part-owner of a Texaco filling station in Harrisburg, was "being forced out of his business through threat of boycott (which is now being carried out)," the Witnesses asserted in their complaint to the solicitor general. One Legionnaire who helped to organize the boycott "stated Mr. Felts would either have to 'compromise' or get out, and he was very sorry this all had to happen." Another Witness lost her job at a Harrisburg bank, a position she had held for fourteen years, because its directors feared a boycott. Since local authorities were colluding with the Legion to suppress the Witnesses' activities, the victims felt that swift federal intervention represented their only hope. "The Constitution gives Jehovah's Witnesses the right to worship God according to the dictates of their conscience," they told Biddle, "and we respectfully request an immediate investigation by the Federal Government of these un-American and un-lawful activities being waged against Jehovah's Witnesses." As would happen so often to Witnesses in the early and mid-1940s, the Harrisburg victims' plea to Biddle went unanswered, and they continued to suffer harassment at the hands of Legionnaires.[32]

No one felt the Legion's hostility more profoundly than Cecil Bevins, a Harrisburg Witness who worked as a miner for the Blue Bird Coal Company. About a month after the George Hart Post passed its anti-Witness resolution, a miners' union official warned Bevins that his union card was about to be revoked because of Legion pressure, according to an account that was forwarded to the solicitor general. The following day, Bevins's fellow miners refused to work with him, and he was discharged. "Bevins was informed later by one of the local members [of the miners' union] his card had been taken away. He has not been able to work—having no mine union card." Bevins's woes continued in December 1940, when Jack Edwards appeared at his home and arrested him for having disturbed the peace several days earlier. If the complaints supplied to the solicitor general by Witnesses in Harrisburg are to be believed, Edwards apparently had few qualms about using his authority as sheriff's deputy to enforce the ban on Witness activities established by his Legion post. Determined to squelch Witness activities in the area, he frequently swore out complaints against Witnesses like Bevins and testified against them in court. In Bevins's case, Edwards's dual roles meshed perfectly: a justice of the peace found the Witness guilty and fined him $100.[33]

In a report issued in 1940, the ACLU offered a blistering critique of the Legion's often savage methods of policing patriotism. According to the organization, a mid-1940 survey of observers in forty-six states "showed agreement on the American Legion as the most active agency of interference with civil rights. The Legion has taken first place in this canvass for several years." After noting that the Legion was significantly responsible for "a wave of intolerance" that threatened to swamp the civil liberties of innocent people like the Witnesses, the ACLU report likened the Legion to "native fascist organizations of the character of the Bund, the Silver Shirts and the Klan." As the ACLU pointed out, the seriousness of the threat posed to civil liberties by organizations like the American Legion was exacerbated when local authorities, themselves caught up in the hysteria surrounding the Fifth Column, empowered groups to "spy on their neighbors and report what they consider subversive activities." In a letter urging Attorney General Robert Jackson to formulate a precise definition of "subversive activities," the ACLU claimed that the American Legion and other groups simply had "no concept of the activities which should be tolerated in the interest of democracy," including the religious work of Jehovah's Witnesses.[34]

To its credit, the American Civil Liberties Union did more than simply criticize members of the American Legion for their fierce attacks on the rights of minorities like the Witnesses. Halfway through June 1940, with incidents of anti-Witness violence being reported almost daily, the ACLU's disgust with heavy-handed attempts to punish "Fifth Columns, Trojan Horses, Communists, German-American Bundists and others" prompted it to call for the formation of "vigilance committees" throughout the country to monitor civil liberties. These monitoring groups were needed, the ACLU claimed, to calm "the present case of jitters" sweeping the country and to preserve the constitutional rights of members of minority groups. Given "the inflamed state of public opinion" and the numerous "calculated incitements of 'patriotic' agencies" reported during that spring, those Americans who genuinely hoped to safeguard civil liberties had an obligation to take action themselves to combat the excesses committed by the likes of the American Legion. After all, the Justice Department's lackluster response to the persecution of Jehovah's Witnesses had vividly demonstrated the futility of relying on the federal government to monitor and control threats to civil liberties.[35]

A fter they had recovered from their harrowing ordeal, the Jehovah's Witnesses who had been tied together, forced to ingest castor oil, and marched through the streets of Richwood, West Virginia, in June 1940 contacted the Justice Department and requested a thorough investigation of the debacle. They claimed that the misconduct of the Richwood assailants—Sheriff's Deputy William Catlette and Police Chief Bert Stewart in particular—warranted an inquiry by the Justice Department's Civil Rights Section, which had been established in February 1939 to investigate and prosecute violations of federal civil rights laws. In framing their protest to the department, the Witnesses contended that both Catlette and Stewart had clearly acted under the "color of law" in depriving them of their civil rights and thus merited prosecution under Section 52 of Title 18 of the U.S. Code. Moreover, it seemed apparent that they and some of the other Richwood assailants also could be prosecuted under Section 51 of that same statute, which prohibited two or more people from conspiring to "injure, oppress, threaten, or intimidate any citizen in the free exercise or enjoyment" of rights guaranteed by the Constitution or federal law.[36]

In 1941, Henry Schweinhaut, the first head of the Civil Rights Section, confessed that mounting a prosecution under those federal measures was "a cumbersome and generally unsatisfactory" approach to guarding civil rights, one that usually ended in frustration for both the victims and the Justice Department.[37] The department maintained that many of its potential prosecutions foundered because it simply lacked the statutory authority to provide substantive protection for civil rights. "It must be borne in mind," Attorney General Frank Murphy said when the CRS came into being, "that the authority of the Federal Government in this field is somewhat limited by the fact that many of the Constitutional guarantees are guarantees against abuses by the Federal Government itself, or by State Governments, and are not guarantees against infringement by individuals or groups of individuals." Two years later, Schweinhaut acknowledged the same limitations, writing, "There are at present few statutes which make federal crimes out of specific violations of civil liberties."[38] Furthermore, the Civil Rights Section's meager resources proved to be as debilitating as its narrow statutory mandate. Housed in a handful of cramped rooms in the Justice Department, the CRS usually employed fewer than ten attorneys and a few stenographers and clerks in the early 1940s. In short, it was "a small agency with limited powers and resources of its own," as one 1947 study noted.[39]

Nothing better demonstrated the Civil Rights Section's limitations than its handling of the numerous complaints reported by Jehovah's Witnesses in the early 1940s. In nearly every instance, the unit concluded that it either lacked jurisdiction under federal law to prosecute or that the victims' formidable unpopularity would make it impossible for the Justice Department to gain an indictment or a conviction. In a 1943 circular distributed to all U.S. attorneys, the CRS outlined its cautious approach to handling the Witnesses' grievances. Because the CRS had such limited resources and so little statu-tory authority, the Justice Department "does not desire to institute wholesale prosecutions against over-zealous public officials who have deprived others of their religious freedom by the unconstitutional application of leaflet distribution ordinances or by persisting in the enforcement of compulsory flag salute regulations against school children whose consciences forbid their participation," the circular noted. In light of statutory constraints and the CRS's scarce re-sources, the U.S. attorneys would do well to respond to the Wit-nesses' many complaints by contacting "the appropriate, responsible state officials, pointing out to them that their actions may involve a denial of constitutional guarantees," and requesting "their coop-eration to the end that the activities complained of may be avoided. It is felt that most of the difficulties involving alleged state interfer-ence with religious freedom can be avoided through the prompt me-diation of the United States Attorneys with the local authorities by letter or personal conference." One point was certain: "Prosecutive action should be reserved for those cases where that remains the only means of alleviating the situation." Prosecutions, in other words, were an absolute last resort.[40]

With the Civil Rights Section begging off prosecutions and me-diating only a handful of disputes, U.S. attorneys were often the Witnesses' most reliable advocates among federal law enforcement authorities. Among them, Clyde Eastus, U.S. attorney for the North-ern District of Texas, proved to be one of the more vocal champions of the Witnesses' civil liberties. Touting himself as "a friend of all of you" and claiming that he was merely "trying to act as a peace-maker," Eastus attempted to curtail the persecution of Witnesses by delivering a series of forceful radio addresses early in 1942. Eastus was nothing if not blunt: he blasted law enforcement, the American Legion, and the Witnesses themselves for distracting their commu-nities from the real task at hand—the nascent war effort—by par-ticipating in "a lot of petty quarrels" and "some serious controver-sies."

He was clearly rankled by the inability of police officers and sher-iffs to shirk off prejudice and discharge their sworn duties by pro-tecting the Witnesses' civil rights. "I know that the peace officers of my district are good, honest, law-abiding patriotic officials," he said in one broadcast, "but it appears that they do not understand their duties. They seem to let their patriotism get the best of their better judgment. . . . I do say that some of the peace officers, good men, are using harsh and improper methods of handling this situation." According to what Eastus had learned from the numerous complaints that had crossed his desk over the preceding two years, "instead of arresting the citizens who provoke the difficulty with the Jehovah's Witnesses, they have arrested the Jehovah's Witnesses, and incarcerated them, tried them and convicted them," in the process making a mockery of the victims' basic democratic freedoms. There seemed to be little question that members of the American Legion were responsible for the Witnesses' suffering in Texas as well. Surely aware that it was a potent force in many small communities, Eastus expressed general admiration for the veterans' organization (at one point he said, "God bless the American Legion"), but he strongly admonished its members for letting themselves get carried away in a reckless effort to protect the United States from spying and subversion. Confronting the Witnesses with the American flag and pressing them to salute was simply begging for trouble, and Legionnaires knew it. "Please leave your flag at your Legion Post," Eastus advised. "If you do not want to hear the Jehovah's Witnesses, do not listen to them. No man should want to fight religion because he does not agree with it."[41]

Yet Eastus, like many U.S. attorneys, had become exasperated by the Witnesses' provocative behavior, and he contended that their own zest for conflict had bred many of their troubles. In a speech broadcast over radio station WFAA, Eastus asserted that the Witnesses

> have a right to speak on the streets of any city in Texas, on the sidewalks, in church houses, or buildings they rent. I say, they have the right to do this unmolested by any chief of police, sheriff, deputy sheriff or any other peace officer. I say they have a right to knock on the doors and ring the door-bells of the citizenship and have a right to pass out their literature—*The Watchtower* magazine.

Yet Eastus also declared in no uncertain terms that the Witnesses could expect little sympathy from federal or state authorities if they continued to engage in intentionally bothersome or even illegal behavior when they proselytized. "I say, you subject yourself to arrest and prosecution," he said directly to his Witness listeners in one radio address. "This has been done in many instances, and you must stop it." Overzealous proselytizers, Eastus knew, sometimes broke the law by refusing to leave private property after they had been asked to do so by a homeowner or tenant. Although the Constitution protected their rights to speak and worship freely, it did not give them license to trespass. "You have no right," he explained, "to force yourself on any citizen," even while worshiping. In Texas, Witnesses could count on receiving the "full protection" of the law only if they respected it themselves and acted like responsible citizens who honored the rights of others.[42]

Eastus was by no means the only U.S. attorney to be irked by the Witnesses' confrontational behavior. If the views expressed in late 1941 by Clinton Barry were typical, many U.S. attorneys shied away from prosecuting Witness cases under federal civil rights laws because they felt that the victims had gone out of their way to court trouble. In October 1941, the American Civil Liberties Union contacted Barry, the U.S. attorney for the Western District of Arkansas, and asked him to investigate the recent harassment of Witnesses in the town of Huntsville. According to ACLU staff counsel Clifford Forster, Witnesses had been badgered for several weeks in Huntsville as they attempted to meet and proselytize, and local authorities, though aware of the danger, "refused to take any action to prevent further attacks." Matters came to a head on 11 October, when a mob of more than a dozen men, led by Hill Everett, Huntsville's acting mayor, set upon the Witnesses as they distributed literature. "Their magazines, bags and literature were forcibly taken from them and burned in the street," Forster informed Barry. "These Jehovah's Witnesses were ordered to leave town immediately and told never to return. . . . The sheriff, Elmo Richie, and Deputy Sheriff Frank Bunch refused to give the Witnesses any protection." In a letter to Barry, the ACLU reviewed the facts of the case and requested a federal prosecution of the guilty parties, claiming that they had obviously run afoul of Section 51 and Section 52.[43]

Barry was unwilling to prosecute the Huntsville assailants, and his response to the ACLU's request for an investigation and prosecutions revealed the kind of ambivalence that many federal authorities experienced when they faced the daunting prospect of prosecuting violators of the Witnesses' civil rights. In a reply to Forster, Barry lashed out at the victims, not the vigilantes who had assaulted them, for precipitating "the frequent clashes which mark the attempts of the Jehovah's Witnesses to proselytize in this section of the United States." He explained:

> The resentment which underlies frequent instances of outright mob action and numerous instances of what amounts to little less than mob action thinly disguised under a cloak of legal process by local officials is not hard to understand when the facts are known. This resentment stems out of the actions and utterances of the members of this sect and cannot be attributed to any other cause.

The Witnesses, many of whom were "plainly imbued with a martyr complex," Barry alleged, almost seemed to invite violence and harassment. For starters, they were "openly antagonistic to the United States of America as a government," and they attempted to "expound principles which are the antithesis of everything that we sum up in the word 'Patriotism.'" Moreover, "they have adopted a policy of abuse and insult toward other denominations and their communicants." Barry vividly remembered seeing a caravan of Witnesses riding through Fort Smith, Arkansas, with banners exclaiming "Religion is a Racket" and "Preachers are Crooks" tied to their cars. Given the tensions generated by the war in Europe (which the United States joined in earnest in a matter of weeks), it was hardly surprising that zealots engaging in such outrageous activities were mobbed.[44]

Writing to Forster, Barry suggested that he was in some ways doing the Witnesses a favor by declining to initiate federal prosecutions under Sections 51 and 52. He maintained that such prosecutions would in fact worsen the Witnesses' suffering, not alleviate it:

> If any local officer is brought into my court for prosecution on account of the illegal search, seizure, arrest or detention of any of [the Witnesses], it will quickly come home to the people of Arkansas that the activities of these people can only be curbed through the action of private citizens outside the pale of law.

When and if this stage of difficulty is reached, there is nothing I know of that can be done in the federal courts to meet the situation.

Witnesses in several Arkansas communities—in part because they had become so frustrated by the Justice Department's unwillingness to enforce federal civil rights laws—had gone to court themselves in order to gain injunctive relief from oppressive local authorities, and Barry believed that it would be a waste of time and effort to complement those civil actions with federal prosecutions. He had taken it upon himself to confer with several Witness plaintiffs, and during those meetings he had "strongly advised them to vindicate their rights" without relying on federal help. He also hinted that if they genuinely hoped to avoid persecution, they might suspend or at least tone down their proselytizing for the duration of the war. As he told Forster, he believed "it would be much better for all concerned if members of this organization would, for the time being, not stress their views and attitude toward the United States of America and would leave the promotion of these matters to a later and happier time."[45]

The tortured logic of Barry's letter disconcerted Clifford Forster. In a cordial but unmistakably firm response, he agreed that not every Witness complaint merited a federal prosecution, and he also pointed to the ACLU's own efforts as an example of how mediation could ease tensions between the Witnesses and their opponents and thus eliminate the need for federal intervention. By submitting amicus curiae briefs supporting their rights to worship, assemble, and speak freely, the ACLU also frequently backed the Witnesses in many of their attempts to obtain justice through civil actions. But, as Forster vehemently maintained, there was a clear and critical role for the federal government to play in the safeguarding of the Witnesses' civil rights. When "the civil remedy will not be made available for technical reasons, and appeals to reason are unanswered, the only method left is to institute criminal proceedings," he told Barry. "Especially should this be true where it appears that great force and violence was used with the active connivance of the local authorities." What troubled Forster even more than Barry's reluctance to enforce Sections 51 and 52 was the U.S. attorney's contention that valid federal prosecutions might be abandoned in order to prevent further anti-Witness disturbances. Obviously shocked by Barry's reasoning, he argued:

> The fact that mob violence may result from Federal action should not be a factor in determining whether a Federal question is involved. Where there is a clear case of a violation of Title 18, Sections 51 and 52, and the local authorities persist in their actions which are calculated to deprive persons of their civil rights, it is the duty of the Federal government to exercise its authority. By failure to use its powers, a bad precedent would be set which would relegate the mentioned statutes to a dead letter office.

Forster believed that federal civil rights laws, however limited or flawed they might be, had to be enforced as a primary means to protect "those whose views are disliked by the majority, or else freedom of speech will no longer have meaning." Turning one of the U.S. attorney's main arguments on its head, Forster asserted that Barry should enforce Sections 51 and 52 precisely *because* the Witnesses were so widely reviled.[46]

Many of Barry's colleagues, including those in the U.S. attorney's office in West Virginia, apparently shared his unwillingness to prosecute anti-Witness vigilantes under federal civil rights laws. Details about the handling of the prosecution are sketchy, but the most reliable account has suggested that Lemuel Via, the U.S. attorney in Huntington, West Virginia, "had no desire to institute criminal proceedings" against Martin Catlette and the Witnesses' other assailants in Richwood, "and the Attorney General's office supported him in this attitude." After nearly two years of wrangling among the FBI, Via, and "high authorities in the Department of Justice," the Civil Rights Section's insistence on prosecution finally carried the day, and the U.S. attorney was persuaded to bring the Richwood case before a federal grand jury and seek indictments of several participants, including Catlette, under Sections 51 and 52. Because their conduct had been so horrifying, the cases against the assailants seemed strong, but Via made a point of requesting assistance from the Justice Department as he presented the case to the grand jury and prepared to take it to trial. The presence of an attorney from Washington, he wrote, "would lend dignity to the proceedings," and it also would "remove the questions of local prejudices and faction from the picture and would have a very fine effect upon the jury." Perhaps because he was so leery of appearing to side with the Witnesses, Via also hoped that having a CRS attorney on hand would serve as "an open avowal to the grand jury and the petit jury that this case was being prosecuted by the Department of Justice, rather than by the United States Attorney." Such overt intervention was usually anathema to U.S. attorneys, but Via apparently hoped to allow the Justice Department to shoulder much of the blame for the prosecutions, which were sure to be unpopular in West Virginia.[47]

The federal grand jury in West Virginia confirmed the Justice Department's worst fears, largely ignoring the evidence against the Richwood defendants and refusing to return an indictment against them. According to a memorandum written by Raoul Berger, the CRS attorney who had been sent from Washington to assist Via, the grand jurors were openly suspicious of the victims of the Richwood disturbance and sympathetic to the defendants. Convening just a few months after the bombing of Pearl Harbor and the formal entry of the United States into World War II, members of the grand jury apparently were more disturbed by the Witnesses' weird beliefs than they were troubled by the abominable behavior of Catlette and the other assailants. Berger reported that

the Jury was patently unfriendly to the "Witnesses" from the very outset, as their queries showed. The witnesses were repeatedly questioned about the particulars of their religion, their refusal to bear arms, their invasion of Richwood in search of "trouble." We were asked if one who refuses to defend his country has constitutional rights, etc.

Undaunted by this setback, the CRS persuaded Via to perform an end run around the hostile grand jury. Displaying resourcefulness that was rare in its handling of Witness cases, the CRS determined that if the federal government abandoned all the Section 51 prosecutions and narrowed its prosecution to Martin Catlette and Bert Stewart under Section 52, it could proceed to trial without first obtaining an indictment from the grand jury. Because the maximum penalty for a violation of Section 52 was a year in prison and a fine of $1,000 (as opposed to a maximum of 10 years and $5,000 for a

violation of Section 51), the U.S. attorney was able to initiate proceedings in federal court simply by filing a trial information against
Catlette and Stewart.[48]

The ploy worked. Tried before Judge Ben Moore in a federal court
in Charleston, West Virginia, Catlette and Stewart were convicted
under Section 52. Fines were imposed on both men—$1,000 for
Catlette, $250 for Stewart—and Catlette received a sentence of
twelve months imprisonment at the federal prison camp in Mill
Point, West Virginia. Catlette appealed, claiming that Section 52
was inapplicable to his case because he had not acted under "color
of law" during the Richwood disturbance, but the Fourth Circuit
Court of Appeals upheld his conviction. The court noted:

> It is quite obvious . . . that Catlette took very active and utterly
> unwarranted steps to subject his victims to affirmative indigni-
> ties. It is equally clear that these indignities were inflicted on the
> victims solely by reason of their membership in the religious sect
> known as Jehovah's Witnesses, and their practices founded on
> their beliefs, particularly their refusal, on religious ground, to sa-
> lute the flag of the United States.

Such actions, the court held, "very clearly" meant that Catlette had
violated both the Constitution and federal civil rights laws in
spearheading the assault on the Witnesses. His conviction affirmed,
Catlette was dispatched to prison for a year.[49] For a man who so bitterly opposed the Witnesses' doctrines, the punishment must have
seemed especially harsh, for a large portion of Mill Point's inmate
population was composed of Jehovah's Witnesses who had been imprisoned by the federal government for violation of the wartime draft
law. In addition to the fine imposed on him for violating Section 52,
Catlette also was compelled to pay a portion of the $1,170 in dam-
ages that was awarded to the Richwood victims in a civil suit. As a
result of that civil action, each Witness received $52.28.[50]

Eager to learn more about how the case was being handled, the
commander of Richwood's American Legion post wrote to Catlette's
attorney while the appeal was still in progress. The attorney, himself a former Legion state commander, responded with a stern letter
urging that all members of the Richwood post "should be admonished that the law enforcing officers have the sole responsibility of

enforcing the law." Anyone who unlawfully assumed that responsibility or who violated the federal civil rights statutes that were designed for "the protection of fundamental rights guaranteed by the Constitution of the United States" could be subject to fines, imprisonment, or both. "You can see how important it is," the attorney wrote, "to keep inviolate our civil liberties which are so vital to the perpetuity of American institutions."[51]

5. Religious Persecutions Under the Guise of Law

On 15 June 1940, when the post-*Gobitis* mistreatment of Jehovah's Witnesses was at its worst, police officers and members of the American Legion waylaid two Witness proselytizers in Connersville, Indiana, and escorted them to the office of Ross Castle, the town's irascible mayor. Castle angrily told the evangelists that local veterans were offended by the un-American and anti-Catholic messages contained in the Witnesses' literature, and he ordered them to quit proselytizing until they gained clearance from the town's Legion post. The Witnesses, eager to dispel rumors that they lacked patriotism, ventured to the Legion hall in Connersville on 19 June, and they spoke at length to the post's Americanism Committee, chaired by Roy Nelson. The Witnesses shared tracts, played recordings of Joseph Rutherford's bombastic speeches, and fielded questions about what motivated them to work so assiduously as proselytizers. "We explained," one of the Witnesses, Grace Trent, later said, "that we were doing this work at God's command." The Legionnaires were courteous to their visitors, but the members of the Americanism Committee remained adamant in opposing the Witnesses' efforts to propagandize in Connersville. Roy Nelson told them, "We don't especially care whether you salute the flag or not, but you are not going to put out any more of that literature."[1]

Nelson's warning went unheeded. The following day, six headstrong Witnesses, all of them women, took to the streets of Connersville and "peacefully engaged in exercising our God-given and constitutionally-guaranteed rights," Trent recalled. "We were going from door to door as Jesus and his disciples did, preaching the gospel of the Kingdom and leaving the message in printed form with those who wished it." Before long, several irate Legionnaires confronted a few of the women and insisted that they refrain from proselytizing. Trent (who was described in several accounts as "elderly" and "aged") refused to abandon the work that brought her so much joy, and she defiantly told the Legionnaires, "We will obey God rather than man." The Witnesses briefly resumed their propagandizing, but, as they had expected, the Legionnaires accosted them again an hour later. This time, the veterans were accompanied by two additional members of their Legion post—Fayette County sheriff Lester Hunt and one of his deputies, Scott Adams. With their fellow veterans' help, Hunt and Adams collected samples of the Witnesses' hyperbolic literature and then hauled the women off to jail. The Witnesses went along but protested vigorously, arguing that their work had been specifically protected by decisions handed down by the U.S. Supreme Court. Hunt and the other Legionnaires on hand laughed at their invocation of the authority of the nation's highest court. "The arresting officers and companions replied," one local Witness said, "that they were the law in that place and were running the town of Connersville and Fayette County, [and] they were not subject to any decision the Supreme Court made."[2] Hunt initially charged Grace Trent, Lucy McKee, Clemmie Evitts, Ruby Revalee, Keziah Ullery, and Frances Laughlin with flag desecration because the Witnesses apparently balked at saluting an American flag lapel pin worn by one of the Legionnaires. At that point, the women faced only a minimal penalty—fines of $10 each.[3]

Arrests such as those made in Connersville plagued Jehovah's Witnesses for decades. The faith's world headquarters in Brooklyn estimated that approximately 3,000 Witnesses were arrested each year in the United States in the early 1940s, with a total of 18,886 arrests being reported between 1933 and 1951.[4] More than 600 Witnesses were arrested in Texas alone in one twelve-month period in 1941 and 1942. During that stretch, the American Civil Liberties Union and the Justice Department were deluged with complaints from Witnesses in that state who had been arrested and jailed, sometimes in groups of several dozen people, simply "for distributing literature explaining the Bible, or refusing to discontinue such distribution when ordered to do so by police," as the ACLU reported.[5] Often acting at the behest of ostensibly patriotic groups such as the American Legion, local authorities in Texas and other states frequently attempted to suppress the Witnesses' proselytizing by charging them with a wide variety of offenses, including disorderly conduct, trespassing, peddling without a permit, and assault and battery (particularly when the Witnesses had the audacity to defend themselves against physical abuse).[6]

In some states, authorities who wished to bridle the Witnesses' civil liberties even used antisedition measures and, perhaps even more incredibly, laws that had been specifically designed to safeguard religious worship. When Paul Mead and several other Witnesses proselytized in Clinton, Iowa, on Sunday 8 December 1940, dozens of that city's residents, including Martin Duffy, the chief of police, had pleasant encounters with them. Nonetheless, shortly after a Witness named Harvey Gregerson visited Duffy's home, police arrested seven Witness proselytizers and charged that they "did unlawfully and willfully and feloniously desecrate the Sabbath." According to the charges filed by the police chief, the Witnesses "did go from door to door . . . knocking on the doors and ringing door bells, arousing persons early in the morning to the disturbance of private families."[7]

Witnesses were characteristically obstinate in responding to such "religious persecutions under [the] guise of law," as they were termed in the *Indiana Law Journal*.[8] At the height of their persecution in the early and mid-1940s, hundreds of Witnesses defended their civil liberties in court, zealously challenging the spurious accusations that were leveled at them so often. When authorities arrested them under bogus charges, Witnesses "refused to take this unlawful action lying down," according to one history published by their faith. "We took our cases to court, pleading not guilty and not giving up when magistrates ruled against us, not abandoning the fight when all the lower courts in the different parts of the country had ruled against us."[9] That the Justice Department usually saw little promise in prosecuting the Witnesses' oppressors only served to heighten the victims' ardor for contesting discrimination in the courts.

In retrospect, it seems apparent that the Witnesses initiated a legal counterattack against religious discrimination primarily to mitigate their own suffering and to use courts as forums for propagandizing. While protecting their own interests, however, they prompted courts at all levels, including the U.S. Supreme Court, to fortify safeguards for this country's most basic democratic liberties, including freedom of religion and freedom of speech. One of the foremost legacies of the persecution of the Jehovah's Witnesses in the United States in the early and mid-1940s thus was a hard-won and remarkably influential body of law, one that strengthened the basic democratic freedoms of all Americans, including the Witnesses' sworn enemies in other faiths. It was an outcome that no one, not even the Witnesses themselves, could have predicted.

The Witnesses' many appeals to the U.S. Supreme Court received widespread attention in the early and mid-1940s, and in later decades their significance has been acknowledged by members of the Court, constitutional scholars, and historians. For all their lasting importance, however, those cases represented only a fraction of the Witnesses' total labors in American courts during the war years. Thanks in part to the herculean efforts of attorney Hayden Covington, Witnesses prevailed in over 100 decisions handed down by various state supreme courts, and they also triumphed in dozens of lower federal court rulings. To be sure, not all of those cases were worthy of headlines, but many were vitally important for Witnesses who were scrambling to preserve their First Amendment freedoms in places like Indiana, Kentucky, and Iowa. A detailed examination of some of these less-prominent cases provides a revealing glimpse of the Witnesses' misery and of the legal strategies that they employed so successfully to combat religious discrimination.

Hayden Covington claimed that the Witnesses who stubbornly defended their civil liberties in court were simply devout Christians following "a Bible precedent." Interviewed in the 1950s, Covington explained that Paul and other early adherents to Christianity "understood that they would be brought before kings and rulers to testify about the faith" because their beliefs were so commonly misunderstood and reviled. Far from dreading such opportunities, Covington said, they welcomed the chance to share their beliefs and assert their right to preach and worship freely. When the apostle Paul was put on trial, the persuasive arguments he advanced were meant not only to secure his own freedom but also to help ensure religious liberty for all Christians. Covington noted that during his trial in Rome, "Paul told the Philippians he was 'defending and legally establishing' the reality and virtue of the good news," regardless of the personal cost. According to Covington, Witnesses who were arrested in the early and mid-1940s came to believe that they had a similar obligation, one rooted in their commitment to bearing any burden in the service of their Creator.[10]

Faithful to that "Bible precedent," the Witnesses who were arrested in Clinton, Iowa, were among the hundreds of members of their faith who successfully defended their imperiled civil liberties in court in the early and mid-1940s. On 4 January 1941, a jury in Clinton convicted four of the seven Witnesses for violating the state's Sabbath desecration law. In an appeal to the Supreme Court of Iowa, the Witnesses maintained that the construction and application of the statute "deprived them of their right of freedom of worship of Almighty God and freedom of press" under both the state and federal constitutions. After all, the Witnesses argued in a brief, since the "plain and clear purpose of this law is to protect everyone in his way of worship on the Sabbath," it would be a gross miscarriage of justice to allow the measure to be used to suppress their form of worship. Impressed by the appellants' arguments, the state supreme court reversed the Witnesses' convictions late in 1941. Its short opinion in *State v. Mead* refuted the state's two primary allegations—that the Witnesses had disturbed residents of Clinton by proselytizing and that they had violated state law by selling property on a Sunday. "We do not think," the court held, "the statute contemplates that the distribution of booklets of this nature and under these particular circumstances constitutes desecrating the Sabbath."[11]

The Witnesses' tenacious efforts in courtrooms in Iowa and dozens of other states were far from improvised. According to a recent Witness history, "Arrangements were made to train all of Jehovah's Witnesses in basic legal procedures. This was done at special assemblies in the United States in 1932, and later, at their regular Service Meeting programs in the congregations." In fact, as the persecution of Witnesses intensified in the 1930s and 1940s, discussions of law and trial practice became an integral part of the Service Meetings.[12] As former Witness Barbara Grizutti Harrison has noted, Witnesses attending such sessions quickly "learned to equip themselves to deal with police and judges." Proselytizers were instructed on how to behave during an arrest, and litigants received training on preserving error at trial (and thus laying the proper foundation for possible appeals to higher courts). "They held mock trials," according to Harrison, "some of them lasting for weeks, with overseers role-playing the parts of prosecution and defense attorneys."[13]

For guidance on specific legal issues and trial practice, Witnesses could turn to a series of publications produced by the faith's headquarters in Brooklyn. The booklets *Jehovah's Servants Defended* (1941) and *Freedom of Worship* (1943) proved to be particularly valuable, providing both concise discussions of relevant cases and supplying the biblical justifications for the Witnesses' conduct. *Jehovah's Servants Defended* furnished citations to and discussions of dozens of cases involving the Witnesses' First Amendment rights, including their many appeals to the U.S. Supreme Court, and it provided suggestions as to how Witness litigants could use those precedents to their best advantage in court. "Using this information, the Witnesses usually handled their own defense in local courts, instead of securing the services of a lawyer," the recent Witness history reports. "They found that in this way they could give a witness to the court and present the issues squarely to the judge, instead of having their cases decided merely on legal technicalities."[14] Unfortunately, because they tended to lack formal training in the law and courtroom experience, the Witnesses' pro se defenses at trial tended to be clumsy and ineffective, particularly when they ignored "legal technicalities" and focused their energies on propagandizing in the courtroom.

Taking over numerous cases on appeal, seasoned attorneys like Hayden Covington, Victor Schmidt, Grover Powell, and Victor Blackwell were an integral component of the Witnesses' legal efforts. Covington oversaw the faith's campaign in the courts, and working below him were what Merlin Owen Newton has termed "a bevy of regional attorneys . . . waiting in the wings to assist those Witnesses who ran into trouble with the law."[15] These attorneys often braved deplorable conditions in order to provide Witnesses with adequate legal representation. Victor Blackwell recalled, "In the 1940s so many cases arose against the Witnesses in Louisiana that I traversed the state from north to south and east to west, arranging bonds for their release, then representing them when their cases came up in court. I was often on the road day and night." Writing in 1976 about his experiences as an attorney, Blackwell remembered that he had "defended these humble folk against every kind of criminal charge." Throughout the 1940s, for instance, he trav-

Attorney Victor Blackwell teaching a course to Jehovah's Witnesses in South Lansing, New York, in 1943.

eled to Alexandria, Louisiana, to defend and arrange bail for Witnesses who had encountered trouble there. Blackwell's first trip to Alexandria (to post bail for four young Witnesses who had been arrested while proselytizing) was by far the most memorable: the city judge brandished a pistol, fixed a pair of "murderous eyes" on him, and screamed, "Get out of my office! Get out of Alexandria! Get out of Rapides Parish! If you ever show your face to me again, I'll kill you!" Blackwell was deeply shaken by this encounter, but it failed to break his spirit; he defended Witnesses in Alexandria for more than a dozen years. He eventually expanded his practice beyond Louisiana, taking numerous Witness cases in Texas, Alabama, Mississippi, Florida, and Tennessee, and he defied intimidation wherever he went. A dedicated Witness himself, Blackwell felt that his mission in court was twofold. "In every case," he wrote, "I tried, not only to defend the right of the Witnesses to preach, but, whenever possible, to give an effective witness respecting God's kingdom."[16]

Victor Schmidt wound up handling the defense of the Witnesses who had been arrested for flag desecration in Connersville, Indiana, and he knew from the start that it would be an uphill struggle. Almost as soon as he arrived from his home in Ohio with his wife, the Witness attorney began sparring with Fayette County Circuit Court judge G. Edwin Johnson, who arraigned the Witnesses on the flag desecration charge. In one bitter colloquy, the volatile Johnson challenged Schmidt's right to practice law in Indiana and stated that he hoped the Witness would "go right back to Ohio where you belong." To make matters even worse, Johnson refused to allow Schmidt to confer with the defendants before they entered their pleas. When Schmidt declared that the women were "entitled to advice of counsel," Johnson rebuffed him by growling, "They had plenty of time to consult local lawyers if they wished to." Schmidt, scrambling for a way to communicate with his clients, was forced to walk past the defendants and loudly whisper that they should plead not guilty, a tactic that Johnson immediately and harshly attacked from the bench. Losing his patience, he asked several of the defendants if they had received advice from Schmidt, who objected that the content of such conversations was "privileged communication between attorney and client." The jousting continued until Schmidt, by then exhausted by Johnson's abuse, left the courtroom with his wife. At that moment, the attorney learned just how vehemently the residents of Connersville detested Witnesses. He recalled, "When I attempted to leave the courtroom, a mob of men followed me and my wife. As we approached our car, they began cussing and swearing at us. . . . We were chased by fifteen or twenty cars out of town."[17]

Things soon went from bad to worse for Schmidt and his defendants. Apparently not satisfied with the modest penalty prescribed by the flag desecration charge, Fayette County authorities filed a second and far more serious set of charges against the Witnesses. Prosecutors asserted that the women had engaged in sedition and fomented insurrection by participating in a scheme aimed at "maliciously inciting the people of Fayette County . . . against all forms of organized government and to disrespect the flag of the United States of America." The intensified prosecution was based largely on Indiana's seldom-used "criminal syndicalism" law, enacted in 1919 to combat political radicalism. The relevant section of that measure prohibited the distribution of printed materials "in or by which there is advocated or incited the overthrow, by force or violence, or by physical injury to personal property, or by the general cessation of industry, of the government of the United States, of the state of Indiana, or of all government." And if the sedition charges were not bad enough, prosecutors also charged that the Witnesses had participated in a "riotous conspiracy" meant to wreak the same kind of havoc. In its beefed-up prosecution of the Witnesses, Fayette County advanced essentially the same argument contrived by vigilantes who set upon the proselytizers in small communities across the country—that the Witnesses represented a grave threat to public safety because they hoped to precipitate the overthrow of American democracy. It was hardly surprising that the new charges carried formidable penalties: the Witnesses now faced up to ten years in prison and fines of up to $2,000 each.[18]

Cowed by the prospect of huge fines and long prison terms, most of the Witnesses gave in and reluctantly struck a deal with prosecutors. They pleaded guilty to the flag desecration count, and the county dropped the more onerous charges. Although they understood their friends' reasons for accepting the lesser charge, Witnesses Grace Trent and Lucy McKee believed that striking such a deal was tantamount to repudiating their faith, and they resolved to go to trial on all counts. Given the charges and the likelihood of guilty verdicts, it was a huge gamble, but the two women believed that they had no other choice but to bear witness in court. Awaiting trial, Trent and McKee had trouble raising bail, and they were forced to spend most of summer 1940 incarcerated on the top floor of Connersville's sweltering jail.[19] John Rainbow, who helped organize Witness activities in Fayette County, complained that despite their age and obvious harmlessness, Trent and McKee were "bullied and treated like criminals, and must languish in a filthy jail for weeks and months." They finally were released on bail in early August.[20]

"Knowing that local sentiment was against the defendants, and that Judge Johnson was prejudiced," Victor Schmidt wisely asked for a change of venue, but Johnson brushed off his request.[21] The trial took place in Connersville in September, and it managed to exceed Schmidt's worst fears. Testifying before a packed and largely hostile courtroom, the defendants patiently cited Watch Tower tracts and the Bible as they attempted to explain their beliefs and their motivation for proselytizing. Both scoffed at the allegation that they had participated in a "riotous conspiracy" designed to precipitate the downfall of the American government. According to Hayden Covington, who defended the Witnesses with Schmidt, the women "point[ed] out that they took no part in political activity, and that if the government was set up, it would be done by the God of heaven" and not ordinary mortals such as themselves. By distributing literature and playing recordings of Joseph Rutherford's speeches, they merely hoped to spread the teachings of Christ, which were desperately needed in such troubled times; fomenting an insurrection was the furthest thing from their minds. As for the flag desecration charge, Trent and McKee "each stated that they did not salute any flag," Covington recalled, "but that they had the greatest respect for the flag and for what it stood." Their refusal to salute, they maintained, should be interpreted as a signal of their devotion to their God, not as a gesture of contempt for their country.[22]

Schmidt and Covington were veterans of such battles, and they did a capable job of defending Trent and McKee. Neither attorney could fathom the ridiculous allegations leveled at the Witnesses by Fayette County, and they believed that the evidence presented at trial demonstrated that the charges were fraudulent. "A review of the record at the trial clearly shows that the two defendants . . . were not guilty of doing any unlawful act," Schmidt later said. "The mere refusal to salute a flag, which they respect but do not worship, is not an unlawful act, and they certainly did not conspire to do an unlawful act. The arrangement to put out and distribute Bible literature, which contains nothing subversive, is not an unlawful act." But both Schmidt and Covington were experienced enough to understand that the verdict was never really in doubt, in part because the trial took place in perhaps the most rancorous environment either attorney had ever seen. According to accounts provided by Witnesses who attended the trial, Fayette County authorities scarcely had control of the courtroom in Connersville. Spectators frequently jeered at the defendants and their attorneys, and at one point the prosecutor, Ralph Helmick, threatened to arrest Covington. "Throughout the trial," Schmidt later said, "there was evidence of a spirit of mob violence, and the officials did not do anything even by suggestion to curb it." During one recess, some Witness spectators and the attorneys were taunted and "stormed with a barrage of fruit and eggs" in full view of the jury.[23] Schmidt was directly threatened by antagonistic spectators, and he feared that vigilantes would run wild after the trial's conclusion, whatever the verdict. Covington had ample reason to worry about his safety as well. As he later wrote to Solicitor General Francis Biddle, Covington learned that one spectator, having missed an opportunity to harass him, had boasted, "We were going to make that big son-of-a-bitch Covington salute the flag or else kill him."[24]

The jury deliberated for nearly six hours on 24 September before it found Trent and McKee guilty on all counts. They were immediately parceled off to the state prison for women in Indianapolis, where they were to serve out the draconian sentence (from two to ten years) prescribed by Indiana's "criminal syndicalism" law.[25] Meanwhile, in a repellent scene that was duplicated throughout the United States in 1940, vigilantes attacked Schmidt and his wife when they exited the courthouse in Connersville. As the couple attempted to walk to their car, "a barrage of fruit and vegetables was thrown on our heads and backs," Schmidt recalled. "A howl that sounded like a pack of wolves was sent up by an infuriated mob. Missiles were thrown as long as the mob had them, but as we approached our automobile, or the place where we thought the automobile was standing, the mob began using its fists." Schmidt later learned that policemen had been content to allow the vigilantes to follow through on their repeated threats against the Witnesses. In an affidavit submitted to the ACLU, the attorney claimed that as police looked on, he was "repeatedly beaten with the fists of mobsters. I staggered several times, feared that it would be my end if I should be knocked down. I began to be cut in the face, and began to bleed from the broken flesh under my eyes. . . . We were repeatedly kicked, hit and pushed." Witness John Rainbow watched in horror as the crowd marched Schmidt and his wife, both of them bruised and bloodied, out of Connersville. Rainbow drove his car to the city limits and waited with Raymond Franz, another Witness, for the besieged couple. Rainbow told the ACLU, "I saw the mob raging along the highway, and I saw a great number of automobiles honking wildly and crowding the highway so that it was a dangerous condition not only for Jehovah's Witnesses but also for anyone else who desired to use it. In fact, the highway was impassible for some time along the route of the mob."[26] Schmidt and his wife eventually made their way into the automobile, and they inspected their injuries as it sped away. "There were five open wounds that I could count. I was

Jehovah's Witness attorney Victor Schmidt after being attacked in Connersville, Indiana, in 1940.

bleeding, and my shirt and coat were spattered and streaked with blood," Schmidt recalled.[27]

The Witnesses responded quickly and angrily to the Connersville trial and its grisly aftermath, enlisting the American Civil Liberties Union's support and calling for a swift federal investigation. Two weeks after the verdicts and the ensuing attack on Schmidt and his wife, the ACLU offered a reward of $500 "to the first person supplying information leading to the arrest, conviction and imprisonment for thirty days or more of any person who took part in mob disorders at Connersville, Ind. on September 24 which resulted in violence upon the person or property of members of Jehovah's Witnesses." In establishing the reward, the ACLU noted that "after the jury's verdict was rendered, members of the sect and the defendants' attorneys were mobbed and beaten" and that local authorities had done nothing to curb the "monstrous" outbreak of violence.[28] As he nursed his wounds, Victor Schmidt reacted to the Connersville mobbing by submitting a nine-page complaint to the Justice Department. His affidavit, which provided a detailed account of the trial and the subsequent assault, ended with a plea for federal prosecutions.

> It is my firm conviction that the mobs that have repeatedly occurred at Connersville, and the oppressive official action that has interfered with innocent people in the exercise of their constitutional rights of freedom of worship, freedom of the press, and freedom of assembly, warrant immediate action on the part of the Department of Justice of the United States by enforcing Sections 51 and 52 of Title 18 of the United States Code Annotated. May we have immediate action?[29]

Witness John Rainbow sent a similar complaint to Washington, noting that "the safety of the public . . . demands that the Federal Bureau of Investigation make careful survey of conditions. It is a deplorable condition when an attorney is not able to defend clients without being mobbed and beaten." As he called for prosecution under Sections 51 and 52, Rainbow asserted that the Justice Department had to investigate conditions in Connersville promptly because "there is grave danger of any attorney representing Jehovah's Witnesses in Connersville [being] foully murdered." The department was swamped with reports of abuse from hundreds of Witnesses, and it failed to muster much interest in the events in Connersville. The complaints voiced by Schmidt and Rainbow essentially went unanswered.[30]

The outcome of the Connersville trial sickened Hayden Covington, and he had no trouble persuading Grace Trent and Lucy McKee to appeal their convictions. Covington was determined to have the verdicts overturned because, as he informed Biddle, the idea that the Witnesses had advocated the forcible overthrow of the federal or state governments was preposterous. The sole basis for their convictions "was that these two elderly women . . . had distributed literature containing explanations of Bible prophecies foretelling the establishment of God's Kingdom on earth for which Jesus Christ had taught his disciples to pray"—hardly an act of rebellion worthy of several years in prison and a hefty fine. From his bustling office in Brooklyn, Covington was disheartened to learn that authorities in Connersville were doing their best to "sandbag" the appeals process, and thus keep the Witnesses in jail, by holding up the preparation of the enormous transcript from the September trial. At the urging of county prosecutors, the court stenographer demanded an exorbitant fee to ready the prodigious document, which would be the cornerstone of any appeal. Compounding the Witnesses' problems was their inability to find a local lawyer brave enough to handle the appeal. According to Covington, there was a concerted effort among authorities in Fayette County to prevent Trent and McKee from obtaining adequate legal representation. He told Biddle, "It has been impossible to get the aid of any Indiana attorney to push the matter to appeal because local officials have threatened and continue to threaten any attorney who comes to Connersville to represent these people with mob violence and arrest."[31]

After several months of wrangling, the Witnesses eventually were able to obtain a trial transcript from the recalcitrant court clerk, and attorney Scott Ging of Indianapolis was persuaded to join with Covington and Schmidt to mount the appeal. Their efforts were bolstered by the American Civil Liberties Union, which filed a friend-of-the-court brief supporting the Witnesses' contention that the impassioned religious proselytizing of two aged women did not amount to either "riotous conspiracy" or "criminal syndicalism," as prosecutors in Fayette County had claimed at the trial. In December 1941, more than a year after the Connersville verdicts, the Supreme

Court of Indiana issued a brief opinion in *McKee et al. v. State*. A dry recitation of relevant facts and law, the court's opinion in no way reflected the extraordinary passions that the case had unleashed among the Witnesses and their oppressors in Fayette County. Writing for the court, Chief Justice Frank Richman doubted that the Witnesses had engaged in any of the illegal behavior proscribed by the statutes invoked by the state. For instance, the state's "riotous conspiracy" law, which apparently had been drafted to curb the night-riding activities of the Ku Klux Klan, barred citizens from "uniting for the purpose of doing any unlawful act in the nighttime or while disguised," he wrote. "There is no evidence of disguise. The most that was done in the nighttime was to unite to distribute or agree to distribute literature that was objectionable to many persons in the community and to discuss doctrine contained in the literature." The criminal syndicalism charge was similarly defective because the state had failed to prove that the Witnesses' literature advocated or incited the overthrow of government "by force or violence," as was required under the relevant Indiana law. The state having failed to produce any credible evidence that the Connersville Witnesses had committed any felony or had conspired to commit one, Indiana's highest court reversed the convictions of Trent and McKee and granted their motion for a new trial. At that, the county finally relented, and the prosecutions apparently were dropped.[32]

While Grace Trent and Lucy McKee appealed their convictions to the Supreme Court of Indiana, Witnesses in Fayette County decided to mount a separate effort to obtain relief from the local authorities who seemed determined to wipe out their religious liberty. Like similarly oppressed Witnesses in Kentucky, Oklahoma, and Iowa, they turned to a federal court for a remedy. In a complaint filed on 27 December 1940, the Witnesses sought an injunction prohibiting a host of county officials from using Indiana's riotous conspiracy, criminal syndicalism, and flag desecration laws to "unlawfully . . . deny and deprive" them of "their 'civil rights' of freedom of speech, of assembly, and freedom to worship Almighty God according to dictates of their consciences, all contrary to the Federal Constitution." Named as defendants were nearly all of the county authorities who had participated in the prosecutions of McKee and Trent (including Hunt, Adams, and Hemlick) and Judge Johnson. Two weeks after the Witnesses filed their complaint, a federal district court in

Indianapolis held a hearing on their petition for a preliminary injunction, which would remain in place until the court rendered a final ruling. That request was denied on 17 March 1941.[33]

What followed was an unfortunate example of the type of crisis that so often resulted from the Witnesses' penchant for confrontation. Witness John Rainbow—who had suffered through the debacle of the Connersville trial and then watched as Victor Schmidt and his wife were mobbed—summoned seventy-five Witnesses from West Virginia, Ohio, and Kentucky to the Kingdom Hall in Cincinnati on the morning of 6 April. Upon arriving, each of the Witnesses was handed a small cardboard map of Connersville, and over the course of the morning they were assigned particular areas in the town for canvassing. After being briefed, the Witnesses piled into several dozen rickety cars and drove sixty miles to Fayette County for a day of defiant worship. It was Palm Sunday, and scores of angry churchgoers complained about the Witnesses' presence in Connersville to William Traylor, the town's police chief, almost as soon as the evangelists hit the streets. Working closely with the county sheriff and his deputies, Traylor wasted little time. He instructed his colleagues and subordinates to fan out in Connersville and take all the Witnesses into custody. By the end of the day, the seventy-five Witnesses—men, women, and children alike—had been jailed. Like Grace Trent and Lucy McKee before them, they were charged with riotous conspiracy and criminal syndicalism.[34]

The mass arrests in Connersville drew howls of protest from the Witnesses and their allies. Just hours after it received word that the group had been taken into custody, the ACLU (which had been closely monitoring events in Fayette County since the arrest of Trent and McKee) expressed its concerns in telegrams to the governor of Indiana, the Justice Department, and the Fayette County prosecutor. "May we urge prompt investigation by your unit of mob violence and arrests of Jehovah's Witnesses in Connersville, Indiana, today?" the ACLU cabled the Justice Department's Civil Rights Section. "Second similar incident in recent months appears to justify vigorous action."[35] Five days later, General Counsel Arthur Garfield Hays wrote to Attorney General Robert H. Jackson to suggest that his "prompt intervention" was needed to prevent the complete eradication of the civil rights of Witnesses who attempted to worship, speak, and assemble in Fayette County. In his letter to Jackson, Hays made it clear that he was profoundly disturbed by the flagrant mistreatment of Witnesses in Indiana and that he hoped the Justice Department would protect them from spurious prosecutions:

> So extraordinary a prosecution has been undertaken at Connersville, Indiana against seventy-five members of Jehovah's Witnesses that we desire to lay the facts before you in the belief that the federal jurisdiction can be invoked to combat what is in effect a conspiracy to deprive members of this religious organization of their civil rights.

Hays reviewed the circumstances of the 6 April arrests in Connersville, noting that the criminal syndicalism charges were based on "the distribution of the usual literature of this religious organization based upon Bible prophecies foretelling the establishment of God's kingdom on earth." He argued strenuously that prosecuting Witnesses on such grounds was unconscionable:

> It is fantastic to charge that this literature constitutes advocacy of the overthrow of the government by force and violence. It is obvious to anyone who knows the prejudice against Jehovah's Witnesses that this charge is merely a device to restrain them in the exercise of their constitutional rights to distribute literature as set forth explicitly in recent Supreme Court decisions.

With local authorities trampling on their civil rights, the most viable solution to the Witnesses' dilemma in Fayette County, Hays suggested, would be federal prosecutions under Sections 51 and 52.[36]

Two days after the Palm Sunday arrests, Covington contacted Biddle and reviewed the Witnesses' misery in Connersville, starting with the arrests of Grace Trent and Lucy McKee ten months earlier. Still seething over the abuse he and other Witnesses had been forced to endure at their trial, Covington reported that the elderly women's convictions had been gross miscarriages of justice and that similar travesties were occurring in Fayette County almost every day, due to the outrageous conduct of local authorities. The dozens of Witnesses who had been arrested on 6 April were in a double bind, Covington told Biddle, since they could neither raise bail (it had originally been set at a whopping $225,000 for the entire group) nor find a local attorney "because the public officials and local rabble element threaten to mob any attorneys as they mobbed others in September." The riotous conspiracy and criminal syndicalism charges leveled at the Witnesses were ridiculous, the attorney maintained, and the only people worthy of prosecution were local authorities who had taken it upon themselves to squelch the victims' First Amendment rights. They had truly entered into a massive criminal conspiracy; the Witnesses had done nothing more sinister than attempt to enjoy the civil rights that were supposedly shielded by the Constitution. Covington told Biddle, "These people are entirely innocent, and it is plain to any honest man that this is a conspiracy to deprive Jehovah's Witnesses of their civil rights in violation of Sections 51 and 52 of Title 18, United States Code." Clearly frustrated by the Justice Department's apparent lack of concern for the Witnesses' welfare, he suggested "that to permit such outrageous violations of constitutional rights by public officials to go unnoticed by the Department of Justice is nothing less than encouragement to anarchy."[37]

In April 1941, the *Christian Century* weighed in with its own assessment of conditions in Connersville, and it was no more sanguine than Covington's. "Preaching the Kingdom of God on earth," the magazine noted in amazement, "constitutes advocacy of the 'overthrow of government by force' in the opinion of the authorities of Fayette County, Indiana." Always a staunch defender of the Witnesses' civil rights, the *Century* reviewed their ongoing mistreatment by local authorities and concluded that "such a display of official tyranny and intolerance as this is a disgrace to democracy and menace to the freedom of all religion." The Witnesses' beliefs certainly were peculiar, and their practices could be bothersome, but the Constitution protected the right of these "harmless but pestiferous people" to nurture their faith and attempts to spread it through proselytizing, provided that they did not disturb the peace themselves. (After all, "liberty of belief under the Constitution is not only for the wise, the tolerant and the respectable.") By so brazenly depriving the Witnesses of their civil rights, Connersville had "exposed its own intolerance to national opprobrium. It has also shown the kind of savagery which is likely to become increasingly common as war hysteria spreads across the country." Though it was tempting to claim that the victims had indeed courted adversity in Connersville, the *Christian Century* was unwilling to fault Grace

Trent, Lucy McKee, and their fellow Witnesses for having the mettle to defy prejudice. "The responsibility for this situation, which is only a part of the most widespread religious persecution which this country has known for a century, lies with the fomenters of war madness," the editorial argued.[38]

Despite the mass arrests of Witnesses in April and the fallacious prosecutions of Grace Trent and Lucy McKee, a federal district court refused to enjoin authorities in Fayette County from enforcing state riotous and criminal conspiracy laws against Jehovah's Witnesses. In its review of the circumstances of the Palm Sunday arrests, the three-judge panel concluded that local officials had acted in good faith by arresting and jailing all the Witnesses. "It is sufficient to say that, in their honest opinion," the court noted, "[local authorities] did what they believed to be necessary in the discharge of their official duties and in accord with their oaths as officials." With Fayette County authorities doing nothing more odious than simply maintaining a semblance of order in Connersville, the Witnesses were not entitled to relief via an injunction, for it was "clear that there are no exceptional circumstances in this case where the danger of irreparable loss or damage to [them] is great and immediate," the court held.[39] The ruling, which strongly suggested that the Witnesses' problems in Fayette County were purely of their own making, infuriated Covington. In a bitter letter to the ACLU's Roger Baldwin, he groused that the opinion was "based upon religious prejudice" and "really amounts to 'pitching the Christians to the lions.'" Stung by the defeat, Covington argued that "something should be done to stop this Nazi advance in the central part of the country around Indiana."[40]

Throughout their lengthy ordeal, the Connersville Witnesses could take a small measure of comfort in knowing that they were by no means the only members of their faith to face spurious charges. For example, early in June 1940, just days before the Witnesses' misfortunes began in Indiana, police officers in Harlan, Kentucky, arrested six local Witnesses and charged them under that state's sedition law. The arrest warrants—signed by L. O. Smith, who served both as Harlan's mayor and commander of its American Legion post—claimed that when the Witnesses handed out Watch

Tower tracts and periodicals in Harlan, they had been "distributing un-American literature and propaganda detrimental to the U.S. government." Interviewed by a local newspaper after he had ordered the arrests, Smith said that he could not abide the Witnesses' flagrant disloyalty. "Any man has the right to worship as he pleases," he said, "but any literature detrimental to the American flag is detrimental to the country, and Harlan is no place for such stuff." Dorothy Carr, the wife of one of the Witness defendants, reported that the atmosphere in Harlan was exceptionally tense, largely because of the mayor's open contempt for the defendants. According to a letter she sent to Solicitor General Biddle (whose office was fast becoming buried under an avalanche of such correspondence), Smith seized local Witnesses' literature, physically abused them, and promised that they would be mobbed if they continued to proselytize in Harlan.[41] At one point, local authorities went so far as to confiscate a shipment of Bibles intended for Carr's husband. "The Harlan County officials' minds are so warped by prejudice, they probably think the Holy Bible is un-American literature," she told Baldwin.[42]

The defendants in Harlan, like many Witnesses who had been charged with crimes, had difficulty finding a local attorney who would defend them. A Kentucky lawyer named R. L. Pope briefly took the case, but he reluctantly dropped it after being "threatened and intimidated," according to Dorothy Carr.[43] In early June, both Victor Schmidt (who soon had his hands full with equally disturbing events in Connersville) and Grover Powell went to Harlan to organize a defense. Schmidt discovered that the Witnesses were being incarcerated in dirty, cramped prison cells as they waited for their steep bail ($10,000 each) to be raised. After meeting with the defendants and assessing the community's attitudes toward Witnesses, the apprehensive lawyer filed a report with the ACLU describing "the deplorable conditions in Harlan, Kentucky." Given the hostility of Mayor Smith, Schmidt wrote, the Witnesses' prospects were bleak:

> The city officials of Harlan, including mayor L. O. Smith and W. L. Rose, the city attorney, are largely responsible for the frenzy of prejudice created against Jehovah's Witnesses. . . . The mayor wants all of Jehovah's Witnesses out of Harlan County and will not endure their work. I am positive that Jehovah's Witnesses

would not get a fair trial in or about Harlan, Kentucky, and it is dangerous for any of Jehovah's Witnesses to be in that county.[44]

Grover Powell wrote a similarly dispirited report linking the Witnesses' woes in Harlan to the *Gobitis* decision. As he informed the ACLU, "The decision of the United States Supreme Court in the Gobitis flag-salute case seemed to be the signal for the onslaught upon faithful Christians. . . . After this decision, [the Witnesses' critics] suddenly saw red."[45]

While the six defendants languished in Harlan's jail during the summer, Covington and other Witnesses pleaded with state authorities and the Justice Department to investigate the misconduct of Mayor Smith and his cohorts. Witness attorneys held largely fruitless conferences with the U.S. attorney in Lexington, Kentucky, and they pleaded with the governor as well, but he "insisted that he is powerless to act officially." When these efforts foundered, Witness officials in Brooklyn asked Biddle to mount a full-scale probe of the mistreatment of Witnesses in Harlan, which was, they claimed, "just one of very many sad and heartrending cases now being reported almost daily from Maine, Oklahoma, Arkansas and many other states, to us." They had chosen to take the matter up with the solicitor general because recent experience had taught them that seeking relief from local authorities was usually pointless. "It must be borne in mind, Mr. Biddle," they wrote, "that in many instances even the officials who can and ought to act from humane impulses are, in fact, moved to withhold acting in that manner by reason of their 'obligation' to safeguard the interests of the Roman Catholic Hierarchy as against the welfare of oppressed individuals."[46]

Hayden Covington sent a separate appeal to Biddle in August 1940, and in it he contended that public officials in Harlan, L. O. Smith in particular, were clearly engaged in a "conspiracy to violate the civil rights" of Witnesses and thus were "deserving of prosecution under Federal laws." As always, Covington was blunt about his purpose in writing: "I should like to see your department make an investigation as soon as possible of this case, with the object of prosecuting the public officials acting under color of law for violation of Section 52, Title 18 of the United States Code."[47] Dorothy Carr contacted Biddle as well because she hoped that "some action will be taken at once in behalf of these six order-loving, harmless and peaceful citizens of the United States."[48]

The Justice Department kept its usual distance, and Witnesses in the area continued to live in fear that local officials would have them arrested for sedition if they dared to defy Mayor Smith by distributing literature. Represented by Covington, Schmidt, and R. L. Pope (who disregarded earlier threats), they fought back by bringing a civil suit in federal court against their primary adversaries. The Witnesses, recognizing that Kentucky's sedition law was a devastating weapon, sought an injunction that would bar authorities in Harlan from wielding the measure unconstitutionally to suppress their freedom of worship. The suit named as defendants not only Mayor Smith but also Harlan's police chief, the city's police court judge, the local commonwealth's attorney, two police officers, and the county sheriff. (Kentucky's attorney general was named as well, but the federal court dismissed the lawsuit against him.) The Witnesses maintained that the defendants, by continually threatening to invoke the state sedition law against them, had participated in "illegal and wrongful interference" with their rights to speak, worship, and assemble freely. The tone of the Witnesses' periodicals and tracts was indeed strident, the plaintiffs admitted in their brief, but the materials were in no way seditious or "un-American," as Smith had charged. "The undisputed evidence shows, and it is admitted by all, that the literature in question does not advocate the use of force by other persons or anyone to overthrow the government." In an opinion issued in June 1941 (a year after the first arrests in Harlan), the federal district court found that "by threatening to continue to arrest, imprison and prosecute" the Witnesses under the state sedition measure, Smith and the other defendants had in fact deprived them of "rights, privileges and immunities secured by the Constitution of the United States." A resounding victory for the Witnesses, the court's order permanently enjoined authorities in Harlan from acting "under color" of the Kentucky sedition law to arrest or jail Witnesses who were merely "circulating, selling or otherwise distributing [their literature] in a peaceable manner."[49]

With the Justice Department so reluctant to mount prosecutions under Section 52, permanent injunctions such as the one granted by the federal court in Kentucky often represented the Witnesses' only real hope of gaining relief from antagonistic public officials, particularly when they enacted and zealously enforced measures that two observers in the *Bill of Rights Review* called "local laws designed to curtail the Witnesses' functions and activities."[50] To suppress the Witnesses' public form of worship, municipalities often drafted or dusted off antiproselytizing ordinances and enforced them mercilessly, arresting and then trying Witnesses by the dozens when they promulgated their beliefs in public. In spring 1941, Witness proselytizers in Muskogee, Oklahoma, ran afoul of that city's Americanism Club, a group comprising mainly war veterans. When Witnesses attempted to preach in Muskogee's downtown area by distributing Watch Tower tracts and periodicals, members of the club berated them as subversives. Pressed by the apoplectic club members, Muskogee's city council drafted and approved an anti-Witness ordinance based on a measure enacted by Oklahoma City the previous fall. The law, touted as an emergency measure, was designed to curb the use of language or the distribution of materials "calculated to cause a breach of the peace or an assault." According to the council, Ordinance 1533 was "immediately necessary for the preservation of the peace, health and safety" of Muskogee residents.[51]

Between 12 April and 4 November 1941, police in Muskogee arrested John Lynch and thirty-nine other Witnesses a grand total of 204 times for violating Ordinance 1533. A few of the more persistent Witnesses were arrested more than a dozen times each during that seven-month span. All but ten of the arrests resulted in convictions in Muskogee's police court, where Judge Elbert Hinds handed out fines ranging from $10.00 to $19.95. The trials in Hinds's courtroom were perfunctory at best: "No particulars other than the fact that the defendant was upon the streets of Muskogee distributing Jehovah's Witness literature were introduced at the trials of these defendants," according to one account. The Muskogee Witnesses, arguing that the law was being enforced in a manner that compromised their First Amendment freedoms (which were protected from encroachment by the state through the Fourteenth Amendment), went to federal court late in 1941 to obtain an injunction prohibiting the enforcement of Ordinance 1533 against them. In an order handed down in January 1942, the court granted the injunction and thus halted the seemingly endless cycle of arrests and trials of Witnesses in Muskogee. The court noted, "It is not the ordinance that is invalid. It is the construction and method of enforcement thereof that is invalid." An injunction blocking the enforcement of the ordinance against the Witnesses was needed because "in effect the ordinance has been construed in such a way as to prohibit the plaintiffs or any members of their society from peaceably disseminating or offering for sale their literature," and that constituted an obvious violation of their constitutional freedoms.[52]

Injunctions were a powerful weapon in the Witnesses' legal arsenal, and victims of discrimination sought them throughout the early and mid-1940s. It was a testament to both the Witnesses' unpopularity and their tenaciousness that they sought injunctive relief in every corner of the country during those years, including Manchester, New Hampshire; Fort Myers, Florida; Colorado Springs, Colorado; Moscow, Idaho; Brookfield, Pennsylvania; Ranger, Texas; and London, Ohio.[53] Even in 1946, long after the peak of their campaign in state and federal courts, Witnesses in Iowa obtained an injunction in federal court prohibiting authorities in Lacona, a small town south of Des Moines, from interfering with their freedoms of speech and assembly.

Although it reached an astonishing climax several weeks later, the origins of the Lacona dispute were fairly routine. On 1 September a handful of local residents pestered a group of approximately fifty Witnesses from Des Moines who had come to a city park to hear a lecture. The next day, the town council responded to complaints about the Witnesses' use of the park by adopting a resolution proclaiming "that the Lacona City Park or Public Square cannot be used for any meetings or congregations of any kind unless it be brought up before the Town Council and voted on." Previously, there had been no real restrictions on the use of the park, and Witnesses had been meeting there for several years. Now, however, they were effectively barred from holding public meetings in Lacona because the town council had made it abundantly clear that they never would be issued the requisite permit. The Witnesses either were not immediately informed of the resolution's passage or they simply chose to ignore it, and they forged ahead with plans to meet again in the park on the following Sunday, 8 September. As they had promised to do throughout the preceding week, a group of roughly twenty-five veterans disrupted the meeting. In a brawl that hearkened back to the worst days of their persecution in spring and summer 1940, the Witnesses fought with assailants for the better part of an hour. "About 30 persons suffered head and face cuts, bloody noses and body bruises as fists, pop bottles, clubs and brass knuckles were used by various persons involved in the dispute," the *Des Moines Register* reported. After the melee, Robert Bowers, a member of the town council, explained to a newspaper reporter why veterans and other patriotic residents were so adamant in opposing the Witnesses' presence in Lacona. "We don't object to their religion," Bowers said, "but we object to the fact that they're too damn yellow to fight [in the armed services] and then expect the rights that we fought for."[54]

The day after the riot, local authorities hatched a scheme to maintain order in Lacona. At a town meeting attended by several hundred local residents, Mayor Lo Goode announced that he and Warren County authorities had agreed to enforce a blockade of the town on the following Sunday, 15 September. Under the plan, Sheriff Lewis Johnson and scores of specially deputized subordinates—close to 200 in all—would man barriers on all the major roads leading into and out of Lacona, and they would prevent anyone who did not have "rightful business" in town from entering. One newspaper report explained that the plan would "place the town under a kind of sheriff-enforced 'martial law'" aimed at keeping both the Witnesses and any potential troublemakers (presumably veterans from nearby communities) from converging on the community and doing battle. Speaking at the town meeting, Johnson brimmed with confidence. "I can assure you," he proclaimed, "that there will be no meeting of Jehovah's Witnesses in the Lacona town park next Sunday."

Later that week, Johnson and Goode met with Jens Grothe, the attorney general of Iowa, and he lent his imprimatur to the plan. They also conferred with the state's director of public safety, who agreed to provide state patrolmen to reroute traffic around Lacona. Eager to learn the details of the proposed blockade, a group of Witnesses apparently followed Johnson and Goode as they made their rounds at the state house in Des Moines. According to one account, Johnson informed them that "they had better not come back to Lacona, that they couldn't hold any meetings there on [15 September]." One of Grothe's subordinates rebuffed them as well, and they were nearly ejected from the capitol. The Witnesses held firm, handing both the mayor and the sheriff letters complaining that their civil rights had been violated during the 8 September riot and that local authorities, motivated by prejudice, had intentionally denied them adequate protection as they attempted to assemble. The letters explained that regardless of the proposed blockade (and the town council's decision to deny them permission to use the city park), the Witnesses were planning to return to Lacona that Sunday.[55]

After crowding themselves into more than a dozen cars, approximately 100 Witnesses drove from Des Moines to Lacona on 15 September. Like nearly everyone else who attempted to enter the town that day, they were turned back "by a road blockade organized by Warren County Sheriff Lewis Johnson, who deputized nearly 200 men," according to the *Register*. Johnson had begun organizing the blockade that morning by swearing in his deputies and giving them makeshift badges fashioned out of red ribbon. The deputies, accompanied by a contingent of state patrolmen, took up their posts at 10:00 A.M. and manned them throughout the day. It seemed as though everyone in town pitched in to support their efforts, and the day took on an almost festive air. In a front-page story sporting the banner headline 200 DEPUTIES STOP WITNESSES, the *Register* reported:

> The town's women served southern fried chicken and all of the trimmings at the American Legion hall in a feed for the men who manned the blockade, making the affair a community project. Besides chicken, the menu included roast pork, roast beef, several varieties of sandwiches, apple, peach and cherry pie, milk, coffee, five types of salad, dill and sweet pickles and five vegetables. About 30 women took care of the serving at the Legion hall. Girls carried the sandwiches and coffee to cars and a jeep was used to deliver food to the four blockade posts about a mile from the town.

Fortified by those ample provisions and the goodwill they symbolized, Johnson and his deputies remained vigilant throughout the day, halting traffic on the main roads until sundown. "Does this constitute being barred from town?" Charles Sellers asked Johnson as the Witnesses were turned away. "Absolutely," the sheriff responded. After the blockaders had left their posts, Johnson told a reporter that he was satisfied with the day's events. "I don't know whether I'm right or wrong, but I wanted to stop trouble and I believe that I accomplished that," he said.[56]

In its second editorial comment on the Lacona dispute, the *Des Moines Register* claimed that Johnson, whatever his intentions, had indeed made a significant error in blockading Lacona. "A sheriff and his deputies are not authorized to tyrannize the highways," the editorial claimed. "The citizens of Iowa towns are not authorized to determine who may and who may not enter their boundaries. Not without a court order based on some charge or evidence, at least." The paper asserted that the "mob methods" employed by local authorities to block the Witnesses amounted to "a sheer display of force," and it urged Johnson, Goode, and other officials "to begin observing the laws that they were sworn to uphold, and confine themselves to that. As leaders of mobs, they don't add much to anybody's pride in Iowa."[57]

In late September, as the town council was again denying them access to the park, the Witnesses asked a federal district court in Des Moines to protect their civil rights by issuing an injunction against the mayor of Lacona, the town marshal, the town itself, and Warren County sheriff Lewis Johnson. As the Eighth Circuit Court of Appeals later described their complaint, Charles Sellers and his fellow Witness plaintiffs requested "an injunction to restrain the defendants . . . from interfering with plaintiffs' rights, from enforcing the resolutions of the Council purporting to require a permit for the use of the park, from barring plaintiffs from the Town, and from interfering with their preaching activities in the park." Beyond the injunction, the Witnesses hoped that the court would issue a declaratory judgment stating that their rights under the Constitution entitled them to full access to the town itself as well as to the park and that the town council's resolution requiring them to obtain a permit before using the park was unconstitutional and thus void.[58]

U.S. District Judge Charles Dewey dismissed the Witnesses' complaint on 30 December 1946. Echoing a passage from Felix Frankfurter's opinion in *Gobitis*, Dewey remarked that he preferred to view the case as a collision between "an irresistible force—the constitutional rights of the Jehovah's Witnesses" and "an immovable body—the right and duty of the police officers to preserve the peace of the community." After listening to the testimony of Lewis Johnson (whom he described as "a man of considerable executive ability"), Dewey was convinced that the sheriff had chosen to blockade Lacona simply because he had been faced with a "grave and serious" threat of violence. It was apparent that Johnson had been responding to a "clear and present danger"—the prospect of an enormous disturbance involving hundreds of local veterans and dozens of Witnesses. With that in mind, Dewey concluded that "his actions were legal and proper and done for the purpose of preserving the peace and preventing bloodshed in his community." The federal judge had high praise for Goode as well, claiming that he was "a kindly disposed, agreeable gentleman with great tolerance." To Dewey, the idea that these two men, who were motivated by a "high regard for the peace of the little community of Lacona," could participate in the type of conspiracy described in the Witnesses' complaint was far-fetched at best. He suggested that the real culprits in the dispute were the Witnesses themselves, for they had courted trouble by choosing to assemble in Lacona on 8 September even though "it was very apparent that there would be opposition . . . as the atmosphere was tense with the expectation of a riot." Dewey acknowledged that the town council's resolution requiring Witnesses to obtain a permit before using the park was unconstitutional, but he brushed that action aside as "slight and inconsequential" because the measure carried no penalty and there was no mechanism for enforcing it. (Besides, he grumbled, the Witnesses had more or less ignored it anyway.)[59]

In October 1947 the Eighth Circuit Court of Appeals reversed Dewey's decision. Written by Judge John Sanborn, the appeals court's ruling pounced on the argument that lay at the heart of Dewey's opinion—that the drastic actions taken by local authorities, including the blockade, had been necessary to prevent a bloodbath in Lacona. "We find no substantial evidence in the record," the court maintained, "to support the conclusion that the proposed religious meetings of the Jehovah's Witnesses in the Town of Lacona were actually fraught with danger to the peace and welfare of the State of Iowa." True, a melee had disrupted the Witnesses' meeting on 8 September, but that fact was "fully consistent with the hypothesis that the disorder was due to the failure of the local and State authorities to police the park as it is with the hypothesis that the unpopularity of the Jehovah's Witnesses was so great that the only means of maintaining order in the future was to deny them access to the Town."

The appeals court did not impugn the motives of Goode and Johnson; from its review of the evidence, it seemed clear that neither man "had any feeling of personal animosity toward the Jehovah's Witnesses, and that each was acting on the advice of counsel and in the belief that what he did to keep the peace was legally permissible." Yet the evidence also indicated that when they had decided to blockade Lacona on 15 September (and thus deprive the Witnesses of their right to assemble and worship), both the mayor and the sheriff had acted on the basis of wild rumors that hundreds of armed veterans from central and southern Iowa would converge on the park if the Witnesses were allowed to meet there. "While we do not question the good faith of the Mayor or the Sheriff . . . we are convinced that evidence of unconfirmed rumors, talk, and fears cannot form the basis of a finding of the existence of such a clear and present danger to the State as to justify a deprivation of fundamental and essential constitutional rights," Sanborn wrote for the court. "We think that is particularly true in a situation where no effort whatever was made to protect those who were attempting lawfully to exercise those rights."

The appeals court also disputed Dewey's assertion that the town council's resolutions, "adopted to prevent the Jehovah's Witnesses from using the park without a permit, were inconsequential. The resolutions obviously were passed to establish a basis for treating the Jehovah's Witnesses as law violators and to justify barring them from the park." Recognizing those clear violations of the Witnesses' civil rights, the court ruled that the plaintiffs were entitled to a decree that would affirm their right to meet in the Lacona park; require that local authorities protect them while they lawfully exercised their constitutional rights; and declare that the blockade had "constituted an unlawful deprivation of the constitutional rights of Jehovah's Witnesses." The decree would also contain language entitling the Witnesses to "injunctive orders" if local authorities attempted to deprive them of their civil rights.[60]

6. Starvation into Patriotism

Many of the Witnesses who weathered persecution in the early and mid-1940s were forced to suffer in public. Mobs brutalized them when they assembled in town squares and parks; vigilantes stormed and sacked their Kingdom Halls and then burned their possessions in the streets; and police officers dragged them off to jail as they proselytized on sidewalks and street corners. Hundreds of people either watched or participated in some of these harrowing spectacles, and they were widely reported in newspapers and magazines. But the persecution of Witnesses was not limited to the flagrant abuses meted out in public spaces by veterans and police officers. Throughout the war years, Witnesses of all ages were forced to brook a wide range of less apparent but equally burdensome forms of discrimination. Adult Witnesses were fired from or forced to quit their jobs, denied relief benefits, and charged with having contributed to the delinquency of minors; their children were expelled from public schools and then prosecuted as delinquents or truants. In responding to these less conspicuous manifestations of bigotry, Witnesses were characteristically stubborn and litigious, repeatedly urging state and federal courts, as well as administrative bodies like the federal Committee on Fair Employment Practice, to protect them from religious discrimination in their workplaces, schools, and homes. As always, they turned to the American Civil Liberties Union for assistance, and it responded by aggressively defending their civil liberties. Although the rulings in these cases usually received scant public attention, they offered powerful evidence of the Witnesses' determination to rely upon the letter and spirit of the Constitution to protect their jeopardized civil rights.

Throughout the World War II era, Witnesses proved to be especially vulnerable to discrimination in their workplaces. Daniel Morgan's travails began in 1939, when his sons refused to salute the American flag at their public high school in Fort Lee, New Jersey, because of their "religious scruples," as Morgan put it. After a local newspaper reported that the boys had been expelled for their intransigence, Morgan was summoned to the office of his boss, the chief inspector of New Jersey's Motor Vehicle Department. "He demanded," Morgan later said, "that I bring parental pressure to bear upon my sons in an effort to change their faith." Morgan, an ardent Witness, believed that the Bible expressly prohibited "salutation to inanimate objects," and he refused to meddle with his sons' behavior. The chief inspector was incredulous; he thought that Morgan's encouragement of the boys' misconduct smacked of disloyalty, and he had no qualms about saying so. Even though Morgan was a veteran of World War I and had been wounded in battle ("I have served the Government well," he pointed out), the chief inspector suggested that anyone who frowned upon the flag salute obviously lacked patriotism. The two men quarreled, and Morgan was charged with insubordination and eventually fired. He later said that the chief inspector had claimed that he was not "a fit man to work for the State."[1]

Morgan's peculiar religious beliefs were again an issue in 1941, when he applied for a job with the state prison system. After receiving his application, New Jersey prison officials subjected him to a rigorous interview. In a contentious session lasting over an hour, they grilled him about his faith, repeatedly asking if he planned to continue to engage in religious proselytizing if the state hired him. Morgan explained that he had every intention of worshiping as he pleased, and he reminded his interviewers that his freedom to do so was clearly protected by the Constitution. According to Morgan, the prison officials who interrogated him also "placed a test upon me to determine whether or not my religious convictions would permit me to salute the national flag. Commissioner [William] Ellis said that now was the time to determine whether or not any of my religious activities would embarrass the state." The Witness completed a training program at the Rahway Reformatory, but he was not offered a permanent job with the prison system. According to the New Jersey Civil Service Commission, which later reviewed Morgan's work history, he failed to earn a job offer primarily because he possessed "a highly nervous disposition" and thus was "temperamentally unsuited to service as a prison and reformatory officer." Morgan, a former sergeant in the marines, ridiculed the idea that he could not handle the rigors of prison work. He was convinced that the prison system had failed to hire him simply because he had espoused an unpopular faith and then refused to be bullied into abandoning it.[2]

Morgan's frustrations finally boiled over when he submitted an application to the Bergen County Board of Freeholders for a job as a bridge attendant. As the lone disabled veteran on the list of certified candidates, Morgan should have been assured of the position, but the Freeholders, appalled by his unwillingness to salute the flag, refused to appoint him. To Morgan's amazement, the New Jersey Civil Service Commission upheld the Freeholders' decision. The commission acknowledged that it was not empowered "to rule on the question of whether his beliefs disqualify him for public employment." Nevertheless, after reviewing Morgan's spotty work history, it held that he could be rejected for the bridge inspector's post because he seemed unable "to devote himself to the daily routine performance of the duties of the position, properly and effectively perform those duties, accept and observe reasonable directions from his supervising officers and work in cooperation with his fellow employees." Furthermore, according to the Civil Service Commission, the Board of Freeholders was "not acting arbitrarily or beyond its reasonable authority when it requires that public employees under its jurisdiction shall salute, and be willing to salute, the Flag on appropriate occasions and otherwise conform to the patriotic practices recognized by law and custom as commendable and proper by the great body of citizens of this State and of the United States." Morgan later obtained a letter in which the Civil Service Commission stated its position more clearly to the Freeholders. "We are directed to advise," the commissioners wrote, "that if a person refuses to salute the flag of the United States, the commission would consider him as being disqualified for a civil service position." In short, if Daniel Morgan wanted to work for the Freeholders, he would have to betray the single most meaningful dimension of his life—his religious faith.[3]

Morgan denounced the Civil Service Commission's ruling as "tyrannical, discriminating and intimidating," and he insisted that its members had "assumed the dangerous position of being a law unto themselves." Working with the Witnesses' characteristic zeal, and enlisting the help of their steadfast allies in the ACLU, he went to state court seeking to rein in the commission and have its decision reversed. In April 1944, the New Jersey Supreme Court handed down its opinion in *Morgan v. Civil Service Commission of New Jersey*, and it provided the Witness with a resounding victory. Given that Morgan had earned a spot on the list of certified candidates by passing the state's civil service examination, no one could legitimately claim that he was unfit to serve as a bridge inspector (even if his performance in earlier jobs had been suspect). In fact, the court noted, the Freeholders had refused to appoint Morgan "on the sole ground, it is conceded, that [he] had declared an unwillingness 'to salute the flag of the United States,'" an aversion firmly rooted in his religious convictions. Neither the Freeholders nor the Civil Service Commission, however, had the authority to require Morgan to forsake his faith in order to obtain a job. The court held that it was "not within the power of officialdom to coerce individual affirmation of a belief and an attitude of mind—to compel the individual to give utterance to what is not in his mind." Viewed within the context of Morgan's religious beliefs, flag-saluting amounted to "a form of utterance," and forcing the Witness to engage in it against his will clearly violated his constitutional rights. Put most simply, "Coerced acceptance of a patriotic creed is beyond official authority. The conscience of the individual may not thus be trammeled. The Bill of Rights enjoins such assertions of official authority."[4]

The most widely reported Witness job-discrimination case of the 1940s involved the dismissal of seven employees of the Pittsburgh Plate Glass Company in Clarksburg, West Virginia. Shortly after the Japanese bombing of Pearl Harbor late in 1941, members of two unions—the Window Glass Cutters League of America and the Glass, Ceramic and Silica Sand Workers of America—began to shun Witnesses who worked at the plant. Paul Schmidt, employed in the cutting room of the plant for more than a decade, was among those ostracized. Halfway through December 1941, Schmidt learned that the men responsible for transporting his cut glass had become so antagonistic that they had "laid down their tools and refused to longer work with me," he later wrote. Once the Witnesses were accused of disloyalty, their jobs were jeopardized "because a small minority of the men at the plant became imbued with the determination that we should be forced to violate our conscience and made to salute the flag or get out." Fearful that the conflict might hamper production, which was sure to skyrocket with the formal entry of the United

States into World War II, Schmidt's supervisors encouraged him to quit. Schmidt appreciated their dilemma, but he was reluctant to yield to intimidation and walk away from a job he loved. "I had spent twelve of the happiest years of my life in the company's service," he explained, "during which I had worked hard and well."

He chose to stay on at the plant, and the harassment only became more intense. At one point, a coworker taunted Schmidt by hanging a small American flag at his work station. "I have too much love and respect for our national emblem to have torn it down, as they probably expected me to do," Schmidt later wrote, "so nothing happened." Schmidt's already tenuous relationship with his fellow employees eroded still further when a local priest was brought to the plant to preside over a flag-raising ceremony. Schmidt and his son Bernard, who also worked for Pittsburgh Plate Glass (PPG), were cautioned to keep their distance from the service, and they left work early "to avoid any possibility of violence." On the morning after the flag-raising ceremony, Schmidt, who "had been warned to expect most anything, even death" when he returned to work, met with officials of the Window Glass Cutters League and beseeched them to ease tensions at the plant. Unfortunately, the union "did nothing for me," Schmidt fumed, and "turned a deaf ear to my plea."[5]

Pittsburgh Plate Glass fired Schmidt on Friday 19 December 1941. His termination notice read: "Now that we are at war, and that your attitude is such that the men refuse to work with you any longer, your services are no longer required. In view of the existing emergency, which has resulted in loss of production, we are obliged to waive your seven days notice." Six other Witnesses, including Schmidt's son, were dismissed as well. Despite the Witnesses' avowed patriotism (Schmidt pointed out that all the men "dearly love our native America with . . . fervor"), both the unions at the plant went along with their firings. On several occasions, an officer of the Window Glass Cutters League local in Clarksburg brought the matter before the union's president and executive board, but "he was severely rebuked and censured" for doing so, according to Schmidt. Abandoned by their unions, the Witnesses were stunned suddenly to find themselves out of work and scrambling to make ends meet. "We are facing a cold hard world with the prospects of losing all we possess, including our homes and all," Schmidt told the ACLU. "You see, we are being ostracized by all other glass plants, here and elsewhere." He added, "It seems outrageous that honest, tax-paying citizens who love their country are denied the privilege of earning their bread in a land that flaunts its 'freedom' to the high heavens."[6]

With the assistance of the American Civil Liberties Union, the men who had been dismissed filed a claim against their employer with the President's Committee on Fair Employment Practice (FEPC), which operated within the War Manpower Commission. The committee investigated the Clarksburg firings, and late in 1942 it ordered Pittsburgh Plate Glass to rehire the Witnesses. "Threatened violence or work stoppage to obtain the dismissal of capable employees whose religious views are unpopular with their fellow-employees," the committee ruled, "does not constitute a valid reason for such dismissal." The press release announcing the order hailed it as "unprecedented," and in fact it was; never before had any agency in the federal government taken such a dramatic step to mitigate the persecution of Witnesses. Chair Malcolm S. McLean explained that the committee had been persuaded to take such an extraordinary effort on behalf of the Witnesses because their mistreatment seemed to be completely at odds with the guiding principles of American democracy, the very principles that the country was defending in battle. He told reporters:

> Our government guarantees equality of right and opportunity without regard to a person's creed. This in an integral part of our democratic way of life, one of our nation's proudest possessions for whose preservation we are fighting this war. This heritage shall not be lightly forfeited at the irresponsible behest of intolerant and misguided persons who seek to impose their will by threats and violence.

The committee also rebuked the unions at the Clarksburg plant and ordered them to "exercise the necessary controls over their members" once the Witnesses returned to work. Union officials were instructed "to secure the proper cooperation for [their] members and to maintain effective control of them who may be inclined to molest these reinstated men or provoke any incident leading to friction or antagonism because of their reinstatement."[7]

Pittsburgh Plate Glass insisted that the return of the Witnesses would disrupt production at the Clarksburg plant, and it fought the federal reinstatement order. The superintendent of the facility predicted that protesting workers would walk off their jobs if the Witnesses returned to work, and the plant would no longer be able to contribute to the war effort.[8] The ACLU dismissed the superintendent's worries as "nonsense," but the FEPC agreed to stay its reinstatement order and to give the company and union officials a chance to air their concerns at a public hearing in Clarksburg.[9] Lawrence Cramer, the committee's executive secretary, attended the rancorous six-hour hearing, and he heard a parade of workers, union officials, and PPG representatives declare, as he later told the ACLU's Roger Baldwin, "that if the seven Jehovah's Witnesses were reinstated, the rest of the workers would walk out." Cramer, however, was not persuaded by what he heard. After the hearing, he told Baldwin, "I don't know how the members of the Committee will vote on this matter, but in my own judgment no facts were produced which support a contention that these Witnesses were not dismissed because of their refusal to salute the flag and because of their religious convictions about this matter, which were alleged to be unpatriotic."[10]

The committee members agreed with Cramer's assessment, and the reinstatement order stood. As it turned out, the Witnesses' victory was bittersweet. Only two of the dismissed men, Paul Schmidt and his son, actually returned to work at the plant; the other five men had been convinced that the federal government would ignore their complaint and had already taken jobs elsewhere when the reinstatement order was issued. Even Bernard Schmidt's days at the Clarksburg plant were numbered: he apparently was classified as a conscientious objector by the Clarksburg draft board and dispatched to a federal work camp in April 1942. For several weeks, though, the two Witnesses were able to work together at the plant and "fully appreciate the greatness of our victory," according to Paul Schmidt. He told the ACLU that even though more than a year had passed since the firings, their unconventional faith was still an issue with many of their coworkers. "The Pittsburgh Plate officials sure treat us fine and seem to be sincere in trying to meet us halfway," Paul Schmidt wrote to staff counsel Clifford Forster, "but most of the men do not speak to us, and that makes a rather unpleasant situation, but I think time will straighten things out and bitter difference will soon be forgotten." Schmidt was genuinely concerned about fostering a harmonious atmosphere at the plant, and he promised to be a gracious victor. He told Forster, "I am doing all in my power to keep the peace and I try to treat [my fellow employees] all kindly and with consideration. I have requested all local Witnesses to refrain from undue boasting over our victory, as such might provoke controversy anew."[11]

When their jobs were jeopardized, Witnesses like Paul Schmidt were often forced to turn to the American Civil Liberties Union for help because the unions that might have championed their rights instead spearheaded efforts to drive them out of workplaces. So many Witnesses were wronged by their unions that Roger Baldwin protested to William Green of the American Federation of Labor (AFL) and Philip Murray of the Congress of Industrial Organizations (CIO). Writing in April 1942, Baldwin noted that in the months following the attack on Pearl Harbor, "a number of cases have been called to our attention in which members of . . . unions have refused to work with men who are members of the religious organization known as Jehovah's Witnesses on the ground that they are unpatriotic because, on religious grounds, they refuse to salute the flag." Baldwin, recognizing that neither the AFL nor the CIO could exercise much disciplinary control over their member unions, urged Green and Murray to "deal with this issue" as best they could. "It is no service to the democratic cause," he reminded them, "when union men are discriminated against on the ground of religion."[12]

That a number of Witnesses suffered from serious discrimination in their workplaces was evident from the American Civil Liberties Union's pamphlet *Jehovah's Witnesses and the War*, which devoted an entire section to "Expulsion from Jobs." Among the cases included in that dismal report was the dismissal of Witness Helge Peterson from his job in the Turlock, California, post office.[13] Like so many Witnesses, Peterson was targeted by members of the American Legion who asserted that he lacked patriotism. Late in 1941, after Peterson came forward at a public meeting and spoke out against a local school district's flag-salute requirement, members of the Legion's Rex Ish Post wrote to U.S. Rep. Bertrand Gearhart and demanded the "removal of a post office employee who was . . . receiving salary from the government of the United States [and] not only was refusing to salute the flag of the United States, and not only stating he would not lift a hand in defense of his country, [but also] was advocating that others refuse to salute the flag and refuse to defend their country." The Legion remarked that "in a time when unity and patriotism are greatly needed," Peterson's activities tended to "undermine the national welfare." Gearhart apparently forwarded the Legion's request to Postmaster General Frank Walker, and he eventually ordered Peterson's dismissal after learning from the Turlock postmaster that the Witness had indeed engaged in "objectionable activity."[14] Peterson defended his behavior ("I merely preached the Gospel as I saw it," he claimed) and pointed out that he had never proselytized while on the job, but he had to find work elsewhere.[15] "All efforts to secure his reinstatement," the ACLU reported, "have been unsuccessful."[16]

Even in the mid-1930s, long before their persecution in the United States reached its peak, Witnesses who owned and operated businesses were targeted by protests and boycotts because their beliefs so offended some members of their communities. In 1936 public school authorities in Atlanta expelled Witness Dorothy Leoles, then a sixth-grader, after she refused to salute the American flag. (The Supreme Court of Georgia ultimately upheld her expulsion.[17]) Soon afterward, members of the Buckhead Klavern of the Ku Klux Klan picketed the hat-cleaning store owned by her father, a naturalized citizen who had been born in Greece. Terming his decision to impart his religious beliefs on his daughter "regrettable and inexcusable from every point of view," one Atlanta newspaper asserted that Leoles had gotten exactly what he deserved for instructing his daughter to refuse to honor the flag, for "withholding obeisance to the natural emblem is not a personal matter within the discretion of any individual to decide for himself." Largely because of the Klan's protest, Leoles was forced to sell his business. The new owner promptly unfurled an American flag outside the store and told a local newspaper that the establishment was now being run by "true Americans."[18]

Although Walter Gobitas and his family did not have to contend with the Ku Klux Klan, they did have to weather a prolonged boycott of the Economy Grocery after the Supreme Court ruled against them in spring 1940. Lillian Gobitas Klose laid the blame for the boycott on a local Catholic priest who reportedly urged his parishioners to avoid the Witnesses' store. "That was a hard one, because business fell off tremendously," she recalled. "One of the local churches boycotted our store, and oh, business fell off." His business in jeopardy from the boycott, Walter Gobitas fell behind on his mortgage, and he had to turn to his sister—ironically, a devout Roman Catholic—for loans. Her beneficence helped carry the family until the boycott "just wore out," as Lillian later put it, and business picked up again. In an account of the boycott, she recognized that her family, despite its struggles to stay financially solvent, had been fortunate. "More than a few Witness families . . . lost businesses and homes during those years," she remembered.[19]

Henry Hopper certainly did not think of himself as being a troublemaker. He was, he wrote in 1940, a tax-paying and law-abiding citizen who held "America's institutions in high honor unmatched elsewhere." Though he respected his country's government and treasured the freedoms it had traditionally safeguarded, Hopper would not salute the American flag; he was a Jehovah's Witness, and a dedicated one at that. Like most members of his faith, Hopper believed that he could best express his devotion to the Creator by heralding the teachings of the Scriptures on front porches and street corners. Hopper explained, "I accept the holy scriptures as the infallible word of God and conform my life wholly to them, to the best of my ability. My form of worship of the Creator is to go from door to door, telling the people that the kingdom for which Jesus taught his followers to pray is the only hope of the world." In the days following the Supreme Court's ruling in Gobitis, however, Hopper and his fellow Witnesses found it next to impossible to worship in public.[20] While proselytizing in Belleville, Illinois, on 15 June 1940, Hopper and eight other members of his faith were arrested and charged with violating an Illinois law prohibiting the sale of publications "criminally exposing the citizens of a race, color, creed or religion to contempt or derision which is productive of a breach of peace or riot." The offense was a misdemeanor and carried a fine of up to $200.[21]

The Witnesses' trial on those charges, slated for 27 June, proved to be the least of Henry Hopper's worries. On 17 June his wife visited a local relief agency and attempted to pick up the family's monthly grocery order and a parcel of secondhand clothing. Hopper, though trained as an electrician, had been out of work for some time because of a physical disability, and his family badly needed the food and clothing. But relief administrator Hugh Edwards, having heard of Hopper's arrest in downtown Belleville, refused to provide any of the materials. He told Hopper's startled wife that her family did not deserve relief from the county because, as he tersely put it, "you're against the government." Edwards later told a reporter that "when Hopper agrees to salute the flag like everyone else in St. Clair County, then he can have relief again. Until then, he's not going to get any of the taxpayers' money."[22] Local Witnesses loudly decried Edwards's actions to various local and state relief officials, and Hopper himself asked Illinois governor Henry Horner to intervene. "I am appealing to you as governor of the state of Illinois to use your influence to see that justice is performed," he wrote in September 1940, three months after Edwards cut off his relief. "I have a wife and five children . . . and they are in desperate need."[23]

Claiming that it was sadly indicative of the suffering of Witnesses throughout the United States, the *Christian Century* reported on Hopper's plight in an editorial, "Starvation into Patriotism." The journal noted that Hopper and his family "have been cut off the relief rolls and will get no more grocery orders until they salute the flag. Such procedure on the part of the authorities would be understandable in Germany. There a man either gives the nazi salute and votes *Ja* when ordered or else he starves." That the Witnesses could suffer from similar abuse in a democracy such as the United States, which so frequently touted its reputation for tolerance, was cause for alarm. And, as the *Century* ruefully noted, the mistreatment of Hopper and his family because of their religious beliefs was by no means an isolated incident for the "ignorant members of this superstitious cult." In the United States, "more than a thousand of their number have suffered physical violence in recent months. Hundreds have had their children banned from the schools, have been cut off from employment and denied relief. All in the name of freedom? . . . Today they are suffering more than any religious minority in the last century of American history."[24] The *St. Louis Post-Dispatch* took up Hopper's cause as well. "The flag salute is a symbol of devotion to democracy," the paper argued in an editorial. "But democracy itself includes in its meaning full respect for every citizen's beliefs, no matter how peculiar, unless those beliefs infringe on the rights of others or the community's welfare. Those who insist on the symbol are losing sight of the substance."[25]

Perhaps no one knew that better than Henry Hopper. About a week after his relief benefits were terminated, he and the other eight Witnesses who had been arrested were found guilty of violating the state law prohibiting the sale of literature "producive of a breach of peace or riot," and they were fined fifty dollars each.[26] Hopper's woes continued in fall 1940, when his son Paul—together with classmates James and Marjorie Baugher, who also were Witnesses—was expelled from his public school after he refused to recite the Pledge of Allegiance or salute the flag. At a contentious school board hearing in October, the mother of the Baugher children relied on Watch Tower tracts, a Supreme Court opinion (most likely Justice Harlan Fiske Stone's dissent in *Gobitis*), and a recording of a speech by Witness leader Joseph Rutherford to help explain why the young Witnesses' faith prohibited them from participating in idolatry. "These children are not bad," said Marie Baugher, a former schoolteacher herself. "They refused to make a ceremony of saluting the flag because they know that all reverence belongs to God." No one had complained that the Witness children were disruptive, Baugher said, or that they had performed poorly in their classes; they were in trouble simply because they had eschewed a ritual that "was contrary to the will of God." After allowing Baugher to say her piece, the school board reaffirmed its decision to expel the Witness children from the Dewey School. The board had little choice but to banish the youngsters because, in the words of its chair, Paul Schrader, "There is no way in which we . . . can excuse a child for an infraction of the rules. We have no desire to dictate to parents what religion to follow, but we will dictate behavior of their children while in school." As the meeting broke up, Hopper made a last-ditch effort to change Schrader's mind, but he was rebuffed. A short time later, the *St. Louis Post-Dispatch* reported that the three young Witnesses were being taught by Marie Baugher in her home.[27]

Caught in a maelstrom of religious discrimination in the early and mid-1940s, numerous Witness families throughout the country shared the Hoppers' predicament. Bigotry harmed not only adults who were struggling to provide for their families but also scores of children who were simply trying to master the basics of learning in public schools. Although their case against the Minersville School

District was probably the most notable of the era, William and Lillian Gobitas were only two of hundreds of Witness children who were expelled for failing to participate in flag-salute exercises. "It is estimated," the American Civil Liberties Union reported in 1942, "that several thousand children have been expelled in the last five years and have been forced to receive very inferior instruction for the sake of conscience."[28] The Witnesses themselves claimed that flag-salute expulsions took place in every state of the Union and that a total of more than 2,000 Witness youngsters had been forced out of public schools by 1943.

It is worth noting that Witness children in some tolerant communities were allowed to remain in public schools without having to compromise their faith. For instance, the school board in Wahoo, Nebraska, adopted a resolution in late 1942 proclaiming "that those children who by reason of religious belief are unable to comply with this [flag-salute] requirement may be deemed to show full respect to the flag when the Pledge of Allegiance is being recited by facing the flag and standing respectfully at attention."[29] A similar agreement was reached late in 1940 in Rochester, Michigan, after school authorities suspended nearly twenty Witness students for failing to participate in the Pledge of Allegiance. In what the ACLU termed "a workable solution," a local judge formulated an agreement whereby Witness students would participate in a separate nonsaluting ceremony and simply omit the words "the flag" when reciting the pledge (and thus avoid committing idolatry). The judge, Arthur Moore, said that he was compelled to broker the compromise because it was "unfortunate and unnecessary that any American child be torn between love of his God and allegiance to his country." Many Witness children suffered, though, when such compromises could not be reached and their families were forced to scramble to provide schooling for them.[30]

As the dispute between the Gobitas family and the Minersville School District demonstrated, Witnesses sometimes responded to expulsions by challenging the constitutionality of flag-salute measures in court. The *Gobitis* case, which was key in touching off the persecution of Jehovah's Witnesses in summer 1940, was the most prominent among numerous suits brought by Witnesses when their children were expelled from public schools. Yet one significant early challenge came in Lynn, Massachusetts, in 1935, when school

A Kingdom School established by Jehovah's Witnesses in Gates, Pennsylvania, after students were expelled from local public schools.

authorities expelled Witness Carleton Nicholls after he refused to salute the flag. Nicholls, a young firebrand, contended that he would not pay tribute to "the Devil's emblem," and his father rose to his defense, arguing, "The Scriptures prove the truth of my assertion that this world, this country, this entire worldly kingdom, is not possessed by any government or any country, but by the Devil. . . . Why, then, should I, or my son, pledge allegiance to the Devil's kingdom?" The youngster had other champions as well, including Joseph Rutherford and Edward H. James, nephew of novelist Henry James and Harvard psychologist William James. (At a protest staged in Nicholls's classroom, James dramatically announced, "Like my ancestors, I will not submit to tyranny." Shortly thereafter, he was hauled off to jail.[31]) With the encouragement of the ACLU, Nicholls's family brought suit against Lynn's mayor and the city's school board, claiming that the flag-salute regulation violated the young Witness's rights under the state and federal constitutions. The Supreme Judicial Court of Massachusetts thought otherwise, and in April 1937 it handed the Witnesses a stinging defeat. Specifically addressing the constitutionality of the school committee's flag-salute regulation and the state law empowering the committee itself, the court ruled that the measures were "well within the competency of legislative authority. They exact nothing in opposition to religion. They are directed to a justifiable end in the conduct of education in the public schools."[32]

Adverse rulings such as *Nicholls v. Mayor and School Committee of Lynn* and *Minersville School District v. Gobitis* were typical of the Witnesses' initial lack of success in challenging the constitutionality of flag-salute regulations in court. Between 1937 and 1940, when the Supreme Court handed down its watershed opinion in *Gobitis*, Witnesses came up short in an abysmal succession of flag-salute cases in state courts in Georgia, New Jersey, California, and New York, among other states. One stern rebuke came from the Florida Supreme Court, which in 1939 upheld the suspensions of Witness Fred Bleich's six children from public schools in Lutz, a small town near Tampa. The court all but mocked the core of the Witnesses' argument against the flag salute. "To symbolize the Flag as a graven image and to ascribe to the act of saluting it a species of idolatry," the opinion held, "is too vague and far fetched to be even tinctured with the flavor of reason." It suggested that should "an objection as remote from religious grounds" as the one offered by Bleich's family be sustained by the courts, "then there is no limit to the reasons that conscientious objectors may advance as grounds for avoiding patriotic duties." In time, the Witnesses scored some stunning victories in flag-salute cases, but not before they suffered a number of humiliating defeats like *State ex rel. Bleich v. Board of Public Instruction.* Such disheartening rulings kept Witness children out of public schools for years and forced their already hard-pressed families to make even greater sacrifices.[33]

More disturbing than the expulsions themselves were the unsparing measures taken afterward by local authorities to punish entire Witness families. Following the dismissals of youngsters who failed to salute the flag, both the children and their parents sometimes became targets for extraordinary prosecutions. These additional charges often carried severe penalties, and the Witnesses resisted them vigorously in court. In fall 1940, for instance, public school officials in Nashua, New Hampshire, expelled Roland, Loretta, and Loraine Lefebvre "because of a refusal to salute the flag on grounds of religious conscience," their mother recalled. The family was simply too poor to pay for private schooling, and so their parents felt they had little choice but to take the youngsters' education into their own hands. As their mother, Gertrude Lefebvre, put it, "they were tutored at home" for several months. This experiment came to an abrupt end late in 1940, when the public school's attendance officer filed a complaint charging the Lefebvre children with delinquency. It was no trifling charge. Municipal Court Judge Frank Clancy found the children guilty and ordered them committed to the State Industrial School in Manchester until they reached their twenty-first birthdays. (Roland Lefebvre was then fifteen years old; Loraine, twelve; and Loretta, ten.) Horrified by the prospect of losing custody of their children, the Lefebvres appealed to the Superior Court of Hillsborough County, which upheld Clancy's order.[34] The children were dispatched to the state reformatory, "where they received no school instruction," their mother complained.[35]

After the superior court upheld Clancy's grim ruling, the Witnesses appealed to the Supreme Court of New Hampshire. From the outset, it demonstrated more compassion for the Lefebvres than the lower courts had, remanding Roland, Loraine, and Loretta to the custody of their parents while the appeal was pending. In their appeal, the Witnesses were aided by a hard-hitting amicus curiae brief filed by the American Civil Liberties Union. In urging the court to dismiss the delinquency complaint, the brief assailed Nashua's motivation for prosecuting the Witnesses:

> It is specious to suggest that the Lefebvre children are charged with delinquency merely because of their non-attendance at school. . . . It is because of their personal religious convictions that Roland, Loraine and Loretta Lefebvre are now threatened with separation from their parents and confinement in the State Industrial School as delinquents.

To permit authorities to further punish young Witnesses after they already had been expelled, the ACLU warned, "would be to deny the rights of minorities and the American principle of religious toleration."[36] The court, in an opinion handed down in May 1941, essentially agreed with the ACLU's arguments and dismissed the complaints against the Lefebvre children. Disturbed by the severity of the punishment that the Witnesses had suffered, the court held that "in view of the sacredness in which the State has always held freedom of religious conscience, it is impossible for us to attribute to the legislature an intent to authorize the breaking up of family life for no other reason than because some of its members have conscientious scruples not shared by the majority of the community."[37]

The ACLU was hopeful that the "important" ruling in *Lefebvre v. New Hampshire* would establish a precedent and "affect many similar situations in many parts of the country. . . . This case raises a new question, as to whether children, after they have been expelled from public school by the authorities, can then be sentenced as delinquents or habitual truants, and treated as criminals because of their non-attendance at school."[38] Although the Witnesses and the ACLU hailed the court's ruling, the youngsters were still barred from Nashua's public schools. At the urging of Gertrude Lefebvre (who confessed to being "very anxious for my children to complete their education"), the youngsters tried to return to classes in the semester after the court handed down its ruling. "In September, 1941, another attempt was made to send these children to school," a disappointed Gertrude Lefebvre wrote, "but the authorities refused to accept them unless they changed their stand in regard to saluting the flag, which they could not do without violating their consciences."[39]

Courts in New York and Massachusetts resolved delinquency and truancy cases similar to *Lefebvre*, and the results for the Witnesses were mixed—the Witnesses' expulsions stood, but they were not further penalized for their refusals to salute the American flag. On 22 October 1940, nine-year-old Witness Doris Jones balked at saluting the flag at her public school in Watertown, New York. Testifying later about her decision to violate a school regulation mandating participation in flag-salute exercises, Jones explained, "I have been taught that saluting the flag is against God's law and anyone who breaks God's law will be slain on Armageddon, and will not be resurrected. I would die." That the young Witnesses' fears were vivid and genuine mattered little to school authorities in Watertown: they not only expelled Jones but also charged her as a delinquent for having failed to obey her school's flag-salute regulation. A judge in the Jefferson County Children's Court conceded that the city's school board had the authority to expel Jones and wondered aloud about the "nonsense" of the Witnesses' beliefs regarding the flag salute. "I am at a loss to understand, as are all reasonable people," he wrote, "why anyone would refuse to salute the flag of the United States, and I think everyone ought to salute it." Yet the judge was reluctant to subject Jones to additional censure beyond expulsion simply because she had chosen her faith (however misguided it was) over the dictates of the school board. In dismissing the delinquency charge, he wrote:

> This little nine-year-old girl finds herself in this position: She has been taught by her parents and the religious society to which she belongs that if she salutes the flag, God will punish her; the school authorities say if she does not salute the flag, the State will punish her. She chooses to obey her God. Is this delinquency? I say no.[40]

Another New York case from the same period yielded much the same result as *In re Jones*. In May 1941 a state appellate court reversed an Onondaga County Children's Court ruling that Anson Reed, an eight-year-old Witness who had resisted flag-salute ceremonies at his public school, was a delinquent.[41]

Three children from a single Witness family in Massachusetts were charged with delinquency as well, and their case went to that state's highest court in 1941. Beginning in September 1938, three of William Johnson's children refrained from saluting the flag at their public school in Deerfield, Massachusetts, because, according to the Supreme Judicial Court of Massachusetts, they "sincerely and honestly believe that to participate in the exercise . . . contravenes the law of Almighty God." Polite and respectful, the Johnson children were not regarded as discipline problems by their teachers, and they "have always been respectful in their refusal to take part in the exercise, and have been studious, industrious, obedient, and well-behaved children in every other respect." Though sincere and well-behaved, the youngsters were expelled and eventually charged with being "habitual school offenders by reason of persistently violating the reasonable regulations of the school they attended," the court observed. In part because of the precedent established in Massachusetts by the *Nicholls* case, the Johnsons' attempt to contest the expulsions failed, but they were more successful in battling the delinquency charges, which carried a burdensome penalty much like that faced by the Lefebvre children in New Hampshire—separation from their parents and commitment to the Hampden County Training School. A judge in the Franklin County Superior Court found the children guilty, but the supreme judicial court reversed the verdicts. Though still barred from public schools in Deerfield, the Johnson children were not dispatched to a state reformatory simply because they had held fast to their religious faith.[42]

After their children were barred from public schools, four pairs of Witness parents in Clallam County, Washington, including Edward Bolling and his wife, were threatened with the loss of custody of their children. The school authorities having rejected their proposed alternative to saluting the flag (like most Witnesses, they had been willing to stand at attention during Pledge of Allegiance ceremonies), the Bollings' three children were expelled from public schools. The youngsters were subsequently charged as delinquents because their parents failed to enroll them in an accredited school after their expulsions. Then, citing the children's purported delinquency, a county superior court judge ruled that Edward Bolling and his wife had "neglected and refused to provide or permit proper training and education," as required by state law. The judge declared the Witness children wards of the state and temporarily placed them in the custody of their older sister, Hazel Tarr.

Three other Witness families in the county—the Fullers, Grittmans, and Parrs—also faced the prospect of being broken up as the result of flag-salute expulsions. These Witness families appealed to the Supreme Court of Washington, and it ruled on their cases early in 1943. In its opinion in *Bolling v. Superior Court for Clallam County*, the court maintained that "respect for our flag as a symbol of our country is part of our way of life, and disrespect to the flag constitutes an offense against our laws." That said, the court acknowledged that the Witnesses, despite their refusal to offer a formal salute to the flag, had shown a genuine willingness to demonstrate their respect for it by standing at attention during the Pledge of Allegiance. Deeply committed to their faith, they failed to salute simply "because of their conscientious scruples." To punish them for acting upon such beliefs, the court held, would be to circumscribe their religious freedom in a manner that had proved nothing short of disastrous throughout the course of human history. The court noted in its opinion,

Too often in times past, persons in authority, who were sincerely convinced that they knew and believed the truth, have felt themselves justified in persecuting persons holding different opinions, believing that the truth should avail itself of all means at its disposal, including the strength of the secular arm, in order to enforce belief, or at least conformity.

Given the protections of religious freedom afforded by the state constitution, authorities in Clallam County could not be allowed similarly to target Witnesses because of their faith. The custody orders against the four Witness families were reversed, and the court also held that the state's compulsory flag-salute law could not be enforced against Witness schoolchildren.[43]

In some communities, parents of expelled Witness schoolchildren were targeted for prosecution as well. Broad attempts to punish these mothers and fathers were contemplated by legislators in several states, including New Hampshire and Rhode Island. In February 1941, State Representative Earle Byrne introduced a bill in the Rhode Island Assembly that was specifically aimed at punishing those parents who "influence or attempt to influence any school pupil in this state against the salute to the flag of the United States of America by instruction printed or otherwise." A misdemeanor, this new offense would be punishable by a fine of up to $100 or as much as three months in jail. When Byrne's bill found its way to the assembly's education committee in April 1941, the American Civil Liberties Union protested emphatically. In a letter to the committee, the ACLU condemned the measure as an unprecedented infringement on the Witnesses' religious liberty and requested that it be "adversely reported"—that is, killed—by the committee. "It is grotesque," the ACLU claimed, "that of all the states in the union Rhode Island, the cradle of religious liberty, should entertain a proposal to make any religious belief a crime." If enacted, Byrne's bill would have catastrophic results: according to the ACLU, the measure would "make a criminal out of every loyal member of Jehovah's Witnesses, the one religious organization which consistently refuses to salute the flag, basing its opposition on religious grounds." Moreover, the bill was "doubtless unconstitutional," and the Witnesses who were certain to contest it in court would be assured of prevailing. Lest anyone doubt the seriousness of the ACLU's opposition, the protest was sent out over the signatures of the organization's three most prominent leaders, John Haynes Holmes, Arthur Garfield Hays, and Roger Baldwin.[44]

When the assembly's education committee announced that it would hold a public hearing on the flag-salute measure, the ACLU encouraged civil libertarians to attend and express their disapproval. Not everyone was enthusiastic about so publicly rushing to the Witnesses' defense. John Baker, a Providence attorney, told Roger Baldwin that he too opposed the bill, which was "silly" and "unnecessary." Yet Baker declined to voice his reservations about the flag-salute bill in public because he could not "become excited about it as something aimed at the destruction of civil liberty." In their "mistaken zeal," Baker asserted, the quarrelsome Witnesses were undermining "a reasonable and important point of national decorum and respect," and it was well within the bounds of the state's authority to try to quell such destructive behavior.[45]

Luckily, Baker's ambivalence was not widely shared among civil libertarians in the Providence area, and several of them appeared at the hearing and offered eloquent testimony against the bill. Among those decrying the measure was S. R. Mayer-Oakes, a minister from Providence who "stated that those who were interested in civil liberties were convinced that passage of the bill would arouse religious antagonism, because it infringed on civil liberties," as he later reported to Baldwin. In part because of such strenuous opposition, the ACLU's strong campaign helped to doom the flag-salute bill. After the hearing, the education committee's chair told Mayer-Oakes that "the bill would not be reported out," and it died before reaching the floor of the assembly.[46]

But even without the benefit of laws directly targeting Witness parents whose children failed to salute the flag, authorities in some communities went out of their way to punish them. For example, after their children violated flag-salute regulations at their public schools, several Witness parents were charged with disorderly conduct, contributing to the delinquency of minors, and other offenses. Witnesses like Charles and Hilda Sandstrom responded to their convictions under such charges by appealing to higher courts. Following the expulsion of their daughter Grace from a public school in Suffolk County, New York, the Sandstroms were charged with having unlawfully kept the youngster out of school. Arthur Garfield Hays, who

defended the Witnesses in court, later commented that the atmosphere at the trial "was not unlike that of Dayton, Tennessee, during
the Scopes trial." (Coming from Hays, this was no idle comparison:
he had been part of John Scopes's defense team during the famed
"monkey trial.") A number of Witnesses sat in the gallery, and because of their frequent outbursts the "proceedings were punctuated
by 'Amens' and 'Blessed be the Lord,'" Hays wrote. Though skeptical
of the tenets of the Witnesses' faith, Hays worked diligently throughout the trial to give them the opportunity to demonstrate the sincerity of their beliefs. Hoping to highlight the Witnesses' earnestness, he engaged in a revealing colloquy with Grace Sandstrom.

> Hays: Why is it you don't salute the flag?
> Sandstrom: Because the flag is an image, and it says in the Bible
> not to bow down to images.
> Hays: Do you love your country?
> Sandstrom: Yes.
> Hays: Do you believe in obeying the laws of your country?
> Sandstrom: Yes, laws that are not in conflict with God's laws.
> Hays: When those are in conflict with God's laws, you would
> obey your conscience?
> Sandstrom: Yes.

Hays was less solicitous of Daniel Terry, the principal who had
expelled the young Witness, asking him at one point, "Do you believe in freedom of religion?"[47] Despite Hays's efforts, the jury returned guilty verdicts against both parents, but they were overturned by a state appeals court. "In like cases where this same
question has arisen, the procedure has always been to expel the student, not to punish the parents unless they in some way have disobeyed the law," the court held. The appeals court did not, however,
doubt the appropriateness of flag-salute regulations such as the one
enforced at Grace Sandstrom's school, and its reticence on that score
was assailed in a concurring opinion. "The salute of the flag is a
gesture of love and respect—fine when there is real love and respect
back of the gesture. The flag is dishonored," the concurrence argued,
"by a salute by a child in reluctant and terrified obedience to a command of secular authority which clashes with the dictates of conscience."[48]

In 1942, the poignant concurrence in *People v. Sandstrom* was cited approvingly by the New Jersey Supreme Court in a case involving Francesco and Raffaele Latrecchia, Witness parents who lived in Fair Lawn, New Jersey. Mario and Josephine, the Latrecchia's teenaged children, were expelled from their public school after they failed to take part in daily flag-salute ceremonies. "The parents were too poor to provide private education," according to the American Civil Liberties Union, and so the youngsters were taught in a makeshift arrangement at their home on Third Street in Fair Lawn. Because Mario and Josephine did not regularly attend an accredited school, their parents eventually were charged with being disorderly persons, and they were convicted in the Juvenile and Domestic Relations Court of Bergen County. The ACLU filed one of its customarily adroit amicus curiae briefs when the Latrecchias appealed their convictions to New Jersey's highest court in 1942. The brief pointed to the *Lefebvre* and *Sandstrom* rulings as apt precedents, and, pressing the larger issue of the constitutionality of the mandatory flag-salute measures, it argued that the state could not hope to foster patriotism in Witnesses "by attempting to coerce them into performing an act which is as repulsive to them as other acts are considered sinful by Catholics, Protestants, and Jews."[49] In a terse ruling, the New Jersey Supreme Court set aside the Latrecchias' convictions. "Liberty of conscience," the court held, "is not subject to uncontrolled administrative action."[50] Witness parents in Illinois faced charges similar to the ones that were dismissed in *Latrecchia*, and they also prevailed in an appeal to their state's highest court.[51]

E. V. and Naomi Davis, Witnesses who lived in Arizona, were less fortunate. After their children—Thelma, age eleven, and Wayne, age nine—were expelled for violating the mandatory flag-salute regulation at their public school, the couple apparently failed to enroll them in an accredited school. Authorities in Maricopa County charged the parents with contributing to the delinquency of minors, and they faced up to a year in prison and a fine of up to $350. Their crime: that by teaching their children the tenets of their faith, they "did . . . teach, instruct, direct and command" their children to refuse to salute the American flag, leading to their expulsions and eventual delinquency from school. The Witnesses were found guilty in a county circuit court, and the Supreme Court of Arizona heard their appeal in 1942. In its opinion in *State v. Davis*, the court noted that the Witness couple had been charged with conduct that "tends to debase and injure the morals, health and welfare" of their children, an accusation they refuted by claiming that "it is their sincere religious belief that to salute the flag of the United States, as required by the school laws and regulations, is an act of idolatry." The Witnesses' argument fell flat with the court, and it upheld their convictions as well as the state's right to enforce flag-salute regulations. In a rebuke to the Witnesses, the court held:

> The vast majority of our people believe, and we think correctly so, that the salute to the flag, which typifies our country and the principles upon which it is founded, is a wise, reasonable and patriotic exercise and that it is in the interest of the welfare of the children of the country that they participate in this simple exercise, and that a failure to follow the most universal custom in this respect does tend to injure the morals and future welfare of the children in ways too numerous to mention.

According to the court's opinion, efforts made by parents to instruct their children "to refuse to follow the national custom" of flag-saluting did in fact "contribute to the delinquency of the child" and could be punished without violating the First or Fourteenth Amendments.[52]

In part because their faith was so widely unpopular, some Witness parents also became embroiled in custody disputes with their non-Witness spouses. Like the prosecutions of parents of expelled Witness schoolchildren, these cases often boiled down to the specious contention that Witnesses were neglectful or "unfit" parents simply because they attempted to pass on the tenets of their religious faith to their children. When she divorced her husband Melvin in spring 1943, Kathleen Cory was awarded custody of the couple's two young children. A year later, Melvin Cory, hoping to gain custody of the youngsters, filed a motion in court alleging that his former wife was unfit to be a parent because she was a zealous Witness. At a superior court hearing in the case, a judge grilled Kathleen Cory about her beliefs and their potentially damaging influence on the children. After she informed him that she would teach her children to respect but not to salute the American flag, the judge probed the Witness's position on a variety of other topics, including the current war.

"Would you teach them that it was against your religion to go to war," he asked, "that they should not support the war?" Yes, Cory said. "In other words," the judge continued, "you would bring the children up so they would be I presume what we call conscientious objectors against the war?" Cory again agreed, noting, "The Bible tells us, 'Thou Shalt Not Kill.'" Her outline of the contours of her faith clearly troubled the judge, and he subsequently awarded custody of the children to Melvin Cory on the ground that he would provide a more "fit and proper" environment for the youngsters, even though no evidence of actual neglect had been introduced in court.[53] The ruling stupefied Clifford Forster, and he complained that "courts are discriminating against Jehovah's Witnesses solely for their religious views." Kathleen Cory agreed and appealed the lower-court ruling.[54]

The Supreme Court of Washington resolved a custody battle much like Kathleen Cory's, and its ruling provided her with a measure of encouragement as she went through her appeal. Lettie Stone, a Jehovah's Witness, divorced her husband on grounds of cruelty and neglect. Mack Stone, described in court documents as having been "indifferent" to his children during the rocky marriage, then claimed that his former wife was unfit to raise their children because her Witness beliefs threatened their well being. Washington's highest court refused to countenance that argument, and custody of the children was awarded to Lettie Stone. "We do not doubt the right of the state to suppress religious practices dangerous to morals . . . and presumably those also which are inimical to public safety, health and good order," the court held, "but so far as appears from the testimony in this case, the teachings of the Jehovah's Witnesses cannot, in our opinion, be classified in any of these categories."[55]

As Kathleen Cory had hoped, a California appeals court reached a similar conclusion and reversed the grant of custody to her former husband. As it attempted to explain why the trial court had so clearly "exceeded the bounds of wise judicial discretion" and stripped Kathleen Cory of custody, the appeals court speculated that the judge might have been swayed by a misguided sense of patriotism and "not unnatural irritation" with the Witnesses' provocative beliefs regarding the flag salute and the war. But in doing so, the appellate court concluded, the lower court had "lost sight of the constitutional provisions which guarantee religious freedom to all."[56]

7. Boundless Courage and Unending Perseverance

When he looked back on his marriage, Newton Cantwell believed that it had thrived because he shared with his wife a set of beliefs and ambitions that were grounded in an unwavering devotion to God. "Both of us," he recalled, "from an early age had entertained a strong desire to be serviceable to God and an aid to our fellow men," particularly those unfortunate souls who were ignorant of the lessons of the Scriptures. Moreover, long before their marriage in 1907, both Newton and Esther shared what he called "early misgivings about the teachings of Christendom's churches," teachings that seemed to be fundamentally at odds with their understanding of the mandates of the Bible. Ill at ease with the tenets of mainstream religions, the Cantwells joined the Jehovah's Witnesses (who were then still known as Bible Students) in the early 1900s. They quickly became ardent students of the Scriptures and avid proselytizers.[1]

As their commitment to their faith grew, the Cantwells made some enormous temporal sacrifices. In the depths of the Great Depression, Newton Cantwell considered selling his farm and accepting an attractive offer to become the manager of a well-funded experimental farm in Tennessee. Around this same time, he also weighed the possibility of focusing all his energies on full-time Witness work. "A family conference was held," Russell Cantwell, one of Newton's sons, recalled, "and after prayerful consideration we agreed to sell the farm and place full trust in Jehovah to provide." With his family's blessing, Newton Cantwell passed up the manager's position and sold the farm at a huge loss; he would fully devote himself to witnessing and make it his life's work. Then tragedy struck, and the Cantwells' faith was momentarily shaken: "An illness in the family took every cent Dad had, leaving us 'broke,'" according to Russell. The resilient family pressed on, scrambling to make ends meet and still nurturing their faith in God. Through it all, Newton Cantwell recalled, they remained confident "that Jehovah would provide as long as we diligently carried out our service." Newton Cantwell's mettle during this crisis left a lasting impression on his son. Though troubled by his financial setback and the havoc it wreaked, the elder Cantwell "said there was only one thing to do, and that was to stay in the full-time witnessing work," Russell later wrote. "This determination and firm resolve . . . strengthened my desire to serve Jehovah." He was so inspired by his steadfast father that he began witnessing in earnest at age fourteen.[2]

The family moved to Tennessee in the early 1930s. "Those were times of depression . . . so that people in general did not have much money," Newton Cantwell recalled. "This meant exchanging literature for all kinds of things—fruits, vegetables, canned goods, grain, and so forth." In time, Newton took to bartering Witness literature for produce and groceries, and so the family "never did have a food problem." If food was plentiful at the Cantwells' table, it also tended to lack variety; as Russell later wrote, "Sometimes we might eat the same menu for several days and desire something more." The children, though, were well aware that many of their neighbors went to bed hungry every evening, and there were few complaints. Resourceful as well as devout, Newton and his sons improvised to keep the family's three cars running every day. The boys mastered auto repair, and their father haggled with gas station operators for cheap fuel. The primitive conditions of local roads—many were unpaved and riddled with potholes—posed perhaps the biggest logistical problem for the Cantwells when they proselytized. Ruts caused innumerable flat tires and more serious mishaps. "On one occasion one of our cars rolled over and was demolished," Newton recalled. "But there was no thought of turning back. We managed to buy a replacement and carry on." They endured such misadventures and proselytized throughout Tennessee, Kentucky, and Virginia.[3]

The family started attending Witness conventions in 1930, when it traveled to a small but lively conclave in Chattanooga, Tennessee. Newton Cantwell welcomed the opportunity to meet with other Witnesses, and he took the family to conventions whenever he could. The trips weren't merely respites for the family; Newton believed that they played a key role in sustaining and reinvigorating his faith. "It has always been a pleasure to attend conventions and experience the strength derived from association with thousands of our fellow members," he wrote near the end of his life. "And especially is this so when one's regular scene of activity is in isolated rural areas." At a Witness convention held in Columbus, Ohio, in 1937, the family learned that Newton had been selected as a "special pioneer" and thus would be, as he later wrote, "assisted financially by the Watch Tower Society to maintain a well-organized campaign of education." With the new position came another move, this time to New Haven, Connecticut, and a host of new challenges. He recalled, "Both physical and spiritual endurance were now necessary. Imagine our situation after spending many years in the warm South, and now [we were] exposed to the bitter winters of the New England coast!" Having already weathered their share of calamities, the Cantwells tackled their new task with their customary vigor. Bundled up against the elements, they quickly adapted themselves to proselytizing in an urban setting.[4]

From the outset, Newton Cantwell realized that his family had far more to more worry about in Connecticut than the climate. In New Haven, he later wrote, "there was considerable religious opposition to our preaching activities," which many viewed as disruptive, irreligious, and un-American. Well aware of their unpopularity, the Cantwells were prepared to encounter trouble whenever they ventured out in public to worship. New Haven's police force was particularly antagonistic. "Each time we went out in our ministerial work in this new assignment," Newton Cantwell remembered, "it was with the realization that we might be subjected to unjust arrest. In fact, we were arrested on many occasions."[5]

Their most memorable confrontation with police came on 26 April 1938 when they attempted to proselytize in a predominantly Roman Catholic neighborhood in New Haven. Newton, Russell, and Jessie, another of the Cantwell children, offered Witness literature to homeowners and passersby. At one point, Jessie Cantwell hailed two men, John Ganley and John Cafferty, and played for them a recording of a speech by Joseph Rutherford that was meant to complement the text of his book *Enemies*. Both Ganley and Cafferty were Catholics, and they were outraged to hear Rutherford pillorying their faith. Ganley was so incensed by the recording that he considered striking the young Witness, but in the end he and Cafferty merely advised Jessie Cantwell to take his fiery propaganda elsewhere. Cantwell wasn't spoiling for a fight; he moved on and continued to worship. Meanwhile, Russell Cantwell preached in vain to a woman named Anna Rigby. When Cantwell appeared at her doorstep and offered her a copy of the book *Riches*, Rigby was, as she later put it, "mad enough to hit him if he did not go away." (She had been offered the book previously by another Witness proselytizer, and she felt that it contained outrageous attacks on the Roman Catholic Church.)[6]

Her patience exhausted, Rigby complained to the New Haven police, and they arrested Newton Cantwell and his sons for soliciting money for a charitable or religious cause without having first received approval from the state's public welfare council. The three Witnesses also faced charges that they "did disturb the public tranquility by certain acts or conduct inciting to violence or tending to provoke or excite others . . . to break the peace." (Decades later, Newton Cantwell bitterly recalled that he and his boys had been arrested for "disturbing the Catholic peace by playing phonograph records in the homes of persons willing to hear them.") A local jury found the Cantwells guilty, and Connecticut's highest court, dismissing the Witnesses' contention that the permit requirement violated their rights under the First and Fourteenth Amendments, affirmed their convictions for violating the permit regulation. Only Jessie Cantwell's conviction for disturbing the peace, however, was upheld; for want of evidence, the court threw out Newton and Russell Cantwell's convictions on that count.[7]

Russell Cantwell later wrote that "although hundreds of our Christian brothers and sisters had been arrested on various occasions, the Watch Tower Society decided to use our case to test the validity of the state law."[8] In their appeal to the U.S. Supreme Court, the Cantwells were represented by Hayden Covington, who handled as many as fifty major cases every year as the persecution of Jehovah's Witnesses reached its apogee in the early and mid-1940s. Years of defending Witnesses against spurious charges eventually convinced Covington that "the legal machinery—at the municipal and state levels—was set up to convert the country to totalitarianism." With the advent of war, many states and cities enacted "a weight of barnacle-like statutes and ordinances" that "virtually nullified the Bill of Rights and wallowed the Constitution in an undemocratic sea," Covington said. For Witnesses, whose public form

Jehovah's Witness attorney Hayden Covington reviewing a brief.

of worship was predicated on the basic democratic freedoms guaranteed by the Bill of Rights, the enactment and sometimes overzealous enforcement of such restrictive measures represented a dire threat. "So they contested legally, full scale, all the way through, the application of these laws," Covington proudly explained. "Their action served like a sieve to strain out insidious by-laws that were cluttering up freedom of worship, speech, and press. Not only for them. But for everybody alike—whether it was realized or not." A graduate of the San Antonio Bar Association School of Law (later St. Mary's University School of Law), Covington was deeply involved in many of these efforts, drafting briefs and delivering oral arguments in numerous state and federal courts. Most significant Witness cases in the early and mid-1940s, as well as innumerable minor ones, bore his imprimatur.[9]

Unleashed in a courtroom, Covington could be a whirlwind. A

brief profile published in *Newsweek* in 1943, marveling at his ath-
letic delivery of oral arguments, compared him to a cyclone. As the
magazine's report noted, Covington was nothing if not blunt when
he championed the rights of Witnesses like Newton Cantwell and
his family before the nation's highest court.

> A precedent-buster extraordinary, the 6-foot lawyer erupted into
> the austere chamber in a bright green suit with padded shoulders
> and a red plaid tie. Linking his hands behind his back and bend-
> ing his body into a right angle, or tucking his thumbs into his
> green vest and lifting his head, he roared, first at the black-robed
> justices and then at the audience: "Jehovah's Witnesses are plain
> people who derive their authority to preach the truth from Jeho-
> vah himself, not from organized wealthy groups. Many of them
> are poor and uneducated." Then, glowering at Justice Murphy, a
> Catholic: "They don't preach in a dead language."

After watching the frenetic Witness attorney argue several cases in
the early 1940s, a Supreme Court clerk cracked, "He may not have
done more talking than anyone I've heard here, but he did more cal-
isthenics."[10] Although Covington's demeanor in the courtroom was
easy to mock, his record was one that any lawyer would envy. Between 1938 and 1955 he prevailed in more than two dozen cases
heard by the Supreme Court, a record that prompted one sympathetic historian to compare him to Thurgood Marshall, the vaunted
NAACP attorney who later served as solicitor general and as a Supreme Court justice.[11]

Covington couldn't help but think that the *Cantwell* case held
enormous promise for his faith. He hoped that a favorable ruling
from the Supreme Court would provide protection for hundreds of
Witnesses who were arrested every year under laws similar to the
permit measure that had been enforced against Newton Cantwell
and his sons. Covington's optimism was fueled by a pair of Supreme
Court rulings in earlier Witness cases. In *Lovell v. City of Griffin*
(1938), the Court had struck down a municipal ordinance requiring
distributors of printed materials to obtain written permission from
the city manager before they took to the streets. Reversing the conviction of Witness Alma Lovell, Chief Justice Charles Evans Hughes
wrote for a unanimous Court that the character of the Griffin ordi-

nance "strikes at the very foundation of the freedom of the press by subjecting it to license and censorship. . . . Legislation of the type of the ordinance in question would restore the system of license and censorship in its baldest form."[12] A year later, in *Schneider v. New Jersey* (1939), the Court had again struck down municipal ordinances regulating the distribution of printed materials, declaring that they violated the due process clause of the Fourteenth Amendment by placing prior restraints on the Witness plaintiffs' freedoms of speech and press.[13] By protecting the Witnesses' expressive activities from infringement by the states, these early cases had served as important steps in the piecemeal incorporation of First Amendment rights into the Fourteenth Amendment's due process clause, which applied explicitly to the states. (This process had begun in 1925 with *Gitlow v. New York*, in which the Court had made the First Amendment's protections of speech and press applicable to the states.[14]) In *Cantwell*, Covington saw an opportunity to continue the process of incorporation. Just as the Fourteenth Amendment prohibited states from placing prior restraints on press and speech freedoms, he argued, it also barred states from wielding measures like the Connecticut permit requirement to abridge the right to free exercise of religion.

As Covington had hoped, the Court decided to take the process of incorporation a step further by holding that the Connecticut permit requirement placed an unconstitutional burden on the Witnesses' free exercise of religion. Justice Owen Roberts noted in his majority opinion in *Cantwell v. Connecticut* that the free exercise clause of the First Amendment "embraces two concepts—freedom to believe and freedom to act. The first is absolute, but in the nature of things, the second cannot be." In certain well-defined circumstances, the state might have reasonable grounds to circumscribe First Amendment freedoms. In the interests of maintaining public order, the time, place, and manner of solicitation could be regulated. But "to condition the solicitation of aid for the perpetuation of religious views or systems upon a license," Roberts wrote, "the grant of which rests in the exercise of a determination by state authority as to what is a religious cause, is to lay a forbidden burden upon the exercise of liberty protected by the Constitution."[15]

The Court also reversed Jesse Cantwell's conviction for disturbing the peace. "No one would have the hardihood to suggest that the principle of freedom of speech sanctions incitement to riot," Roberts wrote, "or that religious liberty connotes the privilege to exhort others to physical attack upon those belonging to another sect." The Court held that Jesse Cantwell's conduct was not illegal because it obviously had not created the kind of "clear and present danger or riot, disorder, interference with traffic upon the public streets, or other immediate threat to public safety, peace, or order" that the state was empowered to prevent or punish. Although he might have annoyed the two Catholic men he had encountered on Cassius Street, Jesse's conduct had not posed an immediate threat to public safety; the record indicated "no assault or threatening of bodily harm, no truculent bearing, no intentional discourtesy, no personal abuse" on his part. "On the contrary," Roberts wrote, "we find only an effort to persuade a willing listener to buy a book or to contribute money in the interest of what Cantwell, however misguided others may think him, conceived to be true religion." Because such activity did not pose a "clear and present danger," the state had no grounds for prosecuting Jesse Cantwell for breaching the peace.[16]

When he reflected on the Supreme Court opinion that bore his family's name, Newton Cantwell was proud but characteristically modest, noting that the decision in *Cantwell v. Connecticut* represented but "one of many legal victories that Jehovah gave his people."[17] In fact, as they campaigned in the courts against religious discrimination in the 1930s and 1940s, Jehovah's Witnesses like the Gobitas children and Cantwell and his sons appealed more than two dozen times to the U.S. Supreme Court. During the course of that unprecedented burst of litigation, which resulted in twenty-three Supreme Court opinions between 1938 and 1946, the Witnesses catalyzed vital and enduring developments in constitutional jurisprudence. One recent study has gone so far as to describe their many appeals during that span as "turning points in the nation's constitutional commitment to individual rights," at least in part because they came at a pivotal moment in modern constitutional history.[18] Finally shifting some of its attention away from economic regulation, which had dominated its docket for decades, the Supreme Court had taken some tentative but important steps in the 1930s to safeguard individual and minority rights, and in the process it "quietly began to work on the agenda of the future," as David P. Currie has written.[19] In *United States v. Carolene Products* (1938), for instance, Justice Harlan Fiske Stone had suggested that the Court might apply a stricter standard of scrutiny to measures that appeared to infringe on the civil rights of members of minority groups. By appealing so often to the Supreme Court in the 1930s and 1940s, the Witnesses sustained this important trend and thus helped to set the stage for an era in which the Supreme Court took dramatic strides to protect civil liberties. One study of the Court has noted that "the great steps taken to protect civil rights in the Warren and Burger Courts would not have been possible without the debates and explorations of their predecessors" in the 1940s and early 1950s.[20] With their focus on basic democratic liberties, including freedom of speech and freedom of religion, Witness cases like *Gobitis* and *Cantwell* played an integral role in this period of discovery and transition for the Court.

At least one member of the Supreme Court acknowledged that the Witnesses' frequent appeals had compelled the Brethren to address matters they had long ignored. Writing to Chief Justice Hughes in 1941, a year after his seminal dissent in *Gobitis,* Justice Stone quipped, "I think the Jehovah's Witnesses ought to have an endowment in view of the aid which they give in solving the legal problems of civil liberties."[21] Even as they shook their heads at the Witnesses' unusual beliefs, observers outside the Supreme Court's chambers also applauded the burgeoning influence of pathbreaking appellants like Newton Cantwell and his sons. A 1942 law journal article lauded the efforts of the Witnesses who had been streaming into the Supreme Court, observing,

> Seldom, if ever, in the past, has one individual or group been able to shape the course, over a period of time, of any phase of our vast body of constitutional law. But it *can* happen, and it *has* happened, here. The group is Jehovah's Witnesses. Through almost constant litigation this organization has made possible an ever-increasing list of precedents concerning the application of the Fourteenth Amendment to freedom of speech and worship.[22]

A year later, A. L. Wirin, a civil libertarian who often defended the Witnesses' rights in court, remarked that their influence had not waned in 1943, thanks in part to their "boundless courage and unending perseverance" in sticking with their appeals until they reached the Supreme Court. According to Wirin, the Supreme Court's most recent term—in which it had handed down its watershed opinion in *West Virginia v. Barnette,* the second Witness flag-salute case—offered further proof that the Witnesses "had won more United States Supreme Court victories for the Bill of Rights than any other single group."[23]

Later assessments have commended the Witnesses' legal campaign as well. In the 1980s, a comprehensive survey of their cases asserted that the Witnesses had had "a profound and extensive impact on the development of our law," contributing to, among other advances, the development of the preferred position doctrine (whereby First Amendment freedoms are accorded special status among constitutional rights), the incorporation of the First Amendment into the due process clause of the Fourteenth Amendment, and the application of a strict scrutiny standard to measures appearing to infringe on minority rights. Acknowledging the long-term impact of the Witnesses' efforts, that study termed them "a catalyst for the evolution of constitutional law."[24] Melvin Urofsky, writing in his recent history of the Court under chief justices Stone and Vinson, similarly observed that the Witnesses "wrote a new chapter into First Amendment jurisprudence" in the early and mid-1940s.[25]

Hayden Covington was proud of noting that ordinary Witnesses like Newton Cantwell had "written their faith into the laws of the land" by calling upon the Supreme Court to protect their civil liberties.[26] To be sure, Covington's boast overstated the Witnesses' influence, but it also contained an undeniable kernel of truth. As William Leuchtenburg has argued in his account of the "constitutional revolution" wrought by the Supreme Court in the Roosevelt era, "it is doubtful that any organization in our history has . . . more affected the course of civil liberties than the Jehovah's Witnesses."[27] In the early and mid-1940s, at the very time they were being persecuted because of their purported anti-American sympathies, the Witnesses repeatedly invoked and ultimately helped to rejuvenate some of the most basic freedoms afforded by the Constitution. The legacy of their efforts—a more vibrant and durable Bill of Rights—has benefited Americans of all faiths for more than five decades.

In 1942, in the wake of the Japanese attack on Pearl Harbor and the formal entry of the United States into World War II, legislators in Mississippi considered two proposals meant to cripple, if not simply eliminate, Witness activities in that state. Unlike many of the anti-Witness measures formulated by city councils and state legislatures in the early and mid-1940s, which were often framed as efforts to combat subversion or foster patriotism, House Resolution no. 28 was nothing more than a brazenly straightforward attack on the Witnesses and their beliefs. Entitled "A House Resolution Declaring Open Season on Jehovah's Witnesses," it noted that "there exists [sic] certain groups of people known as Jehovah's Witnesses, who by spreading alien doctrines and ideals throughout the state are endangering the very fabric and foundation of our state." To mitigate that threat, the house was called upon to formally declare "an open season on all such persons known by the name of Jehovah's Witnesses, and the extermination and extinction of said persons shall be deemed an act meritorious and beneficial to the state. . . . It shall become the imperative duty of the citizenry of this state to exterminate all such persons upon sight." Fortunately for Mississippi's already beleaguered Witnesses, the resolution, which bore more than a passing resemblance to similarly oppressive measures being implemented in Nazi Germany, died in committee and thus never came up for a vote on the floor of the legislature. The fact that it had been introduced at all suggested, however, just how hostile some legislators were to their beliefs and practices.[28]

Although the "open season" measure foundered, Mississippi legislators were more receptive to an anti-Witness bill that was similar to one enacted in Louisiana in the same year. The measure was described in one official legislature publication as an "act to secure peace and safety of the United States and State of Mississippi during war; to prohibit acts detrimental to public peace and safety," but its primary purpose was to suppress Witness activities.[29] The American Civil Liberties Union asserted that some of the bill's provisions "are obviously aimed at the religious sect known as Jehovah's Witnesses." Among them was a ban on the dissemination of any material or the teaching of any principle "which reasonably tends to create an attitude of stubborn refusal to salute, honor or respect" the state or federal flags. The measure similarly prohibited the propagation of words or ideas "designed and calculated to encourage violence, sabotage, or disloyalty" to the state or federal governments. Violators could be jailed for a period of up to ten years, or until a peace treaty ended the current world war.[30] The state legislature passed the bill without much opposition, but at least one law-maker felt that it was "clearly unconstitutional." Appalled by some of its provisions, Rep. Charles G. Hamilton considered amending "the anti–Jehovah's Witness bill," as he called it, but he ultimately "decided it would be better to let the whole thing be unconstitutional" and thus open to a legal challenge by the ACLU.[31]

The American Civil Liberties Union, realizing that the bill posed an immense threat to civil liberties in Mississippi, pulled no punches in opposing what it called "the most sweeping statute aimed at opinion in American history." While acknowledging that state legislators might have had patriotic intentions in passing the bill, the ACLU argued that the measure "so violates constitutional rights as to be void on its face," and it urged Gov. Paul Johnson to exercise his veto. In a telegram to Johnson, Arthur Garfield Hays contended:

The bill . . . violates federal and possibly state guarantees by pe-nalizing speech and publication in absence of acts or incitements, and creates vague offenses open to all sorts of prejudiced con-struction. The bill also would nullify United States Supreme Court decisions in protecting religious liberties in cases of Jeho-vah's Witnesses. [The] bill contributes nothing to wartime pro-tections and would on the contrary arouse strife and persecution.

Disregarding the objections of civil libertarians, Governor John-son—who had ignored the pleas of the Witnesses who were eventu-ally driven from Jackson, Mississippi, in June 1940—signed the bill, and it became Chapter 178 of the Laws of 1942. "A small minority religious group has virtually been outlawed," the ACLU lamented, "under the guise of protecting the state and nation from sabotage." The ACLU was eager to see the new law struck down as unconsti-tutional, and it announced that it would defend any Witness who wished to challenge the measure in court. The ACLU, recognizing the futility of asking the legislature to repeal the law, conceded that "it will take a court proceeding to wipe it off the statute books."[32]

Otto and Roxie Mills provided the ACLU with an opportunity to strike down Chapter 178. The Witnesses were arrested in Lee County, Mississippi, and charged under the new law in March 1942 after they attempted to distribute copies of the Witness tract "God and the State." As the ACLU later reported in *Jehovah's Witnesses and the War*, the prosecution's strategy in the trial was relatively straightforward: with the war in the forefront of the jurors' minds, it hoped to make the defendants look as sinister and unpatriotic as possible. "Mr. Mills," the prosecutor asked at one point, "suppose the United States Army was coming down the streets of Tupelo, to defend your home, and you were standing on the sidewalk when the American flag passed, you tell this court that you would not honor that flag to the extent of saluting it?" Otto Mills said that he would not salute the flag under any circumstances, and he explained that he could not in good conscience support either side in the current war. Incredulous, the prosecutor sputtered, "You mean you are going to stay here and are going to get all the advantages the Government gives you, but you want the other man to do your fighting—then you are just not a fighting man when it comes to defending your home, or your wife, or your baby, or your country?" Although Mills put up a good fight in court, it did him little good; the jury convicted both him and his wife for violating Chapter 178, and they were sentenced to terms of up to ten years in the state prison.[33]

When the couple appealed their convictions to Mississippi's highest court, the ACLU submitted a trenchant amicus curiae brief calling for the elimination of Chapter 178.

> To see this case in its proper perspective, one must see it as part of a wave of hysterical suppression which has vented itself upon the Jehovah's Witnesses, some of it, as in the present case, masquerading as "patriotism." [Throughout the country,] every form of abuse, calumny, official oppression, political persecution and outright brutal assault has been used to intimidate them and to deprive them of their fundamental rights of free speech and religious liberty.

Chapter 178, according to the ACLU, fit perfectly into that pattern of persecution because it clearly violated the freedoms of press, worship, and speech guaranteed to the Witnesses by the state and federal constitutions. The ACLU contended that the Witnesses had been denied a fair trial in Lee County, in part because of the prosecutor's wide-ranging inquiry into some of the more controversial tenets of their faith. The brief argued that it was "apparent from the record of this trial that the conviction was a mere result of prejudice against [the] defendants' religious views, a prejudice inflamed by the prosecution and not adequately avoided by the judge." For the ACLU, the conclusion was inescapable: "This case presents a clear-cut issue of denial of constitutional rights." By charging the Witnesses under an unconstitutional statute and then convicting them in a grossly unfair trial, Mississippi had simply trampled on their civil rights.[34]

In January 1943, the Mississippi Supreme Court reversed the convictions of Otto and Roxie Mills, but it failed to deliver a knockout blow to Chapter 178. The court's brief and narrow ruling freed the couple simply because none of the evidence presented by either side at trial proved they had actually disseminated Witness materials after the law went into effect in March 1942. To the ACLU's dismay, the court explicitly dodged the larger question of the law's constitutionality. "It is not necessary for us to respond to contentions involving the constitutionality of the Act nor of the subversive quality of the matter upon which the prosecution is predicated," the opinion noted. Chapter 178, in other words, remained law in Mississippi, and hundreds of Witnesses remained under its shadow until the ACLU could mount a successful challenge in the courts.[35]

The arrest and conviction of R. E. Taylor and two other Witnesses, Betty Benoit and Clem Cummings, gave the ACLU another crack at Chapter 178. Like most Witnesses in Mississippi, Taylor was no stranger to the authorities; in fact, they seemed to go out of their way to harass him when he attempted to worship in public. In March 1942, for instance, Taylor wrote to Solicitor General Francis Biddle to complain about the abuse he recently had suffered at the hands of authorities in two Mississippi communities. On 16 March police officers and sheriff's deputies confronted Taylor and his wife as they preached from house to house in the town of McComb. The Witnesses were accosted, arrested, and then driven to the town of Magnolia, where they were berated by the local district attorney and several more police officers. As Taylor recalled for the solicitor general, the authorities engaged in "a vicious attack on us by words," with the district attorney "even wanting to engage in personal fist fighting." ("Of course I didn't fall for that trap," Taylor boasted.) After further browbeating and threatening Taylor and his wife, the authorities disappeared into the courthouse in Magnolia but were quickly replaced by a group of five vigilantes who "took turns at ordering us out of the county and threatening us with dire punishment," as Taylor later put it. The Witnesses eventually left town without being arrested, and Taylor felt dejected for having been "run off by a mob."[36]

Several weeks after their ordeal in McComb and Magnolia, Taylor and wife called at the homes of two women in Madison County, Mississippi. As was his habit, Taylor spoke freely about World War II, and he explained in considerable detail how a careful reading of the Bible had led him to oppose the conflict on religious grounds. He also distributed a Witness tract that justified his unpopular position on the war. "Almighty God commands that [Witnesses] must remain entirely neutral in the controversy," it read. "Because his covenant people are servants and representatives of The Theocracy they must hold themselves entirely aloof from warring factions of this world." Taylor also told one of the women, as she later testified in court, "that the President was doing wrong to send our boys . . . to be killed for nothing, and that Hitler would rule, and he wouldn't have to come over here to do it, but he would do it." Taylor was eager to address the topic of idolatry as well, telling her that "it was wrong for us to salute the flag," as she later testified. Another woman who had been approached by Taylor in Madison County reported that he had "said the quicker the people here quit bowing down and worshipping and saluting our flag and government, the sooner we would have peace." A savvy evangelist, Taylor had tracts to back up his claims about the flag salute, and he shared them as he proselytized. One of the pamphlets asserted, "For the Christian to salute a flag is in direct violation of God's specific commandment."[37]

In order to squelch such evangelizing, authorities in Madison County arrested Taylor and wife under Chapter 178. In a dispirited letter to the Justice Department, Taylor described the circumstances of his arrest and requested a prompt investigation by the federal government. He reported that on 3 June 1942, the county attorney and sheriff had led a contingent of men who "came to our rooms with a search warrant, taking six cartons of Watch Tower literature, Bibles, two phonographs, etc." and then had roughly hauled the Taylors off to jail. Despondent over the prospect of a lengthy prison term and separation from his five-year-old daughter, Taylor claimed that the couple's arrest stood as a typical example of the "great amount of persecution against Jehovah's Witnesses going on in the State of Mis-

sissippi," and he resolved to contest the bogus charges in court.[38]
At his trial in Madison County Circuit Court, Taylor discussed his
background at some length, disclosing that he had been a full-time
Witness proselytizer for a dozen years and that he considered himself an ordained minister. He indicated that he was able to support
his wife and daughter because his status as a full-time minister, or
pioneer, entitled him to a modest monthly stipend from Witness
headquarters in Brooklyn.

For Taylor, proselytizing was a labor of love, but he acknowledged
at the trial that practical considerations motivated him as well. "If
we don't work," he said, "we don't eat." Yet it was the purportedly
incendiary nature of Taylor's work as a Witness evangelist, not his
personal history, that dominated the trial. Testimony was heard
from the three Madison County housewives who had been approached by the Witness. The women revealed that Taylor had spoken out passionately against the war and had counseled them to refuse to participate in idolatrous flag-salute ceremonies. When Taylor
learned that two of the women had lost sons during the Japanese
attack on Pearl Harbor, he explained that the boys were not gone
forever; after Satan was vanquished at Armageddon, he said, they
would return and enjoy eternal life on earth. A number of Taylor's
tracts and pamphlets were entered into evidence as well. (A typical
passage read: "All nations of the earth today are under the control
of demons.") Those materials, combined with the testimony of the
women who had been solicited by Taylor, were enough to persuade
the jury of his guilt, and he was convicted of violating Chapter 178.
For the crime of having propagated his unpopular faith in Mississippi, he faced a prison term of up to ten years.[39]

The shaky facts of the *Mills* case had given the Mississippi Supreme Court an excuse to avoid the issue of Chapter 178's constitutionality, but *Taylor v. Mississippi* offered no such escape. To resolve
the case, the justices had to squarely address contentions that the
measure violated the protections of speech and worship guaranteed
by the state and federal constitutions. The battle lines were clearly
drawn: while the Jehovah's Witnesses and the American Civil Liberties Union were allied in an effort to wipe Chapter 178 off the
books, the state of Mississippi, claiming that the measure was an
appropriate exercise of its police power, fought to preserve it. In its
brief, written by Assistant Attorney General George Ethridge, the

state urged the court to uphold Taylor's conviction and find the law constitutional. Reminding the court that the country was engaged in a desperate battle to preserve democracy, Ethridge defended the measure as a harsh but essential part of the war effort, and he praised the state legislature for possessing the "foresight to provide for the common defense in time of possible disturbance or violence during the period of the war, and to promote the peace, safety, and welfare of the state during the war, when many of the male citizens of the state will be called away from home and in the national service." The law, he wrote, "is a war statute and is for the protection of the state and nation from disloyal activities by persons with the intent to obstruct" the country's defenses. Ethridge maintained that the law "is in no sense an anti-religious act and is not intended to interfere with proper religious liberty as recognized and enforced in the courts of this nation and the states." Only those Mississippians "whose religious views conflict with the law of the land as interpreted by the highest courts of the land," that is, Jehovah's Witnesses like R. E. Taylor, violated the law, and it was well within Mississippi's police power to prosecute them.[40]

Hayden Covington, who spearheaded Taylor's defense, took issue with nearly every argument in the state's brief. He maintained that the court should overturn the Witness's conviction because there was simply no evidence to indicate that he had violated Chapter 178. Covington asserted that Taylor's statements and the content of the literature he distributed did not "encourage disloyalty to the government of the United States and did not advocate the cause of the enemies of the United States and did not create an attitude of stubborn refusal to salute, honor or respect the flag." Covington reserved his heaviest fire, though, for Chapter 178 itself, which he lambasted as unconstitutional on several different grounds. By compromising his freedoms of worship, speech, and press, the measure infringed upon Taylor's rights under both the First and Fourteenth Amendments to the U.S. Constitution. It also violated myriad provisions of the state constitution, in part because it "is vague, indefinite, uncertain, too general, does not furnish a sufficiently ascertainable standard of guilt, enables the court and jury trying the indictment to speculate, [and] permits arbitrary and discriminatory action and amounts to a dragnet." For its part, the ACLU filed an amicus curiae brief characterizing Chapter 178 as a "patent attempt to mould a statute to stop

[a] particular religious activity," namely, the proselytizing of the Jehovah's Witnesses, a method of worship protected by the due process clause of the Fourteenth Amendment, thanks to *Cantwell*. Although it was framed in patriotic language, the measure was brutally repressive, and parts of it amounted to little more than "a veiled effort to continue the widespread attacks on this small religious minority," the ACLU contended. Like Covington, it called upon the court to strike down Chapter 178 as unconstitutional and to reverse R. E. Taylor's conviction.[41]

On 25 January 1943, a bitterly divided Mississippi Supreme Court upheld Taylor's conviction, ruling that his rights under the state and federal constitutions had not been compromised. The court's majority opinion held that Chapter 178 had been enacted to "aid in the prosecution of the present war and to meet conditions arising out of the war," not to extirpate a particular form of religious activity. Given the dire circumstances—the "nation is now in a war of self-defense for self-preservation"—the state legislature clearly had the authority to enact such a measure as a means of preserving order and controlling potentially subversive conduct. To the court's majority, there seemed little doubt that Taylor's proselytizing presented a legitimate threat to the war effort. According to the opinion,

> [The] appellant and his co-workers are going about the country and into the homes of the people, of low and high degrees of intelligence, and all races, and advocating disobedience to all laws and disrespect for and disloyalty to all governments, if perchance the particular law or the nature of the government in his opinion is not in accord with Theocracy.

True, the state had a responsibility to respect the Witnesses' civil liberties, but it was not obliged to turn a blind eye to the potentially subversive activities of proselytizers like R. E. Taylor simply because they claimed to be exercising their First Amendment freedoms. This was particularly true in wartime, "when the nation is straining every nerve, muscle and sinew, and mobilizing every resource and person, to defend itself against a treacherous attack of one and the evil designs of all its enemies."[42]

On the same day that it handed down its opinion in *Taylor v. Mis-*

sissippi, the Mississippi Supreme Court ruled in two other cases involving the prosecution of Jehovah's Witnesses under Chapter 178. In *Cummings v. State*, the court's majority affirmed the conviction of Clem Cummings, who had been charged under Chapter 178 after he distributed copies of the Witness book *Children* in Warren County, Mississippi. In *Cummings*, the majority reiterated the basic reasoning from *Taylor*, claiming that the Witness had been convicted for "attempting to persuade the people, at this tragic time, to have disrespect for and disloyalty towards the flag and the state and the nation, and to evince an attitude of disobedience to the laws of the land, thereby undermining the war efforts of the state and national governments." A concurring opinion argued that efforts to discourage flag-saluting were treasonous (and thus subject to sanctions under Chapter 178) because they could be viewed as "a pointed symptom of the disease which lies at the bottom of the subversive and destructive doctrines which [Cummings] and his coworkers are seeking to spread in our state in this time of war, the result of which means everything to us as a state and nation."[43] In his dissent, Justice Julian Alexander disputed the notion that *Children* denigrated the flag, and he pilloried Chapter 178 as unconstitutional. "Constitutional rights are not subject to nullification by reference to a popularity poll," he indignantly wrote. "Men's consciences may not be held hostage by the state to compel conformity to a majority view."[44]

Betty Benoit's was the third conviction under Chapter 178 upheld that day by the Mississippi Supreme Court. As she explained in an anguished letter to the ACLU, authorities in Columbia, Mississippi, frequently harassed her prior to her arrest for violating the state's new antisedition law. Benoit recalled that Bill Owens, Columbia's chief of police, disrupted a Bible-study meeting that was being held at the home of a local Witness on 13 April 1942. According to Benoit, "Owens and two other policemen . . . threatened us with mob violence, told us to get out of town, broke a 14-part phonograph lecture, a phonograph, and burned them together with all the literature in the house." Intent on driving the Witnesses out of Columbia, Owens further pestered Benoit and her roommate, Witness Violet Babin, during the next few days. The police chief warned the women that he would not protect them from vigilantism, and he twice persuaded landlords to evict them. After being pressured by local authorities, one landlord ordered the Witnesses to move out of her building because she "just couldn't afford to have us stay [there] any longer," Benoit wrote. Despite her troubles in Columbia, Benoit knew that her neighbors were good people, and she found it hard to fault them for grudgingly cooperating with the authorities. "The people in general here have been very nice to us," she told the ACLU. "All the threats against us has come by the law officials."

Finally, on 18 April, after a week of harassment, the Witnesses were arrested under Chapter 178 for disseminating literature "tending to create an attitude of stubborn refusal to salute, honor, or respect the national and state flags and governments," as the U.S. Supreme Court would put it. Among the allegedly seditious materials cited in the charges was an issue of *Consolation* containing an editorial from a Lewiston, Maine, newspaper that criticized the Supreme Court's opinion in *Gobitis*. The county attorney released the women on $1,000 bond but warned that "if we went on with our work we would be picked up again, and our bond [would] be set so high we would not be able to make it," Benoit recalled.[45] She was convicted in Marion County Circuit Court for violating Chapter 178, and the Supreme Court of Mississippi upheld the guilty verdict.[46] When the three Witnesses chose to appeal their convictions, the U.S. Supreme Court heard the cases together as *Taylor v. Mississippi.*

Taylor v. Mississippi proved to be a relatively straightforward case for the Supreme Court. In a unanimous opinion handed down 14 June 1943, Justice Owen Roberts noted that the state of Mississippi had wielded Chapter 178 against Taylor, Cummings, and Benoit to prohibit them from "communicat[ing] to others views and opinions respecting governmental policies, and prophecies concerning the future of our own and other nations." The Witnesses were being punished "although what they communicated is not claimed or shown to have been done with an evil or sinister purpose, to have advocated or incited subversive action against the nation or state, or to have threatened any clear and present danger to our institutions or our Government." As they proselytized, these evangelists had simply meant to share "their beliefs and opinions concerning domestic measures and world affairs." As it had in earlier cases, such as *DeJonge v. Oregon* (1937), the Court determined that imposing criminal sanctions for such communications would violate the Witnesses' rights under the Fourteenth Amendment. Consequently, the Court had no choice but to reverse their convictions.[47]

By the time the Supreme Court overturned the convictions of R. E. Taylor and his coreligionists, the peak of the Witnesses' persecution in the United States had passed. Never again would they be so regularly attacked, arrested, and expelled as they had been in summer 1940, when the release of the *Gobitis* opinion and the Fifth Column scare precipitated a wave of anti-Witness incidents. Yet throughout the World War II era, Witnesses continued to suffer at the hands of vigilantes and local authorities who were hostile to their beliefs and practices. "Violence [against Witnesses] declined during 1941 and 1942 but the attacks though less frequent have been shocking," the American Civil Liberties Union reported. "The war has intensified popular antagonism to their refusal to salute the flag and participate in the war." That they still suffered brutal assaults and unjust arrests helped to convince the Witnesses to press forward with their campaign in the courts. They realized that even with victories like *Cantwell* and *Taylor* under their belts, their civil liberties were by no means secure.[48]

In addition to mob attacks, Witnesses continued to endure hundreds of arrests each month. Most of them were spurious, and the Witnesses kept challenging their dubious constitutionality in court. One night late in 1941, Witness Sarah Prince and her nine-year-old niece, Betty Simmons, distributed copies of *Consolation* and *The Watch Tower* on the streets of Brockton, Massachusetts. Prince was Simmons's legal guardian, and they often proselytized together. On this particular evening, George Perkins, an attendance officer in the local public school system, interrupted the Witnesses as they worshiped and berated Prince. As he had done at least once before, Perkins advised Prince that her niece was too young to be engaged in literature sales, and he told her to return home within five minutes. Furious at the attendance officer's meddling, Prince refused to provide him with Simmons's name, and she angrily told him that "neither you nor anybody else can stop me. . . . This child is exercising her God-given right and her constitutional right to preach the gospel, and no creature has a right to interfere with God's commands." Despite this outburst, the Witnesses heeded Perkins's warning and returned home. As she left, Prince fumed, "I'm not going through this any more. We've been through it time and again. I'm going home and put the little girl to bed." Perkins subsequently filed a complaint charging that Prince had violated Massachusetts's child-labor laws by furnishing her niece with literature and then allowing her to peddle it in public. (He also submitted a less serious charge relating to Prince's refusal to provide Simmons's name.) Prince was convicted on all counts in a local court, and a state appellate court upheld the convictions.[49]

At first, the U.S. Supreme Court refused to hear Prince's appeal, but Justice Frank Murphy eventually persuaded the Brethren to grant certiorari. In a memorandum urging his fellow justices to hear the case, Murphy contended that the Court had held on numerous occasions that the public dissemination of religious publications— the Witnesses' fundamental method of worship—was a "sacred franchise" protected by the Constitution. With that in mind, the Court would be making a grievous error if it dismissed as "insubstantial" Prince's contention that Massachusetts's child-labor laws could not be applied to the distribution of religious materials without infringing on the Witnesses' right to free exercise of religion. In part because of Murphy's arguments, the Court voted unanimously to hear *Prince v. Massachusetts*. The case proved to be a struggle for some members of the Court, including Justice Wiley Rutledge, who wrote the majority opinion upholding the Witness's convictions. Like Murphy, Rutledge was ordinarily sympathetic to the claims of Witness appellants, and he saw some merit in Prince's claim that the state's right to regulate the labor of children did not give it license to infringe on her family's First Amendment rights. In a moment of candor, he later confessed that he had been tempted to determine his vote in the case by flipping a coin and that he had nearly felt compelled "to write [the opinion] the other way"—that is, to reverse the convictions rather than affirm them. In the end, however, Rutledge could not "quite step over the line with Murphy," who in fact argued in dissent that the prosecution of Prince under the child-labor measure had been unconstitutional.[50]

Writing for the majority in *Prince*—a case he described as yet "another episode in the conflict between Jehovah's Witnesses and state authority"—Rutledge recognized that in light of the Court's prior decisions in such cases as *Pierce v. Society of Sisters* (1925), "it is cardinal with us that the custody, care and nurture of the child reside first with the parents, whose primary function and freedom include preparation for obligations the state can neither supply nor hinder." Those rulings, he wrote, "have respected the private realm of family life which the state cannot enter," and the current Court had no intention of overturning them. But by the same token, no one could dispute that "the state has a wide range of power for limiting parental freedom and authority in things affecting the child's welfare; and that this includes, to some extent, matters of conscience and religious conviction." Rutledge maintained that in this case, the state's legitimate interest in protecting youngsters like Betty Simmons from "situations difficult enough for adults to cope with and wholly inappropriate for children, especially of tender years, to face" prevailed over the Witnesses' right to exercise their religion freely—a right that was, as the Court had noted in several previous rulings, by no means absolute. Thanks to the protections of the First and Fourteenth Amendments, adult Witnesses like Sarah Prince were free to proselytize as they wished and perhaps "become martyrs themselves," the Court held. "But it does not follow that they are free . . . to make martyrs of their children before they have reached the age of full and legal discretion when they can make that choice for themselves." To prevent such tragedies, the state could intervene, and it could do so without compromising anyone's civil liberties.[51]

When Murphy balked at joining the majority opinion, Justice Felix Frankfurter quipped that Murphy wanted to revel in the "undivided glory of being a dissenter." Murphy himself explained to his clerk that he hoped "to save all that can be saved for the parent as against the state in the right to teach . . . religion to the child." By dissenting, Murphy said, he had "nothing in mind but liberty of religion in a country that was conceived as a sanctuary for oppressed people."[52] After invoking the Court's opinion in *Carolene Products*, Murphy argued in his dissent that "the human freedoms enumerated in the First Amendment and carried over into the Fourteenth Amendment are to be presumed to be invulnerable and any attempt to sweep away those freedoms is prima facie invalid." As the Court had noted on numerous occasions, infringements on such freedoms could occur, but they had to be justified by a compelling state interest. In the case of Sarah Prince, Murphy wrote, Massachusetts had compromised the Witnesses' freedom to worship on the streets of Brockton without "sustain[ing] its burden of proving the existence of any grave or immediate danger to any interest which it may lawfully protect." As Murphy saw it, the dangers faced by Witness children like Betty Simmons while proselytizing under adult supervision were "exceedingly remote, to say the least. And the fact that the zealous exercise of the right to propagandize the community may result in violent or disorderly situations difficult for children to face is no excuse for prohibiting the exercise of that right."[53]

Murphy closed his dissent with a survey of the Witnesses' suffering in the United States in the early and mid-1940s.

No chapter in human history has been so largely written in terms of persecution and intolerance as the one dealing with religious freedom. From ancient times to the present day, the ingenuity of man has known no limits in its ability to forge weapons of oppression for use against those who dare to express or practice unorthodox religious beliefs. And the Jehovah's Witnesses are living proof of the fact that even in this nation, conceived as it was in the ideals of freedom, the right to practice religion in unconventional ways is still far from secure. Theirs is a militant and unpopular faith, pursued with a fanatical zeal. They have suffered brutal beatings; their property has been destroyed; they have been harassed at every turn by the resurrection and enforcement of little used ordinances and statutes. . . . To them, along with other present-day religious minorities, befalls the burden of testing our devotion to the ideals and constitutional guarantees of religious freedom.

With that in mind, Murphy concluded, the Court "should . . . hesitate before approving the application of a statute"—Massachusetts's child-labor law—"that might be used as another instrument of oppression. Religious freedom is too sacred a right to be restricted or prohibited in any degree without convincing proof that a legitimate interest of the state is in grave danger."[54]

As *Prince* demonstrated, the Witnesses suffered some heartrending setbacks when they appealed to the Supreme Court. From case to case, their basic arguments changed relatively little; in describing Hayden Covington's approach to litigating appeals, one observer remarked that he made a practice of "standing flat on the Bill of Rights" and repeatedly invoking its protections of speech, press, and worship, which were being gradually incorporated into the due process clause of the Fourteenth Amendment.[55] In general, the Supreme Court looked favorably on Covington's strategy, but it also handed him some resounding defeats, including *Gobitis, Prince,* and *Chaplinsky v. New Hampshire,* a 1942 decision involving the First Amendment freedoms of a Witness who was mobbed while proselytizing and then arrested. Such setbacks underscored the enormous challenges faced by Witnesses when they attempted to secure their rights through the courts. Already the victims of intolerance, the appellants in those cases suffered still further when the Court overlooked the context of their cases or clung to narrow and increasingly outdated interpretations of the Constitution's protections of civil liberties.

8. Fighting Words

A group of investigators from the Department of Labor's Children's Bureau descended on Walter Chaplinsky's hometown in 1922, when he was eight years old. Brimming with tables, charts, and photographs, their subsequent report, "Child Labor and the Welfare of Children in an Anthracite Coal-Mining District," painted a grim picture of Shenandoah, Pennsylvania, a mining borough located not far from Minersville, the home of the Gobitas family. The investigators wrote that the Shenandoah area was "a black country dominated by the great [coal] breakers which rise above the towns. The streams are black with soot and there are black piles of refuse and culm, and the men returning from work wear masks of coal dust." Hard-coal mining, long the backbone of the local economy, had transformed the region's landscape into something resembling the moon, and the federal investigators came away shaken by its "general desolation." The business center of the area, Shenandoah, was a "congested town shut in by high hills," with "no touch of color or beauty" brightening its cramped streets. Many of the borough's homes were in appalling states of disrepair, and miners and their families were crowded into them like sardines in a tin: in 1920, Shenandoah's population density (43,000 persons per square mile) was more than double New York's (19,000) and triple Chicago's (14,200). To make matters worse, people in the tightly packed borough were forced to compete with animals for breathing room. "Almost every yard had chicken coops," the bureau reported. "In one yard, 12 by 25 feet, an agent of the Children's Bureau counted 11 toilets, and 25 hens, besides dogs and cats."[1]

Barren Shenandoah afforded few chances for recreation. Several years earlier, youngsters had been able to use a park on the northern perimeter of the borough, "but the tennis courts were not kept up, the wading pool for the little children was dry, and the drains became stopped up," according to the bureau. "There was opposition to the playground on the part of some of the neighbors because it was popular with the children and the noise they made was disturbing." With their only local playground in disrepair, children like Walter Chaplinsky were forced to improvise. Dodging automobile and trolley-car traffic, local boys tossed footballs and baseballs in the borough's narrow, steep streets or created makeshift basketball courts by attaching a hoop to a telegraph pole. As one young athlete explained, he and his friends were able to romp on a given thoroughfare "till the cop comes." Impervious to filth, some children gamboled on garbage heaps and culm mounds; for want of anything better to do, others simply loafed. "Everywhere the larger boys loitered on street corners," the bureau noted in dismay, "and gangs of smaller boys swarmed the streets." Outside the borough lay Hooky Dam, which served as a popular swimming hole for Shenandoah's older children. Their younger siblings were forced to make do "wading in the black stream which flowed along two sides of the borough and received the sewages and refuse of the mines."[2]

Like most of the adult men in Shenandoah, Anthony Chaplinsky, Walter's father, labored in the anthracite coal mines. He would leave home near dawn each morning and return twelve hours later, exhausted and covered from head to foot with grime. It was grueling and very often deadly work: between 1916 and 1918, according to the federal Bureau of Mines, 1,688 miners perished in Pennsylvania's hard-coal fields, and thousands more were injured.[3] Mining did not kill the elder Chaplinsky, but over time it wrecked his health. Years of inhaling hard-coal dust ravaged the Russian immigrant's lungs so thoroughly that he was forced to leave the mines altogether. "He worked till his health gave way," Walter Chaplinsky recalled, "and he had a hard time breathing. . . . It was very painful." Devastated by black lung, he sold his house and moved his wife and children, Walter, Mitchell, and Loretta, to a farm located several miles north of Shenandoah. Having grown up in a dingy and overcrowded industrial town that one observer lamented as "a memorial to the age of rampant industry,"[4] Walter Chaplinsky appreciated the eighty-seven-acre farm, and he and his siblings worked diligently to help keep it running smoothly.[5]

Jehovah's Witnesses approached the Chaplinsky family in the early 1930s, after they had moved to the farm. "They came to our home and talked to my parents," Walter Chaplinsky remembered.

"As their message was from the Bible, we were interested. They invited us to come to their Kingdom Hall." Chaplinsky was intrigued by the Witnesses' offer, and he and his brother began walking from their farm to the Kingdom Hall twice each week for Bible-study sessions. Enraptured by their new faith, the brothers did not mind that the trip was more than four miles each way. "What drew us," Chaplinsky explained, "was the wonderful information that is in the Bible. . . . My brother and I wanted to learn how to call on people and present information to them about life that will never end. That's what motivated my brother and I to become Jehovah's Witnesses." As they absorbed Witness doctrines and awakened to the timeless teachings of the Scriptures, the brothers "joined the Witnesses in preaching work from house to house." Like thousands of other members of their faith, they equipped themselves with books, tracts, and Bibles as they proselytized in Shenandoah and neighboring communities in Schuylkill County.[6]

The faith that Walter Chaplinsky forged in Shenandoah was sorely tested in the early 1940s. In April 1940, after being brutalized by a mob as he preached in a public square in Rochester, New Hampshire, Chaplinsky was arrested and convicted under a rarely enforced state law that prohibited the use of offensive language in a public place. Hayden Covington defended Chaplinsky when he appealed to the U.S. Supreme Court, but the resourceful Witness attorney was unable to convince even a single justice that Chaplinsky's conviction should have been vacated because of the unique factual circumstances of the case and the protections of speech provided by the First and Fourteenth Amendments. Chaplinsky lost—and had to spend six arduous months in prison—when the Court unanimously held that the "fighting words" he had uttered after the mobbing were not protected by the Constitution.

Chaplinsky v. New Hampshire is among the most tragic Jehovah's Witness cases of the early and mid-1940s. For the most part, Witnesses were served well during the war years by state and federal courts, which issued dozens of rulings shielding their First Amendment freedoms. In *Chaplinsky,* though, the courts failed miserably, largely because they disregarded many of the essential facts of the case, including the savage context of the Witness's alleged offense. After being ignored by the courts, the disturbing story of Chaplinsky's arrest, conviction, and imprisonment has remained obscure for more than half a century. A full examination of those troubling facts reveals just how badly the Supreme Court stumbled when it ruled against Chaplinsky and introduced the fighting words doctrine into constitutional jurisprudence. Dissenting in another Witness case, Justice Frank Murphy argued that "the law knows no finer hour than when it cuts through formal concepts and transitory emotions to protect unpopular citizens against discrimination and persecution."[7] Judged by that lofty standard, *Chaplinsky* was a singularly dark moment for the First Amendment.

Walter Chaplinsky's commitment to his faith deepened after he attended a week-long Witness convention in Newark, New Jersey, in 1936. Inspired by that meeting, he moved to Philadelphia and became a full-time Witness pioneer, working at least 150 hours a month and "calling on people from house to house," as he later explained. The Kingdom Hall in Philadelphia was large enough to provide space for Bible-study sessions and living quarters, so Chaplinsky boarded there for about two months with several other pioneers. He then headed to Norfolk, Virginia, where he and a partner proselytized for five months. The two men armed themselves with reams of Witness materials and industriously canvassed homes and "all the stores and offices," according to Chaplinsky. "At that time we carried a case of books and a phonograph. We would ring or knock on the door, introduce ourselves, and offer to play the phonograph." His enthusiasm and energy rarely flagging, Chaplinsky redoubled his witnessing after his partner married, and he went on to canvass businessmen in an area covering ten states. He enjoyed the work so much that he eventually assumed still more responsibility. He remembered, "At a Witness convention in St. Louis, I signed up for a different assignment—this was called 'special pioneer.' This type of work was to call on people and conduct Bible studies with them, and the requirement of time was two hundred hours per month. For this work we received twenty-five dollars a month." Chaplinsky's new assignment took him to Manchester, New Hampshire, in 1939.[8]

As many as 100 people participated when Witnesses in Manchester held Thursday evening and Sunday morning meetings at their Kingdom Hall. With Bibles opened on their laps, they talked about their faith and marveled at how the ageless lessons of the Scriptures provided solutions to many of the seemingly intractable problems that the world faced. Mindful that "there is so much proof that the Bible is the word of God," Chaplinsky drew strength from these sessions and continued to proselytize, "working from house to house and conducting private Bible studies with people who were interested," he recalled. "This was one hour a week, and it was done free of charge. This was our method of preaching." A few of Manchester's many Roman Catholic residents were friendly to Chaplinsky as he evangelized, and some were so taken by his message that they discussed the Bible with him or read his pamphlets, tracts, and periodicals. Many rebuked him, however, or hid behind signs warning "No Jehovah's Witnesses." A seasoned proselytizer, Chaplinsky was wary of causing trouble, and he simply walked past homes displaying such notices.[9]

The persistent hostility of local police loomed as one of the Witnesses' chief obstacles in Manchester. Decades afterward, Chaplinsky recalled with some bitterness how one disastrous run-in with police had landed him in jail. "When I was arrested in Manchester, it was for calling on people from door to door," he remembered. "The police asked me if I had a permit to do this work. I explained that I was not selling anything." (Witnesses throughout the country persistently maintained that their proselytizing was a form of worship, not a commercial endeavor, and thus not subject to local registration or licensing ordinances.) Chaplinsky, like hundreds of Witnesses in that era, was convicted for peddling without a license, and a local judge offered him a choice: he "could leave the city or spend forty days in jail," as he recalled. Unwilling to abandon his new post in Manchester, Chaplinsky chose the jail time, and from the outset it was a brutal experience. A prison official reared back and slugged him just after he arrived at the facility. ("What was that for?" Chaplinsky asked. "To show you who is boss around here," he was told.) Wearing a drab gray uniform and old shoes, he spent much of his sentence farming the small parcel of land that surrounded Manchester's jail. "I was teamed up with three other prisoners," he later wrote. "We pulled a cultivator. Four of us pulled it and another prisoner held the handle." Long afterward, Chaplinsky recalled that he and his fellow inmates had been "treated like animals" and physically abused.[10]

So many Witnesses were arrested and convicted under Manchester's peddling ordinance, which required sellers of literature to register with the city and purchase a badge costing fifty cents, that they enlisted the help of Hayden Covington and fought the measure in court. In spring 1940, Milton Leiby and other local Witnesses asked a federal district court to enjoin the city from enforcing the licensing ordinance against them. In their bill of complaint, the Witnesses maintained that they "cannot and will not stop [their] lawful work and cannot and will not apply for a badge or a permit as required by said ordinance because for them to do so would be, as they sincerely believe, an insult to Almighty God, Jehovah, and a violation of His Supreme law and which would result in their everlasting destruction." After the district court, citing the U.S. Supreme Court's ruling in *Lovell v. Griffin*, granted the injunction,[11] the city brought the case before the First Circuit Court of Appeals. That court, to Covington's dismay, distinguished *Leiby* from *Lovell* and reversed the lower-court ruling. In its opinion, the appellate court argued that the Manchester ordinance

> contains no element of prior censorship upon the distribution of literature. It requires only a simple routine act of obtaining a badge of identification before a person can sell on the streets. This reasonable police regulation, in our opinion, imposes no substantial burden upon the freedom of the press or the free exercise of religion.[12]

Witnesses in Manchester battled the city in another case that spring, and they eventually took their appeal all the way to the U.S. Supreme Court. A group of approximately ninety local Witnesses had conducted an "information march" in Manchester in summer 1939. Split into groups of fifteen to twenty marchers, the Witnesses had walked single file through the downtown area on a Saturday night in early July. In addition to distributing tracts and offering printed invitations to a lecture, they had carried signs proclaiming "Serve God and Christ the King" and "Religion is a Snare and a Racket." Following the march, five Witnesses, Willis Cox, Walter Chaplinsky, John Konides, Arvid Moody, and Oliva Paquette, were convicted in municipal court for participating in a parade or procession without having obtained a license from the city. After the

Jehovah's Witnesses in New England being confronted by police during an "information march."

Hillsboro County Superior Court and the Supreme Court of New Hampshire upheld the convictions, the Witnesses, claiming that they had been deprived of their freedoms of worship, speech, press, and assembly, appealed to the U.S. Supreme Court. In spring 1941, it dealt the Manchester Witnesses another loss by unanimously affirming the convictions. Writing for the Court in one of his final opinions (he left the bench three months later, in June), Chief Justice Charles Evans Hughes found that "no interference with religious worship or the practice of religion in any proper sense is shown, but only the exercise of local control over the use of streets for parades and processions."[13]

By the time the Supreme Court handed down its ruling in *Cox v. New Hampshire*, Walter Chaplinsky had moved east from Manchester and settled in Strafford County, New Hampshire, where he continued to proselytize—and to experience bad luck with police. Still a special pioneer, Chaplinsky lived in Dover, New Hampshire, but he frequently preached the lessons of the Bible in nearby cities like Rochester, a mill town not far from the Maine border. On a Saturday morning late in March 1940, Chaplinsky evangelized in Rochester's Central Square. His fiery preaching—about the approach of Armageddon, about the idolatry of saluting the flag, about the perfidy of the Catholic Church—offended several passersby, and they complained to James Bowering, the city's marshal. Like several other members of Rochester's police force, Bowering was a strapping former athlete (he had played football at Springfield College in Massachusetts and then for Rochester's semipro team, the Mountaineers), and he towered over Chaplinsky as he investigated the complaints. Bowering did not charge Chaplinsky, but he took him into custody and warned him in no uncertain terms not to cause a disturbance with his provocative witnessing.[14]

His encounter with Bowering did nothing to dampen Chaplinsky's ardor for evangelizing. The message contained in his periodicals, books, and tracts—that of Jehovah God and his King, Christ Jesus—was the most meaningful that any Christian could relate, and he was not ready to abandon it under duress, especially since Witnesses around the country were at that very moment stepping up their already frenetic proselytizing activities. In February 1940, "street-corner work and publishers' establishing route deliveries for *The Watchtower* and *Consolation* were begun," according to the Witnesses' yearbook. As a result of these new propaganda techniques, devoted ministers of the Gospel like Chaplinsky distributed 3 million pieces of literature that year, and they brought in more than 100,000 new subscriptions for *The Watchtower* and *Consolation*. That the likes of Jim Bowering opposed their reinvigorated proselytizing during this "Battle Siege Testimony Period," as it was called, did not deter many Witnesses. Their yearbook explained that while

> daily suffering cruel persecution at the hands of religious fanatics, Jehovah's Witnesses are not in the least bit discouraged or dismayed. On they joyfully go performing their God-given commission. They know that the persecution which they suffer is indisputable proof that they are the children of God and that nothing can befall them except by the permission of Almighty God and that all things shall work together for the ultimate good of them because they love God and are called according to his purpose.

In the face of sometimes violent opposition, Witnesses kept in mind the lessons of the Scriptures, which explained that they must endure suffering in order to earn life's ultimate reward. An ardent student of the Bible, Walter Chaplinsky might have been thinking of a passage from Acts when Jim Bowering approached him: "We must through much tribulation enter into the kingdom of God."[15]

Accompanied by four boys, Chaplinsky returned to the town square on the following Saturday, 6 April (the eve of his twenty-sixth birthday), and once again preached "the true facts of the situation of the Bible to the people," as he later put it. Chaplinsky stationed himself at the corner of East Wakefield and Main—in the middle of Rochester, near the popular Scenic Theater—and offered Witness tracts. These "Christian publications," as he called them, boldly trumpeted the details of his faith. Some of the pamphlets he distributed that day promised to expose "the real truth about President Roosevelt's envoy to Europe." The tracts condemned the appointment of Myron C. Taylor as the American envoy to the Vatican, decrying it as "the most astounding piece of business thus far perpetrated by an elected servant of the American people." (Given the Witnesses' long-standing hostility to the "harlot" Catholic Church, it was hardly surprising that they opposed sending Taylor to Rome.) While Chaplinsky hawked Witness literature, the boys who had accompanied him toted placards. One of their signs advised, "Read the uncensored news."[16]

For the second Saturday in a row, complaints about Chaplinsky's obstreperous preaching in the town square flooded Jim Bowering's office. "I had possibly fifty or more of either telephone calls or personal complaints from people," the marshal later said, "that there was a man on the street decrying the Catholic religion, calling . . . the priests racketeers, saying that all religion was a racket, and they wanted to know if I could do something about it." Bowering received so many complaints about Chaplinsky that he approached Leonard Hardwick, the city solicitor, and asked, "Is there anything I can do to prevent this?" Hardwick explained that the marshal was powerless to stop Chaplinsky simply because he felt that the content of the preaching seemed offensive. "He said on religious grounds," Bowering recalled of his conversation with the Harvard-educated attorney, "there is absolutely nothing you can do." Meanwhile, men began to cluster around Chaplinsky in the town square, and they

passed threatening notes to the boys who had accompanied him.
(One somewhat cryptic message read, "Don't pass out any more. The
spider.") A menacing group of war veterans and local mill workers,
they taunted the Witness about his purported disloyalty and challenged him to salute an American flag. True to his faith, Chaplinsky
refused, telling the approximately fifty men who surrounded him
that the teachings of the Bible expressly prohibited the worship of
graven images, an answer that did little to mollify his increasingly
hostile audience. Bowering had stationed police officer Gerald
Lapierre at a nearby intersection, but the rookie cop, hired as a patrolman only a few days earlier, ignored the mounting disturbance
and instead concentrated on his assigned task—directing traffic.[17]

Bowering responded to the complaints by lumbering from his
office to the square. Although he "absolutely" knew that trouble was
brewing, the marshal made no attempt to disperse the crowd of men
who surrounded and jeered at the Witness. Instead, he again warned
Chaplinsky to temper his caustic remarks. According to his later
testimony, Bowering informed the Witness that the crowd was in
"an ugly mood" and then asked him "why it wasn't possible for
him to preach his religion without riling the people up so, taking
religion and jamming it down their throats, calling . . . priests racketeers." As he had done a week earlier, Chaplinsky chose to ignore
Bowering's warning. More convinced than ever that he had to fulfill
his sacred obligation to serve as a minister of the Gospel, he explained that he would not allow a mob or an antagonistic cop to disrupt his freedom of worship. "He said," Bowering recalled, "we
preach our religion the way we want." As he attempted to persuade
Chaplinsky to tone down his preaching, the marshal saw firsthand
how incensed some of Chaplinsky's spectators had become over his
refusal to salute the American flag. While Bowering spoke with
Chaplinsky, William Bowman, a former commander of the local
Veterans of Foreign Wars post, throttled the Witness with one hand
and attempted to punch him with the other. According to the marshal's description of the altercation, the irate Bowman "reached over
and got hold of [Chaplinsky's] coat collar . . . and he said, 'Do you
believe in saluting the flag?' Then I pushed him back and told him
go on and mind his own business, I didn't want any riot." Despite
his purported concern about rioting, Bowering took no further action to restrain the veteran; he apparently did not even order Bow-

man to leave the scene. Chaplinsky, believing that he had been assaulted, "wrenched . . . free" and asked the marshal to make an arrest, but Bowering declined. He gruffly told Chaplinsky that it "wasn't necessary."[18]

After he separated Bowman from Chaplinsky, the marshal left the square and headed back to his office in city hall. Bowman momentarily retreated as well, but he returned to the square in a few minutes with an American flag that had been affixed to a long pole. When Chaplinsky resumed preaching his "message of the kingdom of the Bible," elaborating on many of the controversial tenets of his faith, the veteran assaulted him a second time. Testifying later in court, the Witness described how Bowman had attempted to impale him with the flag pole:

> This Mr. Bowman . . . carried this flag in a spear-like position, and he came forward and gave a terrific lunge to plunge me through. I avoided this blow, and as he came by he pushed me into the gutter against an automobile standing there. And he walked by to the corner and offered the flag to a man standing there. . . . And he came back toward me and caught me by the collar and said, "You son of a bitch."

Bowman's charge ignited the crowd, and men swarmed over the prostrate Witness. Chaplinsky "received about seven to ten punches and . . . was cast down between the gutter and the wheels of an automobile," he recalled. Robert Downing, another member of the local Veterans of Foreign Wars post, joined Bowman and other assailants in the fracas, removing Chaplinsky's glasses and striking him repeatedly. The Witness momentarily regained his footing, then collapsed into the gutter after receiving sharp blows from several assailants.[19] As the drubbing progressed, Chaplinsky's attackers flung his tracts and pamphlets around the square, ruining most of them. A few days later, a headline in the local newspaper, the *Rochester Courier*, neatly summarized the brawl and its principal cause: "Chaplinsky Beaten by Irate Mob; Set Upon in Square Here Saturday for Alleged Insult to Flag."[20]

Its rage spent, the mob dispersed. While Chaplinsky attempted to regain his bearings and salvage some of his materials, Gerald Lapierre finally left his traffic post and approached the scene of the

attack. After failing to break up the mobbing, Lapierre made no effort to pursue any of Chaplinsky's assailants. Instead, he grabbed the
Witness by the arm and began leading him toward the police station. Walking up Wakefield Street, the two men were met by Jim
Bowering, who was on his way to the square after receiving a "riot
call." Several other law enforcement officials—including sheriff's
deputies Ralph Dunlap and Lyman Plummer, police officers Vane
Nickerson and Bert Power, and a "special officer" named Stetson—
arrived at the scene within the next few minutes to help lead the
dazed Witness away from the square. Altogether, at least a half-
dozen policemen escorted Chaplinsky as he was "taken to the station for his own protection," in Bowering's words. Although it must
have been clear to everyone present that William Bowman and
Robert Downing had participated in the assault, none of the policemen who converged on the riot scene attempted to detain them or
question any witnesses.[21] "Assailants Unknown, Officers Say," the
Courier reported in a headline. The newspaper harbored little sympathy for Chaplinsky or his faith—few people in Rochester did—but
it was quick to censure Bowering and his subordinates for their lax
policing both before and after the assault. A few days after the mobbing, in the editorial "Why Was It Permitted?" the paper noted,
"The incident which occurred in Central Square here Saturday afternoon, in which a group of overzealous citizens defied the law in
order to right what they believed to be a wrong, leaves several questions to be answered, among them: Why did the police permit the
thing to occur?"[22]

Chaplinsky recalled that "there was about four or five police
officers on top of me" as he was "shoved along roughly" toward the
police station after the attack. Although they ostensibly were taking
him into custody in order to protect him, the policemen berated and
physically abused the Witness as they walked him down Wakefield
Street. In his later testimony, Chaplinsky complained about the
"rough manner" in which he had been treated, claiming that members of his police escort had "caught hold of me . . . as if I had started
a fight, and they swung me over the street staggering." Rochester
resident Gregory Gessis saw the policemen mistreating Chaplinsky
as they led him to the station. "They was roughly handling him,"
Gessis explained. "Pulling him and pushing him." As he stumbled
toward the police station, Chaplinsky realized that one of the men

who was leading him along, Ralph Dunlap, had clouted him during the mobbing. (When asked in court if he was certain that Dunlap, who had not been in uniform that day, had struck him, Chaplinsky said that he was "absolutely positive.") At that point, Chaplinsky's frustrations were beginning to bubble over, and he pleaded with Bowering to pursue and arrest his assailants. "Will you please arrest the ones who started this fight?" he asked. According to Chaplinsky's recollection, the marshal responded to his request by barking, "Shut up you dumb bastard and come along." Exasperated, the Witness shot back, "You are a damn fascist and a racketeer"— not a far-fetched claim, given Bowering's conduct that afternoon.[23] When Dunlap announced that he was a deputy sheriff, Chaplinsky made a similar statement, announcing, "If you are a deputy sheriff, [all of the] city officials of Rochester are fascists." Following these heated exchanges, the policemen hauled Chaplinsky into the marshal's office, where an enraged Bowering called the Witness "an unpatriotic dog." Dunlap added, "You son of a bitch, we ought to have left you to that crowd there and [let] them kill you."[24]

Bowering told Chaplinsky that he was being placed under arrest for having called the marshal a "racketeer and a fascist." At least one piece of evidence suggests, however, that Bowering might not have immediately known exactly which law Chaplinsky had broken in using that epithet. A hand-written docket for Rochester's municipal court listed Bowering as "complainant," Chaplinsky as "respondent," his plea as "not guilty," and the "disposition" of the case as "continued to Apr 10 Bail 25.00." Only the space on the docket reserved for "offense" remained blank—the only such omission on a page listing eight other arrests, and a rarity in the volume as a whole, which covered several hundred arrests.[25] Chaplinsky was eventually cited for violating Chapter 376, Section 2, of the Public Laws of the State of New Hampshire. The law prohibited the use of "offensive, derisive or annoying" language directed at individuals in public places, and it also banned speech meant to "deride, offend, or annoy" any person "pursuing his lawful business or occupation."[26]

Like so many of the accusations leveled at Jehovah's Witnesses in the early and mid-1940s, it was an exceptional charge under a rarely used law. In 1940, police in Rochester, a city of 12,000 residents, made 314 arrests. During the entire year, they charged only two people under the state's abusive language statute—Walter Chaplinsky and another Witness, John Douglas.[27] Douglas's arrest was in many ways a disheartening replay of Chaplinsky's. On 7 September 1940, Rochester patrolman Bert Power took Douglas into custody after he attempted to preach in Central Square. At the police station, marshal Jim Bowering questioned Douglas and concluded that he was intoxicated. "I ordered him to leave the police station," Bowering recalled, "after saying I didn't think it a good idea to preach on the Bible when he had been drinking." Douglas remained, according to Bowering, and lectured him on the evils of Catholicism and the mistreatment of German Witnesses under the Third Reich. After hearing him out, the marshal escorted Douglas from the station, and police officer Wilfred Grenier warned him to stop drinking. Douglas, angered by the suggestion that he was drunk, told Grenier, "You're a liar." The Witness was then arrested for disorderly conduct and for violating the state's abusive language law.[28] Five months after Walter Chaplinsky's arrest, Jim Bowering knew exactly how to charge Douglas. Under "offense," the municipal court docket noted that the Witness allegedly "did address offensive and annoying words in a public place."[29]

Four days after his arrest, Walter Chaplinsky appeared before Gardner S. Hall, a judge in Rochester's municipal court. Unable to find an attorney, he asked for a continuance. Leonard Hardwick, the city solicitor, requested a continuance as well, so Hall slated the Witness's trial for the following week. Testifying before a courtroom tightly packed with fellow Witnesses, Chaplinsky described how he had been drubbed by the mob and how William Bowman had tried to skewer him with the flag pole. "Bowman," he asserted, "attempted to kill me." (For his part, Bowman admitted to having been at the square, but he denied making any attempt to impale Chaplinsky.) Describing his arduous journey from the scene of the mobbing to the police station, the defendant readily admitted to having exchanged angry words with Jim Bowering. "I called the marshal a damned fascist [and] racketeer," Chaplinsky recalled. "He took me into the police station, where he called me a 'damned unpatriotic dog.'" That was enough for Hall: he found the Witness guilty, sentenced him to twelve days in jail, and ordered him to pay $24.78 in court costs.[30]

Chaplinsky was so infuriated by the verdict that he warned the judge, "This court will be responsible to Almighty God," and the Witnesses in attendance staged a brief protest. Hall was unfazed by the reaction to his decision. "I call 'em as I see 'em," he said from the bench. "If I'm wrong, there's a chance for appeal. Thank God." Although he hardly had the resources to pay for a protracted legal battle, Chaplinsky decided to appeal Hall's verdict to the Strafford County Superior Court.[31]

His timing could not have been worse. Chaplinsky's superior court trial, heard by a jury in Dover, New Hampshire, in September 1940, coincided with the widely publicized shooting of a sheriff's deputy in Maine by a Jehovah's Witness. The incident began when two Witnesses, Arthur Cox and Kenneth Carr, proselytized at Dean Pray's garage in North Windham, Maine (a small town located about fifty miles northeast of Rochester). Angered by the proselytizers' message, Pray—a World War I veteran, American Legion member, and deputy sheriff—brandished a tire iron at the Witnesses and chased them from the building. "Dean was still holding the tire iron when [Cox] pulled a gun, apparently from the right hip pocket, and began to shoot, shooting four or five times at Dean," said Perley Varney, who watched the incident. "Dean turned and staggered back toward the garage door facing me and fell." Hit by two shots from Cox's gun, Pray bled to death, and his wife, having witnessed the shooting, had to be hospitalized for shock. With memories of the Kennebunk-area disturbances of June 1940 still fresh in their minds, Cumberland County authorities feared that the gunplay in North Windham would touch off another outbreak of anti-Witness violence. Fully "aware of [the] intense feeling which has been aroused by the slaying of Deputy Sheriff Pray," Albert Knudsen, the county attorney, begged Mainers to remain calm. "In times of high stress and emotion, I plead for moderation," he said. The caution of local authorities paid off, and the lawlessness of the previous June was not repeated. The crisis in North Windham seemed to have passed by 1 October when a jury deliberated for less than four hours and found Cox guilty of murdering Pray.[32]

Pray's untimely death at the hands of a Jehovah's Witness received extensive press coverage in Maine and neighboring New Hampshire throughout August and September. For some newspapers, the shooting, and Cox's apparent lack of remorse afterward, demonstrated all too vividly the dangers posed by Witnesses and their attempts to disseminate un-American doctrines. Commenting on the circumstances of Pray's murder, a newspaper in Dover, New Hampshire, harshly criticized the Witnesses' practices and beliefs, and it hinted that their refusal to salute the American flag signaled a lack of patriotism. "Of course Jehovah's Witnesses represent an extreme of society and of religious intolerance," the paper argued. "They know . . . that all other forms of religion are wrong and worse. They oppose saluting the flag and they are against almost everything for which the average person stands." The editorial in *Foster's Daily Democrat* further suggested that "Jehovah's Witnesses ought to keep the law of the land or else go where they can spread their peculiar beliefs to their heart's content. We cannot here, under any pretext, [tolerate] those who are disloyal to the flag."[33]

Although there is no evidence in the trial record to indicate that the shooting of Dean Pray was an issue in Chaplinsky's superior court trial, it is safe to assume that the furor surrounding the North Windham murder could not have helped his chances with the jury. That Pray's death generated intense anti-Witness sentiments in New Hampshire was demonstrated in another case involving Chaplinsky in 1940. In early September of that year, just before his appeal was heard in superior court, authorities in Dover charged Chaplinsky with disturbing the peace. A municipal court judge in that city found Chaplinsky guilty and then denounced Jehovah's Witnesses as "a dirty bunch of murderers who killed a man in cold blood in Maine." Speaking from the bench, the judge told Chaplinsky, "I despise you and your organization."[34] By that point, Chaplinsky had already dealt with more than his share of hostility and intimidation. For instance, free on bail after his conviction in municipal court, the Witness had been punched in the face while proselytizing in Gonic, New Hampshire. Earlier in the same week, several young men had deflated the tires of his car and removed the valves. "According to witnesses," the *Rochester Courier* reported, "the youths threatened to tip over the car if Chaplinsky and his companions, a woman and two boys, returned to Gonic."[35]

Alfred Albert, Chaplinsky's attorney, believed that he could present a strong case during the superior court trial, in part because the circumstances of the Rochester attack and Chaplinsky's subsequent arrest had been so repulsive. Although they had known that Chaplinsky was in danger, police had failed to prevent the assault, and then they had arrested the victim under a seldom-used law—one that apparently was enforced in Rochester only against Jehovah's Witnesses. Furthermore, of the many people who had been involved in the fracas, only Chaplinsky had been prosecuted; his assailants had been allowed to walk away. Albert decided to make those troubling circumstances the centerpiece of his defense. At the superior court trial, he argued that in light of what had happened to Chaplinsky in Rochester that afternoon, the Witness had every reason to rebuke Jim Bowering as a "damn fascist and racketeer." In his opening statement, Albert contended that the "willful neglect" of Rochester police officers had directly contributed to the attack on Chaplinsky, and he explained that his client had lashed out verbally at Bowering only after he had been "insulted, abused and unjustly and unduly provoked." Chaplinsky's alleged crime was a minor one, Albert maintained, "but the circumstances around that offense are serious," and the jury could consider them as mitigating factors. Albert raised a constitutional issue as well, blasting the abusive language law as an "unreasonable restraint on the freedom of speech, the freedom of the press, and the freedom of worship" that were guaranteed to all Americans by the First and Fourteenth Amendments.[36]

John Beamis, the Strafford County solicitor, voiced objections at several points in Albert's opening statement, and Judge Henri Borque sustained them. And though Borque momentarily headed off Albert's attempt to make police misconduct the central issue of the trial ("The issue is whether or not [Chaplinsky] used these words," the judge admonished), the Witness's attorney never really relented. Throughout his cross-examination of two key prosecution witnesses, Gerald Lapierre and Jim Bowering, Albert was able repeatedly to underscore his contention that the "willful neglect" of the Rochester police had led to the attack on Chaplinsky in Central Square. As they fielded sharp questions from Albert, neither police officer could provide a plausible explanation for the inaction of police during the riot, nor could they account for their slipshod work afterward. In testimony that drew a series of incredulous responses from Albert, Lapierre maintained that although he had been directing traffic "perhaps the length of the [court]room" from the scene of the disturbance, he had noticed nothing unusual until after Chaplinsky had been mobbed, at which point he grabbed the victim and started hauling him off to the police station. Bowering's testimony rang hollow as well. Albert forced the marshal to recount his first trip to the square, when William Bowman had throttled Chaplinsky and angrily demanded that he salute the American flag. He had seen Bowman violently grab the Witness by the collar, the marshal acknowledged, but he had chosen not to arrest the veteran for assault, as Chaplinsky requested.

> Bowering: I said, "It is not necessary."
> Albert: Didn't you consider that a violation of the law?
> Bowering: No.
> Albert: In other words, people in the town that you are marshal of can go around grabbing people by the coat collars, and you don't consider that an offense, do you?
> Bowering: I do in some cases if it is necessary to make an arrest.
> Albert: I am asking whether or not that is an offense.
> Bowering: No.
> Albert: It is not an offense?
> Bowering: Not to me.

The two men engaged in a similarly edgy colloquy when Albert asked Bowering to explain why he had left the square without dispersing the hostile crowd that had gathered around Chaplinsky. Bowering testified that he had merely advised the Witness to tone down his preaching because it was "going to get the public in an ugly mood."

> Albert: You said the public was in an ugly mood?
> Bowering: I knew they were from the complaints I received.
> Albert: You knew the public was in an ugly mood from the complaints you received. Knowing that the public was in an ugly mood, you left the defendant standing on that corner and walked away assuming that everything was serene?
> Bowering: It was when I left.

Albert: It was when you left, yet you knew that the public was in an ugly mood?

Bowering: Oh, yes.

Albert: Didn't you fear that any danger might come to this defendant?

Bowering: Possibly, yes.[37]

Throughout Chaplinsky's trial, Bowering and his fellow police officers attempted to refute Albert's repeated suggestions that they had mistreated the Witness during their journey from Central Square to the police station. None of the policemen, of course, could offer a plausible explanation as to why a half-dozen officers had escorted the battered victim of a mobbing to jail while his assailants were permitted to flee. Yet all the officers who testified at the trial were adamant in denying that they had abused Chaplinsky in the wake of the attack. Chaplinsky himself testified that the officers had manhandled him, and witness Gregory Gessis recalled that he had seen various members of the police escort "mistreating" and "roughly handling" Chaplinsky. The police officers denied it all. Gerald Lapierre—like Bowering, a former member of Rochester's semiprofessional football team—admitted that he and officer Burt Powers "had hold of the defendant," but he maintained that they had not used excessive force. For his part, Bowering asserted that he had done absolutely nothing to provoke Chaplinsky's outburst. Asked by Albert if he had at least addressed the Witness in "a loud tone," the marshal replied, "No, not louder than necessary."[38]

After Albert rested his case, Judge Borque spoke to the jury and offered instructions for its deliberations. If any of the jurors were wrestling with the idea that Walter Chaplinsky's First Amendment freedoms were at stake or that they might seriously have to weigh the defendant's allegations of police misconduct, Borque quickly put their minds at ease. Their job as jurors was uncomplicated, he said.

We are not concerned here with freedom of speech or religious freedom or anything of that kind. The sole question is whether there has been a violation of a statutory law. In other words, whether any statute prohibiting use of offensive, derisive or annoying words to anyone in a public place or a public street has been violated by the respondent. I need not comment on the meaning of the words used. You know what they mean as well as I do. It is for you to determine what the meaning is and whether they were in fact offensive, derisive or annoying.

Making this determination should not be especially difficult, Borque noted, in part because Chaplinsky "practically has admitted what the state charges." The judge's narrow instructions—and his damaging summary of Chaplinsky's testimony—made the jurors' task an easy one; they deliberated for fifteen minutes before finding the Witness guilty. Although Chaplinsky's original sentence had been twelve days in jail, Borque increased the penalty to six months and ordered the defendant, who was already strapped for cash, to pay an additional $42.54 in court costs.[39]

Hayden Covington joined with Alfred Albert to represent Chaplinsky when he appealed his conviction to the Supreme Court of New Hampshire. In his brief, Covington highlighted the issue of police misconduct, remarking that Chaplinsky had testified that he had been "roughly handled" by the officers who had escorted him to the station and that at least one law enforcement official, Deputy Sheriff Ralph Dunlap, had "joined in with the mob" during the attack itself. In light of such evidence, it was apparent that the prosecution of Chaplinsky was little more than

an effort on the part of local officials to get vengeance against [him], and constitutes the "framing of mischief by law" as foretold at Psalm 94:20. They knew that the United States Supreme Court had upheld the right of free distribution of literature, and when they saw that the mob could not drive the defendant off the street they seized upon this law in a desperate effort to put the defendant away "for good."

Realizing, however, that the state supreme court's review of Chaplinsky's conviction might not necessarily hinge on the troubling facts of the case, Covington devoted a large portion of his ten-point argument to assailing the dubious constitutionality of New Hampshire's abusive language statute. His principal contention was that the state measure was "repugnant to the due process clause of the Fourteenth Amendment in that it unreasonably restricts freedom of speech, and as construed and applied [it] unreasonably restricts freedom of press and worship of Almighty God contrary to the Fourteenth Amendment." The law had myriad other flaws as well, including "the fact that it is so vague, indefinite, uncertain, and ambiguous that it fails to set a reasonable standard of guilt."[40]

The brief submitted by the State of New Hampshire—drafted by Strafford County Solicitor John Beamis, Assistant Attorney General Ernest D'Amours, and Attorney General Frank Kenison—was far shorter and more focused than Covington's. Not surprisingly, the state glossed over the circumstances of the mobbing of Chaplinsky and the subsequent misconduct of the police officers who ushered him to the police station. "The evidence concerning the nature of the riot at Central Square is conflicting," the brief claimed, "but all witnesses for the state testified that they did not participate in the riot or in any way provoke, annoy or abuse the respondent." Although it shied away from the facts of the case, the state was eager to refute Covington's blunt attacks on the constitutionality of New Hampshire's abusive language law. According to the state's brief, the measure was in no way "obnoxious to the constitutional guaranty of free speech, free press, [and] free worship," as Covington had asserted. "It is submitted that the statute here in question is simply an exercise of the political authority deemed essential by the legislature to secure and maintain an orderly, tranquil and free society without which religious toleration itself would be a myth."[41]

In their briefs, both the state and Covington attempted to bolster their positions by citing portions of the U.S. Supreme Court's ruling in *Cantwell v. Connecticut*. Having helped to mount the Witnesses' appeal in that case, Covington was quite familiar with the Court's opinion, in which it had completed the incorporation of the First Amendment's protections of speech, press, assembly, and worship into the due process clause of the Fourteenth Amendment. To Covington, one portion of the *Cantwell* opinion seemed particularly germane to Walter Chaplinsky's appeal.

In the realm of religious faith, and in that of political belief, sharp differences arise. In both fields the tenets of one man may seem the rankest error to his neighbor. To persuade others to his own point of view, the pleader, as we know, at times, resorts to exaggeration, to vilification of men who have been, or are, prominent in church or state, and even to false statement. But the people of this nation have ordained in the light of history, that, in spite of the excesses and abuses, these liberties are, in the long view, essential to enlightened opinion and right conduct on the part of the citizens of a democracy.[42]

When viewed within this permissive context, Covington suggested, Chaplinsky's speech, though grating, had to be tolerated in the interests of nurturing religious freedom and protecting the free trade of ideas.[43] But the State of New Hampshire countered with its own passage from the *Cantwell* opinion, one that undercut Covington's assertion that Chaplinsky's speech merited protection. In a citation that must have made Covington cringe, it pointed out that the Supreme Court had held in *Cantwell* that "resort to epithets or personal abuse is not in any proper sense communication of information or opinion safeguarded by the Constitution and its punishment as a criminal act would raise no question under that instrument."[44]

In its unanimous opinion in *Chaplinsky v. New Hampshire*, handed down in March 1941, the Supreme Court of New Hampshire acknowledged that if Chaplinsky's account of his drubbing and arrest was accurate, then "nobody concerned . . . used proper restraint on this occasion." The court also recognized that in the wake of the mobbing, Chaplinsky

> undoubtedly felt resentment because he had been roughly handled by the crowd. His resentment might well enough have extended to the police if they had failed to take any step reasonably within their power to control the crowd, or if they had failed to prosecute anybody who they had reasonable ground to believe had assailed him.

But that Chaplinsky might very well have been provoked—or even that his accusations might have been accurate—did not mean that the Constitution protected his speech, the court held. His outburst, after all, did not

> rise above name-calling. It is not argument. It has no persuasive power. Its only power is to inflame, to endanger that calm and useful consideration of public problems which is the protection of free government. Its tendency is to useless and dangerous disorder in which the object of free speech is lost to view.

Given its role as custodian of public order, the state had every right to limit language that was "plainly likely to cause a breach of the peace by the addressee"—in short, "fighting words"—through measures such as the one under which Chaplinsky was convicted. The law was constitutional, the court held, and the Witness's conviction stood.[45]

Hayden Covington responded to this setback by appealing Chaplinsky's conviction one last time. In the brief he submitted to the U.S. Supreme Court in its October 1941 term, the untiring Witness attorney again condemned the extraordinary circumstances of the attack on Chaplinsky and his subsequent arrest. Covington noted that Chaplinsky had been peacefully distributing literature in Rochester's Central Square, engaging in "Godly and Christlike work," but "because the message contained in the pamphlets and magazines was not suitable to the rabble element of Rochester, including members of the police department, a mob formed and gathered around him, threatening him with violence unless he discontinued his work." A devoted minister of the Gospel, Chaplinsky had kept right on preaching, and he had also refused to commit idolatry by saluting the American flag. As a result, William Bowman, the former commander of the local Veterans of Foreign Wars post, had wielded a flagpole "as a spear or javelin in assault against him," and he had been "assaulted and beaten in the presence of public officers, one of whom actually participated in such mistreatment." Given those circumstances, the harried Witness "was justified in saying what he did say, and such utterances were provoked by the police, one of whom participated in the mob." If the facts of Walter Chaplinsky's mobbing, arrest, and conviction were deeply troubling to Covington, so too was the possibility that the Supreme Court might lose sight of the case's broader constitutional implications and uphold the Witness's conviction. "To permit this conviction to stand," he maintained, "means the end of speech and constitutional liberty in this country."[46]

As the 1940s wore on, Justice Frank Murphy's leniency toward Jehovah's Witness appellants became the subject of good-natured ribbing among his fellow members of the Supreme Court. Assessing Murphy's track record in Witness appeals, one of the

Brethren is said to have commented, "If Frank Murphy is ever sainted, it will be by the Jehovah's Witnesses."[47] Murphy's compassion for the Witnesses dated to his earliest days on the Court. Just months after his appointment, he wrote a dissent in *Gobitis* in which he argued that "it is of vital importance that freedom of conscience and opinion be protected against all considered regulations that have no practical efficacy and bear no necessary or substantial relation to the maintenance of order and safety of our institutions."[48] Although he ultimately bowed to pressure and shelved that effort, Murphy proved to be one of the Witnesses' most reliable and articulate champions during their legal campaign in the early and mid-1940s. In his dissent in *Prince v. Massachusetts*, for instance, Murphy wrote that Witnesses had been "harassed at every turn by the resurrection and enforcement of little used ordinances and statutes," and he warned that the Court should "hesitate before approving the application of a statute that might be used as another instrument of oppression."[49] In another dissent, Murphy acknowledged the seriousness of the Witnesses' suffering by comparing their woes in the early and mid-1940s to the travails of some of this country's earliest religious minorities. "An arresting parallel exists," Murphy wrote, "between the troubles of Jehovah's Witnesses and the struggles of various dissident groups in the American colonies for religious liberty which culminated in the Virginia Statute for Religious Freedom, the Northwest Ordinance of 1787, and the First Amendment."[50] That Murphy was a devout Roman Catholic made his sympathy for Witness appellants, many of whom had run afoul of the law while publicly distributing tracts and pamphlets containing vitriolic attacks on the leaders of his faith, even more remarkable. "It comforts me that with 800 years of Catholic background," he later wrote, "I can speak in defense of a people opposed to my own faith."[51]

Murphy, however, cast a jaundiced eye on Walter Chaplinsky's appeal, and he wrote for a unanimous Supreme Court in affirming the Witness's conviction. In an opinion handed down on 9 March 1942, Murphy spent little time reviewing the disquieting facts of the case. The Court's sole duty, he noted, lay in determining the constitutionality of the New Hampshire abusive language statute under which Chaplinsky had been convicted. And so the appellant's suffering at the hands of the mob in Rochester's Central Square was dealt with perfunctorily, with Murphy briefly mentioning that "a disturbance occurred and the traffic officer on duty at the busy intersection started with Chaplinsky for the police station." He similarly papered over the physically and verbally abusive behavior of Jim Bowering and his compatriots as they dragged Chaplinsky to the police station. Having displayed his indifference to the facts of the case, Murphy eviscerated Covington's contention that Chaplinsky's rights under the Fourteenth Amendment had been compromised. For starters, New Hampshire's abusive language statute was neither overbroad nor vague but rather "narrowly drawn and limited to define and punish specific conduct lying within the domain of state power, the use in a public place of words likely to cause a breach of the peace." There was little doubt that the state had constitutional power to circumscribe such language, Murphy wrote.

> It is well understood that right of free speech is not absolute at all times and under all circumstances. There are certain well-defined and narrowly limited classes of speech, the prevention and punishment of which never have been thought to raise any Constitutional problem. These include the lewd and obscene, the profane, the libelous, and the insulting or "fighting words"— those which by their very utterance inflict injury or tend to incite an immediate breach of peace.

Whether or not they were justified or truthful, the inflammatory words Chaplinsky used as he was led away from Central Square clearly fell into those last two categories, Murphy wrote. In the end, such utterances played "no essential part of any exposition of ideas, and are of such slight social value as a step to truth that any benefit that may be derived from them is clearly outweighed by the social interest in order and morality." To help seal his argument, Murphy cited the *Cantwell* opinion's dictum that "resort to epithets or personal abuse is not in any proper sense communication of information or opinion safeguarded by the Constitution"—the passage that the State of New Hampshire had cited in calling for an affirmation of Chaplinsky's conviction.[52]

If any of Murphy's fellow justices had serious misgivings about his opinion in *Chaplinsky v. New Hampshire,* it appears that they kept their thoughts to themselves. Justice Hugo Black told Murphy that he had "shown much wisdom in deciding the case with such restraint," and Justice Robert Jackson informed him, "The Constitution does not include a right to brawl and that's about all that seems to be involved."[53]

His appeals exhausted, Chaplinsky suffered through a six-month term at a prison farm in Strafford County, New Hampshire. When he arrived at the facility, the warden, fearing that such discussions might cause unrest, cautioned him not to speak with other inmates about his faith. Shortly after his arrival, he ignored the warning during a conversation with a fellow convict. Asked why he had been jailed, Chaplinsky explained that he was a Jehovah's Witness who was so captivated by the truths of the Bible that he preached them wherever and whenever he could. From the time of Christ and the apostles, such messengers had been vilified and persecuted because of their beliefs, and he was no exception. "Another prisoner heard me talking and he went and told the warden that I was preaching," Chaplinsky recalled. "For what I did I served six weeks in solitude." Following his release from solitary confinement, Chaplinsky toiled in the prison's squalid pig barn. His job was simple: each day he had to sweep and shovel away the excrement deposited by dozens of animals. The barn was in dreadful condition, and Chaplinsky worked "over two weeks to clean the filth away and make it a decent place," as he later put it. When he wasn't removing the pigs' waste, the Witness tended to sows who had recently given birth. Having lived on a farm as an adolescent, he knew that sows were capable of crushing or even consuming their newborn, so he moved the helpless piglets out of harm's way.[54] Chaplinsky's spirits remained high throughout his incarceration, and from the prison farm he dispatched a gallant letter to Jehovah's Witness officials in New York. "At all times I shall, by the Lord's grace," he wrote, "stand firm for THE THEOCRACY, and will await the day of my release with joy."[55]

To most contemporary judges and legal scholars, *Chaplinsky v. New Hampshire* is memorable for a single reason: the fighting words doctrine employed by the Supreme Court to uphold Chaplinsky's conviction. As articulated in Murphy's opinion for the Court, the doctrine permits the state to impose criminal sanctions on speech if it can show that the words tend to "inflict injury" or that they are likely to "incite an immediate breach of the peace." Over the past half century, the Supreme Court's two-pronged standard for assessing the constitutionality of fighting words has been modified and reformulated in several cases, including *Terminiello v. Chicago* (1949), *Street v. New York* (1969), *Cohen v. California* (1971), *Gooding v. Wilson* (1972), *Kelly v. Ohio* (1974), and *R.A.V. v. St. Paul* (1992).[56] Thanks to those opinions, the broad restrictions on speech articulated by the Court to uphold Walter Chaplinsky's conviction have been narrowed considerably. The "inflict injury" prong of the fighting words doctrine, for instance, has never been used by the Supreme Court to uphold another conviction, prompting some observers to wonder if anything remains of it.[57] The "breach of peace" prong endures, although it too has been substantially limited over the years.[58]

The erosion of the fighting words doctrine has been demonstrated in two Supreme Court decisions relating to insulting language directed at police officers. In both *Lewis v. City of New Orleans* (1974)[59] and *City of Houston v. Hill* (1987),[60] the Court threw out convictions of defendants who had been arrested for addressing policemen with vituperative speech. That the addressee in both cases had been a police officer was crucial to the Court's determination that the fighting words doctrine was inapplicable. In *Lewis*, Justice Lewis Powell noted that "a properly trained officer may reasonably be expected to 'exercise a higher degree of restraint' than the average citizen, and thus be less likely to respond to 'fighting words.'"[61] Of course, had the Court followed this line of reasoning a half century earlier in *Chaplinsky*, it seems unlikely that the Witness's conviction would have been allowed to stand.

Chaplinsky himself fared far better than the shaky doctrine so closely associated with his name. In the mid-1990s, he was living in St. Petersburg, Florida, and remaining steadfast in his faith. Even in his old age, Chaplinsky was an active proselytizer. One correspondent inquiring about his activities received several thoughtful replies, as well as stacks of Witness tracts and journals. "There is no compromise—all witnesses of Jehovah want to be faithful," he wrote. "My purpose in life is to not lose faith in God."[62]

9. Blot Removed

While Justice Frank Murphy was busy formulating the fighting words doctrine early in 1942, the Supreme Court heard oral arguments in *Jones v. Opelika*, a case consolidating separate appeals from Witnesses in Alabama, Arkansas, and Arizona. The central constitutional issue in the three cases was essentially the same: Could a municipality impose a licensing fee on the Witnesses' proselytizing activities? In three previous rulings—*Lovell* (1938), *Schneider* (1939), and *Cantwell* (1940)—the Court had struck down as unconstitutional measures giving local authorities the discretion to approve or deny peddling and solicitation permits, but it had yet to determine if the Witnesses' rights under the First and Fourteenth Amendments were violated by the payment of a nondiscriminatory tax. (Opelika, Alabama, required payment of a $10.00 annual fee; Casa Grande, Arizona, charged $25.00 every quarter; and Fort Smith, Arkansas, imposed fees ranging from $2.50 a day to $25.00 each month.)[1] An apparently mundane tax case, *Jones* had enormous implications for both the Jehovah's Witnesses and the Supreme Court itself, in part because the justices' prolonged struggle to resolve it led them to readdress what several of the Brethren had come to think of as a grievous mistake—their 1940 ruling in *Minersville School District v. Gobitis.* By mid-1943, a flurry of Witness appeals, including *Jones,* left the court poised to right its glaring error in the Pennsylvania flag-salute case.

In his brief in *Jones,* Hayden Covington vigorously urged the Supreme Court to strike down the licensing ordinances by interpreting the Constitution "fearlessly and impartially so as to promote justice." Describing the work of Rosco Jones, an African-American Witness who had been convicted for failing to pay the licensing fee required of all peddlers of books and tracts in Opelika, Covington informed the Court that Jones proselytized because he was a minister preaching the Gospel. Though ministers in other faiths sermonized from pulpits, Witnesses like Jones and his wife, Thelma, spread their faith just as Christ and the apostles had—by going "throughout every city and village teaching and preaching the Kingdom of God," as it was described in the Scriptures. In effect, by requiring Jones to pay a licensing fee for his proselytizing, the city of Opelika was taxing his form of worship, and that burden clearly violated his First Amendment rights (which were protected from interference by state and local officials via the due process clause of the Fourteenth Amendment).

The American Civil Liberties Union, in its recurring role as friend of the court, buttressed Covington's arguments by asserting that the imposition of licensing taxes on the Witnesses' preaching activities might squelch the free trade of ideas and render the work of itinerant evangelists "impossible." For its part, the city of Opelika claimed that its licensing ordinance was innocuous and lacked "any of the pernicious characteristics attributed to it" by Covington and the ACLU. Distinguishing the tax measure from the ordinance struck down as unconstitutional in *Lovell*, the city maintained that its law posed no threat to anyone's First or Fourteenth Amendment freedoms because there was no danger that it would be wielded as a tool to censor particular points of view; in Opelika, everyone who paid the tax was authorized to sell literature in public. The city told the Court that it should be concerned with shielding "the right of any community to assess and collect . . . revenue needed to carry on the functions and duties of government," not with preserving Jones's civil liberties, especially since the basic nature of his proselytizing activities was in fact more commercial than religious.[2]

Five members of the Supreme Court essentially agreed with the city of Opelika's arguments, and they ruled that its licensing ordinance (along with those in Fort Smith and Casa Grande) was constitutional. Writing for the majority, Justice Stanley Reed noted that in several previous Witness cases, the Court had "den[ied] any place to administrative censorship of ideas or capricious approval of distributors." Yet *Jones* was distinguishable in that the "sole constitutional question considered is whether a nondiscriminatory license fee, presumably appropriate in amount, may be imposed" on the Witnesses' proselytizing activities. That there was a commercial nature to the evangelists' work—they accepted small donations for their books, tracts, and periodicals—was crucial to Reed because no one doubted that municipalities could legitimately regulate and tax commercial activities. He wrote:

> When proponents of religious or social theories use the ordinary commercial methods of sales of articles to raise propaganda funds, it is a natural and proper exercise of the power of the state to charge reasonable fees for the privilege of canvassing. Careful as we may and should be to protect the freedoms safeguarded by the Bill of Rights, it is difficult to see in such enactments a shadow of prohibition of the exercise of religion or of abridgement of the freedom of speech or the press.

Describing the majority's reasoning in a later portion of the *Jones* opinion, Reed explained that "it is because we view these sales as partaking more of commercial than religious or educational transactions that we find the ordinances, as here presented, valid."[3]

The critical response to the majority opinion in *Jones* was reminiscent of the pillorying that the Supreme Court had taken after it handed down its ruling in *Gobitis*. A survey of newspaper editorials revealed that the *Jones* opinion was criticized from Birmingham and Richmond to Racine, Wisconsin, and Lewiston, Idaho, with unfavorable comments exceeding favorable ones at a ratio of nineteen to one.[4] *Time* called it an "ominous decision," and another assessment categorized the opinion as "a black mark on the Supreme Court's record."[5] In an editorial, "Civil Liberty Endangered," the *Christian Century* conceded that the Witness appellants belonged to "a particularly odious and fanatical sect." Even so, the *Jones* opinion was a faulty one, the magazine contended, for

> it promotes the encroachment of government upon legitimate civil rights; it accelerated the tendency, always strong in time of war, toward government by administrative order; it does not strengthen the national unity and morale which it is designed to encourage; and it does not prevent any concrete injuries to society. In short, it does not work.[6]

The reaction to *Jones* in law reviews was scarcely more favorable. A brief but caustic appraisal in the *Yale Law Journal* noted that "with the exception of the West Coast Japanese-Americans, the Wit-

A police officer confronting a Jehovah's Witness as he attempts to proselytize.

nesses are already the most persecuted minority in America. . . . Every conceivable means from mob violence to arrest on charges of vagrancy has been used to silence them or regulate their conduct." Yet another chapter in the lamentable story of the Witnesses' oppression, the *Jones* ruling represented a "serious threat to civil liberties," according to the article, because it would "probably lead to the enactment of similar ordinances throughout the country. If so, the practice of their religion by Witnesses through the distribution of their literature may be curtailed."[7] As it turned out, the fear that *Jones* would spur the widespread enactment of licensing ordinances targeted specifically at Witnesses was not unfounded. Late in 1942, two attorneys from the Justice Department's Civil Rights Section reported that "already letters have been received requesting copies of the [*Jones*] opinion for the information as a basis for drafting peddlers' licensing ordinances for the avowed purpose of putting a stop to Jehovah's Witnesses' activities. The thought is present that most communities will at once resort to this expedient."[8] Thus, although *Jones* did not spark rioting and other acts of vigilantism, as *Gobitis* had, it nonetheless contributed to the continuing suppression of the Witnesses' civil liberties.

Reed's opinion for the majority in *Jones* was perhaps most notable for the three dissents it provoked from the Supreme Court's minority. In his dissent, Harlan Fiske Stone (who had been appointed chief justice by President Roosevelt after Charles Evans Hughes's retirement in 1941) framed the issues presented in *Jones* in starker terms than those employed by Stanley Reed. Stone asserted that the case "presents in its baldest form the question whether the freedoms which the Constitution purports to safeguard can be completely subjected to uncontrolled administrative action." To Stone, it was obvious that those precious individual liberties, so crucial to the success of democracy in America, could not be subordinated to the purported interests of municipalities like Opelika, Fort Smith, and Casa Grande. He had little doubt that the imposition of taxes on the Witnesses' proselytizing activities would be "destructive of freedom of press and religion" and could be levied to suppress the constitutional rights of "peripatetic religious propagandists." That the taxes were levied in a nondiscriminatory fashion mattered little to Stone. "In its potency as a prior restraint on publication," he wrote, "the flat license tax falls short only of outright censorship or suppression. The more humble and needy the cause, the more effective is the suppression."[9]

Stone's dissent also dealt more generally with the particular importance of the freedoms of speech, worship, press, and assembly protected by the First and Fourteenth Amendments. A number of other members of the Supreme Court had shared with Stone the notion that these liberties were of such significance to the maintenance of a free society that they should be considered "preferred freedoms." In 1937, for instance, Justice Benjamin Cardozo had noted that First Amendment freedoms, which "lie at the base of all our civil and political institutions" and comprise "the matrix, the indispensable condition, of nearly every other form of freedom," were "so rooted in the traditions and conscience of our people as to be ranked fundamental."[10] As was evidenced in *Carolene Products* and in his *Gobitis* dissent, Stone believed that the First Amendment's freedoms were so vitally important that they deserved to be accorded an exalted status in the hierarchy of constitutional liberties. The majority's ruling in *Jones*, which seemed to jeopardize the Witnesses' freedoms of press and worship, prompted the chief justice to reiterate his feelings on this score in his dissent:

The First Amendment is not confined to safeguarding freedom of speech and freedom of religion against discriminatory attempts to wipe them out. On the contrary the Constitution, by virtue of the First and Fourteenth Amendments, has put those freedoms in a preferred position. Their commands are not restricted to cases where the protected privilege is sought out for attack. They extend at least to every form of taxation which, because it is a condition of the exercise of the privilege, is capable of being used to control or suppress it.[11]

Justice Frank Murphy joined in Stone's dissent in *Jones* and offered a forceful one of his own. Although Walter Chaplinsky might not have thought so, Murphy was generally sympathetic to the claims of Witness appellants, and in his *Jones* dissent he once again argued for vigorous protections of their civil liberties. Like Stone, Murphy believed that the majority had mischaracterized the basic nature of the Witnesses' proselytizing activities. Disputing a linchpin of Reed's majority opinion, he contended that "it does not appear that their motives were commercial, but only that they were evangelizing their faith as they saw it." Given that the appellants were ministers who were worshiping as they distributed their books, tracts, and periodicals, "the taxes are in reality taxes upon the dissemination of religious ideas, a dissemination carried on by the distribution of religious reasons alone and not for personal profit. As such they place a burden on freedom of speech, freedom of press, and the exercise of religion." With the Constitution protecting from such burdens members of all faiths—even creeds that "are controversial and run counter to the established notions of a community"—taxes such as the ones at issue in *Jones* had to be struck down. Murphy concluded that the freedoms shielded by the First Amendment were such "precious rights" that the Court would do no disservice if it proved overprotective of them when they appeared to be in jeopardy.[12]

The bombshell in the *Jones* opinions lay in the combined dissent authored by Murphy, Justice William Douglas, and Justice Hugo Black. Two years earlier, the three men had been members of the Court's eight-man majority in *Gobitis*. It was now clear, however, that each of the justices was prepared to abandon his earlier vote—an astonishing turnabout that nearly gave Stone's dissenting position in *Gobitis* a five-man majority. Acknowledging their error in having endorsed *Gobitis*, and echoing Stone's preferred position thesis, their dissent in *Jones* read in its entirety:

> The opinion of the Court sanctions a device which in our opinion suppresses or tends to suppress the free exercise of religion practiced by a minority group. This is but another step in the direction which Minersville School District v. Gobitis took against the same religious minority and is a logical extension of the principles upon which that decision rested. Since we joined in the opinion in the Gobitis case, we think this is an appropriate occasion to state that we now believe that it was also wrongly decided. Certainly our democratic form of government functioning under the historic Bill of Rights has a high responsibility to accommodate itself to the religious views of minorities however unpopular and unorthodox those views may be. The First Amendment does not put the right freely to exercise religion in a subordinate position. We fear, however, that the opinions in these and the Gobitis case do exactly that.[13]

With the defections of Murphy, Black, and Douglas, and recent changes in the Court's personnel (Charles Evans Hughes and James McReynolds had retired, and James Byrnes and Robert Jackson had joined the Court), only three members of the *Gobitis* majority—Frankfurter, Reed, and Owen Roberts—remained on the bench.

None of the defectors from *Gobitis* followed identical paths to their dissent in *Jones*. Having only reluctantly given it his imprimatur, Murphy had never fully reconciled himself with the majority opinion in *Gobitis*, and he apparently made no secret of his disaffection for the ruling. Through acquaintances within their faith, the Gobitas family learned that Murphy had returned to the Midwest to sit for an official portrait that was to be hung in the state capitol in Michigan, where he had once served as governor. As it happened, the artist was a Jehovah's Witness. "He had long conversations with Justice Murphy while he was sitting for his portrait," Lillian Gobitas Klose later wrote, "and Murphy was expressing that he surely had second thoughts [about the *Gobitis* opinion]."[14]

Although Murphy's qualms clearly dated to the drafting of the majority opinion in *Gobitis*, Douglas's second thoughts surfaced somewhat later. Douglas apparently had not agonized over his endorsement of the majority opinion, at one point calling it "a powerful moving document of incalculable contemporary and [I believe] historical value."[15] Years later, Douglas attributed his regrettable decision to endorse the *Gobitis* opinion to naivete and poor timing. In his autobiography, he recalled that he and his colleagues Black and Murphy—all of them relative newcomers to the Court—had revered Frankfurter, the esteemed scholar and civil libertarian. "He was indeed learned in constitutional law," Douglas wrote, "and we were inclined to take him at face value." They had done so in *Gobitis*, Douglas admitted, and in the process they had somehow failed to grasp the full import of the majority opinion. Meanwhile, "no one knew for sure where Stone stood" because he had failed to circulate a draft of his dissent until 31 May 1940, just three days before the *Gobitis* ruling was to be handed down. By that time, "the vote for Frankfurter's opinion had solidified," and none of the recent additions to the Court had possessed the mettle to switch their votes. As Douglas later told the story, they had quickly realized their error and resolved to correct it at the earliest possible moment.[16]

Black's recollections about the turnaround mirrored Douglas's. As he later explained to a journalist, Black—an Alabamian who had come to the Supreme Court conspicuously lacking much in the way of intellectual pedigree—had been awestruck by Frankfurter and touched by his approach to *Gobitis*. "Felix mesmerized us," Black recalled, speaking for himself as well as for his colleagues Douglas and Murphy. "Felix was an immigrant, passionate about the flag and what it meant to him. We were so moved by his appeal that we went for it." Unfortunately, Stone had circulated his "brilliant" dissent so late that none of the Court's three newest members could sign onto it in time. Black remembered that he, Douglas, and Murphy had debated their choices while sitting around a swimming pool. "What are we going to do? Stone is right," Black had lamented. As he later said, "But we were wiped out by Felix's emotional appeal. . . . We decided to redress the wrong the next time around."[17]

In a discussion with Frankfurter, Douglas speculated on the precise nature of Black's reflection on *Gobitis*. Later in 1940, when Douglas informed Frankfurter that Black was having second thoughts about the Court's ruling in the case, the latter asked if Black had spent the Court's summer recess rereading the Constitution. Douglas replied, "No—he has been reading the papers"—presumably a reference to both the widespread criticism of the majority opinion in *Gobitis* and the ruling's catalytic role in the persecution of Jehovah's Witnesses throughout the country.[18]

Frankfurter was livid over the *Jones* dissenters' explicit repudiation of *Gobitis*, at least in part because he first learned of their intentions just eight days before the Court's opinion was to be handed down. In an angry marginal comment scribbled on a draft of the dissent, he claimed to have been caught completely off guard. *Gobitis*, after all, "was *not* challenged in the argument and its relevance to these cases . . . never discussed or alluded to in conference."[19] As he reviewed the *Jones* dissent, Frankfurter must have realized that his *Gobitis* opinion now commanded the votes of only three members of the Court. Thanks to *Jones*, Stone would be able to reverse the Minersville flag-salute ruling if he could sway either of the Court's newest members, Robert Jackson or James Byrnes. That prospect sickened Frankfurter, who had begun disparaging the three justices who had abandoned *Gobitis* as "the Axis."[20]

Frankfurter probably recognized that Robert Jackson would vote to reverse *Gobitis*. To be sure, Jackson, unlike his colleague Frank Murphy, was not likely to be sainted by the Jehovah's Witnesses. He sided with the majority in *Jones*, and in an opinion in a later Witness case, *Douglas v. Jeannette*, he authored a lengthy and unflattering critique of their proselytizing activities. ("For a stranger to corner a man in his home, summon him to the door and put him in the position either of arguing his religion or of ordering one of unknown disposition to leave is a questionable use of religious freedom," he asserted in a concurring opinion.[21]) But Jackson had been serving as President Roosevelt's attorney general in summer 1940, and he knew that the *Gobitis* opinion had played an important part in the wholesale suppression of the Witnesses' civil liberties. At least in part because he had observed the devastating impact of *Gobitis*, Jackson had made plain his aversion to the majority opinion in the flag-salute case. Prior to his elevation to the Supreme Court in 1941, Jackson had published *The Struggle for Judicial Supremacy*, and in that volume he had cited the *Gobitis* opinion as an exception to the Supreme Court's usual vigilance "in stamping out attempts by local authorities to suppress the free dissemination of ideas, upon which the system of responsible democratic government rests."[22] He later explained, "When I came on the Court, I agreed with Stone that I didn't think that the compulsory flag salute was constitutional."[23]

Frankfurter's hopes of sustaining a majority that shared his position in *Gobitis* were further jeopardized when James Byrnes left the Supreme Court in October 1942 to serve in a series of posts in the Roosevelt administration. Byrnes's eventual replacement, Wiley Rutledge, had hinted at his disapproval of *Gobitis* in an opinion he had written as a judge on the U.S. Court of Appeals for the District of Columbia. In *Busey v. District of Columbia*, which in many ways paralleled *Jones v. Opelika*, the federal appellate court had upheld as constitutional the convictions of two Jehovah's Witnesses for selling literature in public without having first obtained a license or paid the requisite tax. Rutledge had dissented, arguing that the application of the licensing ordinance to the Witnesses' proselytizing quite possibly "perverted" a measure "designed for regulation of business and trade . . . into one for suppression of unpopular religious and political causes." Obviously dismayed by the expulsions of Witness schoolchildren who refused to salute the flag, he had concluded his dissent by noting that

> Jehovah's Witnesses have had to choose between their consciences and public education for their children. In my judgment, they should not have to give up also the right to disseminate their religious views in an orderly manner on the public streets, exercise it at the whim of public officials, or be taxed for doing so without a license.[24]

Frank Murphy, who was then renouncing the position he had taken in *Gobitis*, had been so impressed by the reasoning of Rutledge's lower-court dissent that he had cited it in his own dissent in *Jones*.[25] (In 1943, when the Supreme Court reversed the *Busey* convictions, Rutledge's position was fully vindicated.[26])

Before the Supreme Court formally readdressed the issue of the constitutionality of compulsory flag-salute regulations, it handled several appeals that dealt primarily with the constitutionality of attempts by municipalities to restrict or eliminate the Witnesses' proselytizing activities. In two separate opinions handed down on 8 March 1943, the Court continued to shield the civil liberties of religious proselytizers by reversing the convictions of two Witnesses who had been arrested while evangelizing in Texas. At issue in *Jamison v. Texas* was a Dallas ordinance prohibiting the distribution of handbills. Citing a number of the Court's previous rulings in Witness cases (including *Lovell, Schneider,* and *Cantwell*), Black wrote for a unanimous court that the measure violated the Witness appellants' freedoms of press and worship. "The right to distribute handbills concerning religious subjects on the streets," Black wrote in a brief opinion, "may not be prohibited at all times, at all places, and under all circumstances."[27] In *Largent v. Texas,* the Court, once again citing *Lovell, Schneider,* and *Cantwell,* struck down as unconstitutional an ordinance in Paris, Texas, requiring peddlers of merchandise to obtain a permit that could be granted or withheld at the mayor's discretion. Under the Paris measure, "Dissemination of ideas depends upon the approval of the distributor by the official," Reed wrote for the Court, which was again unanimous. "This is administrative censorship in an extreme form. It abridges the freedom of religion, of the press and of speech guaranteed by the Fourteenth Amendment."[28]

Two days after the Supreme Court handed down its rulings in *Largent* and *Jamison,* it heard oral arguments in *Murdock v. Pennsylvania,* a case consolidating appeals from eight Witnesses. *Murdock* gave the Court, which now included Wiley Rutledge and not James Byrnes, another opportunity to determine if flat licensing fees violated the Witnesses' constitutional freedoms. Joined by Rutledge, the dissenters in *Jones* were able to form a majority and strike down the taxes as unconstitutional. It was a measure of how far the Witnesses had come in their legal campaign that Douglas, writing for the majority in *Murdock,* went out of his way to acknowledge their proselytizing activities as a form of worship shielded by the First Amendment.

> The hand distribution of religious tracts is an age-old form of missionary evangelism—as old as the history of printing presses. It has been a potent force in various religious movements down through the years. This form of evangelism is utilized today on a large scale by various religious sects whose colporteurs carry the Gospel to thousands upon thousands of homes and seek through personal visitations to win adherents to their faith. It is more

than preaching; it is more than distribution of religious literature. It is a combination of both. Its purpose is as evangelical as
the revival meeting. This form of religious activity occupies the
same high estate under the First Amendment as do worship in
the churches and preaching from the pulpits. It has the same
claim to protection as the more orthodox and conventional exercises of religion. It also has the same claims as the others to the
guarantees of freedom of speech and freedom of the press.

Having established the Witnesses' distribution of tracts, periodicals,
and books as a religious exercise, Douglas argued that the Court had
a duty to "restore to their high, constitutional position the liberties
of itinerant evangelists who disseminate their religious beliefs and
the tenets of their faith through distribution of literature." To do
that, the Court had no other choice but to recognize that "a person
cannot be compelled to purchase, through a license fee or a license
tax, a privilege freely granted in the Constitution," particularly one
holding a preferred position.[29]

The Court applied its *Murdock* ruling to the *Jones* case, which
Hayden Covington had reargued early in 1943, and vacated the decision it had rendered just eleven months earlier.[30] The first *Jones*
ruling had been anathema to many Court-watchers, and its reversal
in *Murdock* and *Jones II* was greeted with widespread praise. Writing in the *New Republic*, Irving Dilliard, a staunch civil libertarian,
called the Court's "outright about-face . . . one of the most notable
acts in the entire span of 154 years of Supreme Court history." An
editorial in the *Washington Post* made much the same point, claiming that the reversal was "of tremendous historical importance." For
its part, the *New York Times* noted that the Court reaffirmed "the
right of Jehovah's Witnesses to agitate for their unusual creed." Like
most papers, the *Times* had little patience for the Witnesses and
their "annoying" methods of propagating their thoroughly unpopular beliefs. "Yet, if we permit extremists of an unpleasant sort to be
deprived of their rights, it is hard to tell where the line can be drawn
and who is to be deemed secure," the paper pointed out. "We think
the rights of all Americans are a little safer because Jehovah's Witnesses have had their second day in court."[31] As it counted the votes
for reversing *Jones*, the *Times* lauded the "decisive" vote of the

Court's newest member, Justice Wiley Rutledge. So did the *St. Louis Post-Dispatch*, which noted that Rutledge had "tipped the scales on the side of the cherished freedoms of the Bill of Rights."[32]

The Supreme Court handed down its rulings in *Murdock* and *Jones II* on what one observer termed a "field-day for Jehovah's Witnesses."[33] In addition to *Murdock* and *Jones II*, the rights of Witness evangelists were shielded in *Martin v. Struthers*. That case centered on the constitutionality of an ordinance in Struthers, Ohio, prohibiting "any person distributing handbills, circulars or other advertisements" from ringing doorbells or knocking on doors in order to summon residents of homes or apartments. The measure effectively outlawed the Witnesses' primary form of worship, and one local member of the faith, having been charged and convicted under it, claimed that it violated her freedoms of press and religion. At first, *Martin* threatened to divide Stone from one of his new allies, Hugo Black. "Can a community be barred by the First Amendment from passing this kind of law?" Black wondered during the Court's discussion of the case during its weekly conference. "The line is not distinct but there are means which appeal to me. If you can't protect a church from interruption, how can you do so with a home?" If not, he feared, "the next case will be Jehovah's Witnesses invading a Catholic Church." At the conference, Black initially voted to uphold the Struthers ordinance as constitutional, joining four other justices (Frankfurter, Reed, Roberts, and Jackson) to form a one-vote majority. But upon reading drafts of dissents circulated by Stone and Rutledge, Black began to have second thoughts about his position.[34] Swayed by their criticism of the ordinance, Black decided to switch his vote, and he was assigned to write the opinion for the new majority. The kind of "stringent prohibition" provided for in the Struthers measure, Black wrote, "can serve no purpose but that forbidden by the Constitution, the naked restriction of the dissemination of ideas."[35] Justice Murphy, having told Chief Justice Stone he found it impossible "to let all these cases involving religious convictions go by without even briefly expressing myself on a subject that touches me profoundly," wrote a concurrence in *Martin* reiterating his usual defense of the right of religious proselytizers to spread the tenets of their faith in public without fear of repression. Acknowledging the Witnesses' reputation for combativeness, he noted that the constitutional protections of such activity extended to "the aggressive and disputatious as well as the meek and acquiescent."[36] Discussing his concurrence, Murphy later told a family member, "I went further than most members of the Court will go but it is my gospel."[37]

Stone wrote for the Court in *Douglas v. Jeannette,* the other opinion handed down on the Witnesses' "field-day." In *Douglas,* a group of Witnesses sought to enjoin the City of Jeannette, Pennsylvania, from enforcing against them an ordinance requiring all "persons canvassing for or soliciting . . . orders for goods . . . wares or merchandise of any kind" to obtain a license and pay a licensing fee. As Witnesses were persecuted throughout the United States in the early and mid-1940s, such injunctive actions had become a central weapon in the faith's campaign in the courts against religious discrimination. Hoping to provide relief for Witnesses whose civil liberties were being abrogated by endless rounds of arrests and convictions under restrictive local measures, Hayden Covington had already spearheaded similar efforts in Connersville, Indiana, and Harlan, Kentucky, and he did so again in Lacona, Iowa, in 1946. As Stone noted in his opinion in *Douglas,* the Court's ruling that day in *Murdock* meant that the disputed ordinance in Jeannette was "an unconstitutional abridgement of free speech, press and religion" and thus unenforceable. A separate jurisdictional issue was not resolved in the Witnesses' favor, so they "lost" the case, but the voiding of the ordinance effectively rendered that setback irrelevant.[38]

The Witnesses could thank the same narrow majority for each of their 3 May 1943 triumphs: Stone, the defectors from *Gobitis* (Black, Douglas, and Murphy), and the newcomer Rutledge. Jackson joined with the bloc of remaining *Gobitis* loyalists (Frankfurter, Reed, and Roberts) in dissenting in the four rulings. In part because they were unwilling to countenance the implications of the preferred position doctrine, the dissenters attacked the majority opinions from a variety of angles. Reed, for instance, invoked the intentions of the framers of the Constitution to claim that by exempting Witness proselytizers from licensing taxes, the Court's opinion in *Murdock* provided an unconstitutional "tax subsidy" for their work. "The distributors of religious literature, possibly of all informatory publications, become today privileged," Reed wrote, "to carry on their occupations without contributing their share to the support of government which provides the opportunity for the exercise of their liberties."[39] Dissenting in *Martin*, Reed was perhaps even more exasperated, claiming that "it is impossible for me to discover in this trivial town police regulation a violation of the First Amendment. No ideas are being suppressed. No censorship is involved."[40]

Reed was comforted by Frankfurter, who grumbled in a letter that the Court's opinions in the 3 May Witness cases were so laden with "large, uncritical, congenial abstraction" that they were sure to make bad law.[41] With his *Gobitis* majority obviously in tatters, Frankfurter clung to the increasingly discredited belief that the Witnesses' rights under the First and Fourteenth Amendments were in no way jeopardized by the enforcement of oppressive regulations that ostensibly had been enacted for the public good. Like Reed, he claimed that exempting Witness proselytizers from licensing taxes meant that their activities "shall be subsidized by the state. Such a claim offends the most important of all aspects of religious freedom in this country, that of the separation of church and state."[42] In effect, Frankfurter asserted that Stone's concept of preferred position had been taken so far by the Supreme Court that the Witnesses' faith would have to be underwritten by local governments across the country.

Robert Jackson came to the Supreme Court in 1941 hoping to emulate the judges he had venerated when he had been a young lawyer in upstate New York, impartial men who had concerned themselves with substantive issues of law and treated everyone who appeared before them equitably. "The kind of judge we admired," he recalled, "was a man that didn't let the personalities on either side interfere with his deciding the case on the facts and the law." Jackson also brought with him to the Court a veneration for precedent, which he regarded as a bulwark against chaos and injustice. "There ought to be a certain adherence to precedence, as Cardozo said. By and large, the way a question was decided yesterday ought to be the way in which it is decided today, even though the personalities have changed sides." But, as Jackson readily admitted, even with the guidance of stare decisis, it was often difficult "to draw the line as to where your views of good policy end and your views of law begin, particularly, as Judge Learned Hand has pointed out so well, in matters of applying the Bill of Rights, where you have simply a series of majestic generalities which you have to apply to concrete situations." That task, an extraordinarily difficult one for most members of the Supreme Court, was even more trying for Jackson. A man who had been a quick-thinking and zealous attorney before joining the Court now found himself having to be far more deliberate. "The problem of anyone who had led the kind of life I've had coming on to the Court," he said, "is to shift his mental gears from advocacy of a position that may quickly impress him to a careful judicial inquiry into which position he'll take before he becomes an advocate." Jackson knew that he had to take a much more cautious approach to cases, but he did not always slow down. He once confessed that his biggest shortcoming as a judge "is that I'm perhaps too quick to make up my mind which way I'll go. Perhaps I don't give enough consideration to it. I pretty quickly make up my mind as to which side of any question I want to be on. Sometimes maybe it's too much of an emotional reaction."[43]

It seems likely that when *West Virginia v. Barnette* reached the Supreme Court in 1943, Jackson determined his vote with his customary swiftness. For all intents and purposes, *Barnette* was a replay of the *Gobitis* flag-salute case, and its core issues were every bit as volatile. Soon after the defections of Justices Black, Douglas, and Murphy in *Jones I,* Hayden Covington had begun searching for a means formally to overturn *Gobitis.* He had found it in West Virginia, where numerous Witness schoolchildren had run afoul of a statewide flag-salute requirement adopted by the state's Board of Education early in 1942. The regulation's language left little doubt that it was targeted specifically at Witnesses: it quoted lengthy portions of the Supreme Court's *Gobitis* ruling, including its contention that "conscientious scruples have not in the long struggle for religious toleration relieved the individual from obedience to the general law not aimed at the promotion or restriction of religious beliefs." After authorities expelled more than a half-dozen Witness children from three families—the Barnettes, Stulls, and McClures—in the Charleston area, their parents asked the West Virginia Supreme Court to bar the education board from enforcing the flag-salute measure. When that court denied their requests, the families initiated a suit against the board in the Federal District Court for the Southern District of West Virginia.[44]

The Witnesses' hopes were buoyed by the dissents in *Jones I* and by Congressional enactment of Public Law 623 in June 1942. That measure, sponsored by the American Legion, was meant to codify the language of the Pledge of Allegiance and establish rules for the observance of the flag-salute ritual. (In the process, of course, the veterans' organization hoped to discourage Americans from offering the kind of stiff-armed salute that Germans were using to honor Hitler.) Crucially for Jehovah's Witnesses throughout the United States, the new law stated that "civilians will always show full respect to the flag when the pledge is given by merely standing at attention, men removing headdress." Although the Legion almost certainly had not meant for it to be construed that way, the new law seemed to suggest that people could participate in patriotic observances without actually reciting words to the Pledge of Allegiance or offering a salute to the flag. The law's broad language was a godsend for the Witnesses, for it appeared to offer sanction under federal law for what they had been willing to do all along—stand in silence and offer "respectful attention" during pledge exercises. Victor Rotnem, head of the Justice Department's Civil Rights Section, helped the Witnesses' cause with a sympathetic interpretation of the measure. Writing with his Justice Department colleague F. G. Folsom Jr., Rotnem later explained his assessment of Public Law 623 and its applicability to Witnesses:

> It is submitted that this law of Congress lays down a federal standard with regard to a matter which is primarily a concern of the national government, and therefore state and local regulations demanding a different standard of performance must give way entirely, or at least be made to conform. Speaking more concretely, a school board order respecting flag salute exercises should not now be permitted to exact more of the pupil with religious scruples against the flag salute than that he should stand at attention while the exercise is being conducted.

Rotnem's position that Public Law 623 in effect preempted all local flag-salute regulations quickly became Justice Department policy, and a memorandum summarizing his interpretation of the measure was distributed to all U.S. attorneys in summer 1942.[45]

The *Jones I* dissents proved to be more crucial to the Witnesses' success than the passage of Public Law 623 when the federal district court ruled in *Barnette v. West Virginia State Board of Education.* In his opinion for the court, Judge John Parker acknowledged that in normal circumstances his court "would feel constrained to follow an unreversed decision of the Supreme Court of the United States, whether we agreed with it or not." However, because of the shuffling of Supreme Court personnel and the change of heart experienced by Justices Black, Douglas, and Murphy in *Jones I,* the court did "not feel it is incumbent upon us to accept [*Gobitis*] as binding authority," Parker wrote. With the majority opinion in *Gobitis* "impaired as an authority," the district court did not feel obliged to "deny protection to rights which we regard as among the most sacred of those protected by constitutional guaranties." The flag salute, Parker asserted, was a splendid ceremony, but it had "at most only an indirect influence on the national safety," and no substantial danger would be posed to the security of the state if Witness children were permitted "to refrain from saluting because of their conscientious scruples, however groundless we may personally think those scruples to be." Furthermore, "It certainly cannot strengthen the Republic, or help the state in any way, to require persons to give a salute which they have conscientious scruples against giving, or to deprive them of an education because they refuse to give it." Although Parker was unimpressed by the Justice Department's interpretation of Public Law 623, he refused to countenance the notion that West Virginia's flag-salute regulation was a valid exercise of the state's authority. "There is not a religious persecution in history," he noted, "that was not justified in the eyes of those engaging in it on the ground that it was reasonable and right and that the persons whose practices were suppressed were guilty of stubborn folly hurtful to the general welfare." In the end, the district court endorsed the position established by Harlan Fiske Stone in his *Gobitis* dissent and later embraced by the dissenters in *Jones I.* In granting the injunction requested by the Witness families, the court held, "If they are required to salute the flag, or are denied rights or privileges which belong to them as citizens because they fail to salute it, [the Witness appellants] are unquestionably denied that religious freedom which the Constitution guarantees."[46]

The West Virginia Board of Education did not request a stay of Parker's injunction, and the state's superintendent of schools issued a statement conceding that "children belonging to religious sects whose belief prohibits their participating completely in giving the Flag Salute" would be able to fulfill the state's flag-salute regulation "by standing at attention." As Witness children began to return to their schools in West Virginia, the state education board decided to appeal the lower-court ruling in *Barnette* to the U.S. Supreme Court. The justices heard oral arguments in the case on 11 March 1943 (the same day that the parties in *Murdock* appeared before the Court). The briefs and oral arguments in *Barnette* demonstrated that the passions unleashed by the flag-salute controversy had not abated in the three years since the *Gobitis* opinion had been handed down. Hayden Covington's ire was directed in part at the American Legion, which submitted an amicus curiae brief supporting the state education board's right to require participation in compulsory flag-salute exercises. (Rejecting the Justice Department's interpretation of Public Law 623, which it had sponsored, the Legion maintained that the enactment of the federal measure did not vitiate the right of state and local authorities to enforce flag-salute regulations.) The Legion, of course, had played a leading role in the persecution of Jehovah's Witnesses in the early 1940s, and to Covington its efforts to preserve *Gobitis* seemed to add insult to injury. Remarking on the intentions of the "non-partisan" veterans' organization, Covington blasted the Legion as "an active, un-American, self-serving and biased interest" determined to suppress the Witnesses' civil liberties.[47]

As he neared the climax of the Witnesses' legal campaign in the early and mid-1940s, Covington did not relent. Because of the procession of Witnesses who had been appearing before the Supreme Court since 1938, most of the justices were familiar with the contours of their faith, but Covington nonetheless devoted a sizable portion of his *Barnette* brief to explaining why Witnesses, based on their reading of the Bible, viewed saluting the flag as a form of idolatry. In his brief and in his oral argument, he lamented both the reasoning of the *Gobitis* opinion and its devastating impact. Covington was disturbed, for instance, by the apparent suggestion in *Gobitis* that members of minority groups could not turn to the judiciary for relief when measures passed by popularly elected legislators encroached on their civil liberties. He confessed to being bewildered by "the new rule that the citizen, regardless of how unpopular, oppressed and persecuted, must trust in the majority popular will to correct 'foolish legislation' which admittedly violates the constitutional liberties of the people." That *Gobitis*—a ruling every bit as "unstatesmanlike" as the notorious *Dred Scott* decision—should be interred was perhaps best proven by the public's savage response to it, Covington maintained in his oral argument. Calling it "one of the greatest mistakes that this Court has ever committed," he told the justices that the ruling in *Gobitis* had done nothing less than ignite a "civil war against Jehovah's Witnesses."[48]

Submitting amicus curiae briefs in *Barnette*, both the ABA's Committee on the Bill of Rights and the ACLU aided Covington in his efforts to bury *Gobitis*. Although the district court had disregarded the impact of Public Law 623, the ACLU argued that its passage preempted states from imposing regulations governing the ceremonies meant to honor the American flag. Only Congress, the ACLU maintained, "can establish the ceremony for saluting the American flag and define and punish the offense of disloyalty to the common emblem of the United States." It also noted some of the devastating consequences of the "unfortunate" *Gobitis* opinion, reminding the Court that authorities in a number of communities had used the ruling "to justify the conviction of children refusing to give the salute on the ground that they are delinquents, and to take such children from their homes and confine them to State Reformatories." Most of the ACLU's brief, however, was devoted to hammering home the argument it had made in *Gobitis* and reiterated in numerous other cases during the following three years: that enforcement of compulsory flag-salute regulations against Jehovah's Witnesses deprived them of religious liberty and violated their rights under the Fourteenth Amendment. To reach such a finding, the full Court would have to follow the lead of Chief Justice Stone and the *Jones I* dissenters and acknowledge that *Gobitis* had been "wrongly decided."[49]

Following oral arguments and the Supreme Court's discussion of *Barnette* in conference, Stone assigned the majority opinion to Jackson. At first blush, this might seem a curious selection. Having advocated constitutional protections of minority rights since *Carolene Products* in 1938, and having dissented so eloquently in *Gobitis* in 1940, Stone himself would have been a natural choice for writing the Court's opinion in *Barnette*, a ruling that was sure to vindicate many of the principles he held so dear. Conversely, Jackson had been uniformly skeptical of—if not downright hostile toward—

many of the Witness appellants who had been appearing before the Court during his tenure. For instance, in his virulent concurrence in *Douglas v. Jeannette* (handed down just a month before the Court ruled in the West Virginia flag salute case), Jackson had been barely able to contain his alarm over the disruptiveness of the Witnesses' most basic form of worship, proselytizing, and he had scoffed at the notion that their sometimes unruly behavior merited constitutional protection. In his *Douglas* concurrence, Jackson had openly wondered if the founding fathers had meant for the Constitution to shield the kind of "forced 'enlightenment'" practiced by the Witnesses. He was appalled by what he called "the singular persistence of turmoil about Jehovah's Witnesses, which seems to result from the work of no other sect," and he had even urged the Court to undertake "a thorough examination of their methods to see if they impinge unduly on the rights of others."[50] Moreover, in spring 1942, Jackson had voted with the majority in *Jones I* and remained mum when three of the dissenters in that case repudiated *Gobitis*. Of the six members of the *Barnette* majority, Jackson clearly had the spottiest record in Witness cases—and that, ultimately, might have been the very reason why Stone selected him to write the opinion. It is probable that the chief justice chose the weakest link in the chain of his majority because he believed that the surest way to keep Jackson in the fold would be to allow him to craft the opinion.

Perhaps mindful of his colleague's checkered history in Witness cases, Stone attempted to keep a tight rein on Jackson during the drafting of the *Barnette* opinion. Prodding him with memorandums and marginal comments, the chief justice tried to make sure that Jackson incorporated into the ruling the central arguments of his *Gobitis* dissent. He advised at one point:

> We, of course, are not concerned with the wisdom or educational utility of the flag salute. That is a matter for the legislative branch to deal with. Our only concern is whether their method of dealing with it violates constitutional limitations. However useful and effective it may be to the majority of children who have no religious scruples and who have faith and belief in what they are compelled to do, I should still think that the powers of government do not extend to compelling children to make statements which they do not believe and which violate their religious beliefs.

In another letter to Jackson, Stone noted that "undoubtedly the Government may coerce citizens to obey constitutional laws, whether they consent or not, but it . . . may not coerce expression of opinions either by suppressing them or compelling them because such acts of government come within the prohibitions of the First Amendment."

And as he watched the *Barnette* opinion evolve, Stone did more than simply endeavor to guide the Court's interpretation of the relevant constitutional issues. After reading early drafts of the opinion, the chief justice wrote to Jackson that he was troubled by "the impression that our judgment of the legal question [in *Barnette*] was affected by the disorders which had followed the *Gobitis* decision." No one on the Court, of course, had been blind to the brutal aftermath of that case, and Stone himself had privately lamented the paroxysm of "religious bigotry and fanatical, unthinking patriotism" that had threatened to overwhelm the Witnesses in spring and summer 1940. Yet Stone was eager to avoid speculation that the Brethren had been persuaded to reverse *Gobitis* by anything except a careful reconsideration of the constitutional issues at stake. Several "rather too journalistic" footnotes referring to post-*Gobitis* rioting had the chief justice especially worried; commenting on some of the quotations within them, he spoke of his "revulsion of feeling." Arguing that the footnotes should be deleted in the final draft of the opinion, Stone told Jackson that if the first flag-salute case had been decided in favor of the Gobitas family, "it is quite possible that the American Legion and other similar minded organizations would have produced similar disorders. But that, I think, should not affect our judgment, and if it doesn't affect judgment, is it worth repeating?" In the end, Stone—who at one point urged Jackson to review his footnotes to make sure that "they really measure up to the dignity which should characterize an opinion of the Supreme Court of the United States"—prevailed. One footnote in the final version of the *Barnette* opinion referred to law review articles that were critical of *Gobitis*, but all references to vigilantism inspired by that ruling were removed.[51]

In a move that was most likely not coincidental, the Supreme Court decided to hand down its ruling in *West Virginia v. Barnette* on 14 June 1943—Flag Day. Jackson's opinion eloquently reversed *Gobitis*, but it did so without fully embracing all the arguments Stone had put forward in his landmark dissent in the first flag-salute case. Perhaps most notably, Jackson maintained that "the issue as we see it [does not] turn on one's possession of particular religious views or the sincerity with which they are held." In other words, the Court did not feel compelled to address one of the central claims that the Witnesses had made in their brief and that Stone had made in his *Gobitis* dissent: that the enforcement of compulsory flag-salute measures violated the Witnesses' right to free exercise of religion, which was protected by both the First and Fourteenth Amendments. Instead, Jackson wrote, the principal question to be answered by the Court in assessing "the flag salute controversy is whether such a ceremony so touching matters of opinion and political attitude may be imposed upon the individual by official authority under powers committed to any political organization under our Constitution." In his opinion for the Court in *Gobitis*, Frankfurter had maintained that legislatures, because of their central role in the democratic process, could exercise such power without undue interference from the judiciary, but now the Court would reexamine that authority within the "broader definition of issues in this case."[52]

Jackson undertook this task by scrutinizing a few of the main underpinnings of the Court's ruling in *Gobitis*. Responding to Frankfurter's quip that the Supreme Court could not meddle in the affairs of local school systems because it had not been empowered to act as "the school board for the country," Jackson noted that "none who acts under color of law is beyond reach of the Constitution." As he addressed the issue of the scope of the powers of local authorities and the duty of the Supreme Court to check them when they were abused, Jackson referred to the passage of Public Law 623 and argued that Congress' action "in making flag observation voluntary . . . contrasts sharply" with the enactment of local regulations dealing with "matters relatively trivial to the welfare of the nation." Here, too, Jackson profoundly disagreed with Frankfurter, who had contended in his *Gobitis* opinion that allowing local authorities to provide for the inculcation of loyalty through ceremonies like the flag salute was crucial both to maintaining national security and sustaining the powers of a healthy, well-balanced democracy. Jackson doubted that "the strength of government to maintain itself would be impressively vindicated by our confirming the power of the State to expel a handful of children from school," and he pointed to several historical examples, including the Inquisition, to highlight the fact that attempts to "coerce uniformity in support of some end thought essential" usually led to "a disappointing and disastrous end." In one of the most powerful passages of the entire *Barnette* opinion, Jackson wrote, "Those who begin coercive elimination of dissent soon find themselves eliminating dissenters. Compulsory unification of opinion achieves only the unanimity of the graveyard."[53]

Although he had not endorsed the view that West Virginia's compulsory flag-salute measure jeopardized the Witnesses' right to free exercise of religion, Jackson did keep his constitutional analysis within the somewhat broader context of the First Amendment and the due process clause of the Fourteenth Amendment. Judging from his opinions in the Witness cases that preceded *Barnette,* it seems clear that Jackson had never fully embraced Stone's assertion that the First Amendment's freedoms were so vital to the survival of democracy that they occupied a preferred position in the hierarchy of constitutional values; in both *Jones I* and *Murdock,* he had passed up opportunities to join opinions that explicitly endorsed that notion. But if Jackson had proven unwilling to privilege First Amendment freedoms, he demonstrated in his *Barnette* opinion that he could not countenance the idea that they could be violated by the whims of popularly elected legislative bodies. "One's right to life, liberty, and property, to free speech, a free press, freedom of worship and assembly, and other fundamental rights may not be submitted to vote; they depend on the outcome of no elections," he wrote. Such rights were by no means absolute, of course, and they could be circumscribed, but "only to prevent grave and immediate danger to interests which the State may lawfully protect." Clearly, the failure of well-intentioned youngsters to participate in flag-salute ceremonies at their public schools did not pose any such hazard:

> It is now a commonplace that censorship or suppression of expression of opinion is tolerated by our Constitution only when the expression presents a clear and present danger of action of a kind the State is empowered to prevent and punish. It would seem that involuntary affirmation could be commanded only on even more immediate and urgent grounds than silence. But here the power of compulsion is invoked without any allegation that remaining passive during a flag salute ritual creates a clear and

present danger that would justify an effort even to muffle expression.

Given those circumstances, Jackson reasoned, the West Virginia Board of Education was in effect asking the Court to hold that "a Bill of Rights which guards the individual's right to speak his own mind left it open to public authorities to compel him to utter what is not in his mind"—and that the Court simply could not do.[54]

Jackson closed his opinion in *Barnette* by contending that the enforcement of West Virginia's compulsory flag-salute measure "invades the sphere of intellect and spirit which it is the purpose of the First Amendment to our Constitution to reserve from all official control." By mandating participation in the flag-salute ceremony, the members of the state education board had "transcend[ed] constitutional limits on their power," and the Court had no other choice but to block their encroachment on the civil liberties of the Witness appellants. "If there is any fixed star in our constitutional constellation, it is that no official, high or petty, can prescribe what shall be orthodox in politics, nationalism, religion or other matters of opinion or force citizens to confess by word or act their faith therein," Jackson wrote in a memorable peroration. "If there are any circumstances which permit an exception, they do not now occur to us."[55]

Jackson later said that Justices Black, Douglas, and Murphy had found Stone's assignment of the *Barnette* opinion to him "plainly distasteful. They wanted to do their own recanting and didn't go along with my opinion."[56] Indeed, Black and Douglas were not fully satisfied with Jackson's majority opinion, and they wound up writing a joint concurrence to explain their endorsement of the Court's first flag-salute opinion and their subsequent change of heart. "Reluctance to make the Federal Constitution a rigid bar against state regulation of conduct thought inimical to the public welfare was the controlling influence which moved us to consent to the Gobitis decision," they wrote. "Long reflection convinced us that although the principle was sound, its application in the particular case was wrong." Unlike Jackson, Black and Douglas viewed the West Virginia flag-salute measure as compromising the Witnesses' right to free exercise of religion, writing, "We believe that the statute before us fails to accord full scope to the freedom of religion secured to the appellees by the First and Fourteenth Amendments." Like Jackson, they ridiculed Frankfurter's suggestion that flag-salute requirements were crucial to the preservation of national security. "Neither our domestic tranquility in peace nor our martial effort in war depend on compelling little children to participate in a ceremony which ends in nothing for them but a fear of spiritual condemnation," they argued. In the end, a measure that required schoolchildren to repudiate their faith and participate in a ceremony they abhorred amounted to "a handy implement for disguised religious persecution. As such, it is inconsistent with our Constitution's plan and purpose."[57]

As he told Stone, Justice Frank Murphy decided to write a concurring opinion in *Barnette* because he believed his thoughts were "not altogether expressed in Brother Jackson's opinion."[58] Like Douglas and Black, Murphy firmly believed that compulsory flag-salute regulations infringed on the Witnesses' right to free exercise of religion, and in his concurrence he reiterated the importance of shielding "freedom to worship one's Maker according to the dictates of one's conscience, a right which the Constitution specifically shelters. Reflection has convinced me that as a judge I have no loftier duty or responsibility than to uphold that spiritual freedom to its farthest reaches." Perhaps thinking back to his own decision to join the *Gobitis* majority, Murphy recognized a few of the reasons why some members of the Court might be reluctant to strike down West Virginia's flag-salute regulation, among them "the emotion aroused by the flag as a symbol for which we have fought and are now fighting again." Yet he professed to being

> unable to agree that the benefits that may accrue to society from the compulsory flag salute are sufficiently definite and tangible to justify the invasion of freedom and privacy that is entailed or to compensate for a restraint on the freedom of the individual to be vocal or silent according to his conscience or personal inclination.

Murphy closed his concurrence by stressing "the desirability of preserving freedom of conscience to the full. It is in that freedom and the example of persuasion, not in force and compulsion, that the real unity of America lies."[59]

One of Frankfurter's biographers has noted that he "prepared for the reversal [of *Gobitis*] as a proud but doomed gunfighter would approach his final shootout." Readying himself for the repudiation of his opinion in the first flag-salute case, Frankfurter began crafting a dissent long before *Barnette* even reached the Supreme Court. "He jotted down sentences while shaving, then stuffed them into a dresser drawer," according to one account. "Later, at the office he dictated isolated paragraphs to his secretary and placed them in a manila folder." Philip Elman, Frankfurter's law clerk, believed that some passages of the nascent dissent lacked coherence, but the justice rebuffed his offer of editorial help by saying, "I have to do this myself." As the dissent neared completion in spring 1943, Frankfurter pieced together the fragments he had been accumulating over the preceding few months and dictated a lengthy opinion to his clerk.[60]

That Frankfurter was stung by the Court's abandonment of *Gobitis* was evident in the extraordinary dissent he composed in *Barnette*. He began it with a remarkably personal statement that stunned some of his colleagues on the Court. "One who belongs to the most vilified and persecuted minority in history is not likely to be insensible to the freedoms guaranteed by our Constitution," Frankfurter wrote. "Were my purely personal attitude relevant I should wholeheartedly associate myself with the general libertarian views in the Court's opinion, representing as they do the thought and action of a lifetime." Yet his religious background was irrelevant, Frankfurter wrote, for all judges

> owe equal attachment to the Constitution and are equally bound by our judicial obligations whether we derive our citizenship from the earliest or latest immigrants to these shores. As a member of this Court I am not justified in writing my private notions of policy into the Constitution, no matter how deeply I may cherish them or how mischievous I may deem their disregard.[61]

When they read drafts of the dissent, several of the Brethren attempted to convince Frankfurter to remove or at least tone down his startling introduction. In his diary, Frankfurter wrote that Owen Roberts told him that he regarded the dissent's opening sentences as "more and more a mistake" and that Frank Murphy cautioned that the opinion's beginning was "too personal" and would be "catapulting a personal issue into the arena." Frankfurter held firm, telling Murphy that "long reflection has left me without doubt that I must disregard my sensitiveness and say in plain language what much needs to be said and express my deepest conviction." He confided to his diary that "the sentences will stay in because they are not the products of a moment's or an hour's or a day's or a week's thought—I had thought about the matter for months and I deem it necessary to say and put into print in the U.S. Reports what I conceive to be basic to the function of this Court and the duty of the Justices of this Court."[62]

After touting his impartiality, Frankfurter launched into a full-bore assault on the majority opinion by reiterating many of the basic arguments he had put forward in his *Gobitis* opinion. "Judicial self-restraint is . . . necessary," he claimed, "whenever an exercise of political or legislative power is challenged." After all, the Supreme Court had only a "very narrow function" within the constitutional system, and it never had been empowered to act as "a super-legislature." As long as a legislative body had a "reasonable justification" for enacting a particular statute, the Court had to defer to its judgment and not "restrict the powers of democratic government," as it was doing in *Barnette.* In a particularly ironic passage of his dissent, Frankfurter—whose opinion in *Gobitis* had so clearly been affected by the spread of war throughout Europe and the emergence of the Fifth Column scare in spring 1940—asserted that the Supreme Court

> has no reason for existence if it merely reflects the pressures of the day. Our system is built on the faith that men set apart for this special function, freed from the influences of immediacy and from the deflections of worldly ambition, will become able to take a view of longer range than the period of responsibility entrusted to Congress and legislatures.

But the stability and credibility of the Court were undoubtedly shaken, Frankfurter suggested, when justices like Black, Douglas, and Murphy ignored precedent and disavowed a ruling they had enthusiastically supported just a few years earlier. "What reason is there to believe that they or their successors may not have another view a few years hence?" he asked. "Is that which was deemed to be so fundamental a nature as to be written into the Constitution to endure for all times to be the sport of shifting winds of doctrine?" The capriciousness of his colleagues left the obdurate Frankfurter wondering what the answers to those questions might be.[63]

Relatively few people shared Frankfurter's bitter views on the Supreme Court's decision to overrule *Gobitis*. *Time*'s story on the *Barnette* decision, for instance, bore the headline "Blot Removed." With Jackson's majority opinion, the magazine noted, "the U.S. Supreme Court this week reaffirmed its faith in the Bill of Rights— which, in 1940, it had come perilously close to outlawing."[64] An editorial in the *Christian Century* was similarly laudatory, remarking that the Court, in reversing *Gobitis*, had done "far more . . . than to set right a legal blunder which had far-reaching consequences for the freedom of conscience of Americans." Portions of the *Barnette* opinion extolling freedom of conscience were so profound, the magazine asserted, that they "should become part of the 'American Scriptures,' to be memorized and taken to heart by every patriot. . . . The constitutional guarantees of religious liberty have been reaffirmed; the encroachments of the state in the realm of conscience have received a salutary check."[65] Writing in the *New Republic*, Thomas Reed Powell of Harvard Law School also noted that Jackson's majority opinion in *Barnette* did far more than simply expunge the stain of *Gobitis*, for "the liberty here given constitutional sanction is not confined to cases where the objections to compulsion to participate in ceremonials are based on religious grounds. The freedom of silence and the freedom of abstention extend to those who have other than religious objections to compulsion of public avowals."[66]

No one was more pleased by the demise of the *Gobitis* decision than Walter Gobitas and his children. The family had traveled to Washington to watch Hayden Covington's oral argument in the *Barnette* case, and the Court's ruling left them feeling vindicated. "I never doubted that we would win," Gobitas exulted to *Newsweek*. "We knew the Lord would arrange it. The victory is His." Nearly eight years after his initial run-in with Minersville's school board, his feelings about flag-saluting remained the same. He said of his children, "America is their country. But God must come first."[67]

Having helped to engineer one of the most dramatic reversals in the Supreme Court's long history, the chief justice must have felt a sense of vindication as well. The majority opinion in *Barnette*, despite its eloquence, had not affirmed all the principles that Stone had articulated in his *Gobitis* dissent, but he praised it in a private note to Jackson as a "good job." Stone reserved warmer praise for the efforts of the justices who had abandoned their earlier position on the flag-salute and authored concurring opinions in *Barnette*. With his characteristic generosity, he wrote to Black, "I wish to express my personal appreciation for your concurring opinion. The sincerity and the good sense of what you have said will, I believe, make a very deep impression on the public conscience. It also states in simple and perfectly understandable form good constitutional law as I understand it." A lone dissenter just three years earlier, Stone had prevailed over Frankfurter, although few people could have predicted the intervening circumstances: the Court's personnel changed; three of his colleagues took the rare step of confessing that they had erred in opposing him; and, tragically, the public's savage response to the *Gobitis* opinion helped to make it a smirch on the Court's reputation. "All's well that ends well," Stone wrote in a letter shortly after the Court handed down its ruling in *Barnette*, "but I should like to have seen the case end well in the first place without following such a devious route to the desired end."[68]

10. A Question of
   Personal Liberty

William Estep's parents were fervent Jehovah's Witnesses who sustained their beliefs by relentlessly reading and interpreting the Bible. Like most Witnesses, they attended regular Bible-study sessions with other members of their faith, and they pored over the Scriptures and Watch Tower tracts most evenings at home. Their enthusiasm for their faith was so intense that the family sometimes even reviewed passages from the Bible when it gathered for meals. "The Bible was read to me by either my father or my mother, and sometimes by both, morning, noon, and night," William Estep recalled. "They taught me the fundamental doctrines to be found in the Bible at a very early age, even before I enrolled in public school." Growing up in Canonsburg, Pennsylvania, Estep shared his parents' devotion to their faith, and in the mid-1930s it landed him in trouble at the Third Ward School. In 1935, shortly after Joseph Rutherford characterized flag-saluting as idolatry, Estep refused to take part in Pledge of Allegiance ceremonies at his school, and he was expelled. To complete his education, he enrolled in a Witness-run Kingdom School in Gates, Pennsylvania, which covered "all the regular school subjects" and provided focused religious instruction. As Estep later explained, the school furnished "a special course in Bible study and the study of Bible dictionaries, the study of Bible characters, the meaning of Bible prophecies, and, in short, a complete Bible education to fit children of that school for further ministerial activities on their graduation."[1]

About a year after his graduation from the Kingdom School in Gates, Estep attended a Witness convention in St. Louis, Missouri, and became, as he put it, "a full-time ordained minister," or pioneer. To him, there was no more sacred calling. "As a minister of the gospel, I am required to go from house to house," Estep said. "Christ

Jesus went from house to house; the Apostle Peter stated that we must follow in the footsteps of Christ Jesus." Assigned to work with a Witness congregation in Washington, Pennsylvania, Estep eagerly performed a variety of tasks, including proselytizing and conducting at-home Bible studies, where he would "preside . . . and counsel those present in the word of the Lord, as a minister of the gospel." Estep's method of evangelizing, as he explained at the time, was straightforward:

> I approach the people at their homes with this [Witness] literature in an orderly and kind way. I introduce myself as a minister, one of Jehovah's Witnesses, preaching from house to house, calling upon the people to leave with them [aids] to enable them to pursue a course of home Bible study. If they are interested, I talk to them about God's kingdom, explain about the battle of Armageddon and the requirements of a Christian. I offer them the literature; if they desire it, they take it. If they are able to contribute, I accept such contributions, [and the] money is used to enable me to distribute literature to more people, including the poor. If the person is unable to contribute, I leave the literature free of charge.

Subsequent assignments in the early 1940s allowed Estep to undertake such work in Manhattan; Uniontown, Pennsylvania; and Akron, Ohio.[2]

Throughout the early 1940s, hundreds of thousands of young Americans rushed to serve their country as it girded for and then fully entered World War II. Devout Jehovah's Witnesses like William Estep were not among them. Firmly believing that, as one Witness put it, "Jehovah does not approve of war between nations today," Estep and other members of his faith resisted the military draft and refused to volunteer for military service.[3] As the Selective Service System reported, Witnesses "usually maintained that military service or alternate civilian duty"—to which most conscientious objectors were assigned—"interfered with their church work and that they therefore could engage in neither."[4] As always, the Witnesses' recalcitrance was dealt with harshly, although in this instance it was the federal government, not vigilantes or hostile policemen, that punished them for holding so steadfastly to their beliefs. By mid-

1944 more than 10,000 men had been convicted for violating the draft law enacted by Congress in 1940. With approximately 4,000 convictions (about 40 percent of the total), Witnesses emerged as the largest single group of draft-law violators, and they streamed into federal correctional facilities across the United States. Several dozen remained behind bars in mid-1947, a full two years after the war's conclusion.[5]

Most Americans scarcely noticed the thousands of Jehovah's Witnesses who were imprisoned for violating the federal draft law. In the early and mid-1940s, the nation's collective attention was fixed on the men who gallantly fought (and often perished) in the war, not on those who remained out of harm's way because they had refused conscription. Yet the Witnesses' resistance to the draft was a dramatic conflict in its own right, a struggle pitting the nation's long-standing commitment to shielding civil liberties against its all-consuming drive to forge national unity and sustain an effective war effort. As so often happens in the United States in wartime, those two undertakings were not easily reconciled, and thousands of young Witnesses were penalized when they refused to compromise their beliefs. Ironically, by imprisoning these Jehovah's Witnesses because they opposed fighting the war, the federal government suppressed the very democratic freedoms it hoped to preserve from the scourge of fascism.[6]

The Witnesses who opposed World War II created their own modest legacy in constitutional law. In a series of appeals that reached the U.S. Supreme Court in the mid-1940s, William Estep and other young Witnesses who had been treated inequitably by their local draft boards protested that their constitutional right to due process of law had been violated after they registered for the military draft. Even in wartime, they asserted, the Bill of Rights protected the civil liberties of all Americans—even members of a pervasively disliked and misunderstood religious minority who fiercely resisted serving in a popular cause that was meant to sustain those very same rights. Although these appeals, with their focus on procedural issues, lacked the emotion and drama of some other Witness cases of the period, they nonetheless highlighted another facet of the evangelists' lives that was disrupted by religious discrimination. Perhaps even more tragically, while those men battled in court to preserve their rights, a few unfortunate ones were inducted into the armed forces and then harshly abused because of their stubborn adherence to their faith. Their mistreatment provided further evidence of the vast and often bitter ideological differences that separated Jehovah's Witnesses and the millions of Americans who fully supported the war.

In response to protests lodged by the American Civil Liberties Union and various religious groups, including the Quakers and Mennonites, Congress tinkered with the Selective Training and Service Act of 1940 after it had been introduced and created provisions for conscientious objector status. According to the final version of the measure (which was the first conscription law ever passed in the United States in peacetime), any person who was "conscientiously opposed to participation in war in any form" because of his religious training or beliefs could be exempted from combatant training and service. Men who were classified as conscientious objectors by their local draft boards could be assigned to noncombatant service or to "work of national importance under civilian direction." Facilities once used by the Civilian Conservation Corps were among the sites eventually designated to serve as Civilian Public Service (CPS) camps for conscientious objectors. During the war, more than 8,000 men were assigned to CPS camps, and they labored on a wide variety of public works and conservation projects. The federal draft law made provisions for ministers as well as for conscientious objectors: once draft boards had reviewed and certified their status, they were free to pursue their religious work or studies.[7]

Jehovah's Witnesses fit awkwardly into this scheme. In keeping with their intention to obey man-made laws whenever possible, Witnesses usually registered with their local draft boards in an attempt to gain ministerial exemptions, but their unorthodox faith and practices often befuddled the men who had been given the task of classifying them. Part of the confusion had to do with the Witnesses' relatively broad definition of "minister." Unlike members of more traditional faiths, Witnesses acknowledged no formal distinction between clergy and laymen; most adult Witnesses proudly identified themselves as "ministers of the Gospel," and they carried certificates attesting to this status when they evangelized. Selective Service officials had no intention of granting exemptions to every single draft-age Witness male, of course, so their claims were carefully scrutinized.[8] As the ACLU noted, federal draft guidelines stipulated that "the ministerial occupation can be recognized only when engaged in full time," meaning that every Witness below the level of a pioneer had little chance of gaining a minister's exemption. The requirement that ministers work full-time at their sacred duties tripped up a number of Witnesses who held part-time secular jobs merely to subsidize their religious proselytizing. The ACLU reported that even when they held secular jobs for the express purpose of supporting their evangelizing, many Witnesses were not recognized as ministers by draft boards because they were "engaged gainfully in other occupations."[9] Some boards were willing to grant these men conscientious objector status, but the Witnesses often rejected it as a wholly inadequate compromise. For many Witnesses, working in a CPS camp would mean neglecting their sacred duty as ministers to preach the Gospel, and they knew from reading the Bible that the punishment for such abandonment promised to be severe. As William Estep explained, "I cannot throw off these covenant obligations for any reasons, for such would mean my everlasting destruction."[10]

Full participation in World War II simply was not an option for most of the Witnesses who failed to gain minister's exemptions from military service. Steadfast Christians, they believed, were to remain aloof from earthly wars, for such conflicts were fought for profane rather than sacred reasons. (The result of the Vatican's machinations, World War II in their view was no exception.) Unlike some who opposed the war, Witnesses were by no means pacifists, but they soldiered in only one army, Jehovah God's, and they fought but a single enemy, Satan. In a letter sent to the Justice Department, Witness officials asked, "Do Jehovah's Witnesses participate in wars between the nations of the world? How could one who is wholly devoted to Almighty God, and to His kingdom under Christ Jesus, take sides in a war between nations, both of which are against God and His kingdom?" Since Witnesses were "wholly devoted to God and His kingdom," they were "separate and distinct as a nation from other nations," and "their citizenship is in the heavenly organization." Loyal servants of God, they would not forsake their opportunity for such an exalted position by bearing arms in the American military.[11]

Such were William Estep's sentiments when he registered with the draft board in Canonsburg, Pennsylvania, in spring 1942. There was little doubt in the Witness's mind that he was a bona fide minister and thus deserved an exemption from any kind of wartime service, including innocuous work in a CPS camp. Asked on a questionnaire to describe his current employment, Estep stated that he performed "missionary and evangelistic service in organizing churches," and that such work entailed "organizing and establishing churches and generally preaching the Gospel of the Kingdom of God" and "proclaiming the gospel of God's Kingdom from house to house and on the streets." Estep did not claim to be a pacifist when he registered with his local draft board. Citing passages from Exodus and Nehemiah as justification, he acknowledged that he believed "in the use of force in defense of my life and property and in defense of my family and fellow Christians." Estep did maintain, however, that he deserved an exemption from wartime service because, as a Witness pioneer, he worked full-time performing ministerial duties. The draft board in Canonsburg disagreed, in part because Estep's name did not appear on a list of full-time Witness pioneers that was circulated by the Selective Service System, and he was classified 1-A, fit for active duty.[12]

Firmly convinced that he deserved the minister's exemption, Estep appeared before the draft board in fall 1942 and pleaded his case. "I asked for a hearing because I felt I have information which bears directly on my case," he told the board. "No doubt the Constitution was framed by men who foresaw the condition that exists now. . . . I am a direct representative of the Jehovah's Witnesses and I am a duly ordained minister." To bolster his case, Estep brought with him a copy of a Selective Service System directive addressing the validity of Witnesses' claims for minister's exemptions. The directive noted that Witness pioneers, because they "devot[ed] their time to the work of teaching the tenets of their religion and in the converting of others to their belief," held a status "similar to that occupied by regular or duly ordained ministers of other religions" and thus could be granted minister's exemptions from wartime service. As he appealed to the draft board, Estep explained that he was indeed the kind of pioneer referred to in the Selective Service directive but that an oversight had caused his name to be omitted from the list circulated to local draft boards. Despite Estep's sincerity, the arguments he made to the draft board fell flat. When the Witness began to describe his ministerial work, one skeptical board member cut in and demanded a specific accounting of his duties over the previous week—where he had worked, for how long, and with whom. Other members of the draft board soon joined in the grilling, pressing Estep with a barrage of questions about his ministerial duties and the basis of his beliefs. ("Is it not true," one board member asked, "that all the members of your society are confined to the teaching of Judge Rutherford?") Estep was clearly flustered by the draft board's antagonism, and he stumbled his way through the hearing without making much of a case.[13]

The Canonsburg draft board's bullying of William Estep was unremarkable. Composed of deeply patriotic men, many of whom were veterans, most wartime draft boards "tended toward strictness" when they judged exemption claims, according to a Selective Service System report, and did their best to ferret out potential shirkers. Because of their widespread unpopularity in the early and mid-1940s, Jehovah's Witnesses were in a particularly disadvantageous position when they asked for exemptions, and their truculent behavior only made matters worse. (As the Selective Service System noted, men who demonstrated such "unreasonable, belligerent, or obnoxious attitudes toward their local board members" usually had little luck when they asked to be exempted from wartime service.)[14] Even when Witnesses authenticated their claims for minister's exemptions with affidavits, certificates, and other documents, some boards simply ignored the evidence and refused to grant them exemptions. A study published in 1945 by the Pacifist Research Bureau contended that some draft boards "seemed determined to grant no ministerial classifications to any Witnesses, regardless of their credentials." According to the study,

some Local Boards refused to recognize them as ministers, which in view of the unusual nature of Jehovah's Witnesses and the hostility of public opinion to them in many communities, is not surprising. In many instances the evidence was overwhelming that Witnesses were engaged in ministerial work for a total of more than the eighty hours a month which the Director of Selective Service set as a minimum for classification as ministers. In some few cases, it was quite clear that Local Boards and Appeal Boards ignored the claim of Witnesses who were spending all their time as ministers.[15]

Members of no other single group faced discrimination so consistently when they registered for the draft. Due to their widespread unpopularity, "it was in the classification of Jehovah's Witnesses that local prejudice was probably most pronounced," one study of the draft concluded.[16]

This point was borne out by William Estep's draft board. A day after Estep's contentious hearing in Canonsburg, board clerk J. W. McNutt informed Estep that his classification remained the same; he was still 1-A. Estep responded by filing a formal appeal and soliciting affidavits from three local Witnesses who could vouch for the seriousness of his ministerial work. In his letter of appeal, Estep told of his commitment to his faith and of his dedication to evangelizing—the sacred work he would have to abandon if the board denied him a minister's exemption from the draft. He also reiterated that he never could in good conscience serve in the armed forces, reminding the board that he believed "it would be impossible for a true Christian to involve himself in any way in a war between any nations at the present time." Further bolstering Estep's arguments, the affidavits noted that he was "a properly ordained Christian minister" and possessed "the scriptural ordination to preach [the] 'Gospel of the Kingdom.'" To Estep's dismay, J. W. McNutt refused to place the affidavits in the Witness's Selective Service file. "I was told," Estep recalled, "that it was impossible to file these affidavits, as my case had gone up before the Appeal Board." Estep, now desperate to gain a minister's exemption, felt that the affidavits were crucial to his appeal, and he virtually begged McNutt to include them in his file. "I said if it was possible at all, I should like these [documents] to go in to the appeal board, that they might be submitted in further evidence of my ministerial classification." As he denied Estep's request to add the affidavits, McNutt explained that the matter was out of his hands because the appeal board already had received Estep's file. At that point, he maintained, it was simply too late to provide additional materials.[17]

As it turned out, McNutt grossly misinformed Estep about the status of his appeal. Contrary to what he told Estep in fall 1942, McNutt had not in fact forwarded the Witness's file to the appeal board. Incredibly, Estep's draft file—the foundation for his appeal—languished in the clerk's office for nearly two years after the Witness formally requested an appeal of his draft classification. Lamely attempting to account for the delay, McNutt later said that he had failed to forward the file because "it was misplaced in our office . . . by either myself or some of the clerks I have in my employ," but his explanation rang hollow. To make matters even worse for Estep, McNutt not only embargoed the file but also added to it several unfavorable items—this while the file supposedly was "misplaced." Among the documents that found their way into Estep's file were an anonymous note and an accompanying newspaper clipping entitled "FOUR DRAFT OBJECTORS GET PRISON TERMS." The note read, "Whats the matter with our own Draft objectors—the Esteps are surely no different from the other boys. Why arent they called—or won't they ever be?" Through incompetence or malice, or perhaps a combination of the two, McNutt crippled Estep's appeal. By refusing to accept pertinent documents to his file, adding damaging materials, and failing to dispatch it to the appeal board, the clerk ensured that Estep's draft classification remained unchanged.[18]

More than a year after Estep had requested an appeal of the draft board's ruling, McNutt instructed him to report for a preinduction physical examination. The order confused Estep, who believed that his appeal was still pending, but he dutifully reported to a local armory, where he was deemed physically fit for military service. Following his unexpected physical exam, Estep became so worried about the status of his appeal that he decided to review his draft file. What he discovered stunned him. Contrary to what he had told Estep, McNutt had failed to forward the file to the appeal board, and he had apparently misplaced several key items as well. Estep scrambled to rectify the draft board clerk's sloppy work by providing the board with copies of the missing documents, copies of the three affidavits that the clerk had rejected earlier, and eight new affidavits attesting to his ministerial work. The affidavits hammered home the point Estep had been making since he registered with the draft board: he was a minister and thus entitled to an exemption from service in the armed forces. One fellow Witness stated, "I [have] recognized him as a sincere and capable minister, meeting the requirements laid upon him, which I am sure equal or exceed in greatness the requirements laid upon ministers of other organizations claiming Christian origin." "He is looked upon . . . by members of Jehovah's Witnesses," another noted, "as an ordained minister."[19]

Late in July 1944, about two months after Estep had discovered that McNutt had stymied his appeal, the draft board clerk finally passed the Witness's file on to the state appeal board. The prolonged delay—Estep had attempted to initiate the appeal in fall 1942—rankled Pennsylvania draft officials, and they made their displeasure clear in several curt letters to the chair of the Canonsburg draft board. When she forwarded Estep's appeal, McNutt's assistant had blamed the standstill on "an oversight," but that explanation failed to satisfy John Smith, deputy director of the state's Selective Service program. Chastising the draft board for fumbling Estep's appeal, Smith wrote that "it is apparent that there has been considerable irregularity in the handling of this case," and he informed the local draft board chair that the state office was "disturbed by the inadequacy of the explanation" offered by McNutt's assistant. In the long run, however, Smith's criticism did not provide much of a boost for Estep. Late in summer 1944, the appeal board upheld his 1-A classification.

Undaunted, Estep continued to press for a minister's exemption, dispatching several increasingly desperate pleas to various state and federal draft officials. In a letter to the state Selective Service director, he complained that his case merited a thorough review because both the Canonsburg draft board and the appeal board had been "arbitrary, unfair, and discriminative" in handling his request for an exemption from military service. "All the evidence shows conclusively that I should be properly placed in Class IV-D as a regular and duly ordained minister, and I ask that you take an appeal in my behalf in order to avoid an injustice." These last-ditch entreaties were ignored, and Estep was told to report for induction. Ironically, it was McNutt who wrote for the local draft board, "You have been ordered for induction; there will be no delay." Estep reported to his induction station as ordered, but, citing his "covenant obligations," he would not formally submit to induction. His refusal resulted in charges that he had violated the Selective Training and Service Act of 1940, and he was tried in federal court late in 1944.[20]

Throughout Estep's trial, Hayden Covington zeroed in on the Canonsburg draft board's mishandling of the Witness's appeal. McNutt was the prosecution's first witness, and Covington subjected him to a withering cross-examination. At one point, Covington asked the clerk how he had responded when Estep had attempted to submit affidavits supporting his assertion that he was indeed a minister.

> Covington: And what did you tell him?
> McNutt: I wouldn't accept them.
> Covington: Why wouldn't you accept them?
> McNutt: Because he hadn't any right to file them. His case had come before the local board and had been considered by the local board.
> Covington: Mr. Clerk, you told him, did you not, that his file was before the appeal board?
> McNutt: I might have told him that, yes.
> Covington: Then you told him a lie?
> McNutt: Possibly.
> Covington: Why did you tell him a lie?

At that point, the prosecutor, Assistant U.S. Attorney George Mashank, objected, claiming that Covington's line of questioning was irrelevant and that "there hasn't been anybody harmed" by McNutt's admitted deception. Covington, highlighting the defense's central argument, retorted by contending that McNutt's testimony demonstrated that he had participated in a conspiracy to deprive Estep of his constitutional right to due process of law. Although the presiding judge sustained Mashank's objection, Covington clung to his strategy throughout the trial. Time and again he maintained that Estep should be found innocent of violating the federal draft measure because his Fifth Amendment right to due process of law had been repeatedly violated as he attempted to gain a minister's exemption.[21] The lower federal court disagreed and found Estep guilty, and the Third Circuit Court of Appeals upheld his conviction early in 1945.[22]

Like William Estep and thousands of other Jehovah's Witnesses, Louis Smith believed that he was entitled to an exemption from military service during World War II. When he registered with the draft board in Columbia, South Carolina, late in 1942, Smith, an active Witness since his baptism in 1938, sought classification as a minister. To support his claim for an exemption, Smith submitted two affidavits signed by a total of forty-six local Witnesses, all of whom maintained that he regularly performed the duties of an ordained minister. When the draft board rejected Smith's contention and classified him 1-A, he complained that he was denied a minister's exemption because, as he later put it, "the board was prejudiced against me," and he appealed. Smith twice argued his case before the draft board in Columbia, but it stuck to its original classification, and he was ordered to report to Fort Jackson, South Carolina, for induction. At that point, Smith's father, who apparently was not a Jehovah's Witness, intervened. The elder Smith believed that his son "ought to be in the Army," but he was firmly convinced that "the boy wasn't going to report" for induction. Hoping to ensure that he would be inducted, Smith's father approached the clerk of the local draft board and asked, as he later put it, "if there was any way we could arrange to have that boy taken out to Camp Jackson." The clerk explained that the draft board lacked such police power, but another draft official informed Smith's father that he was free to make his own arrangements to make sure that the Witness reached the military facility for induction.[23]

Smith's father eventually paid a local magistrate thirty dollars to escort the young Witness to Fort Jackson. On the morning that he was to report for induction, the magistrate and two deputies arrived at Smith's home. "I was at my home in Columbia, in the bathroom shaving," Smith recalled. "While I was shaving I heard a commotion downstairs and opened the door to find out what was the trouble, and I noticed that there were three men coming up the steps." When the officers informed Smith that he was to accompany them to the induction station, he warily asked if they had any kind of a warrant. Apparently caught by surprise, the magistrate and his men equivocated, first claiming that they had left the warrant in their car, then maintaining that they had forgotten it altogether. Smith's mother suspected that no warrant existed, but she encouraged him to cooperate, urging, "Son, don't give them any trouble." Smith heeded her counsel and left with the three men, who escorted him to Fort Jackson. Still objecting to the denial of his claim to a minister's exemption from military service, Smith protested to several officers that he should not be inducted, but they placed him among a group of recruits who were preparing to take their oath of enlistment. The officer in charge told Smith that if he did not wish to take the oath, he could simply stand aside and not participate in the ceremony, and so he and another recruit looked on while the remaining men recited the service pledge. As Smith later learned, the oath-swearing was a formality; by going through the various stages of the induction process, such as the physical examination, he had in fact been inducted.[24]

Like all the other new recruits, Smith was given three weeks' leave after his induction. When he returned to Fort Jackson, he continued to complain that he had been unfairly classified. "I stated that I was a minister of the Gospel," Smith recalled, "and that the board was prejudiced against Jehovah's Witnesses and as a result they refused to classify me as a minister, and I wanted to be released." His ongoing efforts to gain an exemption fell on deaf ears at Fort Jackson. As far as the military was concerned, the time for appealing the draft board's ruling had long since passed, and it was time for Smith to begin soldiering like the other recruits. At one point, an officer ordered the Witness to don an army uniform. Smith refused, proclaiming that he would not wear military garb under any circumstances because doing so would violate his sacred covenant with Jehovah God. "I explained that I had a greater obligation to Almighty God," he later said, "and had to obey his law." Smith's insubordination was dealt with forcefully: a half-dozen men stripped him, then redressed him in a uniform. Stubborn to the end, he "took off the clothes and . . . spent the night in barracks with no clothes and between two mattresses." The following morning, Smith was again ordered to put on the uniform, and he refused once more. Their patience exhausted, officers banished him to the facility's stockade. "I was thrown to the ground and the clothes [were] taken off me and the uniform put on. And I was taken to what was known as the black box, with the door shut," Smith recalled. "I remained there four days with no clothes and no food. Just water." Following a prolonged struggle at Fort Jackson, Smith eventually was tried and convicted in federal court on charges that he had violated the Selective Training and Service Act of 1940.[25]

In their trials and appeals in lower federal courts, both William Estep and Louis Smith were hindered by interpretations of the U.S. Supreme Court's opinion in *Falbo v. United States* (1943), the first major Witness draft case of the World War II era. Classified as a conscientious objector, Nick Falbo, believing that he had been denied a minister's exemption solely because of his draft board's prejudice, refused to report to a Civilian Public Service Camp. (As he considered Falbo's case, one member of the board reportedly said, "I don't have any damned use for Jehovah's Witnesses.") On trial for violating the federal draft law, Falbo attempted to defend himself by asserting that he had been classified incorrectly, but the federal court refused to allow him to present evidence that the draft board had erred. His defense crippled, Falbo was convicted and sentenced to five years in prison, and he appealed to the U.S. Supreme Court after the Third Circuit Court of Appeals upheld his conviction. The American Civil Liberties Union supported Falbo in his appeal, submitting an amicus curiae brief arguing that unless the Court allowed defendants like Falbo to present evidence of draft board errors at their trials, "conscientious objectors will continue to be convicted and imprisoned without the trial at law, the day in court, which has until now been regarded by the courts as the inalienable right of every citizen. The Court is thus confronted in this case with the wholesale destruction of civil rights for an unpopular minority."[26] In an opinion written by Justice Hugo Black, the Court held that Falbo had not been entitled to judicial review of his draft classification because he had not previously exhausted all administrative remedies. According to the Court's reasoning, judicial review of Falbo's draft classification would have been premature because he had not reported to the CPS camp for induction.[27]

The Supreme Court's opinion in *Falbo* startled W. Howard Mann, a former clerk for Justice Wiley Rutledge, who sided with the majority and authored a brief concurring opinion. Clearly disturbed by the ruling, Mann told Rutledge that the opinion had shaken his "ideal of constitutionalism in the protection of civil rights." (Rutledge himself apparently was no great fan of the opinion: he told another member of the Court that the case troubled him and that he had "dodged" by concurring.[28]) *Falbo* also perplexed Justice Frank Murphy, who was then emerging as one of the Jehovah's Witnesses' chief allies on the Court, and he dissented:

That an individual should languish in prison for five years without being accorded the opportunity of proving that the prosecution was based upon arbitrary and illegal administrative action is not in keeping with the high standards of our judicial system. . . . The law knows no finer hour than when it cuts through formal concepts and transitory emotions to protect unpopular citizens against discrimination and persecution.

Murphy's dissent resonated with a conscientious objector who had been assigned to a CPS camp. He wrote Murphy that he had been heartened "to learn that one of the justices of our highest court clearly refused to allow the pressures of war and its emotions to blur his view of what should have been a normal and just legal procedure."[29]

Although the two men had in fact reported for induction, both Estep and Smith were tried in federal court under the *Falbo* doctrine. As a result, neither Witness was permitted to justify his violation of the Selective Service and Training Act of 1940 by presenting evidence that his draft board had erred. Defending Estep before Judge H. P. Schoonmaker (who also had presided over Nick Falbo's trial), Hayden Covington repeatedly tried to highlight the misconduct of John McNutt, the duplicitous clerk of the Canonsburg draft board. Schoonmaker, adhering to *Falbo*, sustained repeated objections to Covington's arguments, at one point telling the attorney, "We rule that this court has no right to pass on the merits of [Estep's] classification." He made much the same point in his instructions to the jury: the sole issue in the case, Schoonmaker said, was "whether or not this defendant complied with the law by submitting to induction."[30] Smith's trial had followed the same course, with attorney Grover Powell failing in his attempts to make the Witness's improper classification the centerpiece of his defense. Clearly relying on *Falbo*, the judge instructed the jury, "Neither you or I have a right to question the judgment and conclusions reached by the draft board or any appeal board that had jurisdiction in this case. That has already been settled once."[31] Barred from making the most compelling argument in their favor—that they had violated the federal draft law only because they had been victimized by the prejudice and chicanery of their draft boards—neither Smith nor Estep was able to muster much of a defense at his trial.

The Witnesses' appeals reached the U.S. Supreme Court in 1946, and they were heard in tandem as *Estep v. United States*. The draft cases required a shift in strategy for Covington, who represented Estep and Smith in the final stage of their appeals. Dozens of times over the preceding decade, Covington had invoked the First Amendment's protections of speech and worship when he defended Witnesses in court. In the draft cases, Covington still built his case around the basic democratic freedoms shielded by the Bill of Rights, but now he cited the procedural rights conferred by the Fifth and Sixth Amendments. In *Estep*, Covington argued that the Witnesses' right to due process of law had been violated when the trial courts had excluded pertinent evidence that might have aided their defenses. He asserted that *Falbo* clearly did not apply to either Estep or Smith because both men, by reporting for induction, had exhausted their administrative remedies before being charged with violations of the federal draft law.[32] As was his habit, Covington maintained that far more was at stake in the appeal than the rights of a few individuals. He wrote in a brief:

Without having had their day in court, approximately 4,000 of Jehovah's Witnesses in the United States have been branded as criminals and put in federal prisons under the Selective Training and Service Act of 1940. They were convicted because the courts refused to permit them to show in their defense that the administrative determinations supporting the indictments were illegal. Such citizens have been incarcerated without a judicial trial, contrary to the Constitution.

This mountain of flesh-and-blood testimony towers high above all other records of wartime prosecutions to stand as a monument of warning to the judiciary that unless that alien doctrine which catapulted them into prison is destroyed now, it will inevitably extend into other fields of administrative law. That one may be denied the right to challenge in court the legality of a final administrative order presents a threat to the liberties of all the people. Indeed . . . it raises a clear and present danger to the judiciary, that it can be destroyed by an administrative hydra over which the courts lose all control.

Allowing the convictions to stand, Covington maintained, would be "a grave error that seriously affects the fairness, integrity, and public reputation of judicial proceedings."[33]

Justice William Douglas, believing that *Falbo* was applicable, initially drafted an opinion upholding the convictions of Smith and Estep, but he reconsidered after reading drafts of dissents circulated by Justices Frank Murphy and Stanley Reed. In his revamped opinion, which carried a majority of the Court, Douglas noted that Estep and Smith, unlike Falbo, had "pursued their administrative remedies to the end" before their cases were litigated. "All had been done which could be done." Judicial review of the draft boards' actions thus was not premature. In fact, in light of the serious criminal penalties meted out to violators of the federal draft law, it was a crucial safeguard of the due process rights guaranteed by the Constitution. "We cannot believe," Douglas wrote for the Court, "that Congress intended that criminal sanctions were to be applied to orders issued by local boards no matter how flagrantly they violated the rules and regulations which defined their jurisdiction." Both men deserved new trials because, as Douglas put it, "we are dealing here with a question of personal liberty."[34]

Reiterating many of the same themes he had developed in his dissent in *Falbo,* Murphy authored a concurrence in which he asserted that upholding the Witnesses' convictions clearly would infringe upon

> the most elementary and fundamental concepts of due process of law. . . . There is something basically wrong and unjust about a judicial system that sanctions the imprisonment of a man without ever according him the opportunity to claim that the charge made against him is illegal. I am not yet willing to conclude that we have such a system in this nation.[35]

Writing later to his brother about his concurring opinion in *Estep,* Murphy acknowledged, "I go further than the rest of the Court," largely because he was eager "to utilize the great charter"—the Constitution—"whenever it is necessary to sustain the rights of man."[36]

Later in 1946, Covington notched another modest victory for Jehovah's Witnesses who hoped to challenge their draft classifications in court. In *Gibson v. United States,* decided by the U.S. Supreme Court in the waning days of the year, Covington represented Taze Gibson and George Dodez, Witnesses who had been convicted for violating the Selective Training and Service Act of 1940. Although the facts of the two appeals were not identical—Gibson had been convicted for deserting a CPS camp, and Dodez had failed to report to his camp altogether—both cases forced the Court to address once more the issues of draft registrants' due process rights. Like Gibson, Dodez considered himself an ordained minister who had been denied the proper exemption from military service because his draft and appeal boards had been biased. (He testified that one draft board member who was "very prejudiced to Jehovah's Witnesses" had informed him that the board simply did not recognize members of his faith as ministers.)[37] As the Supreme Court recognized in its opinion, both Gibson and Dodez had attempted to comply with the *Falbo* ruling, which required draft registrants to exhaust all their administrative remedies before they sought judicial review of their draft classifications, but evidence of their draft boards' bias had been excluded at their trials. In his opinion for the unanimous Court, Rutledge chose to "carry forward another step the sequence" established by *Falbo* and *Estep* and reverse the two Witnesses' convictions. The cases were remanded to lower federal courts, where Gibson and Dodez were able to present evidence challenging the validity of their draft classifications.[38]

Not many Jehovah's Witnesses were as fortunate as William Estep, Louis Smith, Taze Gibson, or George Dodez. For every Witness who gained a minister's exemption or successfully challenged his draft classification in court, hundreds failed. Largely unwilling to serve in the military or labor at public works projects at a CPS camp, most of these men were forced to serve prison terms of up to five years for violating the Selective Training and Service Act of 1940. In 1941 and 1942, approximately 100 Witnesses were dispatched to federal correctional institutions for violating the draft law. The number of Witness inmates skyrocketed in the following years, so that by 1946 approximately 4,000 men had been imprisoned. As the war wound down in mid-1945, nearly 3,000 Witnesses remained behind bars, and a year later, months after the war had ended, the government still held more than 1,300 Witnesses in its correctional facilities in Ashland, Kentucky; Sandstone, Minnesota; and Seagoville, Texas, among other locations. Even in July 1947, two years after the Allies had claimed victory in the war, more than sixty

Jehovah's Witnesses holding services at the federal prison camp at Mill Point, West Virginia, in 1944.

Witnesses woke up each morning in a federal penitentiary, reformatory, or prison camp.[39]

Jehovah's Witnesses remained incarcerated for so long largely because they tended to receive significantly longer sentences than other violators of the federal draft law. In 1944, according to statistics tabulated by the Justice Department, the average sentence for a violator of the Selective Training and Service Act of 1940 was 35.2 months. Men classified as "other," including outright draft-dodgers, received sentences averaging 28 months. With average sentences of 42 months in 1944, Jehovah's Witnesses who were convicted of violating the federal draft measure received the harshest penalties of any group. The trend continued during the following year: Jehovah's Witnesses received sentences averaging 40.1 months, about 7 months longer than the average sentence for all violators of the draft law (32.7 months) and a full year longer than the average sentence for men classified as "other" (28 months). Among men convicted of violating the draft law, "Jehovah's Witnesses appear always to have received the longest sentences," the Justice Department noted. Incredibly, the average sentences meted out to Witnesses were comparable to, and in some cases significantly longer than, those given to violators of federal "white slavery," narcotics, liquor, and motor vehicle theft laws. (In 1946, for instance, the average sentence for a Witness who violated the federal draft law was six months longer than the average sentence for a violator of federal narcotic and drug laws.)[40]

Jehovah's Witnesses began trickling into the federal penitentiary in Danbury, Connecticut, early in 1942. The first of forty-five Witnesses to be sent there that year was a Reading, Pennsylvania, resident, Robert Deysher, who had been convicted under the federal draft statute for failing to report to a CPS camp. The number of Witnesses steadily increased over the next few years, and by mid-1944 more than 200 of them had been dispatched to the facility. The Witnesses were at first dispersed among the prison's housing units, but administrators eventually housed them together in a dormitory known as Concord House. According to a study of the Danbury Witnesses published in 1946 by William Stockdale, "The move was a happy one for the Witnesses. With the acquisition of a dormitory all their own they could now arrange a study schedule. . . . Jehovah's Witnesses settled down to the serious task of studying and preparing themselves for the work of preaching from which they had been taken and to which they desired to return." Over time, the Witnesses were able to establish a daily schedule comprising sessions focusing on "History and Composition," "Theocratic Ministry," "Bible Themes," and other topics. These Witnesses were so zealous about their faith that they supplemented their study sessions by attempting to memorize several hundred significant quotations from the Bible. "On the job, in the mess hall, around the yard," Stockdale wrote, "one could hear the Witnesses testing each other out on the Scriptures."[41]

Stockdale observed that the Danbury Witnesses were somewhat more compliant than their fellow prisoners. During the war, prisoners there staged several well-publicized hunger strikes and work stoppages, but the Witnesses apparently remained largely aloof from such protests. "The attitude of the Witnesses toward the prison system was always one of absolute cooperation," Stockdale wrote. "Never at any time did Jehovah's Witnesses engage in any work strike or policy of non-cooperation with the institution." On the whole, relations between the Witnesses and prison authorities were cordial, although for a time there were tensions over the accessibility of Witness meetings. During the Witnesses' first few years at Danbury, prison officials permitted only men who had entered the penitentiary as Witnesses to attend their frequent Bible-study and lecture sessions. Not surprisingly, the Witnesses, whose faith was built on proselytizing, protested, in part because the services of other faiths within the prison were not subject to similar restrictions. The policy remained until late in 1945, when a new warden arrived and was approached by a sympathetic inmate who had taken up the Witnesses' cause. According to Stockdale's account, this "tolerant agnostic with no interest in Witness theology" was so eager to see "a fair deal for minorities" at the prison that he pleaded the Witnesses' case. Persuaded by his argument, the new warden relented, and the Witnesses were permitted to conduct open meetings in the prison auditorium.[42]

For the most part, the Jehovah's Witnesses who were imprisoned in federal correctional facilities during the war turned out to be cooperative inmates. In a 1946 survey of federal prisons, the Justice Department reported that they had

> proven [to be] tractable prisoners. They have seemed to believe that in refusing both induction and special civilian work, they have done their full duty, and that in prison they need resist no more. Their passive acceptance of imprisonment has enabled us to place them in minimum-custody status where they have done good work on institution farms and camp projects.[43]

A study published in 1945 by the Pacifist Research Bureau also noted that most of the thousands of Witnesses who had been imprisoned for violating the federal draft law were compliant and industrious: "Most Witnesses seem to have submitted willingly to the great bulk of prison regulations and to have worked steadily and well. . . . They seem to have been more assiduous in their work than other inmates." Despite the rigors of prison life, the Witnesses remained extraordinarily devoted to their faith, and in many correctional facilities they banded together to sustain and strengthen their beliefs through ongoing Bible-study sessions. At one prison camp in Arizona, a group of resourceful Witnesses transformed a rocky hillside into a "Kingdom Hollow" and retreated there to discuss Scripture. If the Witnesses weren't the most popular inmates, their deep commitment to their faith left a lasting impression on many who observed them. After being imprisoned for eight months with a group of over 100 Witnesses, a Church of the Brethren pastor remarked, "Much as we may disagree with them, the Jehovah's Witnesses, down to the humblest among them, are developing the sense of a Christian calling for a layman. . . . I am convinced that they have something to contribute to us and the rest of Christendom if we will be humble enough to receive it." Another observer of imprisoned Witnesses concluded that they were "unwittingly doing a greater job of keeping freedom alive in this country than the professional pacifists."[44]

Several Jehovah's Witnesses attempted to reconcile their religious beliefs with the discipline and conformity required by the armed services, and the results were often disastrous, largely because the contradictory demands of soldiering and remaining a devout Witness proved all but impossible to balance. Early in 1941, Witness Frank Moncada reported to a Queens, New York, induction station after bungling an appeal of his draft classification. Reluctant to be inducted, the Brooklyn resident balked at taking the requisite service oath and refused to salute the American flag. News reports of the incident indicated that soldiers at the induction station responded to the Witness's defiance by forcing him into a truck and then hauling him to an army camp on Long Island. When he arrived there, Moncada clung to a Bible, telling an officer who had asked him to surrender it, "I live by the Bible and I always want it with me." Newspaper accounts of the Witness's forcible induction bothered Sen. Burton Wheeler of Montana, a prominent isolationist. In a letter to Attorney General Robert Jackson, Wheeler wrote that he was "seriously concerned over the bare facts carried in press dispatches and the news pictures, showing the registrant being forcibly carried by military police into an army truck and taken away to camp. To me, it is shocking to see pictures of a man crying while his captors, with broad grins on their faces, bodily carry him away." As the army fielded a number of similar protests over Moncada's treatment, including one from the ACLU's National Committee on Conscientious Objectors, it shipped the Witness from Camp Upton to Fort Jay on Governor's Island in New York for a psychiatric evaluation. Thanks in part to the ACLU's efforts, Moncada eventually was released by the army and allowed to complete an appeal of his draft classification with his local draft board. Following Moncada's release, the ACLU's Ernest Angell announced that the National Committee on Conscientious Objectors had been assured by federal draft officials "that hereafter no man who refuses to take the military oath after claiming conscientious objection will be forcibly inducted into the army. We understand that a general order has been issued to this effect."[45]

After being classified as a conscientious objector eligible for noncombatant service, Witness Ernie Strobel reported to Fort McArthur in San Pedro, California. Like three other Witnesses who were stationed at the base, Strobel refused to salute the American flag or wear a military uniform. Moreover, he frequently clashed with his superiors about his workload, which he deemed excessive. Matters came to a head in fall 1942 when a group of soldiers confronted the Witness in the kitchen area of a mess hall. After dousing Strobel with a pail of hot water and dismissing his justifications for refusing to fight for his country, the soldiers, two of them sergeants, set upon him. He later described the beating:

> They started to hit me and . . . would beat me for some minutes. They hit me with their fists and kicked me even when I was knocked to the floor. Then they asked me if I would work and take a uniform, and when I would refuse, they would start in again. They told me they were going to beat me and put me in the hospital or kill me, as they could keep it up all the rest of the day. At one time I hit the ground and was unconscious; when I awoke, one of them was kicking me. . . . They tore my shirt off me and my undershirt also, and my trousers were torn and bloody. I tried to keep the trousers as evidence but could not do so. They were a mess of blood.

The attack, as Strobel later reported, resulted in a variety of wounds. "Cut through the lip in two places—left lip and upper lip—from my teeth," he said after he was thrashed. "Both eyes black—my head with bumps all over it—my face out of shape—my ribs sore and my kidneys and back sore from the kickings."[46]

In a letter to Secretary of War Henry Stimson, the ACLU's Arthur Garfield Hays protested Strobel's beating. Hays described for Stimson the attack on the Witness and its equally disturbing aftermath. "At the end of the beating," Hays wrote, Strobel's assailants dragged him "before three other Jehovah's Witnesses and told them to look at the consequences if they refused to wear uniforms. They warned them to accept the uniforms peacefully." The ACLU believed that the "unwarranted brutality" of the soldiers involved "would bear investigation and that punishment should be meted out if the facts are as they have been related to us."[47] Two months later, Maj. Gen. J. A. Ulio of the War Department's Adjutant General's Office reported back to Hays with the results of an investigation into the attack. Strobel's allegations, Ulio wrote, had "no basis" in fact, and the War Department had concluded that "his statements are false in every detail."[48] Having dismissed Strobel's claims of abuse, the army threw him into a stockade and contemplated initiating court martial proceedings against him. A national publication for conscientious objectors later reported that Strobel eventually was transferred to a hospital and then discharged from the armed services without having to endure a court martial because "his detention in the army stockade had caused a mental condition which made him unable competently to conduct his own defense at a court martial."[49]

Herbert Weatherbee was among the Witnesses who saw the bloodied Strobel after he had been assaulted. Weatherbee himself had been physically abused at Fort McArthur because of his recalcitrance, and word of his mistreatment eventually reached the office of George Outland, a congressman from California. Outland contacted the ACLU, which reported back to him that A. L. Wirin, its counsel in Los Angeles, had met with Weatherbee's worried mother. Responding to her request for an investigation of the mistreatment of the Witnesses at Fort McArthur, the army had reported that "there was not the slightest evidence to bear out the statement that Private Weatherbee or any other soldier was beaten and forcibly put into uniform." Unlike Strobel, Weatherbee could not escape a court martial after the army discounted his claims of abuse. The Witness was charged with "willful disobedience of the command of his superior officer to salute the flag of the United States" and tried in California on 10 March 1943. A military tribunal found Weatherbee guilty and imposed a draconian sentence: confinement at hard labor for life. When the ACLU's National Committee on Conscientious Objectors learned of Weatherbee's harsh punishment, Ernest Angell dispatched a letter of protest to the War Department. "Certainly nothing is gained in the conduct of the war, the morale of the army, nor in the treatment of religious conscience," he noted, "by validating any such unprecedented sentence as this." The ACLU hoped that Weatherbee could be discharged from the army, returned to his draft board, and reclassified as a conscientious objector or minister, a procedure followed in numerous other cases involving Witnesses who had wound up in the military. In part because of the ACLU's strong objections, the Judge Advocate General's Office "disapproved the sentence in its entirety" and reversed it. Spared a life sentence, Weatherbee was returned to his draft board for reclassification.[50]

Throughout World War II, civil libertarians lamented the abuse of Witnesses in the military and their imprisonment for violating the federal draft law. In *Jehovah's Witnesses and the War*, for instance, the ACLU decried the fact that "several hundred [Witness] men of military age are imprisoned for refusing compulsory military service," and it urged that they be granted exemptions from the draft. To the ACLU, the Witnesses' struggles with military service during World War II served as yet another example of how they were "suffering [a] war-time attack on their freedom of conscience."[51] But perhaps the most damning indictment of the federal government's treatment of Witnesses came from a far less likely source. After the Axis powers surrendered to the Allies in 1945, Alfred Rosenberg was among the Nazis tried at Nuremberg for war crimes. At one point in his trial, which took place in spring 1946, Rosenberg likened the Nazis' mistreatment of Bible Students to the imprisonment of thousands of Witnesses who violated the American conscription law.[52] At the time Rosenberg spoke, more than 1,300 Witnesses remained in federal prisons.[53]

11. We Will Obey God First, Last, and All the Time

With her son Harold in tow, Grace Marsh moved from Alabama to Brookhaven, Mississippi, in 1941 and proselytized with fellow Witness Violet Babin.[1] Initially, their witnessing went well, and the two women were able to distribute reams of literature and conduct frequent Bible studies, but "reaction to our work changed dramatically," Marsh recalled, with the Japanese bombing of Pearl Harbor and the formal entry of the United States into World War II late in 1941. "There was a spirit of superpatriotism and a fear of conspiracy. Because of our political neutrality, people were suspicious of us, even accusing us of being German spies." Like thousands of other Witness youngsters throughout the country, Harold was expelled from his public school for refusing to salute the American flag, and vigilantes threatened Marsh and Babin when they attempted to proselytize. Although the Witnesses needed and repeatedly asked for protection, local authorities were slow to come to their aid. In fact, they sometimes proved to be every bit as hostile as the vigilantes who violently disrupted the Witnesses' preaching. "On one occasion," Marsh recalled, "the police shoved us out of a lady's doorway, smashed our phonographs against a tree, broke our records of Bible lectures, tore our Bibles and literature to shreds, and finally set fire to everything they confiscated." Marsh, worried about her son's safety in such a savage atmosphere, dispatched Harold back to Alabama, and he was able to stay out of harm's way with his grandparents.[2]

The harassment did not abate after Marsh's husband Herbert joined her in Brookhaven. Early in 1942, police, acting at the behest of a local Baptist minister who loathed Witnesses, arrested the couple for trespassing and threw them into jail for nearly two weeks. Writing more than fifty years later about her imprisonment, Marsh

285

recalled that conditions in the jail had been deplorable: "One corner of our cell had previously served as a toilet. The place was infested with bedbugs. Food was served on unwashed, dirty tin pans." Authorities released the couple after Grace Marsh caught pneumonia, but threats from vigilantes forced them to return to Alabama until their trial date. Two of Hayden Covington's busiest colleagues, G. C. Clark and Victor Blackwell, defended Marsh and her husband at their trial in Brookhaven, and their constant objections frustrated the prosecution's case. ("Every time the prosecutor opened his mouth, one of our attorneys objected," Marsh recalled. "They objected at least fifty times.") Thanks in part to the dogged efforts of the Witnesses' attorneys, the charges eventually were dismissed.[3]

Marsh's dismal experiences in Brookhaven did not dampen her ardor for witnessing, and she resumed her proselytizing once she regained her health. Eager to be reunited with their son, she and her husband returned to Alabama in 1943 and propagated their faith in Whistler and Chickasaw, two communities located near Mobile. Their work in Whistler went well, and soon more than a dozen people from the community were meeting at the home of Witness Victoria Williams for Bible studies. In time, Witnesses in the community erected a modest Kingdom Hall on a lot donated by Williams, and they were officially recognized by the leaders of their faith as a congregation. Marsh and her husband encountered far more resistance in Chickasaw, a company town owned by the Gulf Shipbuilding Corporation. Late in 1943, a sheriff's deputy, A. I. Chatham, confronted Marsh and fellow Witness Aileen Stephens as they distributed tracts and periodicals in Chickasaw. As Marsh later wrote, the deputy "told us that we had no right to preach, since we were on private property," but the women would not relent. Confident that they were acting within their rights, they informed the deputy that their "work was religious and protected by the First Amendment to the U.S. Constitution." That day and on the following Saturday, when the stubborn Witnesses resumed their proselytizing, Chatham took them into custody but did not file trespassing charges, as he had threatened to do. Determined not to bow to harassment, Marsh and Stephens met with E. B. Peebles, a Gulf Shipbuilding executive, and stressed to him that they were doing important work. "We explained that people had gladly received us into their homes," Marsh remembered. "Could he deny them the right

Jehovah's Witness Grace Marsh with her grandfather in the 1940s.

to study the Bible?" His patience spent, Peebles informed the women that they would be arrested for trespassing if they continued to witness in Chickasaw. He later made good on his threat: throughout late 1943 and early 1944, authorities in Chickasaw arrested Marsh and other Witnesses on numerous occasions when they attempted to distribute literature in the town. The Witnesses' bail increased with each arrest, and they were forced to spend longer and longer periods in squalid jail cells. Marsh's fragile health deteriorated because of the jailings, but she was determined to keep worshiping in Chickasaw.[4]

On 27 January 1944, a half-dozen Witnesses were tried together in a state court for trespassing after they allegedly tried to sell magazines and tracts in Chickasaw without having obtained the necessary permit. Marsh was deemed the lead defendant, and her testimony was allowed to stand for the entire group. Marsh argued that she was worshiping, not selling goods, as she witnessed in Chickasaw; and her attorneys claimed that such activity clearly had been protected from infringement by the First and Fourteenth Amendments. "Even though the trial revealed open discrimination against Jehovah's Witnesses," as Marsh later put it, the state court found the Witnesses guilty of trespassing, and the Alabama Court of Appeals upheld their convictions in an opinion issued early in 1945.[5] According to that ruling, the freedoms shielded by the First Amendment, though precious, hardly "sanction[ed] trespass in the name of freedom." After the Alabama Supreme Court refused to hear the Witness's appeal, Covington petitioned the U.S. Supreme Court for a writ of certiorari.[6] The Court, which by then included Harold Burton, who had replaced the retired Owen Roberts, agreed to hear the case in its October 1945 term.[7]

In both his brief and during oral argument in *Marsh v. Alabama*, Covington urged the Supreme Court to extend the line of reasoning it had been developing since its earliest Witness decisions, *Schneider* and *Lovell*. Beginning with those two opinions and continuing through cases like *Cantwell*, *Murdock*, and *Martin*, the Court had repeatedly upheld the right of Witnesses to proselytize—and thus worship—free from the burdens of permit requirements and licensing fees. In 1944, after the high water mark of the flood of Witness appeals had been reached, the Court had ruled for a Witness in yet another licensing ordinance case, *Follett v. McCormick*. Writing for the majority in *Follett*, which had centered primarily on the applicability of licensing fees to evangelists who were not itinerant, Justice William Douglas had reiterated the Court's opposition to the imposition of restrictions on the Witnesses' most basic act of worship—the public distribution of books, tracts, and other forms of literature. (In reversing Follett's conviction, Douglas had compared the imposition of the flat licensing tax on preaching to the "taxes on knowledge" that had so repulsed the Constitution's framers.)[8] As Covington saw it, the trespassing conviction at issue in *Marsh v. Alabama* was every bit as unconstitutional as the measures struck down in *Follett* and *Murdock* because it similarly fettered freedoms that were explicitly guaranteed by the Constitution. Marsh did not forfeit those liberties, Covington asserted, simply because she had chosen to exercise them within the confines of a company town.[9]

As the Court—minus Justice Robert Jackson, who had gone to Germany to preside over the war crimes trials in Nuremberg—considered *Marsh* during its weekly conference, Justice Hugo Black indicated his approval for Covington's approach. That Gulf Shipbuilding owned Chickasaw "makes no difference to me," Black asserted. "A person has a right to be there and has a right to speak his thoughts."[10] Perhaps because he had spoken so forcefully about the case during conference, Black wrote the court's majority opinion, which reversed Marsh's trespassing conviction. Black asserted that the case boiled down to a relatively straightforward question: "Can those people who live in or come to Chickasaw be denied freedom of press and religion simply because a single company has legal title to all the town?" The answer, as the majority saw it, was no, because "there is no more reason for depriving these people of the liberties guaranteed by the First and Fourteenth Amendments than there is for curtailing these freedoms with respect to any other citizen." Granted, Gulf Shipbuilding did possess rights as a property owner, but, Black maintained, those rights had to be balanced "against those of the people to enjoy freedom of press and religion," and the Court was "mindful that the latter occupy a preferred position." Its argument grounded firmly in the preferred position doctrine, the majority reversed Marsh's conviction and reaffirmed its commitment to protecting the civil liberties of religious evangelists.[11] Ironically, Chief Justice Harlan Fiske Stone shied away from the majority's application of the preferred position doctrine in *Marsh*. He joined in the dissent of Justice Stanley Reed, who expressed concern that the majority sought to advance a "novel constitutional doctrine" by making First Amendment freedoms "absolute and unlimited either in respect to the manner or the place of their exercise." Reed wrote, "The rights of the [property] owner, which the Constitution protects as well as the right of free speech, are not outweighed by the interests of the trespasser, even though he trespasses in behalf of religion or free speech."[12]

The *New Republic*, long an admirer of the Witnesses' legal campaign, praised *Marsh* as "another long step toward the permanent safeguarding of our democratic rights." The dissenters' arguments, the magazine argued, failed to stand up to Black's powerful assertions that "a company town is not ordinary private premises, that the facilities of such communities serve the same public purpose as in a normal town, and that the residents of the town are entitled to the same constitutional rights as other Americans." *Marsh* marked a triumph not only for the Witnesses but also for organized labor, "in that it is the first time that property rights have not been held all-controlling in a company town," the *New Republic* noted. Now, union organizers who ventured into company towns could be confident that their civil liberties "are protected—and by the Constitution, not merely by statute."[13]

On 22 April 1946, just three months after they had handed down their opinion in *Marsh v. Alabama*, the nine members of the Supreme Court sat before a sizable Easter Monday crowd and publicly announced another round of decisions. During the reading of opinions, Chief Justice Stone became disoriented and had to be escorted from the bench by his colleagues Stanley Reed and Hugo Black. They led Stone to a couch, and soon the ailing chief justice was drifting into and out of consciousness and speaking softly to himself. At first, Stone's illness seemed to be a relatively minor one—a physician who had been summoned to the scene speculated that he was merely suffering from a bout of indigestion—but his condition turned grave later that afternoon. Felled by a massive cerebral hemorrhage, Stone died that day at 6:45 P.M. Both the House of Representatives and the Senate honored the chief justice's passing by adjourning, and the Supreme Court recessed for a full week in order to pay tribute to a man who held "a high place in the affection and admiration of all the people," as Black put it. More than 2,000 people, including President Harry Truman and his family, attended Stone's funeral at the Washington Cathedral on 25 April. In a prayer, the Reverend Fleming James told the mourners that his dear friend had been "one to whom we looked for clear direction in perplexity; one who never failed us when we needed him." Later that day, Stone was laid to rest beneath a fir tree in the cemetery of St. Paul's Episcopal Church in Washington.[14]

Stone's unexpected death in spring 1946 helped to mark the end of a remarkable era for the Jehovah's Witnesses. Compared to the frenetic period that had preceded it, the seven years that Stone's successor—former Kentucky congressman Fred Vinson—presided over the Court were relatively uneventful ones for Witness litigants. The patriotic frenzy of the war years had passed, and the Witnesses themselves had become markedly less confrontational and provocative. As a result, their persecution in the United States had abated, and they spent less time defending their civil liberties in court.

A handful of Witness cases reached the Supreme Court in the late 1940s and early 1950s, but the bulk of them dealt with the procedural issues of draft exemption claims. The collective impact of these later cases on constitutional jurisprudence was relatively modest, at least in part because, with Stone gone from the chief justice's chair, the Court entered a period of stagnation in developing its First Amendment jurisprudence. In *Poulos v. New Hampshire* (1953), for instance, the Court passed on an opportunity to expand the preferred position doctrine, relying on narrow procedural grounds to uphold a Witness's conviction for holding a meeting in a municipal park in Portsmouth, New Hampshire, without having obtained the necessary permit.[15] Justices Black and Douglas dissented strenuously, and in doing so they reaffirmed their commitment to the preferred position doctrine. Black contended that the Witness's conviction should be reversed because "the First Amendment affords freedom of speech a special protection,"[16] and Douglas argued that a "citizen can take matters into his own hands" and flout a measure proscribing his civil liberties because of the "preferred position granted freedom of speech, freedom of press, freedom of assembly, and freedom of religion by the First Amendment."[17] If such arguments had been persuasive during Stone's years as chief justice, they were far less resonant during the cautious tenure of his successor. It was a measure of how far the Court drifted under Vinson that in *Kovacs v. Cooper*, an opinion handed down by the Court in 1949, Justice Felix Frankfurter went so far as to deride Stone's preferred position formulation as "a mischievous phrase."[18]

In a recent study of the Supreme Court, Melvin Urofsky has observed that acrimonious debates over the preferred position doctrine, judicial restraint, and other matters "would split the bench throughout the 1940s and 1950s." Disagreements among members of the Court were nothing new, of course, but internecine battles were so constant and venomous during the terms of chief justices Stone and Vinson that Urofsky titled his account of those years *Division and Discord*. Among those responsible for the fractiousness of this period was the sanctimonious Frankfurter, who often went out of his way to bait his ideological adversaries, principally the members of "the Axis"—Murphy, Douglas, and Black, all of whom had broken with him in the Witness flag-salute cases and distanced themselves from his stubborn views on judicial restraint.[19] Black, in turn, engaged in a prolonged and bitter quarrel—one journalist called it a "blood feud"—with Jackson. In tracing the origins of the dispute, Jackson later claimed that "Black felt that he was entitled to be the leader of the New Deal group on the Court" and regarded Jackson as an impediment to his primacy.[20] Whatever its exact cause, the Black-Jackson breach reached a remarkable public climax shortly after Stone's death in 1946, when newspaper columnists reported that Black, Douglas, and Murphy had threatened to resign if President Truman appointed Jackson to fill the chief justice's seat. The ensuing row was unlike anything the Court had experienced before: accounts of a heated conference discussion involving Jackson and Black were leaked to the press, and Jackson attempted to justify his conduct by making public an intemperate cable he had sent to Truman.[21] If such intramural bickering did not paralyze the Court in the Stone and Vinson years, it at least provided ample proof that it was lurching through an agonizing period of transition.

As Jehovah's Witnesses receded from the constitutional stage during this tumultuous interval, members of another embattled minority group came to the fore, and their efforts helped to ensure that individual and minority rights remained a focal point of constitutional jurisprudence. Just as Witnesses had in the early and mid-1940s, African Americans pressed courts at all levels, including the Supreme Court, to safeguard the basic democratic freedoms that were guaranteed to all Americans by the Bill of Rights. Their heroic work in the courts, spearheaded by Thurgood Marshall and the attorneys of the NAACP Legal Defense Fund, hit its stride just as the Witnesses' campaign in the courts was slowing down. In 1947, for instance, the Supreme Court struck down the judicial enforcement of covenants restricting home sales by race as unconstitutional,[22] and over the next several years it further chipped away at the "separate but equal" doctrine sanctioned by *Plessy v. Ferguson* (1896). After Chief Justice Vinson died and was replaced by Earl Warren, the Court handed down its landmark ruling in *Brown v. Board of Education* (1954). *Brown*, of course, hardly marked an end to African-Americans' struggles to achieve equality, and they continued to battle throughout the 1950s and 1960s in the courtrooms of America—and, increasingly, on its streets and in its lunch rooms—for their civil rights.

During Warren's tenure as chief justice, the Supreme Court at last became a zealous guardian of individual and minority rights. In a succession of landmark opinions that began with *Brown* and lasted until Warren's retirement in 1969, the Court revitalized Reconstruction-era civil rights laws, validated contemporary civil rights measures like the Voting Rights Act of 1965, and continued to incorporate the protections of the Bill of Rights into the due process clause of the Fourteenth Amendment, thus shielding those freedoms from state action. African Americans were by no means the only citizens to benefit from the transformation of constitutional jurisprudence wrought by the Warren Court. In cases like *Mapp v. Ohio* (1961)[23] and *Gideon v. Wainwright* (1963),[24] the Court bolstered the due process rights of criminal defendants by extending the protections of the Fourth, Fifth, Sixth, and Eighth Amendments to state proceedings. Through its rulings in several reapportionment cases, the Court also ensured that citizens were more fairly represented by their elected legislatures.

Some of the seeds of this revolution had been sown decades earlier, when Jehovah's Witnesses repeatedly tested the boundaries of the Bill of Rights. Determined to preserve their civil liberties by contesting religious discrimination "legally, full scale, all the way through," as Hayden Covington put it, they brought dozens of ap-

peals before the Supreme Court in the early and mid-1940s. In grap-
pling with cases like *Cantwell, Murdock,* and *Barnette,* the Court
started to address a range of questions it had long overlooked, and in
the process it "cautiously but deliberately . . . began to examine issues of individual liberty and constitutional guarantees that shaped
the concept of human freedom within the Constitution," according
to one account. To be sure, the Court sometimes made only erratic
progress as it attempted to define the limits of the Witnesses' individual rights, as was evidenced by the *Gobitis* and *Jones* cases, in
which the justices handed down opinions and then abruptly reversed
themselves. Nonetheless, their struggles with the Witness cases
were critically important because they allowed the Court to nurture
a fledgling body of constitutional jurisprudence. Profiting from that
spadework, the Warren Court took a succession of historic steps in
the 1950s and 1960s to further reinvigorate the protections afforded
by the Bill of Rights. The "aid which [the Witnesses] give in solving
the legal problems of civil liberties," as Justice Stone put it in 1941,
thus proved to be invaluable as the Court fortified judicial protections of civil and minority rights over the second half of the century.[25]

While the legacy of their campaign in the courts began to influence constitutional jurisprudence, the Jehovah's Witnesses enjoyed a period of rapid growth. The expansion was due at least partly
to the fact that, as M. James Penton has noted, "as a people [they]
gradually became more tactful and effective in their evangelizing."
Although they were still viewed by many as nuisances, Witness
proselytizers began to see the wisdom of employing less aggressive
tactics when they distributed literature in public. Moreover, those
books, tracts, and periodicals were generally less hyperbolic than the
fiery materials they had disseminated in the early 1940s. "Over the
past ten or fifteen years this remarkable group has quietly under-
gone a facewashing and hair-combing," a Jesuit priest wrote in 1955.
"Jehovah's Witnesses have done a tactical about-face with far-rever-
berating results."[26] Under the stewardship of Nathan Knorr, who
succeeded Joseph Rutherford as Watch Tower leader in 1942, the
faith inched closer to the mainstream, and in the process it claimed
tens of thousands of new adherents every year. In Knorr's first year

at the helm, there were roughly 115,000 active Witnesses worldwide. That number skyrocketed to 207,000 in 1947; 456,000 in 1952; and 716,000 in 1957. Over that period, no other Western religion expanded more quickly. The Witnesses' phenomenal growth in the 1940s and 1950s was perhaps best evidenced by the massive convention they held in New York in summer 1958. In late July and early August, Watch Tower leaders had to rent two of the biggest ballparks in the country—Yankee Stadium and the Polo Grounds—in order to accommodate the thousands of Witnesses who swarmed into the city from more than 100 countries. The high point of the convention was a speech delivered by Knorr ("God's Kingdom Rules—Is the World's End Near?") to a throng of more than 250,000 people.[27]

With the faith's expansion, however, came friction. As Penton has written in *Apocalypse Delayed*, his insightful history of the Witnesses, "just as [they] were beginning to gain a very favorable reputation as champions of freedom of speech and worship, and were beginning to revel in it, the Watch Tower Society began to establish a system of 'theocratic law' which was illiberal in the extreme." In the mid-twentieth century, the process of "disfellowshipping"—or excommunicating—members of the faith emerged as a particularly onerous aspect of this system. Described by Penton as "a terrible weapon," disfellowship suppressed dissent within the faith by weeding out those "persons who disagreed openly with the society's teachings and policies." In time, Witnesses who had been branded as immoral because of their drunkenness or participation in adultery were targeted for disfellowship as well. According to Barbara Grizutti Harrison, the procedures for disfellowshipping provided scant protection for those who were forced to defend themselves before the "judicial committees" established in each congregation, and they often left other Witnesses in the dark as to why someone had been banished from the faith. "Trial proceedings are confidential; members of the congregation are not permitted to question the decision of the committee and must comply with the committee's judgment," she has written. "If they act in contravention of the committee's ruling, they become candidates for disfellowshipping on the ground of 'rebelliousness.'"[28] According to Watch Tower leaders, those who had been expelled from the faith were to be spurned and treated as pariahs by loyal Witnesses. "Witnesses in good standing were not to speak to disfellowshipped persons or even to greet

them," Penton has written. "In business dealings, they were to relate to them as little as possible. When [the disfellowshipped] died,
they were not to attend their funerals. To all intents and purposes,
they were regarded as eternally damned." Through repentance, disfellowshipped Witnesses could be rehabilitated, but they were rele-
gated to second-class status within the faith and forced to endure a
lengthy and humiliating probationary period.[29]

Although the Witness opinions aged well, time was less kind to
Hayden Covington, the attorney who had represented so many Jehovah's Witnesses, and eventually he was among those who felt the
sting of disfellowship. Some of Covington's woes apparently were of
his own making. According to Penton, Covington "was a rather
proud, sometimes arrogant man who could combine libertarian arguments, which he characteristically used in courts of law, with the
most completely authoritarian views imaginable when speaking of
the spiritual and organizational authority of the board of directors
of the Watch Tower Society," on which he served. Sometimes too
strong-minded for his own good, Covington often quarreled with
Nathan Knorr, and in time the two men "developed a deep sense
of resentment toward one another." Penton has claimed that Covington, overworked and exhausted, developed a "severe drinking
problem" and was disfellowshipped for several years. Speaking at
Covington's funeral in 1980, a friend maintained that he was a
"workaholic rather than an alcoholic," and Penton has suggested
that "there is some evidence that Covington may have suffered from
an inner-ear disease which was affected dramatically by any inges-
tion of alcohol."[30] Even as he floundered, Covington managed briefly
to return to prominence as an attorney in the late 1960s by helping
the boxer Muhammad Ali contest his military draft classification in
court. After a much-publicized battle with the federal government,
Ali finally triumphed (the Supreme Court ruled unanimously in his
favor in 1970), and in his autobiography he acknowledged that Covington had contributed to "the biggest victory of my life."[31]

Victor Blackwell, the attorney who served as one of Covington's
most able lieutenants in the 1940s, also experienced troubles. Ironically, they stemmed in part from his decision in the mid-1970s
to publish, largely at his own expense, a book exploring the Witnesses' legal campaign and its impact. In *O'er the Ramparts They
Watched*, Blackwell praised the valor of the Witnesses who fought

in the courts and claimed that they had effected significant changes in constitutional jurisprudence. As a result of the book, "he became quite popular with many of his brethren," according to Penton. The faith's governing body, however, began to view him with disfavor, and "he was accused of trying to 'exalt himself.'" In time, Blackwell was stripped of his status as an elder within the faith, and "he came close to being disfellowshipped," Penton has reported. In describing Blackwell's travails (which included struggles with his congregation), Penton has written that "there can be no doubt that he suffered directly from the publication of his book"—a harsh irony, given its subject matter.[32]

Most of the Witnesses who were represented by Covington and Blackwell thrived in the years after the Supreme Court heard their appeals, although they too had to endure a fair share of tribulations. Rosco Jones continued to proselytize in the South after the courts wrestled with his case against the City of Opelika, Alabama, and he encountered some fierce opposition. Authorities in LaGrange, Georgia, brutalized Jones after he protested the jailing of his wife, who had been arrested while distributing Witness books and tracts. Writing later about the incident, Jones recalled that "a group of policemen grabbed me . . . and beat me without mercy. Four of them held me, one on each arm and leg, and, raising me off the ground, started kicking me in the stomach and ribs, all of them taking turns. They also beat me over the head with an old bicycle tire." Jones survived that thrashing and redoubled his preaching activities. When a variety of ailments—a duodenal ulcer and hemorrhoids among them—landed Jones in the hospital in the mid-1960s, a physician instructed him to "take things easy from now on," as he remembered. Still devoted to serving his faith, Jones barely broke stride, and a few years later he wrote that, at age seventy-three, he had "not slowed down much yet."[33]

True itinerant evangelists, the Cantwell family had moved on from New Haven, Connecticut, by the time the Supreme Court rendered its verdict in *Cantwell v. Connecticut* in 1940. Newton Cantwell, as deeply committed to his faith as ever, packed up and relocated once again, first to Staten Island and then to various other posts in New York and New England. In each new town or city, he and his wife immersed themselves in witnessing, and they never seemed to weary of disseminating tracts or meeting with other Witnesses for Bible-study sessions. Yearning to serve their Creator in a more temperate climate, Newton and Esther moved to Chase City, Virginia, in 1950, and Newton became overseer of the local Witness congregation, a position he enjoyed immensely. He remained in that post until 1964, when he felt obliged to step aside and let younger men in the congregation take over his duties. Age, however, did not blunt Cantwell's enthusiasm for his life's work, and he continued to proselytize well after he had reached his ninetieth birthday. In his old age, knowing that his children had followed their parents' example and become "devoted servants of God" gave Cantwell great comfort. His son Russell, for instance, proselytized all over the country and eventually became an instructor at the Witnesses' Kingdom Ministry School, "a training center for Christian elders," as he called it. Russell apparently had few regrets about following in his father's footsteps. Reflecting in *The Watchtower* about his forty-three-year career as a Witness minister, he remarked that he would "strongly . . . encourage young folks to make the full-time Witnessing work their goal, yes, to make serving Jehovah God their life's career."[34]

After moving around the South for several years, Grace Marsh and her husband Herbert "finally settled down in Fairhope, Alabama, and continued to work for Kingdom interests throughout the years," she wrote recently. Marsh's husband died in 1981, and Harold, her son, passed away three years later. Although both deaths stung Marsh, Harold's seemed especially tragic to her because he had "stopped serving Jehovah later in life." As she passed her ninetieth birthday in the late 1990s, Marsh took comfort in the fact that her sisters, grandchildren, and great-grandchildren were devoted Witnesses. Her sister Crystal, married to Lyman Swingle, a member of the Witnesses' Governing Body, "remained a wonderful example and an encouragement to me," Marsh wrote, because of her unswerving commitment to her faith. Marsh herself was admired by many Witnesses, at least in part because of her unflagging bravery. "In my more than ninety years," she wrote, "I have learned never to fear what man can do, for Jehovah is stronger than any sheriff, any judge, any man."[35]

Among those who looked to Marsh for inspiration was Lillian Gobitas Klose. Writing in the 1980s, Klose asserted that she had been fortunate enough to live a "storybook life" in the decades after the Supreme Court handed down its opinion in the Minersville flag-salute case. She witnessed in the Bronx in the 1940s ("That was *very* interesting," she later mused) and then worked at her faith's world headquarters in Brooklyn. At that time, the Witnesses broadcast an afternoon radio program called "Rachel and Uncle John," and Nathan Knorr tabbed Lillian to play Rachel "because of the flag salute case," she recalled. Traveling in Europe in the early 1950s, she met Erwin Klose, a German Witness who had been arrested eleven times by the Gestapo during World War II. They married in Vienna in 1954 and eventually settled in Atlanta, where they raised two children, Stephen and Judith. Although the children "did not have the problems my brother and I had in school as Jehovah's Witnesses," Lillian noted, they were occasionally "attacked for their convictions" by classmates and teachers. As their parents had, both Stephen and Judith "showed the courage to take their stand for what is right."[36]

Four decades after the Supreme Court ruled in their cases, some of the Jehovah's Witnesses whose civil liberties were at the heart of *Gobitis* and *Barnette*, including Lillian Gobitas Klose's brother, were called upon to comment on compulsory political exercises at public schools. In 1988, Vice President George Bush made the Pledge of Allegiance a centerpiece of his campaign for president, chiefly by excoriating his Democratic opponent, Massachusetts governor Michael Dukakis, for having vetoed a proposal that would have fined public school teachers in his state who failed to lead their classes in pledge exercises. Jehovah's Witnesses, along with millions of other Americans, were staggered by Bush's tactics. Bill Gobitas, then a piano tuner living in Belgium, Wisconsin, told the *New York Times,* "It's hard to comprehend why they're raising this issue again. They're ignoring our constitutional development and history." Gobitas claimed that the resurfacing of the flag-salute controversy made him think of a fitting passage from the Book of Revelation. "To the Jehovah's Witnesses," he maintained, "all this political fanfare boils down to is 'the croaking of frogs and expressions inspired by demons.'" Paul Stull, uncle to the Barnette children, said of politicians like Bush, "They are beating a dead horse. The bunch of them are hypocrites. They all sing the national anthem at ball games, but how many would stay and sing if they didn't play it until the game was over?"[37]

But it was Stull's niece, Martha (Barnette) Snodgrass, who spoke most tellingly for the Witnesses on the reemergence of the pledge issue. "We believe the end is coming very near, and this is one more sign," she told a reporter. "That's the only thing I can think."[38]

Notes

INTRODUCTION

1. My understanding of the Witnesses' beliefs and practices has been greatly influenced by the standard history of the faith: M. James Penton, *Apocalypse Delayed: The Story of Jehovah's Witnesses*, 2d ed. (Toronto: University of Toronto Press, 1997).

2. Statement of Barton Ensley, 22 July 1942, American Civil Liberties Union Papers, Seeley G. Mudd Library, Princeton University (hereafter ACLUP), vol. 2423. Excerpts from the statements of the Witnesses who were assaulted in Imperial were published in American Civil Liberties Union, *Jehovah's Witnesses and the War* (New York: American Civil Liberties Union, 1943), 14–15.

3. Statement of Ensley; statement of John Golinie, 22 July 1942, ACLUP, vol. 2423; statement of G. C. Flick, 22 July 1942, ACLUP, vol. 2423.

4. Statements of Ensley, Flick, and Golinie; statement of Steve Chornenky, 22 July 1942, ACLUP, vol. 2423.

5. Statements of Chornenky, Ensley, Flick, and Golinie.

6. Ibid.

7. Ibid.; statement of Frank Kikosicsky, 22 July 1942, ACLUP, vol. 2423.

8. Statements of Chornenky, Ensley, Flick, Golinie, and Kikosicsky; statement of William Comodor, 22 July 1942, ACLUP, vol. 2423.

9. Statements of Chornenky, Comodor, Ensley, Flick, Golinie, and Kikosicsky.

10. Ibid.

11. Ibid.; statement of Walter Vrusk, 22 July 1942, ACLUP, vol. 2423.

12. Statements of Chornenky, Comodor, Ensley, Flick, Golinie, Kikosicsky, and Vrusk.

13. Ibid.

14. Ibid.; statement of John Kikosicsky Jr., 22 July 1942, ACLUP, vol. 2423.

15. Marley Cole, *Jehovah's Witnesses: The New World Society* (New York: Vantage Press, 1955), 111.

16. Victor Rotnem and F. G. Folsom, "Recent Restrictions upon Religious Liberty," *American Political Science Review* (December 1942): 1061–1075; American Civil Liberties Union, *Jehovah's Witnesses and the War*, 1–10; American Civil Liberties Union, *The Persecution of Jehovah's Witnesses* (New York: American Civil Liberties Union, 1941), 1–3.

17. *Minersville School District v. Gobitis*, 310 U.S. 586 (1940). The family who brought the *Gobitis* case before the Supreme Court in fact spelled its sur-

name "Gobitas." Throughout this work, I will refer to the case as *"Gobitis"* and to the family as "Gobitas."

18. "Jehovah's Witnesses—Victims or Front?" *Christian Century* (26 June 1940): 813.

19. Rotnem and Folsom, "Recent Restrictions upon Religious Liberty," 1061–1075; American Civil Liberties Union, *The Persecution of Jehovah's Witnesses,* 22.

20. Rotnem and Folsom, "Recent Restrictions upon Religious Liberty," 1061–1075; American Civil Liberties Union, *The Persecution of Jehovah's Witnesses,* 1–10.

21. In the most exhaustive study of the anti-Witness violence of the war years, David Manwaring examined the complaints received by the Justice Department and concluded there had been 843 "incidents of alleged persecution" involving Jehovah's Witnesses between May 1940 and December 1943 (*Render unto Caesar: The Flag Salute Controversy* [Chicago: University of Chicago Press, 1962], 163, 166–170, 185). In 1978, Barbara Grizutti Harrison estimated that a total of 2,500 attacks had occurred between 1940 and 1944 (*Visions of Glory: A History and Memory of Jehovah's Witnesses* [New York: Simon and Schuster, 1978], 190). The Witnesses themselves essentially split the difference between Manwaring's and Harrison's estimates, claiming that "at least 1,500 mobbings" occurred during the World War II era ("Modern History of Jehovah's Witnesses, Part 19: Christian Neutrals in America During World War II," *Watchtower* [1 October 1955]: 588).

22. Robert Carr, *Federal Protection of Civil Rights: Quest for a Sword* (Ithaca, NY: Cornell University Press, 1947).

23. *Prince v. Massachusetts,* 321 U.S. 158, 176 (1944) (J. Murphy dissenting).

24. United States Department of Justice, *Federal Prisons 1946* (Washington, DC: U.S. Department of Justice, 1947).

25. *Lincoln (NE) Journal,* 26 June 1940.

26. Merlin Owen Newton, *Armed with the Constitution: Jehovah's Witnesses in Alabama and the U.S. Supreme Court* (Tuscaloosa: University of Alabama Press, 1995), 8, 146.

27. *Cantwell v. Connecticut,* 310 U.S 296 (1940).

28. *Chaplinsky v. New Hampshire,* 315 U.S. 568 (1942).

29. *Jones v. Opelika (Jones I),* 316 U.S. 586 (1942) (J. Stone dissenting).

30. *Murdock v. Pennsylvania,* 319 U.S. 105 (1943); *West Virginia v. Barnette,* 319 U.S. 624 (1943).

31. Melvin I. Urofsky, *Division and Discord: The Supreme Court Under Stone and Vinson, 1941–1953* (Columbia: University of South Carolina Press, 1997), 113.

32. Francis H. Heller, "A Turning Point for Religious Liberty," *Virginia Law Review* 29 (1943): 440, 459.

33. Newton, *Armed with the Constitution,* 8, 146.

34. William F. Swindler, *Court and Constitution in the Twentieth Century* (Indianapolis: Bobbs-Merrill, 1970), 101–103.

35. Barbara Grizutti Harrison, "Life with Jehovah," *Ms* (December 1975): 56–59.

36. William J. Schnell, *Thirty Years a Watch Tower Slave* (Grand Rapids, MI: Baker Book House, 1956).

37. Jerry Bergman, "The Modern Religious Objection to the Flag Salute in America: A History and Evaluation," *Journal of Church and State* (spring 1997): 215–236.

38. Harrison, *Visions of Glory,* 197–198, and "Life with Jehovah," 56–59.

1. JEHOVAH IS MY GOD AND THE BIBLE IS MY CREED

1. Schollenberger quoted in Leonard Stevens, *Salute! The Case of the Bible vs. the Flag* (New York: Coward, McCann and Geoghegan, 1973), 36–38.

2. Interview with Lillian Gobitas Klose (14 May 1998) (hereafter LGK interview).

3. Ibid.; Lillian Gobitas Klose, "The Courage to Put God First," *Awake!* (22 July 1993): 12–17; Lillian Gobitas Klose, "Here Comes Jehovah!" in Peter Irons, *The Courage of Their Convictions: Sixteen Americans Who Fought Their Way to the Supreme Court* (New York: Penguin, 1990): 25–27.

4. LKG interview.

5. Richard Keller, *Pennsylvania's Little New Deal* (New York: Garland Publishing, 1982), 159.

6. LGK interview; Klose, "The Courage to Put God First," 12–17, and "Here Comes Jehovah!" 25–27.

7. LKG interview; Klose, "The Courage to Put God First," 12–17, and "Here Comes Jehovah!" 25–27.

8. Ibid.; Watch Tower Bible and Tract Society, *Jehovah's Witnesses in the Twentieth Century* (Brooklyn, New York: Watch Tower Bible and Tract Society, 1989), 1–10.

9. LGK interview; Klose, "The Courage to Put God First," 12–17, and "Here Comes Jehovah!" 25–27.

10. LGK interview.

11. J. S. Conway, *The Nazi Persecution of the Churches* (New York: Basic Books, 1968), 195–200.

12. Klose, "The Courage to Put God First," 12–17.

13. LGK interview; Klose, "The Courage to Put God First," 12–17, and "Here Comes Jehovah!" 25–27; Lillian Gobitas Klose to author, 15 May 1998 (on file with author).

14. Stevens, *Salute!* 29–33.

15. LGK interview; Klose, "The Courage to Put God First," 12–17, and "Here Comes Jehovah!" 25–27; Lillian Gobitas Klose to author, 15 May 1998.

16. LGK interview; Klose, "The Courage to Put God First," 12–17, and "Here Comes Jehovah!" 25–27; Lillian Gobitas Klose to author, 15 May 1998.

17. My understanding of these earlier American millennialists has been shaped in part by *The Disappointed: Millerism and Millenarianism in the Nineteenth Century,* ed. Ronald L. Numbers and Jonathan M. Butler (Bloomington: Indiana University Press, 1987). I also benefited greatly from conversations with

Ronald L. Numbers of the University of Wisconsin during spring, summer, and fall 1998.

18. Charles H. Lippy, "Millennialism and Adventism," in *The Encyclopedia of the American Religious Experience: Studies of Traditions and Movements*, ed. Charles H. Lippy and Peter W. Williams, vol. 3 (New York: Charles Scribner's Sons, 1988), 831–844.

19. Manwaring, *Render unto Caesar*, 17–34; Newton, *Armed with the Constitution*, 25–49; Milton G. Henschel, "Who Are Jehovah's Witnesses?" in *Religions in America*, ed. Leo Rosten (New York: Simon and Schuster, 1963), 95–102.

20. Harrison, *Visions of Glory*, 41–71.

21. In reviewing the Witnesses' early history and the development of their major doctrines, I have profited from the following sources: Penton, *Apocalypse Delayed*, 13–46; Manwaring, *Render unto Caesar*, 17–34; Newton, *Armed with the Constitution*, 25–49; and Herbert Hewitt Stroup, "Jehovah's Witnesses," in *Encyclopedia of Religion*, ed. Mircea Eliade, vol. 7 (New York: Macmillan and Company, 1987), 564–566.

22. Harold Bloom, *The American Religion: The Emergence of the Post-Christian Nation* (New York: Simon and Schuster, 1992), 159–170.

23. Harrison, *Visions of Glory*, 41–71.

24. Manwaring, *Render unto Caesar*, 17–34.

25. Penton, *Apocalypse Delayed*, 197–199.

26. For more on Rutherford's background, see ibid., 47–76.

27. Newton, *Armed with the Constitution*, 25–49; Watch Tower Bible and Tract Society, *Jehovah's Witnesses—Proclaimers of God's Kingdom* (Brooklyn, NY: Watch Tower Bible and Tract Society, 1993), 650–656.

28. Manwaring, *Render unto Caesar*, 18–20; Watch Tower Bible and Tract Society, *Jehovah's Witnesses*, 1–10.

29. Watch Tower Bible and Tract Society, *Jehovah's Witnesses—Proclaimers of God's Kingdom*, 72–89.

30. In the Supreme Court of Iowa, *State of Iowa v. Paul E. Mead*, Appellants' Abstract of Record and Notice of Oral Argument, 47.

31. These statistics have been compiled from Stanley High, "Armageddon Inc.," *Saturday Evening Post* (14 September 1940): 18–19, 50, 52–54, 58; Timothy White, *A People for His Name: A History of Jehovah's Witnesses and an Evaluation* (New York: Vantage Press, 1967), 315–316; Jerome Beatty, "Peddlers of Paradise," *American Magazine* (November 1940): 52–54, 69–71; "Jehovah's Witnesses: Holding Doomsday's at Hand, Sect Steps up Propaganda," *Newsweek* (26 June 1939): 29; and "Modern History of Jehovah's Witnesses," 588.

32. Watch Tower Bible and Tract Society, *Jehovah's Witnesses—Proclaimers of God's Kingdom*, 692.

33. Rutherford's book *Religion* is quoted in *Douglas v. Jeannette*, 319 U.S. 157, 172–173 (1943) (J. Jackson concurring).

34. John Haynes Holmes, "The Case of Jehovah's Witnesses," *Christian Century* (17 July 1940): 896–898.

35. Beatty, "Peddlers of Paradise," 52–54, 69–71; American Civil Liberties Union, *The Persecution of Jehovah's Witnesses*, 1–5.

36. Joseph Rutherford, *Enemies* (Brooklyn, NY: Watch Tower Bible and Tract Society, 1937), 223, 274.

37. Rutherford, *Enemies*, 100–101.

38. American Civil Liberties Union, *Jehovah's Witnesses and the War*, 7.

39. Klose, "The Courage to Put God First," 12–17.

40. Margiotti quoted in Manwaring, *Render unto Caesar*, 82–84.

41. Stevens, *Salute!* 32–33.

42. Irons, *The Courage of Their Convictions*, 17; Lillian Gobitas Klose to author, 15 May 1998.

43. William Gobitas to "Our School Directors," 5 November 1935, William Gobitas Papers, Manuscript Division, Library of Congress.

44. School board and Roudabush quoted in Manwaring, *Render unto Caesar*, 82–84.

45. LGK interview; Klose, "The Courage to Put God First," 12–17, and "Here Comes Jehovah!" 25–27; Lillian Gobitas Klose to author, 15 May 1998.

46. Stevens, *Salute!* 33–34.

47. *Gobitis v. Minersville School District*, 21 F.Supp. 581, 583 (E.D. Pa. 1937); Manwaring, *Render unto Caesar*, 85–87.

48. Manwaring, *Render unto Caesar*, 85–91.

49. *Gobitis v. Minersville School District*, 21 F.Supp. at 583–588.

50. Klose, "Here Comes Jehovah!" 30; LGK interview; Klose, "The Courage to Put God First," 12–17; *Gobitis v. Minersville School District*, 24 F.Supp. 271, 272–275 (E.D. Pa. 1938).

51. Roudabush quoted in Manwaring, *Render unto Caesar*, 95–100.

52. Klose, "Here Comes Jehovah!" 30; LGK interview; Klose, "The Courage to Put God First," 12–17.

53. *Gobitis v. Minersville School District*, 24 F.Supp. at 272–275.

54. Ibid.

55. Manwaring, *Render unto Caesar*, 106–108.

56. LGK interview; Klose, "The Courage to Put God First," 12–17, and "Here Comes Jehovah!" 27–28; Stevens, *Salute!* 36–46.

57. LGK interview; Klose, "The Courage to Put God First," 12–17, and "Here Comes Jehovah!" 25–27; Stevens, *Salute!* 36–46.

58. LGK interview; Klose, "The Courage to Put God First," 12–17, and "Here Comes Jehovah!" 25–27; Stevens, *Salute!* 36–46.

2. FELIX'S FALL-OF-FRANCE OPINION

1. In the United States Circuit Court of Appeals for the Third Circuit, October Term, 1938, no. 6862, *Minersville School District v. Gobitis*, Brief for the American Civil Liberties Union, *Amicus Curiae*, 1–7.

2. *Minersville School District v. Gobitis*, 108 F.2d 683, 684–694 (3d Cir. 1939).

3. Manwaring, *Render unto Caesar*, 116–123.

4. Ibid.

5. In the Supreme Court of the United States, October Term, 1939, no. 691,

Minersville School District v. Gobitis, Brief for the American Civil Liberties Union, *Amicus Curiae*, 1–34.

6. Irving Dilliard, "The Flag-Salute Cases," in *Quarrels That Have Shaped the Constitution*, ed. John A. Garraty (New York: Harper and Row, 1987), 285–306.

7. "Dred Scott and the Flag," *Consolation* (24 July 1940): 19–24.

8. Klose, "The Courage to Put God First," 12–17.

9. J. Woodford Howard, *Mr. Justice Murphy: A Political Biography* (Princeton: Princeton University Press, 1968), 250.

10. Manwaring, *Render unto Caesar*, 132.

11. Howard, *Mr. Justice Murphy*, 287; Alice Fleetwood Bartee, *Cases Lost, Causes Won: The Supreme Court in the Judicial Process* (New York: St. Martin's Press, 1984), 56–58; Merlo Pusey, *Charles Evans Hughes*, vol. 2 (New York: Macmillan, 1951), 728–729; Sidney Fine, *Frank Murphy: The Washington Years* (Ann Arbor: University of Michigan Press, 1984), 187.

12. Howard, *Mr. Justice Murphy*, 287; Bartee, *Cases Lost, Causes Won*, 56–58; Pusey, *Charles Evans Hughes*, 2:728–729; Fine, *Frank Murphy: The Washington Years*, 187.

13. Melvin Urofsky, *Felix Frankfurter: Judicial Restraint and Individual Liberty* (Boston: Twayne Publishers, 1991), 64. My understanding of Frankfurter's judicial philosophy has been shaped in large part by Urofsky's excellent study.

14. *Minersville School District v. Gobitis*, 310 U.S. at 596.

15. Felix Frankfurter, "On Being an American," 21 May 1944, Felix Frankfurter Papers (microfilm) (Frederick, MD: University Publications of America), 1987.

16. Richard Danzig, "How Questions Begot Answers in Felix Frankfurter's First Flag Salute Opinion," *Supreme Court Review* (1977): 257–274, and "Justice Frankfurter's Opinions in the Flag Salute Cases: Blending Logic and Psychologic in Constitutional Decisionmaking," *Stanford Law Review* 36 (1984): 675.

17. Danzig, "How Questions Begot Answers," 267.

18. Max Freedman, ed., *Roosevelt and Frankfurter, Their Correspondence, 1928–1945* (Boston: Little, Brown and Company, 1967), 520–525.

19. Harold L. Ickes, *The Secret Diary of Harold Ickes*, vol. 3, *The Lowering Clouds, 1939–1941* (New York: Simon and Schuster, 1954), 185–199.

20. Freedman, *Roosevelt and Frankfurter*, 523.

21. Felix Frankfurter to Harlan Fiske Stone, 27 May 1940, Frankfurter Papers.

22. Ibid.

23. Ibid.

24. *Minersville School District v. Gobitis*, 310 U.S. at 591–600.

25. Ibid.

26. James F. Simon, *The Antagonists: Hugo Black, Felix Frankfurter and Civil Liberties in Modern America* (New York: Simon and Schuster, 1989), 111–112.

27. Alpheus Mason, *Harlan Fiske Stone: Pillar of the Law* (New York: Viking Press, 1956), 525–534.

28. Ibid.

29. William Leuchtenburg, *The Supreme Court Reborn: The Constitutional Revolution in the Age of Roosevelt* (New York: Oxford University Press, 1995), 215.

30. John W. Johnson, "Harlan Fiske Stone," in *The Supreme Court Justices: A Biographical Dictionary*, ed. Melvin Urofsky (New York: Garland Publishing, 1994), 425–434.

31. *United States v. Butler*, 297 U.S. 1, 78–89 (1936) (J. Stone dissenting).

32. Frankfurter to Stone, 27 May 1940.

33. *United States v. Carolene Products*, 304 U.S. 144, 152 (n. 4) (1938).

34. Frankfurter to Stone, 27 May 1940.

35. *Minersville School District v. Gobitis*, 310 U.S. at 606 (J. Stone dissenting).

36. Frankfurter to Stone, 27 May 1940.

37. *Minersville School District v. Gobitis*, 310 U.S. at 601–607 (J. Stone dissenting).

38. Ibid.

39. Ibid.

40. John Frank, "Review of *The Brandeis/Frankfurter Connection*, by Bruce Allen Murphy," *Journal of Legal Education* (September 1982): 442.

41. Fine, *Frank Murphy: The Washington Years*, 185–190.

42. *Minersville School District v. Gobitis*, 310 U.S. at 601–607 (J. Stone dissenting).

43. Mason, *Harlan Fiske Stone: Pillar of the Law*, 525–534.

44. John Haynes Holmes to Harlan Fiske Stone, 14 June 1940, Harlan Fiske Stone Papers, Manuscript Division, Library of Congress.

45. Thurman Arnold to Harlan Fiske Stone, 7 June 1940, Stone Papers.

46. Charles Hager to Harlan Fiske Stone, 4 June 1940, Stone Papers.

47. *Washington Post*, 4 June 1940.

48. Mason, *Harlan Fiske Stone*, 525–534.

49. Dilliard, "The Flag Salute Cases," 298.

50. *Des Moines Register*, 4 June 1940.

51. "The Court Abdicates," *Christian Century* (3 July 1940): 845–846.

52. "The Flag Salute Case," *Christian Century* (19 June 1940): 791–792.

53. Mason, *Harlan Fiske Stone*, 525–534.

54. News Release, American Civil Liberties Union, 7 June 1940.

55. "Frankfurter vs. Stone," *New Republic* (24 June 1940): 843; "The Supreme Court Today," *New Republic* (5 August 1940): 178–180; "Unser Gott and Jehovah's Witnesses," *New Republic* (5 August 1940): 173–174; "Salute to the Court," *New Republic* (1 March 1943): 276–277.

56. Katharine Graham, *Personal History* (New York: Alfred A. Knopf, 1997), 121–122.

57. LGK interview; Klose, "The Courage to Put God First," 12–17; *Pottsville Republican and Evening Herald*, 22 September 1988.

58. LGK interview; Klose, "The Courage to Put God First," 12–17, and "Here Comes Jehovah!" 25–27; Stevens, *Salute!* 36–46.

59. Irons, *The Courage of Their Convictions*, 22.

3. THEY'RE TRAITORS—THE SUPREME COURT SAYS SO

1. Francis Michael MacDonnell, *Insidious Foes: The Axis Fifth Column and the American Home Front* (New York: Oxford University Press, 1996), 3–9, 107–121. MacDonnell's study of the Fifth Column scare is indispensable, and it has been crucial to my understanding of this topic.

2. "The Fortune Survey: XXXII—The War," supplement to *Fortune* (July 1940): 1–10.

3. Franklin D. Roosevelt, *Complete Presidential Press Conferences of Franklin Roosevelt*, vol. 15 (New York: Da Capo Press, 1972), 420, 484–489.

4. Franklin D. Roosevelt, *The Public Papers of Franklin Roosevelt*, vol. 9 (New York: Harper and Row, 1950), 238.

5. See "War and Peace," *Time* (3 June 1940): 12.

6. *New York Times*, 23 and 24 May 1940.

7. News Release, American Civil Liberties Union, 23 May 1940.

8. *Del Rio News Herald*, 26 May 1940.

9. American Civil Liberties Union, "Brief Case History of Some Recent Arrests," 8 June 1940, ACLUP, vol. 2215.

10. *Washington Post*, 3 June 1940.

11. News Release, American Civil Liberties Union, 4 June 1940.

12. *New York Times*, 4 June 1940.

13. Statement of Virgil Walker, 12 August 1940, ACLUP, vol. 2215.

14. Statement of H. C. Beattie, 23 August 1940, ACLUP, vol. 2215.

15. Ibid.

16. Statement of Virgil Walker, 12 August 1940.

17. Statement of J. O. Spaulding, 24 August 1940, ACLUP, vol. 2215.

18. Holmes, "Case of Jehovah's Witnesses," 896–898. Responding to one of the many letters of protest that reached his office in the weeks after the Witnesses were expelled from Odessa, O. E. Cerron, the Ector County Attorney, angrily claimed that the Witnesses "stormed our peaceful, law abiding, Christian town and undertook to force their German propaganda upon the people. We as County officials did not interfere until our local citizens undertook to mob and lynch them." According to Cerron, the Witnesses had been fortunate; before the "necktie party" could be organized, Sheriff Webb and his deputies jailed the potential victims "in order to protect their . . . lives." Although the Witnesses had escaped the lynch mob, the widely publicized incident gave Odessa an undeserved black eye and left Cerron "bitterly opposed to German agents using a bunch of ignorant, illiterate people as a means of spreading their propaganda in this nation." He told his correspondent—a Witness named R. D. James from Kansas City, Missouri—that it would be easy enough to neutralize the Witnesses' Fifth Column activities: "I am not speaking as a County Official but as an American citizen, and I say to you very frankly that I believe that Jehovah's Witnesses should be herded like a drove of cattle and driven in[to] the sea if they persist in their belief of not fighting for the defense of our great and glorious nation. I believe it will be only a matter of weeks until all of your kind will be forced by the United

States Government to salute the flag and pop your heels together and give the oath of allegiance to the flag or be placed in concentration camps where you belong." Cerron ended his missive by issuing a thinly veiled threat to James, sneering that the two men "may be able to settle these differences" of opinion if the Witness was ever foolish enough to "visit our little city" (O. E. Cerron to R. D. James, 6 June 1940, ACLUP, vol. 2246).

19. Holmes, "Case of Jehovah's Witnesses," 896–898.

20. Statement of Gertrude Bobb, June 1940, ACLUP, vol. 2231. An amended version of Bobb's statement appears in ACLU, *The Persecution of Jehovah's Witnesses*, 16–19.

21. Statement of Gertrude Bobb.

22. *New York Herald Tribune*, 13 June 1940.

23. John Haynes Holmes to Roger Baldwin, 20 June 1940, ACLUP, vol. 2231.

24. *New York Times*, 9 June 1940.

25. American Civil Liberties Union, "Summary of Sanford incident," 12 June 1940, ACLUP, vol. 2231.

26. John Haynes Holmes to Roger Baldwin, 10 June 1940, ACLUP, vol. 2231.

27. Statement of Gertrude Bobb, June 1940.

28. *Boston Globe*, 10 June 1940; *Portland Press Herald*, 10 June 1940.

29. Holmes to Baldwin, 10 and 20 June 1940.

30. Statement of Gertrude Bobb, June 1940.

31. Holmes, "Case of Jehovah's Witnesses, 896–898; *Boston Globe*, 10, 11, and 13 June 1940; *New York Times*, 10 June 1940.

32. Holmes to Baldwin, 20 June 1940.

33. *Boston Globe*, 10 June 1940.

34. Ibid., 11 and 12 June 1940.

35. "Witnesses in Trouble," *Time* (24 June 1940): 54.

36. *Portland Express*, 10 June 1940.

37. *Boston Globe*, 10 and 11 June 1940.

38. "Witnesses in Trouble," 54.

39. *New York Herald Tribune*, 13 June 1940.

40. "Witnesses in Trouble," 54.

41. News Release, American Civil Liberties Union, 11 June 1940.

42. *New York Herald Tribune*, 13 June 1940.

43. Holmes, "Case of Jehovah's Witnesses," 896–898.

44. Beulah Amidon, "Can We Afford Martyrs?" *Survey Graphic* (September 1940): 457–460.

45. Ibid.

46. Holmes, "Case of Jehovah's Witnesses," 897.

47. Rotnem and Folsom, "Recent Restrictions upon Religious Liberty," 1062.

48. ACLU, *The Persecution of Jehovah's Witnesses*, 3; John Haynes Holmes, "Jehovah's Witnesses—Cases Received to August 26, 1940," ACLUP, vol. 2215.

49. *New York World-Telegram*, 22 June 1940.

50. *St. Louis Post-Dispatch*, 17 June 1940; *Chicago Tribune*, 17 June 1940.

51. Statement of Clara Morford, 14 September 1940, ACLUP, vol. 2229.

52. Statement of Will Mittendorf, 14 September 1940, ACLUP, vol. 2229.

53. Statement of Bob Fischer, 14 September 1940, ACLUP, vol. 2229. An amended version of Fischer's statement appears in ACLU, *The Persecution of Jehovah's Witnesses*, 15-16.

54. Statement of Virginia Jordan, 14 September 1940, ACLUP, vol. 2229.

55. *St. Louis Post-Dispatch*, 17 June 1940; *Chicago Tribune*, 17 June 1940; statements of Edward Stuteville, Sam Kirkpatrick, Lester Agnew, Joe Witkowski, Cebert Elder, Claire DeBacco, Otto Hayden, Bob Fischer, Paul Edwards, and St. Louis Company Servant, 14 September 1940, ACLUP, vol. 2229; Watchtower Bible and Tract Society to Ira Latimer, 27 June 1940, ACLUP, vol. 2229.

56. *Washington Post*, 20 and 22 June 1940.

57. *Rockville (MD) Star*, 20 June 1940; Watch Tower Bible and Tract Society to Herbert O'Conor, 21 June 1940, ACLUP, vol. 2231.

58. *Washington Post*, 20 and 22 June 1940.

59. Ibid., 21 June 1940.

60. Ibid., 30 June 1940.

61. Ibid., 6, 9, and 11 July 1940.

62. Ibid., 23 June 1940.

63. Statement of C. A. Cecil, 8 July 1940, ACLUP, vol. 2249; *Catlette v. United States*, 132 F.2d 902, 903-907 (4th Cir. 1943).

64. Statement of C. A. Cecil; *Catlette v. United States*, 132 F.2d at 903-907.

65. Ibid.

66. Ibid.

67. Ibid.

68. Frederick Gibson to Leon Thompson, 2 July 1940, ACLUP, vol. 2237.

69. Ibid.

70. Oliver Siebenlist to Robert Leroy Cochran, 23 June 1940, ACLUP, vol. 2237.

71. *Lincoln (NE) Journal*, 26 June 1940.

72. S. A. Senk to American Civil Liberties Union, 10 August 1940, ACLUP, vol. 2237.

73. Mrs. J. C. Kantz to Francis Biddle, 6 July 1940, ACLUP, vol. 2237.

74. American Civil Liberties Union to Sheriff, Otoe County, Nebraska, 8 July 1940, ACLUP, vol. 2237; American Civil Liberties Union to County Attorney, Hall County, Nebraska, 8 July 1940, ACLUP, vol. 2237.

75. Statement of Albert Walkenhorst, 28 August 1940, ACLUP, vol. 2237. Nat Hentoff featured Walkenhorst's horrific experience in "Castrated for Refusing to Pledge," *Village Voice* (11 October 1988): 42.

4. A SHOCKING EPISODE OF INTOLERANCE IN AMERICAN LIFE

1. American Civil Liberties Union, *The Persecution of Jehovah's Witnesses*, 22.

2. Holmes, "The Case of Jehovah's Witnesses," 898.

3. American Civil Liberties Union, *Jehovah's Witnesses and the War*, 8–9.

4. "We have insisted upon the propagandizing rights of various groups—Communists, IWW's, evolutionists, birth-controllers, union organizers, industrialists, freethinkers, Jehovah's Witnesses," Arthur Garfield Hays later wrote, "and even of Fascists, Nazis, and Lindbergh" (Arthur Garfield Hays, *City Lawyer: The Autobiography of a Law Practice* [New York: Simon and Schuster, 1942], 221).

5. Manwaring, *Render unto Caesar*, 163–186.

6. American Civil Liberties Union, *The Persecution of Jehovah's Witnesses*, 21.

7. Ibid., 1–24.

8. American Civil Liberties Union, *Jehovah's Witnesses and the War*, 1–36.

9. American Civil Liberties Union, *Freedom in Wartime: The Work of Local Civil Liberties Committees, 1942–1943* (New York: American Civil Liberties Union, 1944), 4–9, 30; American Civil Liberties Union, Bulletin no. 1033, 13 July 1942.

10. Open letter of Robert Mathews, Ohio League for Constitutional Rights, 27 June 1940, ACLUP, vol. 2240.

11. C. F. Ransom to American Civil Liberties Union, 16 June 1940, ACLUP, vol. 2230; *Des Moines Register*, 4 and 9 June 1940.

12. John Haynes Holmes, *I Speak for Myself: The Autobiography of John Haynes Holmes* (New York: Harper and Brothers, 1959), 289.

13. Holmes, "The Case of Jehovah's Witnesses," 896–898.

14. Ibid.

15. John Haynes Holmes to Roger Baldwin, 10 June 1940, ACLUP, vol. 2231.

16. Ibid., 20 June 1940, ACLUP, vol. 2231.

17. American Civil Liberties Union, *The Persecution of Jehovah's Witnesses*, 2, and *Jehovah's Witnesses and the War*, 2–3.

18. Watch Tower Bible and Tract Society, *1941 Yearbook of Jehovah's Witnesses* (Brooklyn, New York: Watch Tower Bible and Tract Society, 1940), 42–44.

19. Clyde Eastus, "Speech Delivered over Radio Station WFAA," 22 February 1942, ACLUP, vol. 2386.

20. Manwaring, *Render unto Caesar*, 175–176.

21. H. Rutledge Southworth, "Jehovah's 50,000 Witnesses," *Nation* (10 August 1940): 110–112.

22. William Pencak, *For God and Country: The American Legion, 1919–1941* (Boston: Northeastern University Press, 1989), 302–321.

23. Arthur Garfield Hays to Henry Schweinhaut, Raymond Kelly, and Paul Johnson, 26 June 1940, ACLUP, vol. 2235.

24. H. L. Chaillaux to Arthur Garfield Hays, 27 June 1940, ACLUP, vol. 2235. Documents in the ACLU Archives at Princeton University clearly indicate that Hays's telegrams, including the one he dispatched to the American Legion, mentioned Jackson, not Jacksonville.

25. *New Orleans Times Picayune*, 28 June 1940.

26. ACLU, *The Persecution of Jehovah's Witnesses*, 13–15. For more on the Witnesses' travails in Jackson, see this pamphlet and H. M. S. Dixon to Watchtower Bible and Tract Society, 26 June 1940, ACLUP, vol. 2235.

27. Southworth, "Jehovah's 50,000 Witnesses," 111; American Civil Liberties Union, Bulletin no. 928, 6 July 1940.

28. Pencak, *For God and Country*, 302–321.

29. Lynn Stambaugh to Arthur Garfield Hays, 31 December 1941, ACLUP, vol. 2386.

30. See Southworth, "Jehovah's 50,000 Witnesses," 111.

31. Ibid.

32. The Harrisburg Company of Jehovah's Witnesses to Francis Biddle, 8 July 1940, ACLUP, vol. 2229.

33. Statement of Cecil Bevins, 13 December 1940, ACLUP, vol. 2229. A year of harassment drove the Witnesses to take action in federal court. The Harrisburg plaintiffs, led by Cecil Bevins, brought a suit in federal district court that was fairly typical of the tenacious legal efforts mounted by members of their faith. In court, Bevins and his coreligionists did not take direct aim at the George Hart Post of the American Legion, although its antagonism was largely responsible for their misery. Instead, they sought relief from the unconstitutional enforcement of an Illinois statute that had been used time and again as the basis for arrests of Witnesses in the Harrisburg area. (The law prohibited the distribution of materials exposing "the citizens of any race, color, creed or religion to contempt, derision, or obloquy or which is productive of breach of peace or riots.") Anyone convicted of this misdemeanor was subject to a fine of up to $200—a huge sum for most Witnesses. In its summary of the Witnesses' request for an interlocutory injunction prohibiting the enforcement of the state law, a three-judge federal panel noted that Bevins and the other plaintiffs feared that their freedoms of worship, speech, press, and assembly would "suffer irreparable damage" if local sheriff's departments continued to use the law to batter their First Amendment rights. In June 1941, a year after the George Hart Post had begun its campaign to drive the Witnesses out of Harrisburg, the federal court denied the plaintiffs' request for the interlocutory injunction. In a ruling that must have infuriated Cecil Bevins, the panel claimed that authorities in St. Clair and Saline Counties—including Legionnaire Jack Edwards—had acted in "good faith" in enforcing the statute in question because they "honestly believed that the publication of the virulent attacks upon churches and religious leaders contained in the Watchtower literature being distributed by [the] plaintiffs constituted a violation" of the law (*Bevins v. Prindable*, 39 F.Supp. 708 [E.D. Ill. 1941], 709–713).

34. *New York Times*, 10 and 16 June and 15 July 1940.

35. Ibid.; Samuel Walker, *In Defense of American Liberties: A History of the ACLU* (New York: Oxford University Press, 1990), 135–169.

36. Victor Rotnem, "Criminal Enforcement of Federal Civil Rights," *Lawyers Guild Review* (May 1942): 18–23.

37. Ibid., 125–136; Henry A. Schweinhaut, "The Civil Liberties Section of the Department of Justice," *Bill of Rights Review* 1 (1941): 206.

38. Rotnem, "Criminal Enforcement of Federal Civil Rights," 18–23; Schweinhaut, "The Civil Liberties Section of the Department of Justice," 206–216.
39. Carr, *Federal Protection of Civil Rights,* 121–133, 137.
40. Ibid., 130.
41. Eastus, "Speech Broadcast over Radio Station WFAA," 22 February 1942.
42. Ibid.
43. Clifford Forster to Clinton Barry, 27 October 1941, ACLUP, vol. 2317.
44. Clinton Barry to Clifford Forster, 25 November 1941, ACLUP, vol. 2317.
45. Ibid.
46. Clifford Forster to Clinton Barry, 5 December 1941, ACLUP, vol. 2317.
47. Carr, *Federal Protection of Civil Rights,* 133–146, 155–159.
48. Ibid.
49. *Catlette v. United States,* 132 F.2d at 903–907.
50. Carr, *Federal Protection of Civil Rights,* 133–146, 155–159.
51. Ibid.

5. RELIGIOUS PERSECUTIONS UNDER THE GUISE OF LAW

1. Statement of Grace Trent, 8 August 1940, ACLUP, vol. 2230.
2. Statement of John C. Rainbow, 19 July 1940, ACLUP, vol. 2230.
3. Statement of Grace Trent, 8 August 1940.
4. Watch Tower Bible and Tract Society, *Jehovah's Witnesses in the Divine Purpose,* 181; "Modern History of Jehovah's Witnesses, Part 19," 588.
5. American Civil Liberties Union, Bulletin no. 983, 28 July 1941; Arthur Garfield Hays to Walter Suttle, 30 August 1940, ACLUP, vol. 2215; Statement of D. T. Arbuckle, 24 August 1940, ACLUP, vol. 2215.
6. For three typical Witness arrests, see *State v. Wagner,* 44 A. 2d 821 (Me. 1945); *Commonwealth v. Richardson,* 48 N.E.2d 678 (Mass. 1943); *State v. Sanford,* 14 So. 2d 778 (La. 1943).
7. In the Supreme Court of Iowa, *State of Iowa v. Paul E. Mead,* Appellants' Abstract of Record and Notice of Oral Argument, 1–31, 54–58, 73; *State v. Mead,* 300 N.W. 523, 524 (Iowa 1941).
8. "Civil Liberties: Religious Persecutions Under Guise of Law," *Indiana Law Journal* 17 (1942): 435.
9. Watch Tower Bible and Tract Society, *Jehovah's Witnesses in the Divine Purpose,* 176.
10. Cole, *Jehovah's Witnesses,* 122–123.
11. *State v. Mead,* Appellants' Abstract of Record, 1–31, 54–58, 73; *State v. Mead,* 300 N.W. at 524.
12. Watch Tower Bible and Tract Society, *Jehovah's Witnesses—Proclaimers of God's Kingdom,* 690–691.
13. Harrison, *Visions of Glory,* 191–192.
14. Watch Tower Bible and Tract Society, *Jehovah's Witnesses—Proclaimers of God's Kingdom,* 690–691.
15. Newton, *Armed with the Constitution,* 48.

16. Victor Blackwell, "Defending God's Truth and His People," *Watchtower* (15 February 1973): 117–122, and *O'er the Ramparts They Watched* (New York: Carlton Press, 1976), ix–xxi, 220–228.

17. Statement of Victor Schmidt, 22 December 1940, ACLUP, vol. 2230.

18. *McKee v. State*, 37 N.E.2d 940 (Ind. 1941).

19. Statement of Grace Trent, 8 August 1940.

20. Statement of John Rainbow, 19 July 1940; statement of John Rainbow, December 1940, ACLUP, vol. 2230.

21. Statement of Victor Schmidt, 22 December 1940.

22. Hayden Covington to Francis Biddle, 8 April 1941, ACLUP, vol. 2230.

23. Statement of Victor Schmidt, 22 December 1940.

24. Hayden Covington to Francis Biddle, 8 April 1941.

25. *McKee v. State*, 37 N.E.2d at 940–942.

26. Statement of John Rainbow, December 1940.

27. Statement of Victor Schmidt, 22 December 1940.

28. News Release, American Civil Liberties Union, 5 October 1940.

29. Statement of Victor Schmidt, 22 December 1940.

30. Statement of John Rainbow, December 1940.

31. Hayden Covington to Francis Biddle, 8 April 1941.

32. *McKee v. State*, 37 N.E.2d at 940–942.

33. *Trent v. Hunt*, 39 F.Supp. 373 (S.D. Ind. 1941).

34. Ibid. at 374–381.

35. Arthur Garfield Hays to Henry Schweinhaut, 6 April 1941, ACLUP, vol. 2230.

36. *New York Times*, 7 April 1941; Arthur Garfield Hays to Robert Jackson, 11 April 1941, ACLUP, vol. 2230.

37. Hayden Covington to Francis Biddle, 8 April 1941.

38. "No Kingdom of God for Connersville," *Christian Century* (30 April 1941): 581.

39. *Trent v. Hunt*, 39 F.Supp. at 374–381.

40. Hayden Covington to Roger Baldwin, 17 June 1941, ACLUP, vol. 2230.

41. Mrs. L. E. Carr to Francis Biddle, 5 July 1940, ACLUP, vol. 2230.

42. Mrs. L. E. Carr to Roger Baldwin, 15 June 1940, ACLUP, vol. 2230.

43. Ibid.

44. Statement of Victor Schmidt, 11 June 1940, ACLUP, vol. 2230.

45. Statement of Grover Powell, 12 June 1940, ACLUP, vol. 2230.

46. Watchtower Bible and Tract Society to Francis Biddle, 13 June 1940, ACLUP, vol. 2230.

47. Hayden Covington to Francis Biddle, 24 August 1940, ACLUP, vol. 2230.

48. Mrs. L. E. Carr to Francis Biddle, 5 July 1940.

49. *Beeler v. Smith*, 40 F.Supp. 139, 140–142 (E.D. Ky. 1941); American Civil Liberties Union, *Jehovah's Witnesses and the War*, 28.

50. John F. Mulder and Marvin Comisky, "Jehovah's Witnesses Mold Constitutional Law," *Bill of Rights Review* 2 (1942): 262.

51. *Lynch v. City of Muskogee*, 47 F.Supp. 589, 590–592 (E.D. Okla. 1942).

52. Ibid.

53. *Leiby v. City of Manchester,* 33 F.Supp. 842 (D. N.H. 1940); *City of Manchester v. Leiby,* 117 F.2d 661 (1st Cir. 1941); *Donley v. City of Colorado Springs,* 40 F.Supp. 15 (D. Colo. 1941); *Zimmerman v. Village of London,* 38 F.Supp. 582 (S.D. Ohio 1941); *Borchert v. City of Ranger,* 42 F.Supp. 577 (N.D. Texas 1941); *Reid v. Borough of Brookfield,* 39 F.Supp. 30 (W.D. Pa. 1941); *Hord v. City of Fort Myers,* 13 So.2d 809 (Fla. 1943); *Kennedy v. City of Moscow,* 39 F.Supp. 26 (C.D. Idaho 1941); *Zimmerman v. Village of London,* 38 F.Supp. 582 (S.D. Ohio 1941).

54. *Des Moines Register,* 9 September 1946.

55. *Indianola (IA) Record-Herald,* 12 September 1946; *Des Moines Register,* 11 September 1946; *Sellers v. Johnson,* 69 F.Supp. 778, 780–783 (S.D. Iowa 1946).

56. *Des Moines Register,* 16 September 1946.

57. Ibid., 17 and 21 September 1946.

58. *Sellers v. Johnson,* 69 F.Supp. at 780–788.

59. Ibid.

60. Ibid., 163 F.2d 877, 878–883 (8th Cir. 1947).

6. STARVATION INTO PATRIOTISM

1. Daniel Morgan to Francis Biddle, 5 January 1943, ACLUP, vol. 2621; statement of Daniel Morgan, December 1942, ACLUP, vol. 2621; *Morgan v. Civil Service Commission,* 36 A.2d 898, 900–903 (N.J. 1944).

2. Morgan to Biddle, 5 January 1943; *Morgan v. Civil Service Commission,* 36 A.2d at 900–903.

3. Ibid.

4. *Morgan v. Civil Service Commission,* 36 A.2d at 900–903; *New York Times,* 21 January 1943 and 15 April 1944.

5. American Civil Liberties Union, Bulletin no. 1012, 16 February 1942; Paul Schmidt to ACLU, 26 January and 6 March 1942, ACLUP, vol. 2428.

6. Schmidt to ACLU, 26 January and 6 March 1942.

7. President's Committee on Fair Employment Practice, War Manpower Commission, Press Release, 24 November 1942, ACLUP, vol. 2428.

8. *New York Times,* 22 December 1942.

9. News Release, American Civil Liberties Union, ACLUP, 24 December 1942.

10. Lawrence Cramer to Roger Baldwin, 2 January 1943, ACLUP, vol. 2428.

11. Paul Schmidt to ACLU, 15 April 1943, ACLUP, vol. 2428.

12. Roger Baldwin to William Green, 17 April 1942, ACLUP, vol. 2386; Roger Baldwin to Philip Murray, 17 April 1942, ACLUP, vol. 2386.

13. American Civil Liberties Union, *Jehovah's Witnesses and the War,* 33–35.

14. "Won't Salute Flag, Postal Clerk Fired," *Conscientious Objector* (March 1942): 5.

15. Mrs. Helge C. Peterson to Ernest Besig, 29 November 1941, ACLUP, vol. 2320; "Postal Employee Fired Following Legion Protest," 25 November 1941, ACLUP, vol. 2320.

16. American Civil Liberties Union, *Jehovah's Witnesses and the War,* 34.

17. *Leoles v. Landers*, 192 S.E. 218 (1937).

18. *Atlanta Journal*, 18 October 1936; Manwaring, *Render unto Caesar*, 63.

19. LGK interview; Klose, "The Courage to Put God First," 12–17.

20. Henry Hopper to Henry Horner, 4 September 1940, ACLUP, vol. 2229; S. S. Goodin to Francis Biddle, 5 July 1940, ACLUP, vol. 2229.

21. *St. Louis Post-Dispatch*, 16 and 28 June 1940.

22. Ibid., 11 October 1940.

23. Henry Hopper to Henry Horner, 4 September 1940.

24. "Starvation into Patriotism," *Christian Century* (30 October 1940): 1333–1334.

25. *St. Louis Post-Dispatch*, 12 October 1940.

26. Ibid., 28 June 1940.

27. Ibid., 4 and 5 October 1940.

28. American Civil Liberties Union, *Jehovah's Witnesses and the War*, 28–29.

29. American Civil Liberties Union, Bulletin no. 1056, 28 December 1942.

30. American Civil Liberties Union, Bulletin no. 951, 14 December 1940.

31. Manwaring, *Render unto Caesar*, 56–59; Stevens, *Salute!* 30–33.

32. *Nicholls v. Mayor and School Committee of Lynn*, 7 N.E.2d 577, 578–581 (Mass. 1937).

33. Manwaring, *Render unto Caesar*, 63–80; *State ex rel. Bleich v. Board of Public Instruction*, 190 So. 815, 816–817 (Fla. 1939).

34. *State v. Lefebvre*, 20 A.2d 185, 186–188 (N.H. 1941).

35. Gertrude Lefebvre to Alexander Murchie, 30 November 1942, ACLUP, vol. 2416.

36. The State of New Hampshire, Supreme Court, *The State of New Hampshire v. Roland, Loraine and Loretta Lefebvre*, Brief for the American Civil Liberties Union, *Amicus Curiae*, 7.

37. *State v. Lefebvre*, 20 A.2d at 186–188.

38. American Civil Liberties Union, Bulletin no. 973, 19 May 1941.

39. Gertrude Lefebvre to Alexander Murchie, 30 November 1942.

40. *In re Jones*, 24 N.Y.S.2d 10, 11–15 (Chld. Ct. Jefferson Co. 1940).

41. *In re Reed*, 28 N.Y.S.2d 93 (N.Y. 1941).

42. *Commonwealth v. Johnson*, 35 N.E.2d 801, 802–806 (Mass. 1941).

43. *Bolling v. Superior Court for Clallam County*, 133 F.2d 803, 804–810 (Wash. 1943).

44. Roger Baldwin to Chairman, Committee on Education, Rhode Island House of Representatives, 8 April 1941, ACLUP, vol. 2309.

45. John W. Baker to Roger Baldwin, 9 April 1941, ACLUP, vol. 2309.

46. S. R. Mayer-Oakes to Roger Baldwin, 16 April 1941, ACLUP, vol. 2309; American Civil Liberties Union, Bulletin no. 970, 28 April 1941.

47. Hays, *City Lawyer*, 199–202.

48. *People ex rel. Fish v. Sandstrom*, 18 N.E.2d 840, 841–847 (Ct. App. N.Y. 1939).

49. American Civil Liberties, Bulletin no. 1023, 4 May 1942.

50. *In re Latrecchia*, 26 A.2d 88, 882 (N.J. 1942); *New York Times*, 1 July 1942.

51. *People v. Chiafreddo*, 44 N.E.2d 888 (Ill. 1942).

52. *State v. Davis*, 120 F.2d 808, 809–813 (Ariz. 1942).

53. *Cory v. Cory*, 161 P.2d 385, 387–391 (Cal. App. 3d 1945).

54. Clifford Forster to Gurney Edwards, 11 July 1945, ACLUP, vol. 2707.

55. *Stone v. Stone*, 133 P.2d 526, 527–529 (Wash. 1943).

56. *Cory v. Cory*, 161 P.2d at 387–391.

7. BOUNDLESS COURAGE AND UNENDING PERSEVERANCE

1. Newton Cantwell, "Jehovah Provides," *Watchtower* (1 July 1970): 410–413.

2. Ibid.; Russell Cantwell, "We Are Given a Goal in Life," *Watchtower* (15 March 1977): 168–171.

3. Newton Cantwell, "Jehovah Provides," 410–413; Russell Cantwell, "We Are Given a Goal in Life," 168–171.

4. Newton Cantwell, "Jehovah Provides," 410–413; Russell Cantwell, "We Are Given a Goal in Life," 168–171.

5. Newton Cantwell, "Jehovah Provides," 410–413.

6. *State v. Cantwell*, 8 A.2d 533, 535–537 (Conn. 1939).

7. Ibid.

8. Russell Cantwell, "We Are Given a Goal in Life," 168–171.

9. Ibid.; Cole, *Jehovah's Witnesses*, 109–123.

10. "Witnesses's Angle," *Newsweek* (22 March 1943): 68–69.

11. Walker, *In Defense of American Liberties*, 107, 172.

12. *Lovell v. City of Griffin*, 303 U.S. 444, 451–452 (1938).

13. *Schneider v. State of New Jersey*, 308 U.S. 147 (1939).

14. *Gitlow v. New York*, 268 U.S. 652 (1925).

15. *Cantwell v. Connecticut*, 310 U.S. 296, 300–311(1940).

16. Ibid.

17. Newton Cantwell, "Jehovah Provides," 410–413.

18. Newton, *Armed with the Constitution*, 8, 146.

19. David P. Currie, "The Constitution in the Supreme Court: Civil Rights and Liberties, 1930–1941," *Duke Law Journal* (1987): 800–830.

20. Urofsky, *Division and Discord*, 263.

21. Harlan Fiske Stone to Charles Evans Hughes, 24 March 1941, Stone Papers.

22. Mulder and Comisky, "Jehovah's Witnesses Mold Constitutional Law," 262.

23. Cole, *Jehovah's Witnesses*, 112.

24. William Shephard McAninch, "A Catalyst for the Evolution of Constitutional Law: Jehovah's Witnesses in the Supreme Court," *Cincinnati Law Review* 55 (1987): 997–1077.

25. Urofsky, *Division and Discord*, 106.

26. Cole, *Jehovah's Witnesses*, 109–123.

27. Leuchtenburg, *The Supreme Court Reborn*, 251.

28. The Mississippi Legislative Reference Bureau provided the author with a

copy of House Resolution no. 28, "A House Resolution Declaring Open Season on Jehovah's Witnesses," in a letter dated 6 March 1995.

29. *Journal of the Senate of the State of Mississippi, 1942* (Jackson, MS: Hederman Brothers, 1942), 797.

30. News Release, American Civil Liberties Union, 28 March 1942.

31. Charles Hamilton to unidentified, March 1942, ACLUP, vol. 2414.

32. News Release, American Civil Liberties Union, 28 March 1942; News Release, American Civil Liberties Union, 6 April 1942; Mississippi Supreme Court, *State of Mississippi v. Otto Mills, and wife, Roxie Mills*, Brief of American Civil Liberties Union, *Amicus Curiae*, 14.

33. American Civil Liberties Union, *Jehovah's Witnesses and the War*, 25–28.

34. *State v. Mills*, Brief of American Civil Liberties Union, 1–15.

35. *Mills v. State*, 11 So.2d 439 (Miss. 1943).

36. R. E. Taylor to Francis Biddle, 17 March 1942, ACLUP, vol. 2414; R. E. Taylor to United States Department of Justice, 9 June 1942, ACLUP, vol. 2414.

37. Taylor to Biddle, 17 March 1942; Taylor to United States Department of Justice, 9 June 1942; *Taylor v. State*, 11 So. 2d 633, 664–683 (Miss. 1943).

38. R. E. Taylor to United States Department of Justice, 9 June 1942.

39. *Taylor v. State*, 11 So.2d at 664–683.

40. Ibid., 194 Miss. 1, 7–16 (1943).

41. Ibid.

42. Ibid., 11 So.2d at 664–683.

43. *Cummings v. State*, 11 So. 2d 683, 684 (Miss. 1943).

44. Ibid., at 684–689 (J. Alexander dissenting).

45. Betty Benoit to American Civil Liberties Union, 29 April 1942, ACLUP, vol. 2414.

46. *Benoit v. State*, 11 So.2d 689 (Miss. 1943).

47. *Taylor v. Mississippi*, 319 U.S. 583, 584–590 (1944).

48. American Civil Liberties Union, *Jehovah's Witnesses and the War*, 9–10.

49. *Prince v. Massachusetts*, 321 U.S. 158, 159–171 (1944).

50. Fine, *Frank Murphy: The Washington Years*, 382–387.

51. *Prince v. Massachusetts*, 321 U.S. at 159–171.

52. Fine, *Frank Murphy: The Washington Years*, 382–387.

53. *Prince v. Massachusetts*, 321 U.S. at 171–176 (J. Murphy dissenting).

54. Ibid. Murphy's fear that the application of child-labor laws might be wielded as yet "another instrument of oppression" against the Witnesses was borne out by a case decided later in 1944 by the Supreme Court of Oregon. After proselytizing on the streets of Portland with her ten-year-old daughter, Witness Rowena Thornton was convicted under a municipal ordinance similar to the Massachusetts law used to prosecute Sarah Prince. Asserting that Oregon's constitution protected her right to free exercise of religion from such infringements, Thornton's attorneys—who included Hayden Covington—urged the state supreme court to ignore *Prince* and reverse the conviction. This the court refused to do. "We think the ordinance of the city of Portland was enacted for the same purpose as the statute of Massachusetts," the court held, "and that it

should receive the same construction as that announced by the Supreme Court of the United States" (*City of Portland v. Thornton,* 149 P.2d 972, 973–974 [Ore. 1944]).

55. "Witnesses's Angle," 68–69.

8. FIGHTING WORDS

1. U.S. Department of Labor, Children's Bureau, *Child Labor and the Welfare Children in an Anthracite Coal-Mining District* (Washington, DC: U.S. Government Printing Office, 1922), 1–4, 48–64.

2. Ibid., 65–66.

3. Ibid., 19.

4. George R. Leighton, "Shenandoah, Pennsylvania: The Story of an Anthracite Town," *Harper's Monthly Magazine* (January 1937): 131–147.

5. Walter Chaplinsky to author, 22 July and 24 September 1994 (on file with author).

6. Ibid.

7. *Falbo v. United States,* 320 U.S. 549, 555–561 (J. Murphy dissenting) (1944).

8. Ibid.

9. Walter Chaplinsky to author, 16 October 1994 (on file with author).

10. Ibid.

11. *Leiby v. City of Manchester,* 33 F.Supp. 842 (D. N.H. 1940).

12. *City of Manchester v. Leiby,* 117 F.2d 661, 666 (1st Cir. 1941).

13. *Cox v. New Hampshire,* 312 U.S. 569, 578 (1941).

14. *Rochester (NH) Courier,* 4 January and 11 and 18 April 1940; transcript, the State of New Hampshire Superior Court, Strafford, SS., September Term, 1940, no. 2119, *State vs. Walter Chaplinsky,* at Dover, New Hampshire, 16 September 1940 (hereafter *Chaplinsky* Transcript), 11–16.

15. Watchtower Bible and Tract Society, *1941 Yearbook of Jehovah's Witnesses,* 46–47.

16. *Rochester (NH) Courier,* 8 February, 7 March, and 11 and 18 April 1940; *Foster's Daily Democrat* (Dover, NH), 3 April 1940.

17. *Chaplinsky* Transcript, 11–16, 28–32.

18. Ibid., 11–16.

19. Ibid., 28–32.

20. *Rochester (NH) Courier,* 11 and 18 April 1940.

21. *Chaplinsky* Transcript, 5–31.

22. *Rochester (NH) Courier,* 11 and 18 April 1940.

23. Bowering and Chaplinsky disagreed on the precise wording of Chaplinsky's accusation, Bowering claiming that the Witness had said "God damn fascist." Given Chaplinsky's candor about the incident—and Bowering's almost complete lack thereof—I am inclined to believe the Witness.

24. *Chaplinsky* Transcript, 24–32.

25. Docket of Rochester, NH, District Court, January to December 1940. I am grateful to the clerks in Rochester who unearthed this volume for me.

26. *Chaplinsky* Transcript, 1.

27. Arrests in Rochester in 1940 are broken down by offense in Jim Bowering's "Report of the City Marshal," which appears in the 1940 *City of Rochester Annual Report*, 66–67.

28. Docket, Rochester District Court, 10 September 1940.

29. *Rochester (NH) Courier*, 12 September 1940.

30. *Chaplinsky* Transcript, 1–4.

31. *Rochester (NH) Courier*, 18 April 1940.

32. *Lewiston (ME) Daily Sun*, 21 and 23 August and 2 October 1940.

33. *Foster's Daily Democrat* (Dover, NH), 27 August 1940.

34. Ibid., 18 September 1940.

35. *Rochester (NH) Courier*, 9 May 1940.

36. *Chaplinsky* Transcript, 2–4, 23–24.

37. Ibid., 6–9, 11–16, 23–24.

38. Ibid., 5–33.

39. Ibid., 1, 33–35; *Foster's Daily Democrat* (Dover, NH), 18 September 1940.

40. The State of New Hampshire Supreme Court, February Term, 1941, *State v. Walter Chaplinsky*, Brief for Appellant, 1–32.

41. Ibid., Brief for Respondent, 1–11.

42. *Cantwell v. Connecticut*, 310 U.S. at 300–311.

43. New Hampshire Supreme Court, *State v. Walter Chaplinsky*, Brief for Appellant, 1–32.

44. Ibid., Brief for Respondent, 1–11.

45. *State v. Walter Chaplinsky*, 18 A.2d 754, 757–763 (N.H. 1941).

46. Covington's brief is reproduced as "The Chaplinsky Case, in New Hampshire," *Consolation* (10 June 1942): 20–22.

47. Fine, *Frank Murphy: The Washington Years*, 372–395.

48. Ibid., 185–190.

49. *Prince v. Massachusetts*, 321 U.S. at 171–176.

50. *Jones v. Opelika*, 316 U.S. 584, 622 (1942) (J. Murphy dissenting).

51. Fine, *Frank Murphy: The Washington Years*, 372–395.

52. *Chaplinsky v. New Hampshire*, 315 U.S. 568, 569–573 (1942).

53. Fine, *Frank Murphy: The Washington Years*, 372–373.

54. Walter Chaplinsky to author, 22 July 1940.

55. "The Chaplinsky Case," 22.

56. *Terminiello v. Chicago*, 337 U.S. 1 (1949); *Street v. New York*, 394 U.S. 576 (1969); *Cohen v. California*, 403 U.S. 15 (1971); *Gooding v. Wilson*, 405 U.S. 518 (1972); *Kelly v. Ohio*, 416 U.S. 923 (1974); *R.A.V. v. City of St. Paul*, 505 U.S. 377 (1992).

57. "The Demise of the Chaplinsky Fighting Words Doctrine: An Argument for Its Interment," *Harvard Law Review* 106 (1993): 1129.

58. John F. Wirenius, "The Road Not Taken: The Curse of Chaplinsky," *Capital University Law Review* 22 (1995): 331.

59. *Lewis v. City of New Orleans*, 415 U.S. 130 (1974).

60. *City of Houston v. Hill*, 482 U.S. 451 (1987).
61. *Lewis v. City of New Orleans*, 415 U.S. at 135.
62. Walter Chaplinsky to author, 16 October 1994.

9. BLOT REMOVED

1. *Jones v. City of Opelika (Jones I)*, 316 U.S. 584, 586–600 (1942).
2. Briefs quoted in Newton, *Armed with the Constitution*, 75–91. I would direct any reader interested in a more thorough account of *Jones* and *Marsh v. Alabama* to Newton's excellent study, which I have found invaluable throughout my research on the Witnesses' legal campaign.
3. *Jones v. City of Opelika*, 316 U.S. at 586–600.
4. Rotnem and Folsom, "Recent Restrictions upon Religious Liberty," 1066.
5. "Ominous Decision," *Time* (22 June 1943): 55; Newton, *Armed with the Constitution*, 96–97.
6. "Civil Liberty Endangered," *Christian Century* (24 June 1942): 798–799.
7. "Use of Taxation and Licensing in the Suppression of Freedom of Religion and the Press," *Yale Law Journal* 52 (1942): 168–175.
8. Rotnem and Folsom, "Recent Restrictions upon Religious Liberty," 1061–1075.
9. *Jones v. Opelika*, 316 U.S. 584 at 600–611 (C. J. Stone dissenting).
10. *Palko v. Connecticut*, 302 U.S. 319, 325–327 (1937).
11. *Jones v. Opelika*, 316 U.S. 584 at 600–611 (C. J. Stone dissenting).
12. *Jones v. Opelika*, 316 U.S. 584 at 611–623 (J. Murphy dissenting).
13. *Jones v. Opelika*, 316 U.S. 584 at 623–624 (J. Black, J. Douglas, and J. Murphy dissenting).
14. Klose, "Here Comes Jehovah!" 33.
15. H. N. Hirsch, *The Enigma of Felix Frankfurter* (New York: Basic Books, 1981), 150; Urofsky, *Division and Discord*, 107.
16. William O. Douglas, *The Court Years: 1939–1975* (New York: Random House, 1980), 43–46.
17. Harrison, *Visions of Glory*, 190.
18. Hirsch, *The Enigma of Felix Frankfurter*, 152.
19. Newton, *Armed with the Constitution*, 95–96.
20. Urofsky, *Division and Discord*, 35–40.
21. *Douglas v. Jeannette*, 319 U.S. 157, 166–182 (1943) (J. Jackson concurring).
22. Robert H. Jackson, *The Struggle for Judicial Supremacy* (New York: Alfred A. Knopf, 1941), 284.
23. Robert H. Jackson, "Justice Jackson's Story" (manuscript of tape recording taken by Dr. Harlan B. Phillips, Oral History Research Office, Columbia University, 1952–1953), Robert H. Jackson Papers, Manuscript Division, Library of Congress.
24. *Busey v. District of Columbia*, 129 F.2d 24, 28–38 (D.C. Cir. 1942).
25. *Jones v. Opelika*, 316 U.S. 584 at 611–623 (J. Murphy dissenting).
26. *Busey v. District of Columbia*, 319 U.S. 579 (1943).

27. *Jamison v. Texas*, 318 U.S. 413, 413–417 (1943).

28. *Largent v. Texas*, 318 U.S. 418, 418–422 (1943).

29. *Murdock v. Pennsylvania*, 319 U.S. 105, 106–117 (1943).

30. *Jones v. Opelika* (*Jones* II), 319 U.S. 103 (1943).

31. *New York Times*, 4 May 1943.

32. Fowler V. Harper, *Justice Rutledge and the Bright Constellation* (Indianapolis and New York: Bobbs-Merrill, 1965), 64–67.

33. Edward F. Waite, "The Debt of Constitutional Law to Jehovah's Witnesses," *Minnesota Law Review* 28 (1944): 209.

34. Roger K. Newman, *Hugo Black: A Biography* (New York: Pantheon Books, 1994), 295–297.

35. *Martin v. City of Struthers*, 319 U.S. 141, 141–149 (1943).

36. Ibid. at 149–152 (J. Murphy concurring).

37. Fine, *Frank Murphy: The Washington Years*, 377–378.

38. *Douglas v. Jeannette*, 319 U.S. 157, 159–165 (1943).

39. *Murdock v. Pennsylvania*, 319 U.S. 105 at 117–134 (J. Reed dissenting).

40. *Martin v. Struthers*, 319 U.S. at 154–157 (J. Reed dissenting).

41. Urofsky, *Division and Discord*, 111.

42. *Martin v. Struthers*, 319 U.S. at 152–154 (J. Frankfurter dissenting).

43. Jackson, "Justice Jackson's Story."

44. *West Virginia v. Barnette*, 319 U.S. 624 (1943).

45. Rotnem and Folsom, "Recent Restrictions upon Religious Liberty," 1063–1064.

46. *Barnette v. West Virginia State Board of Education*, 47 F.Supp. 251, 252–255 (S.D. W.Va. 1942).

47. Manwaring, *Render unto Caesar*, 208–224.

48. Ibid.

49. In the Supreme Court of the United States, October Term, 1942, no. 591, *West Virginia State Board of Education v. Walter Barnette*, Brief for the American Civil Liberties Union, *Amicus Curiae*, 1–23.

50. *Douglas v. Jeannette*, 319 U.S. 157 at 166–182 (J. Jackson concurring).

51. Harlan F. Stone to Robert Jackson, 31 March and 24 May 1943, Stone Papers.

52. *West Virginia v. Barnette*, 319 U.S. 624 at 625–642.

53. Ibid.

54. Ibid.

55. Ibid.

56. Jackson, "Justice Jackson's Story."

57. *West Virginia v. Barnette*, 319 U.S. at 643–644 (J. Black and J. Douglas concurring).

58. Fine, *Frank Murphy: The Washington Years*, 381–382.

59. *West Virginia v. Barnette*, 319 U.S. at 644–646 (J. Murphy concurring).

60. Simon, *The Antagonists*, 117–119.

61. *West Virginia v. Barnette*, 319 U.S. at 646–671 (J. Frankfurter dissenting).

62. Joseph Lash, ed., *From the Diaries of Felix Frankfurter* (New York: Norton, 1975), 253–254.

63. *West Virginia v. Barnette*, 319 U.S. at 646–671 (J. Frankfurter dissenting).

64. "Blot Removed," *Time* (21 June 1943): 16.

65. "Court Upholds Freedom of Conscience," *Christian Century* (23 June 1943): 731.

66. Thomas Reed Powell, "The Flag Salute Case," *New Republic* (5 July 1943): 16–18.

67. "God's in His Heaven," *Newsweek* (5 July 1943): 81–82.

68. Mason, *Harlan Fiske Stone*, 600–602.

10. A QUESTION OF PERSONAL LIBERTY

1. United States Circuit Court of Appeals, Third Circuit, no. 8810, *United States v. William Murray Estep*, Appendix for Appellant's Brief (hereafter *Estep* Appendix), 77–82, 88–91.

2. Ibid., 92–93.

3. Cynthia Eller, *Conscientious Objectors and the Second World War: Moral and Religious Arguments in Support of Pacifism* (New York: Praeger, 1991), 58, 90.

4. Selective Service System, *Conscientious Objection*, Special Monograph no. 11, vol. 1 (Washington, DC: U.S. Government Printing Office, 1950), 19.

5. United States Department of Justice, *Federal Prisons 1946* (Washington, DC: U.S. Department of Justice, 1947), 38.

6. In researching the Witnesses and the draft, I have benefited from reading the following works: Nathan T. Elliff, "Jehovah's Witnesses and the Selective Service Act," *Virginia Law Review* 31 (1945): 811; J. B. Tietz, "Jehovah's Witnesses: Conscientious Objectors," *Southern California Law Review* 28 (1955): 123; and Claud H. Richards, "Religion and the Draft," in *Law and Justice: Essays in Honor of Robert S. Rankin*, ed. Carl Beck (Durham, NC: Duke University Press, 1970), 47–75.

7. American Civil Liberties Union, *Jehovah's Witnesses and the War*, 5; John W. Masland et al., "Treatment of the Conscientious Objector Under the Selective Service Act of 1940," *American Political Science Review* (August 1942): 697–701.

8. Elliff, "Jehovah's Witnesses and the Selective Service Act," 818–819.

9. American Civil Liberties Union, *Jehovah's Witnesses and the War*, 5–6.

10. *Estep* Appendix, 169.

11. American Civil Liberties Union, *Jehovah's Witnesses and the War*, 7; Nathan Elliff, "The Prosecution of Conscientious Objectors Under the Selective Service Act," *Federal Bar Journal* 6 (1942): 44.

12. *Estep* Appendix, 161–164, 194–197.

13. Ibid., 169–173, 200–211.

14. Selective Service System, *Conscientious Objection*, 136–137; Department of Justice, *Federal Prisons 1946*, 13.

15. Mulford Sibley and Ada Wardlaw, *Conscientious Objectors in Prison, 1940–1945* (Philadelphia: Pacifist Research Bureau, 1945), 24.

16. Mulford Sibley and Philip Jacob, *Conscription of Conscience: The American State and the Conscientious Objector* (Ithaca, NY: Cornell University Press, 1952), 71.

17. *Estep* Appendix, 99–100, 167–169, 175–177.

18. Ibid., 9–30, 218–219.

19. Ibid., 167–169, 181–189, 217, 220–221.

20. Ibid., 227, 229–232.

21. Ibid., 16.

22. *United States v. Estep*, 150 F.2d 768 (3d Cir. 1945).

23. United States Circuit Court of Appeals, Fourth Circuit, no. 5329, *The United States of America v. Louis Dabney Smith*, Appendix for Appellant's Brief (hereafter *Smith* Appendix), 13; *Smith v. United States*, 148 F.2d 288, 289–292 (4th Cir. 1945); *Smith v. United States*, 157 F.2d 176, 178–185 (4th Cir. 1946).

24. *Smith* Appendix, 9–25.

25. Ibid.; *Smith v. United States*, 148 F.2d 288.

26. Supreme Court of the United States, October Term, 1943, no. 73, *Nick Falbo v. United States of America*, Brief of *Amicus Curiae*, National Committee on Conscientious Objectors of the American Civil Liberties Union, 2.

27. *Falbo v. United States*, 320 U.S. 549, 549–561 (1944); "War: Judicial Review of Classification by Local Draft Boards Under Selective Service Act of 1940," *California Law Review* 30 (1942): 226.

28. Fine, *Frank Murphy: The Washington Years*, 430–432.

29. *Falbo v. United States*, 320 U.S. at 555–561 (J. Murphy dissenting).

30. *Estep* Appendix, 19.

31. *Smith* Appendix, 33.

32. The Supreme Court of the United States, October Term, 1945, no. 292, *William Murray Estep v. United States of America*, Brief for Defendant-Appellant, 38–40.

33. The Supreme Court of the United States, October Term, 1945, no. 66, *Louis Smith v. United States of America*, Brief for Defendant-Appellant, 203.

34. *Estep v. United States*, 327 U.S. 114, 115–125 (1946).

35. Ibid., at 125–132 (J. Murphy concurring).

36. Fine, *Frank Murphy: The Washington Years*, 432–433.

37. *Dodez v. United States*, 154 F.2d 637 (6th Cir. 1946); *Gibson v. United States*, 149 F.2d 751 (8th Cir. 1945).

38. *Gibson v. United States*, 329 U.S. 338 (1946).

39. Department of Justice, *Federal Prisons 1946*, 8–15, 41, 66; Tietz, "Conscientious Objectors," 123–137.

40. Department of Justice, *Federal Prisons 1946*, 8–15, 41, 66; Tietz, "Conscientious Objectors," 123–137.

41. William Stockdale, *Jehovah's Witnesses in American Prisons* (Putnam, CT: Wilda Press, 1946), 1–25.

42. Ibid.

43. Department of Justice, *Federal Prisons 1946*, 13.

44. Sibley and Wardlaw, *Conscientious Objectors in Prison*, 25–27.

45. *New York Times*, 20, 21, and 24 March 1941; "Wheeler Blasts Army Bru-

tality," *Conscientious Objector* (June–July 1941); 8; News Release, American Civil Liberties Union, 29 March 1941.

46. Statement of Ernie Strobel, 24 October 1942, ACLUP, vol. 2520; "CO Describes Army Beating," *Conscientious Objector* (November 1942): 1.

47. Arthur Garfield Hays to Henry Stimson, 21 October 1942, ACLUP, vol. 2520; American Civil Liberties Union, Bulletin no. 1048, 2 November 1942.

48. J. A. Ulio to Arthur Garfield Hays, 30 December 1942, ACLUP, vol. 2520.

49. "CO Serving Life Freed by Army," *Conscientious Objector* (July 1943): 6.

50. Clifford Forster to A. L. Wirin, 5 January 1943, ACLUP, vol. 2520; Roger Baldwin to George E. Outland, 14 January 1943, ACLUP, vol. 2520; American Civil Liberties Union, Bulletin no. 1070, 5 April 1943; American Civil Liberties Union, Bulletin no. 1074, 3 May 1943; "Life Term Revoked on Committee Protest," *Conscientious Objector* (May 1943): 1; "CO Serving Life Freed by Army," 6; Sibley and Wardlaw, *Conscientious Objectors in Prison,* 9.

51. American Civil Liberties Union, *Jehovah's Witnesses and the War,* 2–3.

52. *New York Times,* 17 April 1946.

53. Department of Justice, *Federal Prisons 1946,* 50–51.

11. WE WILL OBEY GOD FIRST, LAST, AND ALL THE TIME

1. Babin also worked with Betty Benoit, one of the appellants in *Taylor v. Mississippi.*

2. Grace Marsh, "Our Fight for the Right to Preach," *Awake!* (22 April 1998): 20–24. As with *Jones v. Opelika,* I would direct any reader interested in a more thorough account of *Marsh v. Alabama* to Merlin Owen Newton's excellent *Armed with the Constitution.*

3. Marsh, "Our Fight for the Right to Preach," 20–24.

4. Ibid.

5. Ibid.

6. *Marsh v. Alabama,* 21 So.2d 558 (Ala. 1945).

7. Newton, *Armed with the Constitution,* 106–132.

8. *Follett v. Town of McCormick,* 321 U.S 573, 574–579 (1944).

9. Newton, *Armed with the Constitution,* 106–132.

10. Newman, *Hugo Black,* 331–332.

11. *Marsh v. Alabama,* 326 U.S. 501, 502–510 (1943).

12. Ibid., at 511–516 (J. Reed dissenting).

13. "Civil Rights v. Property," *New Republic* (21 January 1946): 9. As the historian Merlin Owen Newton has maintained in her excellent study of *Marsh,* the opinion's "potential in litigation expanding the areas of 'public forum' to privately owned facilities open to the general public lay largely dormant for more than twenty years." In 1968, however, *Marsh* was given new life by the Supreme Court in *Amalgamated Food Employees Local 590 v. Logan Valley Plaza.* The appellants in *Logan Valley Plaza* were union members who had been barred by an injunction from picketing at an enormous shopping center in Pennsylvania because, as the lower courts hearing the case had ruled, their conduct constituted

trespassing on private property. Relying heavily on *Marsh*, Justice Thurgood Marshall's opinion for the Court reversed the lower court rulings and struck down the injunction against the union picketers. Because of its immense size, Marshall wrote, Logan Valley Plaza was "the functional equivalent" of Chickasaw, the company town in *Marsh*, and those people who attempted to exercise their First Amendment freedoms there could expect to have their rights shielded by the Constitution. Justice Hugo Black, the author of *Marsh*, contended that his opinion in that case "was never intended to apply in this kind of situation," and he dissented. His narrow reading of *Marsh* was vindicated just four years later, when the Court overruled *Logan Valley Plaza* in *Lloyd Corp. v. Tanner* (Newton, *Armed with the Constitution*, 140; *Amalgamated Food Employees Local 590 v. Logan Valley Plaza*, 391 U.S. 308, 309–326, 327–334 [J. Black dissenting] [1968]; *Lloyd Corp. v. Tanner*, 407 U.S. 551 [1972]).

14. Mason, *Harlan Fiske Stone: Pillar of the Law*, 799–809.

15. *Poulous v. New Hampshire*, 345 U.S 395 (1953).

16. Ibid., at 396–414 (J. Black dissenting).

17. Ibid., at 422–426 (J. Douglas dissenting).

18. *Kovacs v. Cooper*, 336 U.S. 77, 90 (1949).

19. Urofsky, *Division and Dissent*, 37, 137–145.

20. Jackson, "Justice Jackson's Story."

21. Newman, *Hugo Black*, 333–348.

22. *Shelley v. Kraemer*, 334 U.S. 1 (1948).

23. *Mapp v. Ohio*, 367 U.S. 643 (1961).

24. *Gideon v. Wainwright*, 372 U.S. 335 (1963).

25. Herbert A. Johnson, editor's preface to Urofsky, *Division and Discord*, x.

26. Neil G. McCluskey, "Who Are Jehovah's Witnesses?" *America* (19 November 1955): 204–208.

27. Penton, *Apocalypse Delayed*, 84–87.

28. Harrison, *Visions of Glory*, 150–157.

29. Penton, *Apocalypse Delayed*, 89–90.

30. Ibid., 79, 354 (nn.6 and 7).

31. Muhammad Ali, *The Greatest: My Own Story* (New York: Random House, 1975), 160–163, 174–175.

32. Penton, *Apocalypse Delayed*, 105.

33. Rosco Jones, "Putting Kingdom Interests First," *Watchtower* (15 January 1968): 57–62.

34. Newton Cantwell, "Jehovah Provides," 410–413; Russell Cantwell, "We Are Given a Goal in Life," 168–171.

35. Marsh, "Our Fight for the Right to Preach," 20–24.

36. LGK interview; Klose, "The Courage to Put God First," 12–17, and "Here Comes Jehovah!" 31–35.

37. *New York Times*, 11 September 1988.

38. Ibid.

Bibliography

MANUSCRIPT COLLECTIONS

American Civil Liberties Union Papers, Seeley G. Mudd Library, Princeton University
The Papers of Felix Frankfurter (microfilm), Frederick, MD: University Publications of America, 1987
William Gobitas Papers, Manuscript Division, Library of Congress
Robert H. Jackson Papers, Manuscript Division, Library of Congress
Harlan Fiske Stone Papers, Manuscript Division, Library of Congress

BOOKS, ARTICLES, AND GOVERNMENT DOCUMENTS

Ali, Muhammad. *The Greatest: My Own Story.* New York: Random House, 1975.
American Civil Liberties Union. *Freedom in Wartime: The Work of Local Civil Liberties Committees, 1942–1943.* New York: American Civil Liberties Union, 1944.
———. *Jehovah's Witnesses and the War.* New York: American Civil Liberties Union, 1943.
———. *The Persecution of Jehovah's Witnesses.* New York: American Civil Liberties Union, 1941.
Amidon, Beulah. "Can We Afford Martyrs?" *Survey Graphic* (September 1940): 457–460.
Bartee, Alice Fleetwood. *Cases Lost, Causes Won: The Supreme Court and the Judicial Process.* New York: St. Martin's Press, 1984.
Beatty, Jerome. "Peddlers of Paradise." *American Magazine* (November 1940): 52–54, 69–71.
Beck, Carl, ed. *Law and Justice: Essays in Honor of Robert S. Rankin.* Durham, NC: Duke University Press, 1970.
Bergman, Jerry. "The Modern Religious Objection to the Flag Salute in America: A History and Evaluation." *Journal of Church and State* (spring 1997): 215–236.
Black, Hugo. *A Constitutional Faith.* New York: Alfred A. Knopf, 1969.
Blackwell, Victor. "Defending God's Truth and His People." *Watchtower* (15 February 1973): 117–122.

———. *O'er the Ramparts They Watched.* New York: Carlton Press, 1976.

Bloom, Harold. *The American Religion: The Emergence of the Post-Christian Nation.* New York: Simon and Schuster, 1992.

"Blot Removed." *Time* (21 June 1943): 16.

Cantwell, Newton. "Jehovah Provides." *Watchtower* (1 July 1970): 410–413.

Cantwell, Russell. "We Are Given a Goal in Life." *Watchtower* (15 March 1977): 168–171.

Carr, Robert. *Federal Protection of Civil Rights: Quest for a Sword.* Ithaca, NY: Cornell University Press, 1947.

"The Chaplinsky Case, in New Hampshire." *Consolation* (10 June 1942): 20–22.

"Civil Liberties: Religious Persecutions Under Guise of Law." *Indiana Law Journal* 17 (1942): 435–437.

"Civil Liberty Endangered." *Christian Century* (24 June 1942): 798–799.

"Civil Rights v. Property." *New Republic* (21 January 1946): 9.

"CO Describes Army Beating." *Conscientious Objector* (November 1942): 1.

"CO Serving Life Freed by Army." *Conscientious Objector* (July 1943): 6.

Cole, Marley. *Jehovah's Witnesses: The New World Society.* New York: Vantage Press, 1955.

Conway, J. S. *The Nazi Persecution of the Churches.* New York: Basic Books, 1968.

"The Court Abdicates." *Christian Century* (3 July 1940): 845–846.

"Court Upholds Freedom of Conscience." *Christian Century* (23 June 1943): 731.

"A Crisis in the Supreme Court." *Christian Century* (13 January 1943): 38.

Currie, David P. "The Constitution in the Supreme Court: Civil Rights and Liberties, 1930-1941." *Duke Law Journal* (1987): 800–830.

Danzig, Richard. "How Questions Begot Answers in Felix Frankfurter's First Flag Salute Opinion." *Supreme Court Review* (1977): 257–274.

———. "Justice Frankfurter's Opinions in the Flag Salute Cases: Blending Logic and Psychologic in Constitutional Decisionmaking." *Stanford Law Review* 36 (1984): 675–723.

"The Demise of the Chaplinsky Fighting Words Doctrine: An Argument for Its Interment." *Harvard Law Review* 106 (1993): 1129–1146.

Douglas, William O. *The Court Years: 1939-1975.* New York: Random House, 1980.

"Dred Scott and the Flag." *Consolation* (24 July 1940): 19–24.

Eliade, Mircea, ed. *Encyclopedia of Religion.* Vol. 7. New York: Macmillan and Company, 1987.

Eller, Cynthia. *Conscientious Objectors and the Second World War: Moral and Religious Arguments in Support of Pacifism.* New York: Praeger, 1991.

Elliff, Nathan. "Jehovah's Witnesses and the Selective Service Act." *Virginia Law Review* 31 (1945): 811–834.

———. "The Prosecution of Conscientious Objectors Under the Selective Service Act." *Federal Bar Journal* 6 (1942): 41–50.

Fine, Sidney. *Frank Murphy: The Washington Years.* Ann Arbor: University of Michigan Press, 1984.

"The Flag Salute Case." *Christian Century* (19 June 1940): 791–792.

"The Fortune Survey: XXXII—The War." Supplement to *Fortune* (July 1940): 1–10.

Frank, John. "Review of *The Brandeis/Frankfurter Connection.*" *Journal of Legal Education* (September 1982): 442–445.

"Frankfurter v. Stone." *New Republic* (24 June 1940): 843.

Freedman, Max, ed. *Roosevelt and Frankfurter, Their Correspondence, 1928–1945.* Boston: Little, Brown and Company, 1967.

Garraty, John A., ed. *Quarrels That Have Shaped the Constitution.* New York: Harper and Row, 1987.

"God's in His Heaven." *Newsweek* (5 July 1943): 81–82.

Graham, Katharine. *Personal History.* New York: Alfred A. Knopf, 1997.

Harper, Fowler V. *Justice Rutledge and the Bright Constellation.* Indianapolis: Bobbs-Merrill, 1965.

Harrison, Barbara Grizutti. "Life with Jehovah." *Ms* (December 1975): 56–59.

———. *Visions of Glory: A History and Memory of Jehovah's Witnesses.* New York: Simon and Schuster, 1978.

Hays, Arthur Garfield. *City Lawyer: The Autobiography of a Law Practice.* New York: Simon and Schuster, 1942.

Heller, Francis H. "A Turning Point for Religious Liberty." *Virginia Law Review* 29 (1943): 440–459.

Hentoff, Nat. "Castrated for Refusing to Pledge." *Village Voice* (11 October 1988): 42.

High, Stanley. "Armageddon, Inc." *Saturday Evening Post* (14 September 1940): 18–19, 50, 52–54, 58.

Hirsch, H. N. *The Enigma of Felix Frankfurter.* New York: Basic Books, 1981.

Holmes, John Haynes. "The Case of Jehovah's Witnesses." *Christian Century* (17 July 1940): 896–898.

———. *I Speak for Myself: The Autobiography of John Haynes Holmes.* New York: Harper and Brothers, 1959.

Howard, J. Woodford. *Mr. Justice Murphy: A Political Biography.* Princeton: Princeton University Press, 1968.

Ickes, Harold L. *The Secret Diary of Harold Ickes.* Vol. 3. *The Lowering Clouds, 1939–1941.* New York: Simon and Schuster, 1954.

Irons, Peter. *The Courage of Their Convictions: Sixteen Americans Who Fought Their Way to the Supreme Court.* New York: Penguin, 1990.

Jackson, Robert H. *The Struggle for Judicial Supremacy.* New York: Alfred A. Knopf, 1941.

"Jehovah's Witnesses: Holding Doomsday's at Hand, Sect Steps up Propaganda." *Newsweek* (26 June 1939): 29.

"Jehovah's Witnesses—Victims or Front?" *Christian Century* (26 June 1940): 813.

Jones, Rosco. "Putting Kingdom Interests First." *Watchtower* (15 January 1968): 57–62.

Journal of the Senate of the State of Mississippi, 1942. Jackson, MS: Hederman Brothers, 1942.

Keller, Richard. *Pennsylvania's Little New Deal.* New York: Garland Publishing, 1982.

Klose, Lillian Gobitas. "The Courage to Put God First." *Awake!* (22 July 1993): 12–17.

——. "Here Comes Jehovah!" In Peter Irons, *The Courage of Their Convictions: Sixteen Americans Who Fought Their Way to the Supreme Court,* 25–35. New York: Penguin, 1990.

Lash, Joseph, ed. *From the Diaries of Felix Frankfurter.* New York: Norton, 1975.

Leighton, George R. "Shenandoah, Pennsylvania: The Story of an Anthracite Town." *Harper's Monthly Magazine* (January 1937): 131–147.

Leuchtenburg, William. *The Supreme Court Reborn: The Constitutional Revolution in the Age of Roosevelt.* New York: Oxford University Press, 1995.

Levine, Samuel J. "Toward a Religious Minority Voice: A Look at Free Exercise Law Through a Religious Minority Perspective." *William and Mary Bill of Rights Journal* 5 (1996): 153–184.

"Life Term Revoked on Committee Protest." *Conscientious Objector* (May 1943): 1.

Lippy, Charles H., and Peter W. Williams, eds. *The Encyclopedia of the American Religious Experience: Studies of Traditions and Movements.* Vol. 3. New York: Charles Scribner's Sons, 1988.

MacDonnell, Francis Michael. *Insidious Foes: The Axis Fifth Column and the American Home Front.* New York: Oxford University Press, 1996.

Manwaring, David. *Render unto Caesar: The Flag Salute Controversy.* Chicago: University of Chicago Press, 1962.

Marsh, Grace. "Our Fight for the Right to Preach." *Awake!* (22 April 1998): 20–24.

Masland, John W. et al. "Treatment of the Conscientious Objector Under the Selective Service Act of 1940." *American Political Science Review* (August 1942): 697–701.

Mason, Alpheus. *Harlan Fiske Stone: Pillar of the Law.* New York: Viking Press, 1956.

McAninch, William Shephard. "A Catalyst for the Evolution of Constitutional Law: Jehovah's Witnesses in the Supreme Court." *Cincinnati Law Review* 55 (1987): 997–1077.

McCluskey, Neil G. "Who Are Jehovah's Witnesses?" *America* (19 November 1955): 204–208.

"Modern History of Jehovah's Witnesses, Part 19: Christian Neutrals in America During World War II." *Watchtower* (1 October 1955): 588–596.

Mulder, John F., and Marvin Comisky. "Jehovah's Witnesses Mold Constitutional Law." *Bill of Rights Review* 2 (1942): 262–268.

Newman, Roger K. *Hugo Black: A Biography.* New York: Pantheon Books, 1994.

Newton, Merlin Owen. *Armed with the Constitution: Jehovah's Witnesses in Alabama and the U.S. Supreme Court.* Tuscaloosa: University of Alabama Press, 1995.

"No Kingdom of God for Connersville." *Christian Century* (30 April 1941): 581.

Numbers, Ronald L., and Jonathan M. Butler, eds. *The Disappointed: Millerism and Millenarianism in the Nineteenth Century.* Bloomington: Indiana University Press, 1987.

"Ominous Decision." *Time* (22 June 1943): 55.

Pencak, William. *For God and Country: The American Legion, 1919–1941.* Boston: Northeastern University Press, 1989.

Penton, M. James. *Apocalypse Delayed: The Story of Jehovah's Witnesses.* 2d ed. Toronto: University of Toronto Press, 1997.

Powell, Thomas Reed. "The Flag Salute Case." *New Republic* (5 July 1943): 16–18.

Pusey, Merlo. *Charles Evans Hughes.* Vol. 2. New York: Macmillan, 1951.

Roosevelt, Franklin D. *Complete Presidential Press Conferences of Franklin Roosevelt.* Vol. 15. New York: Da Capo Press, 1972.

———. *The Public Papers of Franklin Roosevelt.* Vol. 9. New York: Harper and Row, 1950.

Rosten, Leo, ed. *Religions in America.* New York: Simon and Schuster, 1963.

Rotnem, Victor. "Criminal Enforcement of Federal Civil Rights." *Lawyers Guild Review* (May 1942): 18–23.

Rotnem, Victor, and F. G. Folsom. "Recent Restrictions upon Religious Liberty." *American Political Science Review* (December 1942): 1061–1075.

Rutherford, Joseph. *Enemies.* Brooklyn, NY: Watch Tower Bible and Tract Society, 1937.

"Salute to the Court." *New Republic* (1 March 1943): 276–277.

Schnell, William J. *Thirty Years a Watch Tower Slave.* Grand Rapids, MI: Baker Book House, 1956.

Schweinhaut, Henry A. "The Civil Liberties Section of the Department of Justice." *Bill of Rights Review* 1 (1941): 206–216.

Selective Service System, *Conscientious Objection* (Special Monograph no. 11, Vol. 1). Washington, DC: U.S. Government Printing Office, 1950.

Sibley, Mulford, and Philip Jacob. *Conscription of Conscience: The American State and the Conscientious Objector.* Ithaca, NY: Cornell University Press, 1952.

Sibley, Mulford, and Ada Wardlaw. *Conscientious Objectors in Prison, 1940–1945.* Philadelphia: Pacifist Research Bureau, 1945.

Simon, James F. *The Antagonists: Hugo Black, Felix Frankfurter and Civil Liberties in Modern America.* New York: Simon and Schuster, 1989.

Southworth, H. Rutledge. "Jehovah's 50,000 Witnesses." *Nation* (10 August 1940): 110–112.

"Starvation into Patriotism." *Christian Century* (30 October 1940): 1333–1334.

Stockdale, William. *Jehovah's Witnesses in American Prisons.* Putnam, CT: Wilda Press, 1946.

Stevens, Leonard. *Salute! The Case of the Bible vs. the Flag.* New York: Coward, McCann and Geoghegan, 1973.

Stroup, Herbert Hewitt. *The Jehovah's Witnesses.* New York: Columbia University Press, 1945.

"The Supreme Court Today." *New Republic* (5 August 1940): 178–180.

Swindler, William F. *Court and Constitution in the Twentieth Century.* Indianapolis: Bobbs-Merrill, 1970.

Tietz, J. B. "Jehovah's Witnesses: Conscientious Objectors." *Southern California Law Review* 28 (1955): 123–137.

United States Department of Justice. *Federal Prisons 1946.* Washington, DC: U.S. Department of Justice, 1947.

United States Department of Labor, Children's Bureau. *Child Labor and the Welfare Children in an Anthracite Coal-Mining District.* Washington, DC: U.S. Government Printing Office, 1922.

"Unser Gott and Jehovah's Witnesses." *New Republic* (5 August 1940): 173–174.

Urofsky, Melvin. *Division and Discord: The Supreme Court Under Stone and Vinson, 1941–1953.* Columbia: University of South Carolina Press, 1997.

———. *Felix Frankfurter: Judicial Restraint and Individual Liberty.* Boston: Twayne Publishers, 1991.

———, ed. *The Supreme Court Justices: A Biographical Dictionary.* New York: Garland Publishing, 1994.

"Use of Taxation and Licensing in the Suppression of Freedom of Religion and the Press." *Yale Law Journal* 52 (1942): 168–175.

Waite, Edward F. "The Debt of Constitutional Law to Jehovah's Witnesses." *Minnesota Law Review* 28 (1944): 209–246.

Walker, Samuel. *In Defense of American Liberties: A History of the ACLU.* New York: Oxford University Press, 1990.

"War and Peace." *Time* (3 June 1940): 12.

"War: Judicial Review of Classification by Local Draft Boards Under Selective Service Act of 1940." *California Law Review* 30 (1942): 226–230.

Watch Tower Bible and Tract Society. *Jehovah's Witnesses in the Divine Purpose.* Brooklyn, NY: Watch Tower Bible and Tract Society, 1959.

———. *Jehovah's Witnesses in the Twentieth Century.* Brooklyn, NY: Watch Tower Bible and Tract Society, 1989.

———. *Jehovah's Witnesses—Proclaimers of God's Kingdom.* Brooklyn, NY: Watch Tower Bible and Tract Society, 1993.

———. *1941 Yearbook of Jehovah's Witnesses.* Brooklyn, NY: Watch Tower Bible and Tract Society, 1940.

"Wheeler Blasts Army Brutality." *Conscientious Objector* (June–July 1941): 8.

White, Timothy. *A People for His Name: A History of Jehovah's Witnesses and an Evaluation.* New York: Vantage Press, 1967.

Wirenius, John F. "The Road Not Taken: The Curse of Chaplinsky." *Capital University Law Review* 24 (1995): 331–383.

"Witnesses in Trouble." *Time* (24 June 1940): 54.

"Witnesses's Angle." *Newsweek* (22 March 1943): 68–69.

"Won't Salute Flag, Postal Clerk Fired." *Conscientious Objector* (March 1942): 5.

Index